Empire's Legacy

Recent Titles in
OXFORD STUDIES IN CULTURE AND POLITICS
CLIFFORD BOB AND JAMES M. JASPER, GENERAL EDITORS

Situational Breakdowns
Understanding Protest Violence and other Surprising Outcomes
ANNE NASSAUER

Democratic Practice
Origins of the Iberian Divide in Political Inclusion
ROBERT M. FISHMAN

Contentious Rituals
Parading the Nation in Northern Ireland
JONATHAN S. BLAKE

Contradictions of Democracy
Vigilantism and Rights in Post-Apartheid South Africa
NICHOLAS RUSH SMITH

Plausible Legality
Legal Culture and Political Imperative in the Global War on Terror
REBECCA SANDERS

Legacies and Memories in Movements
Justice and Democracy in Southern Europe
DONATELLA DELLA PORTA, MASSIMILIANO ANDRETTA, TIAGO
FERNANDES, EDUARDO ROMANOS, AND MARKOS VOGIATZOGLOU

Curated Stories
The Uses and Misuses of Storytelling
SUJATHA FERNANDES

Taking Root
Human Rights and Public Opinion in the Global South
JAMES RON, SHANNON GOLDEN, DAVID CROW, AND ARCHANA PANDYA

The Human Right to Dominate
NICOLA PERUGINI AND NEVE GORDON

Some Men
Feminist Allies and the Movement to End Violence Against Women
MICHAEL A. MESSNER, MAX A. GREENBERG, AND TAL PERETZ

Empire's Legacy

Roots of a Far-Right Affinity in Contemporary France

John W. P. Veugelers

Oxford University Press is a department of the University of Oxford. It furthers the University's objective of excellence in research, scholarship, and education by publishing worldwide. Oxford is a registered trade mark of Oxford University Press in the UK and certain other countries.

Published in the United States of America by Oxford University Press
198 Madison Avenue, New York, NY 10016, United States of America.

© Oxford University Press 2020

All rights reserved. No part of this publication may be reproduced, stored in a retrieval system, or transmitted, in any form or by any means, without the prior permission in writing of Oxford University Press, or as expressly permitted by law, by license, or under terms agreed with the appropriate reproduction rights organization. Inquiries concerning reproduction outside the scope of the above should be sent to the Rights Department, Oxford University Press, at the address above.

You must not circulate this work in any other form
and you must impose this same condition on any acquirer.

CIP data is on file at the Library of Congress
ISBN 978-0-19-087566-1

9 8 7 6 5 4 3 2 1

Printed by Sheridan Books, Inc., United States of America

In memory of
Georges Boutigny
(Algiers 1947–Rocbaron 2007)

CONTENTS

Preface   ix
Acknowledgments   xv
Abbreviations   xvii

Introduction   1

PART I: Sedimentation of a Political Affinity
 1. Settler Relations and Identities in Colonial Algeria   15
 2. The Unmaking of the Colony   29

PART II: Ex-colonials in the Metropole
 3. From Newcomers to Incipient Constituency   47
 4. New Political Configurations   61

PART III: Shift in Opportunities
 5. Gaullism Loses Ground   77
 6. Building a Base for the National Front   89
 7. The Far Right Organizes in the Var   103
 8. A City under the Far Right   117

PART IV: The Far Right Endures
 9. Discourse and Politics   133
 10. Transmitting a Far-Right Affinity   153
 11. Holding Off the National Front   163

Conclusion   175

Appendix   187
Notes   191
References   237
Index   251

PREFACE

Karl Marx wrote that the tradition of all the dead generations weighs like a nightmare on the brains of the living. Does this not depend? Many traditions have vanished. The weight of the past is itself historical: some societies inherit more history than do others. Tradition seems to be fading nowadays. Collective memory plays tricks on us. It selects and embellishes, represses and confabulates. A nightmare may never outweigh a mote.

Curiosity about the unfixed weight of the past motivates this book, an inquiry into the development of a political potential: the possibility, big or little, that a group of people will support an option like a movement, pressure group, or party. No political potential in a complex society exists in isolation. Situations, options, and resources matter. Many potentials never ripen into solid support.

Some do, though.

Before it happened, the rise of the contemporary far right was a possibility none in France foresaw. The time for reactionaries and fascists seemed long gone. The country's far right came out of World War II reviled and damaged. After 1945, usually its candidates got few votes. Suddenly, during the 1980s, the National Front became a serious competitor. Entering the party system, it upset the balance of forces. Its opponents responded with new tactics and strategies. Political debate became obsessed with immigration, Islam, and national identity. Not a flash party, the National Front endured.

Before the far right broke through, this book argues, a subculture had kept its potential alive. Societies are not uniform wholes with one way of making sense. We are code switchers: each milieu has its own way of organizing words and other symbols. As this book shows, subcultures shape *cognition*—recognizing features, setting boundaries, and classifying people, things, events, and other phenomena; *evaluation*—tying classes of phenomena to appraisals; and *emotion*—connecting the foregoing to responses (sensitivities, moods, passions, and humors) of varying intensity on the pleasure–pain continuum.

Skill enacts identity. When people put a code into practice, their very act conveys meaning: "I am like others who talk like this, and unlike those who lack this ability." Members of a subculture may not share the same skill in using its vernacular. All know about tact, though. Effects that give spice to life—such as humor, gaucheness, and insult—result when, purposely or not, discourse is out of joint with what the situation calls for.

Discourses that mark identity never arise fully blown. The superficial identity of a loose subculture is like a wardrobe item: thrown on and off, as befits the occasion. Other identities are not so light and switchable. A subculture may have performance standards that make authenticity and belonging exacting. Becoming adept at using a code may require insider knowledge and years of practice. Putting the foregoing together suggests a line of inquiry. The codes that define a tight subculture might be rooted in lasting relations of inclusion and exclusion. In France, as we will see, a subculture with an affinity toward the far right grew out of relations between colonizers and colonized. Codes enable meaning through practices as diverse as ritual behavior and visual representation. At its core, though, the subculture that kept a far-right potential alive in France did so with words. Using a language of sturdy gloom and hurt pride, it upheld ideas now disreputable. Allotting honor and blame, it separated friend from foe. Looking back at the past to see into the future, it fashioned threats and hopes. Out of joint with a mixed-race France, it hid a political affinity.

External scrutiny, control, and interaction corrode subcultures. If shielded from these intrusions, all kinds of milieus (such as the family, village, gang, neighborhood, school, sect, religious community, and online network) can uphold eccentricity, autonomy, and closure. Another milieu that can shield is the voluntary association. In institutional and semi-institutional political processes, associations may act as lobby groups or cogs in patron-client systems. In addition, this book shows, associations can protect subcultures of dissent. They do so when they inhibit multiple group memberships and cross-cutting connections. When this happens, associations join the set of milieus that harbor hidden political potentials.

This book asks why the breakthrough of the National Front caught observers off guard. The answer, I will suggest, was a blindness to latent potentials. This does not mean that analysts had ignored the past. On the contrary, we knew much about the ties of ideology and organization that linked the National Front to earlier strands of the French far right. Still not appreciated, though, was the potential of a current below the surface: a subculture not expressed in party politics yet thriving socially.

During the decades of post-1945 decolonization, millions of European settlers migrated from former dominions to imperial metropole—to Belgium, Britain, France, Italy, Portugal, Spain, and the Netherlands. By far the greatest flow—1 million settlers, or *pieds noirs*—departed from Algeria during the late 1950s and early 1960s. Most resettled in parts of France that later became the heartland of the National Front.

Although not all became supporters of the far right, the *pieds noirs* were carriers of a legacy shared by others in French society. From ancient Rome and the British Empire to Shōwa Japan and Communist China, imperial powers have spun myths about civilization and its opposite (with civilization cutting both ways, lest we forget, for anti-imperialists condemn empire as barbaric). Through various channels—literature, schools, newspapers, exhibitions, advertising, and film—a generous appraisal of conquest and colonization spread through nineteenth- and twentieth-century France. This propaganda did not persuade everyone. Still, it has had a lasting influence.

In addition to the settlers, imperialism shaped others who spent years of their life overseas, sometimes with their family: soldiers, merchants, missionaries, educators, doctors, engineers, and administrators. The Algerian War mobilized some 1.7 million French conscripts and regulars. Businesses and politicians from the republican left to the conservative right joined in an imperial lobby that, until Algerian independence, bridged interests in the metropole with those in the colony. In the making of an imperial legacy, then, evaluation meshed with experience on both sides of the Mediterranean.

For reasons soon clear, this study starts with the conquest of Algeria, France's biggest settler colony and frontline of a brutal, divisive war. It ends in 2018—when, hoping to improve her party's image, the leader of the National Front decided to change its name to the National Rally. Ranging across nearly two centuries, *Empire's Legacy* consists of four parts that progress through time.

Searching for the roots of a far-right potential, Part I (1830–1962) looks at social relations in colonial Algeria. Chapter 1 examines how thousands of European settlers from different lands became the French of Algeria, a people that defined itself in opposition to the native Arabs and Berbers. Chapter 2 probes the years from World War II until the onset of Algerian independence, an unsettled time for notions of them and us. Once dominant in the social order of the colony, in 1962 the settlers ended up on the losing side. Relations with natives, metropole, and each other would condition their postcolonial identity and far-right availability.

Part II (1962–1968) begins with the flight of the settlers. Shifting the focus to Toulon—the greatest experiment in municipal right-wing extremism in Europe since 1945—I trace the transformation of colonial refugees into political clients. Chapter 3 shows why opposition to Algerian independence and sympathy toward the *pieds noirs* set leading politicians in Toulon against the dominant Gaullist party. Chapter 4 charts strategies—in civil society, city council, and electoral politics—by which the *pieds noirs* formed a political bloc. It also shows how disunity within the *pied noir* community limited their influence. By winning the *pieds noirs* over, mainstream politicians had shrunk the space for the far right. An affinity went underground.

Part III (1968–2001) shows how the far right changed from political outsider into challenger. Chapter 5 begins with its response to the regime's troubles in May 1968. While the regime recovered, Gaullist dominance over the right slipped. This opened opportunities for the non-Gaullist right and the *pieds noirs*. Chapter 6 surveys the National Front's founding and early challenges. Turning to Toulon, Chapter 7 examines how changes in national politics combined with initiatives by the far right and errors by local politicians to turn this city into a stronghold for the National Front. Seizing a rare chance to study the contemporary far right when it governs, Chapter 8 reviews the problems that marred its term of office in Toulon. Still, the National Front had proven it could endure. With its loyal electorate, active members, and organizing efforts, in parts of southern France it had overtaken the left as the main opposition.

Part IV (2001–2018) examines in finer detail the culture of the *pieds noirs*. Focusing on the link between situation and practice, Chapter 9 isolates the affinity between their subcultural language and the insider discourse of the far right. Chapter 10 analyzes the connection between group boundaries, cultural practices, and political choices. Despite claims that voluntary associations are good for democracy, *pied noir* groups nurtured a far-right potential by shielding their members from cross-pressures. Chapter 11 distills lessons, for mainstream politics, about how to keep the far right at bay. Despite the continued success of the National Front in southern France, since 2001 the conservative right has held power in Toulon by avoiding scandal, governing well, and controlling partisanship.

This Preface opened with a wary nod to Marx; it closes with a wee bow in his direction. Believing it indispensable to connect theory with practice, Marx treated utopian socialism with contempt (better, he asserted, to analyze the real prospects for revolution in light of the concrete situation of the proletariat). Not an exercise in Marxist analysis, *Empire's Legacy* does not assign a central role to class conflict; but it does take a swipe at what we can call utopian liberalism. Enthusiasm for liberal democracy lacks gravity unless anchored in a sound assessment of its real potential next to other possibilities. What do we gain by plumbing the contradictions of our time? An alternative to unilinear readings of contemporary history, which squeeze out conflict and make outcomes inevitable. The past is more than a series of victories by the strong over the weak—an inexorable march that would explain, allegedly, our situation today. In taking stock of how we got here, let us be on the lookout for subterranean currents, countervailing forces, and lost causes. This has little to do with a sentimental partiality for underdogs. Against bullish optimism or soothing gloominess, shuttling between the mainstream and what lies beyond expands our vision of what remains possible, for better *and* for worse.

ACKNOWLEDGMENTS

For funding, I am grateful to the Faculty of Arts and Science at the University of Toronto as well as the Social Sciences and Humanities Research Council of Canada. For quiet in which to write and community in which to deliberate, my thanks to the Camargo Foundation in Cassis; the Department of Political Science at the University of Siena; and the Maison Suger of the Fondation Maison des Sciences de l'Homme in Paris. For access to material on which this book depends, I am indebted to the library of the Institut d'Études Politiques in Paris; the library of the Maison méditerranéenne des sciences de l'homme in Aix-en-Provence; and the Archives Municipales and the Bibliothèque du Centre Ville in Toulon.

In France, I was fortunate to receive all kinds of support—moral, material, and scholarly—from Georges Boutigny, Marie-Lou Boutigny, Emmanuelle Comtat, Antoine Di Iorio, Stephan Di Iorio, Jean-Marie Guillon, Guy Hello, Jean-Jacques Jordi, Bernadette Lombard, and Nonna Mayer. I am also grateful to the *pieds noirs* who agreed to my interviews. They gave graciously of their time, hospitality, and thoughts, even when they must have guessed that our views differed. Likewise, I am indebted to those who participated in the post-electoral surveys of 2002, 2007, and 2012.

Along the way, talented students at the University of Toronto provided invaluable help: Nadine Abd El Razek, Aya Bar Oz, Edana Beauvais, Amanda Foley, Gabriel Menard, Gavin Nardocchio-Jones, and Pierre Permingeat. Young people like these brighten our future. Colleagues at the University of Toronto who, despite their learning, could not rescue this project from its imperfections include Zaheer Baber, Dean Behrens, Joseph Bryant, Robert Brym, Clayton Childress, James DiCenso, Ron Gillis, John Hannigan, Eric Jennings, Charles Jones, Vanina Leschziner, William Magee, Jeffrey Reitz, and Lorne Tepperman.

The café at 321 Bloor Street West that the Mercurio family runs with Tony Macri supplied good cheer and daily fuel.

Work on this book may have put to the test my bonds with Domenico Cuomo, Lawrence Hill, Christopher Kevill, Bernard Maciejewski, and Bruce Veugelers. Gladly, most of these bonds more than resisted.

ABBREVIATIONS

ANFANOMA	Association Nationale des Français d'Afrique du Nord, d'Outre-Mer et de leurs Amis
CNIP	Centre national des indépendants et paysans
CODUR	Comité de Défense et d'Union des Rapatriés
EU	European Union
FLN	Front de libération nationale
FN	Front national
FNC	Front national des Combattants
FNR	Front national des rapatriés
FRAN	Front des Réfugiés d'Afrique du Nord
FSR	Fédération du Sud des Rapatriés
LR	Les Républicains
MSI	Movimento sociale italiano
NATO	North Atlantic Treaty Organization
OAS	Organisation armée secrète
ON	Ordre Nouveau
PACA	Provence-Alpes-Côte d'Azur
PFN	Parti des forces nouvelles
PR	Parti républicain
PS	Parti socialiste
RANFRAN	Rassemblement National des Français Rapatriés d'Afrique du Nord
RECOURS	Rassemblement et coordination unitaire des rapatriés et spoliés d'outre-mer
RI	Républicains indépendants
RPR	Rassemblement pour la République
TPM	Communauté d'agglomération Toulon Provence Méditerranée

UAVFROM	Union des Amicales Varoises des Français Rapatriés d'Outre-mer
UDCA	Union de défense des commerçants et artisans
UDF	Union pour la démocratie française
UMP	Union pour un mouvement populaire

Introduction

During the two centuries after the French Revolution, no problem mattered more for domestic politics in Europe than conflict between the social classes. Other divisions—the landed interests against commerce and industry, the subject cultures of the peripheries against the centralizing state, the religions against each other or against the secularists—also shaped alliances and oppositions. Still, above all, domestic politics consisted of left versus right: those who dreamed of a broader distribution of wealth—if not an overthrow of the capitalist system—opposed the propertied classes, who feared a revolutionary upheaval that would unseat them.

Sometimes hidden, sometimes open, another opposition pitted the native against the outsider. Largely dormant after World War II, today this cleavage is back. Out of solidarity with race or nation, social classes are closing ranks and choosing the xenophobic option; to oppose the politics of exclusion, likewise, opponents of nativism are crossing lines of class. The opposition over nativism has not eliminated other cleavages, it overlays them, thereby making politics more complicated.[1]

Many countries are feeling this tectonic shift, but the shockwaves have hit longest and hardest in France. Its far-right party has offered a model for anti-immigrant parties across the continent. The dominant party of the left—the Socialist Party—has made its peace with capitalism while chasing the ethnic vote. Blurring the lines between extremism and moderation, politicians of the conservative right have upheld the nativist cleavage by borrowing from the rhetoric of the far right. During the 2017 presidential election, the leading liberal candidate—Emmanuel Macron—declared that colonialism had been a crime against humanity. Setting himself apart from the patriotic right, he was competing for the anti-nativist vote.

This book will succeed if it persuades the reader that the social roots of nativist politics in France lie in imperialism and its legacy.

After World War I, the history of France consisted of a mostly unwanted and sometimes bloody exit from the ranks of the great powers. Legacies of empire endure today—in French sovereignty over islands across the seas as well as the presence, in the metropole, of millions of people whose origins lie in former dominions such as Senegal, Morocco, Tunisia, or Vietnam. This book focusses on the Europeans of French Algeria, who lived in that land for over a century before fleeing to the metropole at the time of decolonization. Their story provides the guiding strand for *Empire's Legacy*, which connects cultural codes to social milieu and political choice. Relations between colonizer, colonized, and French state inculcated among the Europeans of Algeria an affinity toward the far right, I will argue, but only later—in a kind of delayed reaction—did this affinity translate into actual support for the National Front.

During the first decades after World War II, France conformed to the dominant pattern in Europe: an anti-liberal, extreme right survived, but in a space much constricted by comparison with the interwar period. In eastern Europe, the single-party, communist regimes barely tolerated rival political organizations or ideologies (whether conservative, liberal, social-democratic, or fascist). In southern Europe—Portugal, Spain, Italy, and Greece—the postwar far right found the terrain more fertile. Elsewhere in Europe, though, support for a brand of politics now associated with Nazism proved absent, weak, or transitory. During the 1970s, moreover, even Portugal, Spain, and Greece traded right-wing authoritarianism for parliamentary democracy.

By the 1980s, the European far right seemed on the way to extinction. Anachronistic, irrelevant, and illegitimate, instead of valuing social equality its advocates believed in a hierarchy of races deemed natural, inevitable, and legitimate. Instead of valuing parliamentary democracy, they put the interests of race, nation, or state ahead of liberal rights and freedoms. Impatient with social conflict, they reacted with hostility not only toward their critics but also toward the pluralistic principle that an open society should value and protect the right to hold or express divergent opinions. In a fashion often eccentric, they ranked emotion and honor ahead of material well-being and peaceful coexistence.[2] In public, members of the postwar far right tended to avoid nostalgia for their predecessors; in private, they proved less circumspect.[3] Stigmatized by its association with the worst episodes of barbarity in the West's collective memory, the far right clung to the edges of social and political life.

Rather than remaining passive or clinging to outmoded ways, the far right adapted. Its rejection of democratic politics softened into demagogy.

Some in the far right kept their support for parliamentary democracy either ambiguous or conditional.[4] Others presented themselves as champions of populist protest.[5] Instead of overthrowing democracy, they wanted to clean up the system by throwing out the elites: establishment politicians out of touch with the people, corrupt scoundrels who line their pockets with bribes, and nepotistic opportunists for whom political office is a sinecure.[6]

The far right also learned to blame differently. To the Jew, the Freemason, the Bolshevik, and the plutocrat, it added the "immigrant"—a specious label for immigrants, refugees, and ethno-racial minorities with full citizenship.[7] Issuing crude disparagements of people of African, Caribbean, or South Asian ancestry in the United Kingdom, during the 1970s the British National Front led the way. After it all but disappeared from the political scene, a more viable prototype surfaced in France, the National Front of Jean-Marie Le Pen. Inspired by its example, since the 1980s far-right politicians in the rest of Europe have adopted the nativist formula, with Muslims, Sinti, and Roma joining the list of aliens to blame for a host of problems: rising crime; scarce jobs; cultural decline; urban decay; heavy taxes; and shortcomings in housing, education, and health care. Among voters, in turn, opposition to immigration is the dominant motivation for supporting the far right.[8]

THE PENETRATION OF PARTY POLITICS

The far right has adjusted its image and its message, but to what effect? "The far right is on the rise!" warn the news media. Journalists have been recycling this message for years, after each surge in support for the far right: in France one year, Italy or Belgium another year, then Switzerland, next Greece, Hungary, Poland, Austria, Italy, Germany, and—looking across the Atlantic—the United States. Their diagnosis makes the alarm bells ring: the failure of mainstream parties to deal with serious economic problems due to globalization has made extreme solutions more attractive to an alienated, suffering, and desperate segment of the electorate. The wave is swelling, and it threatens to submerge democracy.

This—the losers of globalization thesis—lacks credibility given voting trends over the past decade. If the alarmists were correct, a marked increase in far-right support should have followed the jarring economic crisis that hit Europe in 2008. Its after-effects are still afflicting youths and pensioners, workers and families, firms and communities. Yet of 28 European Union (EU) member countries, 10 still have no far-right party. Among the other 18 countries, after 2008 only nine saw an increase in far-right support. Among these nine, the increase topped 5 percent in only four (Austria,

France, Hungary, and Latvia); among the nine countries where support dropped, again the decrease topped 5 percent in four (Belgium, Italy, Romania, and Slovakia).[9] The pattern is inconsistent and contradictory. Economic conditions have had effects on far-right voting that are neither uniform (the same across different societies) nor straightforward (unaffected by other conditions).

Consider Spain, which each year between 2009 and 2013 received 6.7 immigrants per 1,000 inhabitants (compared with 2.4 in France); and in 2014, received 265,800 immigrants (compared with 168,100 immigrants who went to France).[10] Between 2008 and 2013, its unemployment rate surged from 8 to 26 percent (more than twice the EU average). In 2000, surveys suggest, Spaniards were more accepting of immigration than were the citizens of any other country in Europe.[11] Today, three-quarters of them say their country has too many immigrants. In national elections, though, Spaniards have given the far right hardly any support.[12]

The far right has gained, in fact, but at a deeper level. In free elections held during the decades after World War II, party systems remained frozen. From one election to the next, the options on offer hardly changed. Brief exceptions aside, to vote meant choosing between the parties of the liberals, the conservatives, the farmers, the workers, the Catholics, or the Protestants. Despite their different labels, programs, and electorates, these options had built mass organizations and penetrated systems of local politics before the final thrust toward universal suffrage in the late nineteenth and early twentieth centuries. Space for another option—the communists—opened after the Russian Revolution. Then the freeze set in.

Starting in the 1950s, non-party movements of the left and the right posed a new challenge. Through a process of survival by adaptation, though, the established parties deflected or absorbed the messages, cadres, and supporters of their challengers.[13] During the 1980s, by contrast, party systems thawed as other options—the new left, ecologists, and far right—became relevant. The far right broke through in France, then in other countries: Austria, Belgium, Italy, Denmark, and Norway. In some places (Britain, Greece, Ireland, Portugal, and Spain), it remained absent, transient, or marginal. Like the new left and ecologist parties, still, it challenged the strategy of adaptation that had served the established parties for so long. Between 1960 and 1994, the vote for established parties shrank an average of 24.5 percent in four European countries with patronage politics (Austria, Belgium, Italy, and Switzerland) and 9.2 percent in eight others.[14] Between 2000 and 2016, similarly, electoral support for Europe's mainstream parties (social democrats, Christian democrats, conservatives, and liberals) fell from 75 to 64 percent.[15] Levels of support for the challengers (new left, ecologists, and far right) have varied. Yet the established parties would have declined even more had they not reacted by adopting new messages and strategies. Along with the rise of the new left and the ecologists, in sum, the far right has contributed to the thawing of party systems. The fortunes of these upstarts will continue to wax and wane, but they have reconfigured the political landscape.[16]

Where the far right has become entrenched in party politics, we should not expect it to disappear. This need not represent a threat to democracy, whose stability rests on a consensus: an agreement, between those who govern and those who do not, to abide by the rules of the game. These rules permit open but peaceful challenges to those who govern. Although not without fissures, the consensus on these rules is now stronger than during the interwar period: democracy has been sliding lately but remains in the saddle. Some argue that incorporating the far right into party systems is better than their exclusion, which tempts them toward extremism, violence, and subversion. A difficulty remains, of course: far-right parties are intolerant. They oppose pluralism of opinion and peoples. An ascendant far right emboldens hateful speech and action.

A CONSTANT DEMAND

This book does not attempt to resolve the conundrum of whether a defense of democracy can justify a militant intolerance of political extremism (by suspending the right to free speech or freedom of association, for example).[17] Anchored in an interdisciplinary approach at the juncture between history, sociology, and political science, instead this book addresses a paradox.

Scholars who study the contemporary far right look at two families of factors: (1) *demand-side factors that pertain to electorates* (such as social atomization, relative deprivation, ethnic competition, popular xenophobia, or political discontent); and (2) *supply-side factors outside of electorates* (such as party messages, party organizations, interparty dynamics, electoral systems, elite alliances, or media messages).[18] At first glance, it would seem sensible not to rule out causes of either kind: How could explanation do without both? According to this line of reasoning, far-right voting depends on the interaction between demand and supply. A good part of the electorate must share an appetite for the far right; and the party system (as well as mass media and other opinion shapers) must whet and satisfy that appetite.

Sensible as this composite theory seems, one of its premises turns out to be weaker than expected. Explanations focused on the demand side risk overestimating the importance of demand. This is because attitudes sympathetic to the far right are always in plentiful supply.[19] Far-right success may have less to do with change in demand than with change in party politics. This provides a cue for *Empire's Legacy*, which charts a new direction by treating far-right affinities as a relative constant within the electorate. It asks how much can be explained by the supply side alone.

Saying some factors do not change while others vary is still vague, though. What also matters is the significance of change or continuity, as well as the place and period in question. Since the early 1960s, a socially rooted affinity toward the far right has proven less changeable than have parties, party systems, and other elements of the environment that shapes electoral competition. *Empire's Legacy* charts the birth, development, and maturation of this affinity in France before its channeling into support for the far right.

TOULON

The story that unfolds in this book turns on a single event: the victory, on 18 June 1995, of the National Front in Toulon. On that day, this Mediterranean port of some 170,000 inhabitants became the largest city in Europe to come under the far right since 1945. Victory had eluded the National Front in elections with higher stakes (whether departmental, regional, parliamentary, or presidential). The party of Le Pen thus scored a coup in 1995: the chance to show it was not merely a protest party but one that could govern well. Its opponents feared the south of France would become a showcase for the politics of reaction and intolerance.

To explain the victory of the National Front in Toulon, I return to the development of a complex and multilayered sense of belonging and exclusion among the Europeans of colonial Algeria. Herein lie the roots of an affinity for the French far right. Other parties received the support of the ex-colonials during the two decades that followed the independence of Algeria. During the 1980s, though, many ex-colonials turned to the far right. Whether members of this group supported the National Front depended on closed social ties that sealed them within a subculture.

PAST AND PRESENT

Born in the same year in the 1940s, Monsieur Bertou and Monsieur Ollières both grew up in Algiers. They migrated to the metropole during the summer of 1962, and both reside in Toulon, where they know each other. These men are lukewarm Catholics: they go to church for baptisms, marriages, and funerals, but not for Sunday mass. When I interviewed Monsieur Bertou and Monsieur Ollières separately, I asked if some races possess superior aptitudes (past research found the answer a powerful predictor of far-right support). Each denied a belief in racial differences. Similar in so many ways, politically the two men differ.

For the past three decades, Monsieur Bertou tells me, people in his neighborhood have known that he votes for the National Front.[20] He admits the media could be telling the truth when it accuses this party of racism. He denies that he is a racist, though, and says he has yet to see racism at National Front rallies. This also holds for the Algeria of his youth. A few landowners may have lived far above the rest of the population. Still, the colony was a symbiosis of communities:

> Even with the Arabs—people with whom we would have many quarrels later on—we all lived together, each community contributed its own customs, its traditions, and everything was mixed together, was really mixed together and it made for a melting pot that worked well.

At the Algiers Forum in May 1958, Monsieur Bertou joined the thousands of settlers who called out "Long Live De Gaulle!" They counted on this man—who thanks to their insurgency soon became president—to save their colony:

> Four years later, he kicked us out. In this regard, I think that we *pieds noirs*, we're all the same. We were manipulated by the Gaullists. They came to power by making us think they would restore order but in the end, after four years, they let everything go.

As a teenager, Monsieur Bertou joined in clandestine activity. This led him to Pierre Sergent, an OAS leader who later entered the National Assembly as a deputy for the National Front.[21] Remembering Sergent and other nationalists who opposed Algerian independence reminds Monsieur Bertou of losses that seared his soul:

> You know militants who are dead, people who were fighting with you, they were from my neighborhood, and now they were dead.

Honoring such sacrifices means not turning the page. He calls the National Front a protest party, not a governing party. But honor entails duties:

> I am loyal, no matter what. I am loyal to the people who fought the same fight I did. And in the National Front there are many people who fought the same fight we did. I don't

share every single one of their ideas, but I am loyal. I vote for them even if I haven't known them personally. I happened to meet them by chance, after coming to France. Already in Algeria these people were more or less always on our side, you know, the only ones.

Monsieur Bertou cannot let bygones be bygones. For him, a French ex-colonial who supports the left is a sellout.

Monsieur Ollières, who prefers the moderate left, understands people like Monsieur Bertou:

> They were hurt badly, really torn apart. They were told: "You are going to fight for France," and then suddenly they were told, "You have won on the battlefield, but you must retreat." They had friends who had died, children who had died, so they came back here with a rancor that is understandable, a rancor they still hold onto, they still hang onto. I understand all that, for sure, I understand. Even if I can't agree, I understand.

Still, Monsieur Ollières pleads for the need to move on:

> They need to understand too. They need to turn the page. Life can't stay stuck in the past forever. The English did some bad things to the French too. But if you keep going back, it never ends. Same thing with the Germans. When I see a twenty-year-old German, I don't blame him for what Hitler did. He is not responsible. The English too. They fought against the French—at Mers-El-Kébir, for example. It never ends. I think people need to know when to turn the page. A time comes when people need to say, "Okay, we won't forget, but we need to change."

If by chance the Socialist candidate in an election fails to qualify for the run-off, Monsieur Ollières transfers his support to the moderate right. He never supports the far right:

> In the National Front, you find former members of the Waffen-SS, and you find former members of the OAS. The National Front incites people to look for scapegoats who are responsible for every problem. It used to be the Jews, now maybe it's the blacks, maybe it's the Arabs. They always say, "It's not me, it's their fault."

He denies that foreigners are stealing jobs from the French:

> When one looks at the projections, our workforce will need more and more foreigners. Look, we are living longer, right, and we are having fewer children, because we prefer well-being and tranquility.

This is why Monsieur Ollières questions the program of the far right:

> It's easy to unite resentments, but that only amounts to exclusion. It's not constructive, it's all about criticism, that's all. National Front politicians don't provide any solutions. When you read their program, it has no solutions. Or when they put some in, they are completely utopian.

Why, then, do so many ex-colonials vote for the far right?

> Their memory is stuck. It cannot move ahead. Their memory does not evolve. Instead of looking around, they only want to look back. But that doesn't work, it's not useful. We might not like many things, we don't have to agree with everything, not at all, but the Euro, the European Union, are good things. We can't retreat inside ourselves. We can't do that anymore. It does not help. The past is over.

Shared historical experiences—life in colonial Algeria, wounds caused by independence, flight to the metropole—nurtured an affinity for the far right. So did collective forgetting, as we will see.[22] Keeping this affinity alive required community. Absent a fertile social setting—communities of discourse, interaction, and ritual—ex-colonials became more like Monsieur Ollières, ready to forgive. For people like Monsieur Bertou, by contrast, the march of history is not a synonym for progress.

This book does not argue that all of France's ex-colonials have supported the far right.[23] Instead, it identifies social ties that kept a far-right potential alive within a segment of this group. Specifically, I focus on membership in patriotic associations of ex-colonials or military veterans. Membership of this kind had a triple effect. Cutting contact with outsiders, it shielded members from dissonant values and opinions. Through shared practices such as talk and ritual, it upheld and updated subcultural codes. Curbing outside contact and keeping codes alive, in turn, membership raised the likelihood of far-right voting. Without participation in this segregated milieu, the far-right potential faded.

In certain localities and regions of France, we will see, European ex-colonials have given the far right a decisive boost. In Toulon, they decided the outcome of a municipal election won by the National Front. Traditionally, the French far right has suffered from a weak social base. A latecomer in a field already occupied by others, its capacity to mobilize mass support was weak and transitory. The ex-colonials helped the far right gain the solid social base it never had.[24] Concentrated among them are remnants of a colonial culture that penetrated the metropole until the early 1960s, and still persists.[25] Only change in political context, though, can explain why this legacy came to affect voting instead of remaining latent.

A HIDDEN UNDERCURRENT

Today it is easy to forget that the breakthrough of the National Front came as a surprise. Since its formation, the party had remained weak and nearly invisible. During the 1980s, suddenly, it moved out of the shadows. Outside as well as inside France, its ascent caught observers off guard. The reason for surprise inhered not in the events, but in the lenses used to view them. Overlooking deep and enduring patterns in society, observers had missed an undercurrent.[26] Unlike communism (above the surface, even after the consolidation of Gaullism), right-wing resentment against the regime had slipped from view. It re-emerged when relations between voters and politicians unraveled. To see this required a lens that did not cut empire, colonization, and decolonization from its field of vision.

The National Front consolidated its breakthrough by building its voter base. Coupled with citizen alienation from the established parties, a mix of voter concerns—crime, unemployment, economic liberalization, and European integration—ensured the party's ongoing competitiveness. Today, in depressed mining and industrial areas of the north and northeast, the party of Le Pen is replacing the Communists and the Socialists as the voice of the weak and vulnerable. In towns and cities of the Mediterranean, by contrast, European ex-colonials provided a reservoir of support. Studying Toulon, then, opens the lid on regional variation in the party's strategy.

The fortunes of the far right have fluctuated, yet it remains competitive. Other parties try to match its appeal, yet it refuses to disappear. Politicians take a risk when they mimic the far right: opportunism harms credibility. Stealing votes from the far right in one election, they lose them in the next. For those who oppose the far right, the lesson is sobering. A quick fix to the challenge of nativist politics is chimerical. By connecting France's colonial past to contemporary politics, we see why the demand that allowed the far right to penetrate the party system will persist.

THE LOSING SIDE AND ITS ANACHRONISTIC REMNANTS

This book tells the story of a poisoned legacy, a betrayal of liberty, equality, and fraternity. Shaping this story is a vision that transcends its subject. Ignoring the losers of history, I submit, results not merely in blind spots—a forgetting of the past—but also a thin and potentially distorted understanding of politics and social change, whose direction depends on interactions between the losers of history and those who occupy positions that confer influence, esteem, or power.[27]

I am not the first with this vision. Explaining the attraction of Nazism to social classes that felt threatened, in 1932 Ernst Bloch wrote:

> Germany in general, which did not accomplish a bourgeois revolution until 1918, is, unlike England, and much less France, the classical land of nonsynchronism, that is, of unsurmounted remnants of older economic being and consciousness.[28]

By unsurmounted remnants, the neo-Marxist thinker meant fractions of the German peasantry, urban bourgeoisie, and Junker nobility that, each in its own way, with its own myths and memories, idealized the past because the capitalist economy was ruining them. Writing that "[n]eeds and elements from past ages break through the relativism of the general weariness like magma through a thin crust," Bloch wondered if the ghost of history did not have more volcanic power in Germany than in France.[29]

Many decades after Bloch linked cultural traditions in Germany to politics in the Great Depression, his assessment stands ready for revision: France harbors its own unsurmounted remnants. I am not claiming that a Le Pen is like a Hitler or that the party of a Le Pen is akin to the Nazi Party. Although effective, perhaps, when contemporary anti-fascists wish to demonize their opponents, often parallels of this type are unreliable. In France, indeed, far-right propaganda that defends the exclusion of minorities or the primacy of the general will has invoked ideals that are republican, so mainstream.[30] My point is instead this: in France too, the past—the past of a former imperial power that conquered and ruled, colonized and then decolonized—continues to haunt the present. Bloch's insight—*people have different conceptions of historical time, thus of the meaning of the present, and this affects their politics*—remains as true today as it did for Weimar Germany. Further, it applies across the political spectrum.

A considered awareness of how historical time affects the political affinities of groups that make up our societies is sorely lacking, I believe. This awareness should be recovered and revitalized. Before reaching this conclusion, a memory had dogged me for years: the shock, among observers of French politics during the 1980s, at the breakthrough of a far-right party that seemed to come from nowhere. This book looks to where it came from.

PART I
Sedimentation of a Political Affinity

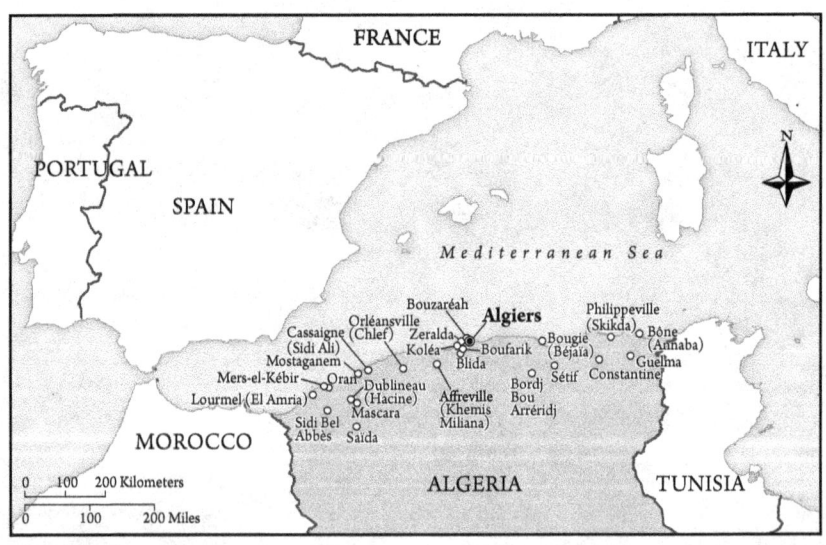

Map 1. Colonial Algeria.

CHAPTER 1
Settler Relations and Identities in Colonial Algeria

Sometimes a bureaucratic report can be like the organ of a sacrificial animal: not very alive, but full of omens. In 1954, the Government-General of Algeria conducted a broad survey of local officials. In addition to land reform, agricultural output, and vocational training, it asked about relations between colonizers and colonized. An official from Blida responded:

> The most bothersome point is the absence of any affective and spiritual contact between the French and the Muslims. Two populations live side-by-side, go about their common business, without making serious efforts to understand and respect each other. Cultural events organized by one part leave the other part completely indifferent. This is the most preoccupying point, because indifference can sometimes be more durable than open hostility.[1]

This report came just months before the Algerian war of independence, a conflict that would make contact across the ethno-religious divide more difficult yet.

Far-right parties are obsessed with the threat from aliens living inside the national borders. Sometimes they paint this threat as hidden and mysterious, other times as plain to anyone with common sense. Aliens threaten cherished values and traditions, say the nativists, because they are unable or unwilling to assimilate. Intolerant, authoritarian, sexist, and potentially violent, aliens threaten progress and peaceful coexistence. Many are agents of Islamic fundamentalism, allegedly. They take jobs away from natives, and they take advantage of the welfare state. Their criminality erodes public safety. Immigration serves a plan that disregards the interests of the average citizen. Combined with anti-elitism, nativism offers ready-made diagnoses and remedies for a host of problems.[2]

Why has this language resonated with a sizeable part of the French electorate? The National Front is the continuator of an intellectual and political tradition fixated on Jews, Bolsheviks, and Freemasons. Yet these scapegoats it hardly mentions in public. Instead, it targets "immigrants"—a euphemism that includes refugees and a good number of French nationals but excludes people of, say, Portuguese, Italian, or Armenian descent. Immigrant is code for nonwhite, above all people of Maghrebi origin.[3] The far right in contemporary France, I will argue, has exploited stereotypes, hopes, and fears planted during the colonial period.[4]

Among the three countries that form the Maghreb, Tunisia and Morocco came under French domination half a century later than Algeria. Neither attracted anywhere near as many European settlers as did Algeria. Tunisia and most of Morocco were protectorates (the rest of Morocco went to Spain). French Algeria—the "Jewel of the Empire"—was not a colony in law because it was subdivided into departments with a civilian administration, just like the rest of France. During the 1950s, Tunisia and Morocco made the transition to independence relatively smoothly. Algeria became independent after a brutal war that cost many lives and upset many others. Dividing public opinion and creating political crisis, like the Dreyfus Affair it belonged to the series of periodic conflicts that have pitted French against French since 1789.

When he visited Algiers during the 1840s, the writer Théophile Gautier found chaos and confusion. "The black cloak of the Parisienne," he wrote, "brushes in passing against the white veil of the Moorish woman; the embroidered sleeve of the officer scratches the naked arm of the Negro rubbed with oil; the rags of the Bedouin jostle the frock coat of the elegant Frenchman."[5] Colonial Algeria was a caste society whose European inhabitants could count on political rights, social courtesies, and material prospects unknown to the vast majority of those they referred to as *les Arabes*. The settlers did not form a unified mass, clearly. Half or more possessed Spanish, Italian, or Maltese origins. Rural life offered one formative context, life in one of Algeria's cities or towns another. The party choices of the Algerian settlers spanned the left-right spectrum. Fault lines between Europeans did not disappear during the war that led to independence in 1962, but crossing them became easier. The French of Algeria set aside ethnic differences and came closest to forming one people with a shared consciousness of its collective destiny.[6] By then the colony's survival was uncertain. With the unravelling of French Algeria, 1 million settlers found themselves among the losers of twentieth-century history.

Social identity is about them and us, according to psychologists and sociologists, who agree on the following. All things being equal: group members tend to view those outside their group as antipathetic and inferior; and each person is an identity bundle—they belong to multiple groups whose symbolic salience depends on the situation. When threat recedes, friendly intergroup contact can lessen bias and prejudice toward outsiders.[7] Proceeding from these premises, we ask how exclusion and inclusion made settler identities in Algeria. Concentrated among those 1 million settlers were orientations the far right would exploit decades later.

1830–1914: THE FRENCH CONQUEST AND COLONIZATION

When Alexis de Tocqueville sat in the Chamber of Deputies, his peers regarded him as an expert on the Algerian question. Twice the author of *Democracy in America* had visited the North African colony, whose submission to France he championed in the name of glory and national interest. Yet when he addressed a parliamentary commission on Algeria in 1847, he declared, "We have made Muslim society far more miserable, more disorganized, more ignorant, and more barbaric than before we arrived."[8] His words came too late and hardly mattered.

Along with a Bourbon king's wish to divert attention from political problems in Paris, geopolitics—especially the Great Power rivalry with Britain—had motivated the invasion of Algiers, which fell to a French expeditionary force in 1830. The French proceeded to capture more towns along the Mediterranean but met with defeat in the interior. Applying lessons learned in combats against the counterrevolutionary Vendéens in 1793–1796 and the Portuguese and Russian guerillas during the Napoleonic wars, they decided to press on. To regain the initiative, they switched to mobile columns that brought the skirmish into enemy territory. To deprive the enemy of food and supplies, they pursued scorched earth tactics: burning crops, felling trees, slaughtering herds, and destroying granaries. Rape, pillaging, and mass murder that offended public opinion in France left hundreds, if not thousands, of dead civilians.[9] Afterward, an oral tradition of songs, poems, and stories that celebrated resistance to the French would feed the mistrust and animosity of the subject population.[10]

Unlike its plantation colonies in the Caribbean or later possessions in Southeast Asia and sub-Saharan Africa, France envisioned a "pacified" Algeria as a pioneer society of European smallholders working their own land.[11] Cholera, malaria, and malnutrition afflicted immigrants, though, with less than a third settling permanently in the first decades. To encourage others, Paris suspended duties with Algeria and built roads, dams, ports, railroads, and villages. Despite a slow start, the settler population grew rapidly.[12] After early experiments with cotton, the *colons* found wheat and tobacco—and eventually wine and citrus fruits—more profitable.[13] Still, many Europeans who came to Algeria lacked skill in agriculture. A report from two villages lists only nine farmers among the 82 men who arrived in January 1849. The rest included a metal caster, a confectioner, a café owner, a waiter, a postman, a barber, a stationer's clerk, and a wigmaker.[14] Contrary to plan, most of the European population became urban and in the biggest cities—Algiers, Oran, Constantine, and Bône—they would form a slight majority.[15]

Differences in class, politics, and ethnicity made the migrants a mix: aristocrats and officials on the losing side when the Bourbon regime fell, republican opponents to the Second Empire, and loyalists fleeing Alsace-Lorraine after its annexation by the German Empire.[16] The mix also included migrants that the French mistrusted:

> We have not conquered Algeria to make it into a cosmopolitan country: French land it is, and French land it shall remain. It is imperative to monitor carefully the arrival of emigrants, especially the Spanish; to admit only those with proper documentation and certified morals; and to deport vagabonds and miscreants. All the hospitality in the world could not oblige us to accept in our land the cast-offs of other peoples.[17]

Many of those the French settlers referred to derogatively as Neo-French came from the Balearic Islands and the Spanish mainland.[18] Well represented in Algiers, Spaniards formed the majority of the European population in Oran. Less numerous and less urban were the Maltese and Italians, who tended to settle along Algeria's eastern seaboard. Italians from Campagna, Sicily, and Puglia worked mostly in fishing while Maltese became market gardeners. Settlers of non-French stock entered the working class that would build and maintain the colony's roads, ports, dams, railroads, warehouses, and public buildings.[19]

A nationalization law of 1889 extended French citizenship to the Algerian-born children of non-French Europeans. Algerians of French stock did not approve: "By virtue of the law of 1889, each year about 8,000 individuals of foreign origin are becoming French without making a request, without any evidence they are worthy, without any possibility for the government to oppose their admission into our country."[20] Before this political sleight of hand, less than half the settler population was French.[21] Afterward, the non-French share of the European population would shrink steadily—according to the census, at least.[22] Settlers with metropolitan origins kept their disdain for the Neo-French.[23] How could the Neo-French be truly French? In their ignorance of French culture, it seemed that some equaled Arabs or Kabyles.[24]

In practice, settlers of Spanish, Italian, or Maltese descent adapted: "A settler may have been 'French' when requesting aid at the public assistance office in central Algiers, a 'Valencian' at the café in his local Bab-el-Oued neighborhood, and an 'Algerian' around election time."[25] Contrary to those who dreamed of a fusion between the Europeans, endogamy persisted.[26] Apart from mutual mistrust, language difference and residential segregation delayed intermarriage. Eventually, though, a good number of Europeans did marry outside their group. According to a Frenchman living in Algeria:

> In mixed European marriages, nearly always the man was French. The prestige French nationality bestowed served as an attraction to women from the southern Mediterranean shores, in particular the Hispanic-Algerian women, who were gratified to marry into "the conquering race."[27]

While taking a French spouse allowed social climbing for the Neo-French, finding a non-French spouse from a higher class might rescue from social decline a French person with dim economic prospects.[28] Though never achieved, a melting pot of Europeans—the French of Algeria—was in the making.

RELATIONS BETWEEN EUROPEANS AND *LES ARABES*

For all the differences between Europeans, they would pull together in defending a system that made the lowest among them superior to almost any native. Those lumped together as *les Arabes* included not only people of Arabian descent but also the first inhabitants of the region, the Berbers, who had converted to Islam after the Arab incursions of the seventh century.[29] Through war, famine, sickness, and emigration, during the four decades after 1830 the subject population shrank from an estimated 3 or 4 million to 2.1 million.[30] This number never fell below that of the settler population, though, a condition that made Algeria different from Australia, Canada, and the United States.

Beyond the enmity born of violent conquest, religious difference, forced loans, and punitive levies, the opposition between colonizer and colonized fed off the land question.[31] The French seized the lands of tribes in exile or at war with them. Estates of the Ottoman oligarchy as well as uncultivated lands (including fallow fields and common pastures) reverted to the French state as well. The colonial administration imposed a system of private property that overturned Ottoman, Islamic, and tribal systems of land use; and adopted a policy of tribal consolidation that freed up more land. To aid settlement, in turn, the administration created villages and granted land to

Europeans. By expropriating and commodifying land, the French destroyed an intricate system of rights on which tribal economies had depended. Their communal lands lost, some tribes surrendered their last scraps of territory and moved away. Loss of land drove insurgencies that harried the French until the early twentieth century.[32] Collective representations were discordant, then: settlers lived in a pacified land; natives lived under an alien power.

Unlike French colonies in Oceania, Indochina, and sub-Saharan Africa, to calm the Maghreb the authorities barred conversion by Catholic missionaries. The incommensurability of Islamic society hinged on its male-female relations. Polygamy was not widespread in Algeria but accepted; so were divorce and arranged marriage. By comparison with Europeans, spouses in a Muslim marriage tended to be further apart in age.[33] The rarity of Muslims—particularly girls—in public schools raised an additional barrier to intermarriage. Others came from residential segregation in the cities and the rural concentration of the Muslim population. Absence of opportunity meshed with attitudes. After visiting Algeria during the early 1860s, one French journalist wrote:

> Opinion in the cities of Africa is indulgent toward romantic peccadilloes; it shows no mercy toward misalliances between the races. So great was the scandal around a European woman of Oran, discovered under orange trees in an intimate conversation with a *caïd* of the Hachems during an evening celebration, that she had to leave that city.[34]

During the quarter century after 1880, only 139 marriages joined a Muslim man and a European woman; and only 126 joined a European man and a Muslim woman. Most Europeans believed that unyielding cultural differences doomed such unions to failure.[35]

By the early twentieth century, the native represented a diminished threat to the physical security of the settler:

> It was now a question of creating a society in the image of the newcomer, and this could only work to the detriment of the society already *in situ*. The settler ideology that evolved denigrated and marginalized indigenous society better to anchor its own. This ensured the exclusion, with a few individual exceptions, of the indigenous population from the European social pyramid. Indigenous society evolved at its own pace, and with its own hierarchies, alongside European society but not within it.[36]

Administrators and military officers in the colony might show sympathy toward the Berbers, deemed closer than the Arabs were to civilization, thus within range of the secularizing norms and ideals of republican France.[37]

Further, military, administrative, and political elites included men with a practical or scholarly knowledge of the history, language, and customs of the Arabs and Berbers.[38]

Such knowledge and curiosity showed less in the *Cayagous* series of mass-circulation novels and cartoons, published in weekly installments between 1891 and 1920.[39] Popular enough for republication as books, the *Cayagous* series did not simply bear the imprint of colonial society; upholding linguistic boundaries, it acted back on its milieu.[40] The series was in *pataouète*, a French idiom with borrowings from Arabic, Judeo-Arabic, Spanish, and Italian.[41] Among the Europeans of Algeria, possessing the ability to fathom *Cayagous* by understanding its language, grasping its references, and appreciating its humor provided living evidence of their difference from others (including the French of the metropole). The *Cayagous* series presents its readers with childlike *Arabes* who speak clumsy French. Alternately picturesque or ridiculous, they lack individualizing features such as personal names (except for the ubiquitous Ahmed). They perform work that is menial and subservient. European youngsters play tricks on them. Doubts about cleanliness and probity abound:

> The gentleman: Look here! Find me two Arabs who are no thieves to whom I can entrust two bundles of laundry to bring to my house.
> The native: Such Arabs are not to be found, sir![42]

The *Cayagous* series pokes fun at the impossibility of a marriage or a sexual liaison between a European woman and an Arab man: better for the subject people to keep to their proper place.[43]

In Indochina as well as the military regions of Saharan Algeria—parts of the empire where European women were rare, and the subject population was phenotypically distinct—the legal and social position of the offspring of mixed relations was an important question. Not so in the bulk of Algeria, where the sex ratio of the settler population was near parity; the offspring of sexual relations across the settler-Muslim divide were less easy to recognize; and sequestration limited the sexual freedom of Muslim women. Provocatively, the unimportance of the *métis* question in colonial Algeria suggests that ethnicity and religion—not phenotype—provided the main principle of differentiation between the colony's peoples.[44]

Under France's neo-mercantilist policy, primary goods moved to the metropole, while manufactured goods found an outlet in Algeria. Responding to calls for self-government, in 1898 Paris transferred control over the Algerian budget to a delegation in Algiers. Defending big interests in wine, cereals, and livestock, the delegation's budgets (which parliamentarians in Paris approved after scarce debate) set the priorities for

Algerian development: ports, roads, railroads, shipping lines, irrigation, and communication. Creating an infrastructure for large-scale commercial agriculture oriented toward metropolitan markets prevailed over industrialization, universal education, and social services.[45] The delegation included a section of *indigènes*, their position a reward for loyal military service to the French. When a European proposed an increase in native representation on the delegation, a fellow delegate objected:

> If an *indigène* should wish to act independently, where will we be? He, a French subject, would want to question the basis of sovereignty! I challenge him on his right to do this. I am the conqueror, with the goodness of a Frenchman, but I wish to remain the conqueror and to say to him, "Your place is not in the same assembly as mine."[46]

Solidarity with their own made few Muslims apply for French citizenship. To prove assimilation, in any event, an applicant needed to know French and have professional or friendly relations with a European. Because it showed devotion to France, service in the military, schools, or administration helped. After a background check, though, the police might conclude that career advancement had motivated an application. The administration treated polygamy or a criminal record as a sign of poor character. Education also raised suspicion—the applicant might be an independent thinker. During the entire colonial period, perhaps 6,000 Muslims crossed to the other side and acquired French citizenship.[47]

THE JEWISH MINORITY

The Ottoman regime had tolerated Judaism but subjected its adherents to legal and economic discrimination. France also recognized its subjects' right to practice their religion. Just as Muslims came under the jurisdiction of *cadis* who upheld Islamic codes mixed with Berber customs, the Jewish minority came under the authority of rabbis and the Mosaic codes.[48] After the conquest, young Jewish men took advantage of new opportunities for schooling, but French nationality remained a condition for public employment or entry into professions like law and medicine.[49]

Pressure for the naturalization of Jews did not originate within the colony, where military elites feared it would antagonize the Muslim majority.[50] The metropole held precedents: the emancipation of the Jews in 1791; and the civil code of 1804, which had granted religious freedom. In 1806, Bonaparte had convened an assembly of Jewish notables in Paris to ascertain if the civil code were compatible with the Mosaic code. Foremost among the issues discussed were polygamy, divorce, and intermarriage.

This assembly had found insufficient reason to reverse the 1791 law that granted civic equality to Jews. Advocates of naturalization drew an invidious distinction: unlike Islam, Judaism belonged within the realm of civilization. The Israelite Central Consistory emphasized the decency of Jewish mores around marriage and the family.[51] Under the Crémieux decree of 1870, then, the Jews of Algeria won a status barred not just to Muslims but also to the colony's Spanish, Italians, and Maltese. Their naturalization sparked anger across the board: among the Arabs, Berbers, French *colons*, and Europeans still barred from citizenship.[52]

Collective action against Jews broke out in 1895, when settlers in Oran attacked Jews and their property. Anti-Jewish politicians won elections in Oran and Constantine. Students at the University of Algiers protested against the appointment of a Jewish professor. During the Dreyfus Affair the Ligue antijuive d'Alger turned anti-Semitism into a popular movement among the Neo-French.[53] When Zola published *J'accuse* in January 1898, anti-Semitic demonstrations across France peaked in Algiers, Oran, and Constantine.[54] Algerian voters elected four anti-Jewish deputies to the National Assembly, including Edouard Drumont, who in a bestseller from the 1880s wrote, "The Semite is mercantile, greedy, scheming, cunning, and sly; the Aryan is enthusiastic, heroic, chivalrous, generous, open, trusting to the point of naïveté."[55] Little of this turmoil seems to have mobilized Muslims, whose leaders joined the Jewish community in calling for a restoration of order. The administration responded by successfully monitoring, prosecuting, and banning the colony's anti-Semitic organizations.[56]

The anti-Jewish crisis and its aftermath revealed the unsettled state of ethnic relations at the turn of the century. Settlers of French origin might refer to those of Spanish or Italian origin as "foreign vermin" beneath the Arabs. A new governor-general recommended that applicants of French stock receive preference over "foreigners" (naturalized French) in hiring for public works.[57] Even if expressed less crudely than toward Muslims, marriage between a Christian and a Jew met with resistance.[58] According to one official report, in Algeria the French encountered "difficulties that we experience in no metropolitan city . . . nowhere do we find such a diversity of races . . . all in conflict."[59]

1914–1939: CHANGE AND CONTINUITY IN A DIVIDED COLONY

Between 1914 and 1918, more than 172,000 men left Algeria to fight for France (with some 22,000 Europeans and 25,000 Muslims killed). Wartime service unified the European soldiers from Algeria by putting their attachment to France above differences in locality and ethnicity. Within the segregated units of the *tirailleurs*, meanwhile, Muslim infantrymen discovered a France less overbearing and prejudiced than back home.[60] To cope with labor shortages in the metropole, the authorities pressed another 119,000 Muslims to work in mines and factories, where the commandeered laborers learned firsthand about union organization and strike tactics. Exposure to international developments furthered their political education: when the Ottoman Empire aligned with Germany, it declared a *jihad* against France and its allies; in Russia, a revolution overturned the czarist regime; and President Wilson affirmed the right of every people to self-determination. Police in Algeria worried about the subversive potential of the repatriated colonial worker and soldier, who re-entered a caste system hardly changed.[61]

After the war, the flow of migrant workers to the metropole intensified.[62] Older anti-Christian and anti-French traditions rubbed against socialism, republicanism, nationalism, trade unionism, and pan-Arabism. In Algeria, *ulema* reformers sought unity among the cults of the countryside. Their secular counterparts called for equal rights for all in a French Algeria that lived up to republican ideals. With the Algerian Communist Party dominated by settlers, a nationalist group founded by Algerians living in Paris (the Étoile nord-africaine) aligned itself with the French Communist Party in the metropole, and then split off and went its own way.[63]

To recognize wartime service, a 1919 decree had enlarged to about 100,000 the number of natives eligible to vote.[64] The French did not completely dismantle the native nobility, whose remnants won status as rural administrators. In urban politics, Muslim representatives sat on local assemblies and campaigned for full citizenship.[65] Yet famine, forced migration, and tribal disintegration had been transforming peasants and pastoral herdsmen into a semi-proletariat of sharecroppers and day laborers. Nomadism persisted, but even rural Muslims were becoming more sedentary, with nearly half living in dirt huts.[66] A poverty commission reported that of 3.5 million natives, only 14 percent enjoyed a minimally acceptable standard of living and another 50 percent were malnourished.[67] A 1931 report to the prefect for Constantine warned:

> The *indigène* is at the end of his rope. He is running out of food and cash; debt is paralyzing him; the mortgage on his lands has reached the extreme limit; the lack of pasture has reduced livestock by 60 percent; and to provide for his family, which he can no longer feed on his own, he has no choice but to sell the rest. All around are rock and bare earth.[68]

The administration increased relief funds, but population growth was worsening the problem of scarce land.[69]

The Jewish population remained small, but flare-ups of anti-Semitism exposed the tensions in intergroup relations. During the 1920s—when Jewish groups were organizing for self-defense but also pressing for recognition that one could be both Jew and French in public spaces and civic affairs—attacks in the press and the street came mainly from European settlers. To preserve order, officials and police stepped in. The vigilance of local authorities proved weaker during the 1930s, when another wave of anti-Semitism arose. Muslim leaders were pressing for liberal reforms from Paris. The Radical Republicans were losing influence to the Communist Party and the proto-fascist Croix de Feu. Already in 1933, graffiti with swastikas and slogans like "Long Live Hitler" started to appear on Jewish shopfronts. This time the attacks, including violence that cost dozens of lives, issued mainly from Muslims. The changing face of anti-Semitism corresponded to relations of belonging and exclusion that were insecure and contested.[70]

While some nine-tenths of Muslims remained rural in the 1930s, in most major cities they outnumbered Europeans.[71] Households of colonizer and subject fit into a pattern of residential segregation, with Muslims living mainly in the crammed Kasbahs of the old cities or the burgeoning shantytowns of the periphery.[72] Education attracted Jews, who gained an induction into French ways and a ladder to success; among Muslims, the interwar rate of school attendance for children stood at less than 1 percent.[73] Rather than chipping away at the divide between European and Muslim, then, the French reinforced it—not only by maintaining the distinction between citizen and subject but by upholding the authority of the Islamic code, hence of Muslim officials, over the native population. Through separate beliefs, rituals, holidays, and places of worship—as well as distinct understandings of relations between sacred and secular—religion kept the peoples apart.[74]

This was not an apartheid regime, yet invisible barriers turned city quarters and public spaces—cafés, parks, beaches, sports facilities, and swimming pools—into European preserves.[75] To prevent ethnic battles, before a soccer match the authorities might insist on diluting an all-Muslim team by including a few European players.[76] Intermarriage remained rare, with mixed couples facing rejection on both sides. One observer claimed that a Franco-Muslim couple made Europeans feel uneasy and almost humiliated, as if the spouse belonging to the dominant group had lost their respectability.[77] Some integration might be possible in the workplace, perhaps when a domestic worker entered the intimacy of the private realm:

> Even if pure friendship was exceptional between women, cordial relations might sometimes grow between European women and their Muslim domestic helpers. When they

did occur, these relations could be closer than in the case of European and Muslim men because they arose in the household context.... Beyond social and ethnic differences, the life of women remained regulated by a common biological destiny. There might be an exchange of confidences, woman to woman. Moments of shared identity might develop that still left unquestioned neither the social distance separating *patronne* from *domestique*, nor perceptions of the Muslim community.[78]

Patriarchal pressures placed limits on female friendship across ethno-religious lines; so did patterns of paid work, which as elsewhere upheld female segregation in the home.[79]

Proclaiming social and political equality, the Second Republic (1848–1852) had made Algeria an integral part of the French territory. Henceforth the laws of the metropole would apply in the colony, whose provinces became departments under the administration of prefects.[80] The French of Algeria had the right to elect municipal councilors as well as deputies in the National Assembly.[81] A Berber or an Arab could become a French citizen with equal political rights, but they must renounce the legal authority of Islam, an apostasy, so between 1865 and 1937 only 2,468 Muslims became French citizens.[82] Lifting this condition would have made the settlers into a minority not just demographically but also politically. One man, one vote fit with the republican logic, but not the settler logic:

> Would it be possible to grant complete political rights to the Algerian *indigènes*, in particular the right to be electors and candidates for the Houses, without running a serious danger? Would this not run the risk of provoking a kind of plebiscite against our domination? Would this not place a weapon in the hands of people who would not know how to use it?[83]

One French critic put the problem succinctly: the Europeans of Algeria did not want liberal reforms that would submerge them under the greater number of Muslims.[84]

Here lay the contradiction of a republic single, indivisible, equal, and free—in principle. Algeria formed a part of France, yet rights and freedoms in the colony depended on religion, hence ethnicity. Republican liberalism upheld not just the exclusion of the majority of the people but also a regime that served the interests of a dominant people. In 1937–1938, Algerian mayors and municipal councilors threatened to resign unless the National Assembly in Paris withdrew the Blum-Viollette bill, which would have extended the franchise to select Muslims (civil servants, elected officials, those with a higher level of education, and veteran war officers). The senator from Oran declared, "The French of Algeria will never accept such a bill because ... it would place them sooner or later under Arab domination."[85]

After parliament withdrew the bill, the vast majority of Muslims remained subjects, not citizens.

In the early 1930s, after finishing his posting at a *lycée* in Algiers, the historian Fernand Braudel wrote: "Next to our mistakes and errors, which it would be imprudent not to recognize, is our work of civilization. . . . Fortune, which is a great force, led us into North Africa. There we accomplished great things. In my opinion we can consider the past without remorse."[86] The historian's assessment matched the official view, which was decidedly triumphalist. In 1930, the colony organized a grand, six-month celebration for the centenary of the conquest. Depicting an epic movement from tribalism to civilization, its symbolism took delight in the status quo. Ceremonies and images showed the gratitude and loyalty toward France of the colonized.[87] Not all agreed with this exercise in collective forgetting.[88] Even among those who measured the colony unfavorably against the ideals of the republic, though, a desire for reform rather than independence prevailed.[89]

ETHNOCRACY AND THE REPUBLIC

Although they overlap, personal identity is not reducible to social identity. A small number of Europeans married non-Europeans. Friendship could cross the lines of religion. At work, in the market, and around the neighborhood, Muslim might harmonize with Christian. A doctor, nurse, teacher, administrator, or soldier might care deeply for the Muslims in their charge. Algeria was a caste society but without the walls between the Brahmin and Dalit in India. Unlike North America and Australasia, the towns and cities of Algeria bred contact between native and nonnative. Every European had their Good Arab, a cynic might wisecrack. This seems too formulaic. For starters, it dismisses the duties that honor might impose on a European's relations with others. The civilizing mission democratized *noblesse oblige*. It misses the overlaps between groups, moreover, the multiple ways that social circles intersected—sometimes fleetingly, other times not.[90]

Usually contained, tensions in defining who was French would persist beyond the 1930s. French in name, the Jews provided a counterweight to the Muslim majority; yet anti-Semitism persisted among the Europeans. The French from France enjoyed prestige relative to other Europeans. Outside the colony, the metropolitans might consider their Algerian compatriots like the Corsicans: French, yes, but not as civilized. Living alongside *les Arabes*, native expressions and folkways rubbed off on the French. Alongside such manifestations of hybridity, comparison with so much that was not French provided an everyday reminder of difference.[91]

Rather than contradicting French institutions, ethnocracy coexisted with liberal republicanism.[92] Political authority and armed force backed a system of unequal rights integral to the colonial order. When the state suffered shocks, therefore, the colonial system trembled. In the next chapter, we will see the debilitating effects of France's defeat by the Germans; the division of the country into zones; the Allied landing in North Africa; and the Indochinese War. The weakening of France and the fight for Algerian independence did not erase earlier understandings of them and us. Instead, it overlaid new ways of making sense. Some sharpened stereotypes and tensions whose development this chapter has traced. Others altered meaning as the gap between colonizers and colonized widened. New fears and hatreds appeared. When common enemies pressed upon the Europeans of Algeria, differences among them lost salience: Algerian independence bred new resentments, this time against not only *les Arabes* but also the Fifth Republic. This mix contained traits later exploited by the National Front, many of whose leaders and cadres fought to keep Algeria a part of France.

CHAPTER 2

The Unmaking of the Colony

During the bloody years between 1954 and 1962—when kidnappings, mutilations, murders, and bombings by Algerian nationalists kept them on edge—the French of Algeria would project, onto Muslims at large, hidden fears and fresh resentments.[1] In 1958, they formed a collective actor that would topple the regime in Paris.[2] Many defenders of French Algeria claimed the same love of country that during 1940–1944 had inspired the Resistance against the German occupier. When the metropole turned against them, this patriotism made them enemies of the republic. The victory of the Algerian nationalists turned the tables: the last became the first. In addition to hardening ethnic identity, the war created an affinity with French Algeria among activists in the metropole who would later form the National Front.

This chapter begins by tracing the weakening, between 1940 and 1962, of France's hold over Algeria. It proceeds to show the war's effects on society, politics, and ideology. Before 1956, voters in Algeria and the metropole chose among the same parties. Parties of different kinds (including the Communists, Socialists, and Radicals) won local and parliamentary elections on both sides of the Mediterranean. During the war, the Algerian electorate shifted to the right. The range of electoral alternatives narrowed, with parties not opposed to independence almost disappearing. Except for the short-lived Poujadist movement, no far-right party competed for the settler vote. Imperialism and decolonization fostered a far-right potential, this chapter shows, but it found no outlet in old style, anti-republican parties that were anti-Semitic, royalist, or Pétainist.

CRACKS IN FRENCH CONTROL

Unlike Australia, Canada, and New Zealand, settler societies able to survive without special arrangements with Great Britain, French Algeria was like Northern Ireland: to survive, it needed the mother country.[3] To control the Muslim majority, the military alternated between policies of paternalism and repression. The ministries supplied the bureaucratic apparatus. Paris upheld the colonial pact (the colony offered an outlet for French industry, while the metropole offered a protected market for Algerian agriculture). Under this arrangement, Algeria could not industrialize. Liberals hoping that economic development would forestall a nationalist revolution lacked a realistic appreciation of the situation. If the pact between Paris and the big *colons* no longer held, neither would the colonial system.[4]

Setbacks during World War II weakened French control over its colony.[5] After the Germany victory, the British air force bombed the Mers-el-Kébir naval base near Oran. A fratricidal conflict under Vichy pitted one part of France against another. In 1942, an Anglo-American force defeated the French at Oran and Algiers. One colonial official observed:

> The Muslim populations, which respect strength and authority, saw our armies crushed in one month by the German army, and witnessed the spectacle of the armistice commissions in Algeria; they saw the American troops stationed in North Africa, and they compared our respective strengths.[6]

High food prices; forced labor requisitions; diseases like typhus; material scarcities; and rations lower than for Europeans added to Muslim hardships.[7] With French power and authority diminished, privations emboldened resistance and disobedience. Sometimes contact between the peoples increased, but in tense situations like waiting for food rations in long queues or cramming into trams and buses made scarce by fuel shortages.[8]

Between 1940 and the Allied landings in 1942, Algeria belonged to Vichy France, which abrogated the Crémieux Decree and imposed quotas and other discriminatory measures against Jews in education, professions, and public service. The regime defended the abrogation of the Decree as fair, given its preferential treatment of Jew over Muslim; Muslim leaders countered that taking rights away from Jews did not make Algeria equal for all.[9]

An incident at Zeralda in 1942 had a profound effect on Muslim opinion. Wanting to attract vacationers by restricting its beach, the town's administration posted signs forbidding access to Arabs and Jews (with at least one sign appearing next to others that prohibited dogs and horses). After a few Europeans complained of thefts at the beach, the police arrested dozens of

Muslims, some on their way to gather wood in a nearby forest. That night, 25 boys and men held as prisoners in the poorly ventilated basement of the town hall died of suffocation.[10] The image of the colonizer was crumbling.[11] Muslims protested their exclusion from local committees and authorities' failure to punish torture by the gendarmes.[12] As relations degenerated, in 1944 the prefect for the Department of Algiers issued this reminder:

> I realize that in dealing with the Muslim population, most public servants have displayed an attitude of courtesy that nonetheless does not preclude firmness. I wish nonetheless to insist on the need for an end to certain bad habits, characterized by excessive haughtiness, contemptuous familiarity, and sometimes even brutal behavior.[13]

Patriots bragged that France, ravaged by the Germans, would rise again thanks to its empire.[14] Still, the settler nightmare of submersion by *les Arabes* would not go away.[15] Leadership and organization of native demands for change had grown before the war, with failure of the Blum-Viollette reform sharpening the call for independence from France. As in World War I, colonial troops made heavy sacrifices. The program of the French Resistance called for the extension of rights in the colonies.[16] Invincible no more, France could either let go of its colonies and protectorates, or push back. It did both: withdrawing from Lebanon and Syria but remaining in Indochina and Africa.[17]

On May Day in 1945, authorities in Algiers, Oran, Bougie, and Guelma used violence to repress marches for freedom and equality. On Germany's surrender a week later, police in Sétif fired to disperse a nationalist march, killing three. Muslims reacted by hunting down European, leaving over 200 dead or injured. Backed by army, navy, and air force, settler vigilantes retaliated fiercely, with hundreds—possibly thousands—of Muslims killed. Long contained, the potential for violence had erupted.[18] In his official report, the general who headed the inquiry into the Sétif massacres wrote:

> We learned of three incidents that reveal the state of mind of the Muslim population. A schoolteacher in the Bougie area gave his students an example for composition: "I am French, France is my country." The Muslim children wrote down, "I am Algerian, Algeria is my country." When another teacher was giving a lesson on the Roman Empire, he talked about the slaves. "Like us," shouted a boy. The city of Bône, finally, prevented a riot by suspending a football match between European and Muslim teams.[19]

The metropole was recovering from war, so invested little in the colony's housing, schooling, health, farming, and training.[20] No significant political reforms came from the bargaining between Algerian officials, Muslim leaders, and parliamentary parties. Settler elites opposed changes that might appease the movement for equality, and France let them be.[21] Meanwhile, a new generation of Algerian nationalists was working to unite their movement.

SOCIAL DISTANCE PERSISTS

As interwar antisemitism had shown, relations between Jew and Muslim depended on those with Europeans. Most Jews were citizens, but not full members of the dominant caste.[22] Still, the boundary between French and non-French was rigid enough to exclude most Berbers and Arabs. In school, shop, market, stadium, and workplace, European and *Arabe* might become companions. Every day, French teachers, soldiers, technicians, administrators, and medical personnel worked among Muslims; and educational opportunity and administrative service pulled Muslim elites into French institutions. Yet tenacious differences—in language, schooling, religion, residential location, family mores, political rights, collective memories, and economic opportunities blocked a full fusion of these peoples.[23]

Consider private life: of the 3,971 marriages celebrated in Algiers in 1948, only 2.5 percent joined spouses of different faiths.[24] Language still divided the colony, for some 80 percent of Muslims did not know French.[25] The Government-General's report of 1954 refers to a mutual estrangement. In the rural town of Cassaigne, one administrator wrote, the war and its aftermath had deepened the trench between European and Muslim.[26] Another official wrote:

> During four years spent living in the backcountry, I have never encountered a single citizen who would admit that an Arab, even if civilized and educated, could be their equal. In general, the *colon* confuses French sovereignty with the defense of his personal interests and condemns any administrative practice for which the defense of these interests is not the sole objective.[27]

Settlers felt especially vulnerable in areas without a military presence, where Muslims ("often impulsive and violent") possessed revolvers, rifles, and even explosives.[28]

Religion still posed a barrier. From the French side, Islam seemed to block progress because its confraternities dominated villages, subjugated women, and oppressed *haratins* (former black slaves).[29] Unequal access to education squared with this view, for among Muslims only one in sixteen girls attended school (for boys, the ratio was one in five).[30] According to an official from Orléansville:

Islam is a man's religion. The code of Islam still denies women their full emancipation. For them this represents a barrier to equal rights with men, which they desire. Respect of women and their equality with men are inherently Christian and Western notions. It will take some time before they can alter ways of thinking.[31]

Undoing the backwardness of the Muslim woman should be a priority, French administrators wrote, because she was the guardian of tradition.[32]

The political class put its faith in economic reforms. From the Sahara, an official wrote that the well-being and happiness of the native population depended on the productivity of their date palms and the health of their herds.[33] Administrators expected that material comfort would erase pan-Islamism and Algerian nationalism.[34] Once living conditions in the colony approach those of migrant workers in the metropole, an official from Djurdjura wrote, Algerians would look upon the French presence more favorably.[35] Because Muslims were not yet ready for rapid change, reforms should mix fidelity to "the generous ideas of the Republic and its ideals of liberty, equality, and fraternity" with prudence.[36] What complicated the situation, according to administrators, was the waiting game played by a segment of the native population that was ready to follow the nationalists. Reforms, they concluded, must not signal a slackening of French authority.[37]

Settler attitudes were complex, yet equal rights for the colony's subject population were not a priority. At a time of Cold War rivalries, Third World movements, and domestic communist challenges, political elites hoped that economic development would dissolve backwardness, eradicate grievances, and reinforce consent. This was asking a lot from change in material conditions. Events soon overtook their hopes.

THE FOURTH REPUBLIC UNRAVELS

In November 1954, shortly after the victory of Vietnamese rebels over the French military at Dien Bien Phu, a few hundred guerrillas in Algeria launched coordinated attacks against warehouses, factories, electrical facilities, telephone lines, army barracks, and police stations.[38] So began the conflict that would lead to independence in 1962. In the National Assembly, the minister of the interior, François Mitterrand (a Socialist), declared that a firm policy in Algeria would "make of Africa the finest demonstration of the transcendence of French civilization."[39] Reacting decisively, Paris increased the military contingent in Algeria and banned a leading nationalist party, whose leaders it imprisoned. The government also promised reforms: expansion of voting rights, political representation, and public service employment; reallocation of land for agriculture; and construction of housing and schools. Some reforms it did implement—along with anti-guerrilla repression, security checks, forced relocations, and concentration camps.[40]

According to French polls, public support for the fight to keep Algeria in France peaked at 49 percent in 1956. Conscription and casualties inflamed antiwar opinion. Conscripts returning from the war spread nasty images of the settlers: exploitative, violent, and for the most part not truly French.[41] Further, the future of Algeria became an international affair. In 1955, the Front de libération nationale (FLN) participated in the Bandung Conference. Alongside Britain and Israel, in 1956 France attacked Egypt, which was supplying weapons and other support to the nationalists in Algeria. France relied on the Marshall Plan, and the United States insisted on a withdrawal from Egypt.[42]

In a private letter to the metropole dated 15 December 1955, a European of Algiers begins by apologizing for not writing sooner. After an update on money and health problems, the letter turns to wartime conditions:

> Life goes on. The holidays are behind us, like in a photo album. Still, the difficulties under which we struggle at present are unbearable. At any moment, we might rebel against the incomprehensible actions of the authorities and the French government. The *Arabes* know this well and take full advantage of it. I believe it is not necessary to tell someone like you the extent of their barbarity; you know them as well as we do, if not better. Show the people around you who think they are "an underprivileged people" the enclosed photos, which have the sad merit of being true. Despite this, no reaction on the part of the government. We have a clear feeling of betrayal and abandonment by the Metropole. A certain rancor has even developed between Algerians and Metropolitans following the lack of conviction among the conscripts called to help us even though we showed ourselves to be more generous in 1945. The way things are going, by this spring we can expect a vile solution similar to the one in Indochina, Tunisia, and Morocco. I find it hard to see myself making deep bows to "*Messieurs les Arabes*." Poor France. There really is no more dynamism and energy left in France. Grandeur and decadence. To stay out of harm's way, we are getting ready to pass a sad New Year's Eve locked inside. All the same, it would be a real shame to leave this lovely country in the hands of those lazy idlers. Lately Algiers has made itself quite attractive, a rival of the great capitals. My greatest desire would be to leave Algeria as the French found it when they arrived. The *melons* would be entirely incapable of doing anything. Obviously, a foreign power would gladly "help" them. Maybe that is one of the reasons for our generous surrender.[43]

To provoke the French into responses of blind violence that made it difficult for Muslims to sit on the fence, nationalists resorted to terrorism. Rebels in the Philippeville area raped, mutilated, and killed dozens of settlers and Muslim "traitors." French civilians and soldiers reacted indiscriminately, killing hundreds of natives.[44] In Algiers, rebels attacked

Europeans at random and planted bombs in crowded cafés. After the funeral for youths blown to pieces in a packed dancehall, settler activists in Algiers imposed a one-day closure on businesses and then marched on the Casbah, harassing Muslims and sacking their stands and shops along the way. With fear and suspicion constant, every unknown *Arabe* became a potential terrorist.[45] At entrances to shops and public buildings, security searches became routine. Government offices took special measures:

> We have been asked to provide ourselves with defensive weapons. In response, we have purchased revolvers, which have been distributed to the department heads. It seemed to us necessary to adopt this minimal precaution.[46]

Feelings of insecurity seeped into everyday life:

> When one boards a trolley, one checks instinctively for unaccompanied bags or packages. At the slightest noise out of the ordinary, everyone jumps. Wherever one looks, one sees suspicious signs: the man who bends over, the one who leans against a wall, the automobile that slows down, or the package lying about. To prevent a mistake that might be fatal, people in the street take care to avoid running or shouting. We seem as lively as always, but the war is inside us and it is fraying our nerves.[47]

A European woman admitted:

> When I go out to buy groceries, suddenly I surprise myself imagining that a man I cannot see is aiming for the back of my head. I have not done anything wrong, yet I too only want someone to do me the favor of eliminating me.[48]

Les Arabes reciprocated with gestures of disrespect. In markets, old women jostled settlers and shoeshine boys spat toward them.[49] Deepening the wedge between colonizers and colonized, terrorism did its job.

The insurgents suffered military setbacks in 1958, when paratroops under General Jacques Massu curbed the attacks in Algiers.[50] Yet attitudes and opinion in the metropole kept turning against the war. Ultimately, about 1.7 million soldiers would serve in Algeria, most of them conscripts.[51] For families, friends, and neighbors, military service and battle casualties meant worry, sacrifice, and suffering. In 1956, when journalists revealed the military's use of torture, outrage grew over practices that evoked Nazi brutality. International pressure mounted after French troops crossed the border between Algeria and Tunisia. Backed by Britain and the United States, the United Nations called on France to find a solution that was "peaceful, democratic, and fair."[52]

The war was tearing the country apart. It divided the military from the politicians, the French in the metropole from those in Algeria. Even the left fractured, for neither Socialists nor Communists could reach a consensus on Algeria's future. As the Algerian question became intractable, one government followed another. For the post-1945 tasks of material reconstruction, economic modernization, and European integration, the party system had worked: with each major challenge, the government of the day had found a new majority in Parliament. The defense of French Algeria stymied this system.[53] In May 1958, a new prime minister, Pierre Pflimflin, seemed ready to negotiate with the separatists. This threatened the very survival of French Algeria, where Pflimlin's appointment prompted a vivid reaction among those now called the *pieds noirs* (the Europeans of Algeria, with the Jewish minority included) as well as career soldiers unwilling to separate this struggle from the one against Germany during World War II or, since 1945, the conflicts in Madagascar, Vietnam, and Egypt. The Fourth Republic would fall after civil unrest orchestrated by the military.

DAYS OF HOPE: MAY 1958

On the afternoon of 13 May 1958, work stopped at one o'clock in Algiers. High-ranking officers had negotiated in secret with politicians who wanted General Charles De Gaulle in power. The assassination of three French prisoners by Algerian rebels provided the pretext for a mass mobilization by the military's psychological warfare unit. Patriots—mostly European men—gathered at meeting places across Algiers, then marched toward the city center (unhappy with international calls for peace, along the way one group sacked the American Cultural Center). Some 100,000 people filled the public square at the war memorial. After a ceremony in honor of the dead prisoners, they moved against the nearby headquarters of the Government-General. Vehicles rammed its gates, and hundreds of demonstrators streamed in. Instead of ejecting the occupiers, the army acceded to their request that General Massu head a Committee of Public Safety (a label that showed the rebels' kinship with the Sans Culottes of the French Revolution rather than Napoleon Bonaparte, General Boulanger, or Marshall Pétain). Over the next three weeks, the unrest spread across Algeria.[54]

According to the partisans of French Algeria, the participation of non-Europeans in the marches, demonstrations, strikes, and occupations that unfolded across the colony during May 1958 displayed the unity of colonized and colonizer.[55] Muslims, many of them transported by the military, joined tens of thousands of Europeans in the Forum of Algiers on

May 16. At a rally the next evening, Muslim women stripped off their *haïk* (cloth head and body wrap) and threw it onto a bonfire. Not just an element of dress, it was a flashpoint between rival models of society.[56] The war was subverting femininity. Muslim women had joined the rebels; they had transported and planted bombs that sowed terror.[57] Mounted for propaganda purposes by the French military, for an instant the shedding of veils recalled the night of 4 August 1789 (the moment of collective effervescence in the National Constituent Assembly when nobleman joined commoner in ending feudalism). Scenes in which Muslim women removed and burned their head covering repeated themselves.

The European woman enjoyed more public freedom than did her Muslim counterpart (for Muslims, by contrast, the private sphere provided a refuge against the French).[58] Among the believers in French Algeria, this was the apotheosis: as if by magic, a fusion of peoples.[59] According to European propaganda, the presence of Muslim men and women proved that customs blocking the progress of Muslim society had fallen. The new Algeria had arrived.[60] May 1958 was thus a time of myth: not just of fraternity between peoples but also of surrender to a superior civilization. In a private letter, a resident of Algiers wrote:

> We know that in the Metropole you are getting distorted information about the events in Algeria. If you could receive the signal from Radio Algiers, you would have had a faithful soundtrack of all the rallies. It was grandiose. The Forum became the promenade of the people of Algiers. We are grateful to Lyon for electing someone like Soustelle. If only you could see this city with flags flying, it is unbelievable. Everywhere there are flags with the V for Victory and the Cross of Lorraine, entire balconies draped with the tricolor flag. Now we really have hope again. All our hopes are concentrated on De Gaulle. I can honestly say that everything unfolded in peace and dignity, when the Moorish women took off their veils the Muslim population took part. Wild cheering for Generals Massu, Soustelle, and Salan goes on each day. Algeria is on a mission to save France. We have been living days we will never forget, what a feeling, better even than at the Liberation of France. It's all indescribable, really. I have kept the newspapers that I will send to my dad and I will ask him to show them to you when there is a chance. We sense a complete shift among the Muslim masses and can't help asking if it is for real. Our idiots in Parliament needed a lesson. Unfortunately, those shitty Communists refuse to give up, so the reaction in France is less calm than in Algeria. Don't listen to the lies of the defeatists.[61]

Pied noir leaders proclaimed that governments in Paris—not Muslims in the colony—were pressing for the abandonment of Algeria to a fanatical, foreign-backed minority. "The uprising of May 13 has prepared the resurrection of France," clamored the federation of Algerian mayors.[62] Believers in French Algeria held that France now offered an alternative to communism and pan-Islamism. This was the chance for France to become a Muslim power, a global leader in the mission to reconcile the West with the Orient.[63] These sentiments proved to be chimerical; the civil unrest and military insubordination of May 1958, less so.

DE GAULLE BETRAYS THE FRENCH OF ALGERIA

Enjoying the support of settlers and military, in June 1958 De Gaulle became prime minister with emergency powers. Three days after his investiture, he thrilled thousands at the Forum in Algiers with a speech that began: "I have understood you." The *pieds noirs* had toppled the Fourth Republic, so he mollified them: "In the name of France, I declare that, starting from today, France considers that across the whole of Algeria there is only one category of people, those who are fully French, fully French with the same rights and the same duties."[64] His eager audience overlooked that he did not close the door on independence.

In retrospect, his thinking has become clearer. Extracting France from the Algerian quagmire would allow De Gaulle to modernize his country's armed forces. The birth of the Common Market was imminent: by comparison with the colony in North Africa, Europe offered better economic prospects. De Gaulle wanted autonomy from the United States and the USSR, and decolonization would boost his country's prestige in the Third World. As in his discourse, duplicity in his policies (a renewed military campaign in Algeria, but leniency toward imprisoned rebel leaders) bought time. Now desperate, the partisans of French Algeria called for equal political rights, with a single electoral college instead of the system that had disenfranchised the colony's majority. Still, coercion had its place. As French Algeria politicians said:

> For a Muslim, sovereignty resides not in the will of the people but in the will of God. And nothing takes place that He has not willed. Thus, the man who triumphs because he is the strongest will also win full legitimacy. This explains why, if left to itself, every Islamic country will submit to those who are power-hungry. Dictators follow one after another because they cannot govern peacefully, in the name of what we consider the good of the people.[65]

Independence, then, would bring not only poverty but also dictatorship.[66] De Gaulle reasoned differently. A large population of Muslims, he told confidantes, should not enjoy equality with an overwhelmingly Christian people.[67]

The honeymoon with the *pieds noirs* lasted little more than a year. In his inaugural speech as president of the Fifth Republic, De Gaulle proclaimed (again using ambivalent language) that "a special place is destined for an Algeria of tomorrow, pacified and transformed, developing by itself its own personality and tightly bound to France."[68] In the 1958 referendum on a constitution that increased the power of the president, fully 97 percent of the Algerian electorate (Europeans and non-Europeans alike) voted "yes" (by comparison with 79 percent in the metropole). In a radio speech from Algiers in early 1959, likewise, Prime Minister Michel Debré praised the insurrection of May 1958:

> Thanks to Algiers, the nation found herself and started to rise up again. Our rebirth is underway, naturally, and it will continue thanks to General de Gaulle. . . . No doubt problems remain and nowhere is this better understood than in Algeria. From now on, still, we will bring a fresh resolve to liberty and French sovereignty, which apply here as much as across the Mediterranean. In the name of the government, I have come here to give a guarantee, a guarantee contained in these few words: "France will stay in Algeria."[69]

Still hiding the truth, De Gaulle repeated that negotiations were out of the question.[70] In March 1959, however, a deputy who represented Algiers in the National Assembly voiced a troubling question:

> What does General De Gaulle really want? Anybody can read anything into his statements. Because they hear what they want to hear, everybody is happy. The Head of State should stop equivocating. Algeria is at war. With each day that passes in this land, the loss of life only increases.[71]

The *pieds noirs* held hope until September 1959, when De Gaulle broached in public the right to Algerian self-determination. Tired of war and prepared to sacrifice the colony in exchange for peace, in the metropole the Communists, Socialists, and most of the right supported him.[72]

THE END OF FRENCH ALGERIA

Early in 1960, French authorities reacted to a week of civilian insurgency in Algiers by declaring a state of siege. This put the military in a difficult position. Its officers sympathized with the settler cause. Yet Paris wanted them to restore order. The gendarmerie took over, with casualties on both sides. This pushed the settlers and the military in Algeria even further from De Gaulle, whose visit to Algeria later that year stirred up more violence (with over 100 killed). Believing that French military superiority made compromise unnecessary, the partisans of French Algeria were out of tune with the metropole, where parties, unions, and churches called for talks with the rebels.[73] In a referendum on Algerian self-determination in early 1961, finally, 75 percent of voters chose "yes."[74]

Unwilling to let politicians interfere in a war that they were winning, four generals (Salan, Challe, Jouhaud, and Zeller) launched a coup d'état. The *pieds noirs* treated them as heroes, but parts of the military refused to follow. Putschists not arrested, tried, and imprisoned either went underground or fled abroad.[75] Calling itself an heir to the French Revolution, the Paris Commune, and the World War II Resistance, the Organisation armée secrète (OAS)—a group of renegade officers, soldiers, and civilians— swung into action.[76] Its message mixed Cold War rhetoric with that of the anti-Dreyfusards: "Algeria and France are in a state of mortal peril, and with them the entire Western world. The army (the only true guarantor of national independence) has been decapitated, broken, ridiculed."[77]

Enjoying broad support among the *pieds noirs*, the OAS sowed terror.[78] It asserted that the racism of De Gaulle, who did not want Muslims to be French, contrasted with its own battle for equal rights.[79] One OAS handbill describes as "espionage on behalf of the Gaullist Gestapo" the crime of a man the organization assassinated.[80] A bomb intended for André Malraux, the minister of state for cultural affairs, blinded the four-year-old daughter of his Parisian neighbors. OAS activities deepened the colonial divide: Europeans avoided Muslim neighborhoods; in European areas, Muslims feared OAS attacks.[81] Since the late 1950s, pessimism had driven tens of thousands to leave the colony. Now a mass exit loomed.[82]

In March 1962, Paris signed the Évian Accords, which recognized the right of Algerians to self-determination. With time running out for French Algeria, OAS activists ambushed and killed soldiers in units loyal to Paris. The army—now an occupying force, said the OAS—responded by sealing off Bab El Oued, a working-class district of Algiers suspected of harboring the killers. In response, the OAS declared a general strike. On March 26, as hundreds of *pieds noirs* filed past military checkpoints on the Rue d'Isly to join a rally in Bab el-Oued, colonial troops opened fire, killing or wounding dozens of civilians. The Rue d'Isly massacre smothered the last hope that settler mobilization would save the colony. In the referendum of April 1962, fully 91 percent of French voters supported the Évian Accords.[83] With independence now certain, *pieds noirs* doubted a new Algeria would respect their civil rights. With their trust in the army waning, the *pieds noirs* felt more vulnerable than ever.[84]

During the following weeks, anarchy broke out as army, police, OAS, and rebels fought separate battles. Each day brought new reports of people killed for no apparent reason other than ethno-religious antagonism. A Parisian daily gave this update on two days of incidents in the Oran backcountry:

> In the Mascara area, at Aïn Farès, Mr. Villaret was kidnapped by Muslims and found with his throat slit. At Rio Salado and Laferrière, on the Tlemcen road, 16 farms and residences owned by Europeans were looted and vandalized. At Lourmel, a European woman was seriously wounded when Muslims stole three weapons from soldiers after damaging their vehicle. Also in this village, two Muslims were wounded by unknown assailants. A curfew was imposed already at 9 a.m. At Sidi-Bel-Abbès, late on Saturday afternoon Mr Benabdallah came to the public hospital for the discharge of his brother Amar, wounded in an earlier attack. The two men were machine-gunned as they exited, leaving Mr. Benabdallah killed and his already seriously wounded brother in critical condition. Other attacks left four Muslims dead. At Saïda, an OAS commando in military uniform attacked two guards at the sub-prefecture and escaped with their two submachine guns. At Perrégaux, numerous packing crates were damaged at the train station. A fire destroyed a newsstand owned by a Muslim, and Muslims looted and burned the food and clothing depot of the Catholic Aid. At Dublineau, an explosion interrupted service on the Oran-Sahara railroad.[85]

Two days later, under a headline that read "Algiers: A Ghastly Exchange of Killings," the *pieds noirs* learned about a mass grave with the mutilated remains of 20 victims of the FLN.[86] Similar reports issued from the rest of Algeria, where bands of Muslims kidnapped, raped, and murdered Europeans. When fearful Europeans abandoned neighborhoods, Muslims claimed their homes.[87]

The OAS responded with hit squads against "moderates"—French soldiers charged with enforcing the post-accord ceasefire and settlers leaving the colony without OAS permission. The group also targeted Muslims, often at random, with 230 murdered during a single day in Algiers. By June, when a transition government was pleading for peaceful coexistence, most *pieds noirs* had decided that independence dictated a departure.[88] As they deserted homes, schools, shops, restaurants, and offices, the OAS resorted to a scorched-earth policy (the group torched the University of Algiers library, set oil refineries alight, and dynamited the Oran city hall).[89]

Zones of calm did persist. During the week before Independence Day—days and nights of celebration when *mujahideen* walked the streets, Algerian flags bloomed on buildings, and women's ululations issued—a French reporter in Algiers commented on the absence of violence:

> I stayed outdoors and mixed with crowds in every neighborhood. Almost never was I the object of an insult, of a sign of hatred or mere antipathy. Yet I plunged deep into the dusty alleyways of the Clos Salembier shantytown, the narrowest mazes of inclined

steps in the Casbah. I was the only European and ready to chat under the slightest pretext. People selling miniature flags or white-and-green caps called out to me often, saying, "Shout out with us: 'Yahia FLN!'" and I would respond with a "no" and explain why. They would understand. They would smile and remain quiet, and then we would go our separate ways.[90]

Two days after independence, some 800 Muslims marched on the Cathedral of Algiers, which they damaged and looted until the arrival of Algerian soldiers, who upbraided them by citing from the Quran. Wary of the OAS and now posted on foreign soil, many French troops and gendarmes stayed in their barracks. On Independence Day—5 July 1962—hundreds of unprotected *pieds noirs* died in Oran. Elsewhere, Algerians shamed, tortured, and murdered thousands of *harkis*, Muslims who had served as French Army auxiliaries.[91]

A sociological study that spring had found that young *pieds noirs* felt much less attached to Algeria. When one respondent said he wanted "to live and die where my ancestors have lived and died," he meant a place where most *pieds noirs* had never set foot: the metropole.[92] Two weeks before independence, *pied noir* politicians in the National Assembly issued a communiqué:

> We declare that all those who, like us, wish to remain solely French have no other option than withdrawal to the metropole. They should move to safety as soon as possible and without trusting in deceptive promises.[93]

Advice of this kind the authorities did not take seriously.[94] That spring and summer, though, the *pieds noirs* would clog the seaports and airports of Algeria, ready to leave.[95]

SHIFTS IN SETTLER POLITICS

Since the nineteenth century, labor unions, party politics, patron-client relations, and a good dose of electoral fraud had spread the settlers between left, center, and right.[96] Their ancestors included not only economic migrants but also left-wing political refugees from France, Spain, and Italy.[97] Labor strikes began before the Depression, when the number of unionized Europeans in Algeria's ports, railways, trading firms, and public administration rose to about 28,000.[98] Like the metropole, from 1920 to 1934 voters in the colony tended to support the center-left Radical Party.[99] Amidst resurgent anti-Semitism and rejection of the Popular Front (whose leader, Léon Blum, co-sponsored the bill to extend citizenship and voting rights to more of the colony's Muslims), during the late 1930s the Europeans of Algeria moved toward the right. Divisions in settler politics hid a consensus: Muslims should not have equal rights.[100]

After World War II, voters in Algeria and the metropole still chose between similar parties. In 1946, the colony elected 11 candidates from the right and four from the left (two Socialists and two Communists, who campaigned against a reform granting parity to non-Europeans).[101] In the 1951 parliamentary elections, similarly, Algeria elected 12 right-wing candidates and three left-wing candidates (one Socialist and two Communists).[102] Communists denounced the colonial regime in Algeria and fought for the rights of Muslim workers but held that Algeria was not yet ready for independence.[103]

During the Algerian War, by contrast, the colony went its own way in party politics.[104] In 1955, French authorities banned the Algerian Communist Party.[105] In the 1958 parliamentary elections, moreover, most of Algeria's 18 electoral districts had slates peculiar to the colony.[106] The left-right cleavage became almost redundant: the left fielded few slates and some districts had only a single, anti-independence slate.[107] In 1958, the colony's Electoral College voted entirely for De Gaulle (who in the metropole attracted 78 percent of the vote).[108] As the struggle for the survival of French Algeria intensified, the settlers pulled together and moved rightward—but toward the Gaullist right, not the far right.[109] Party labels mattered less than a politician's stand on independence. Algerian politics had shifted: as past alignments between parties and voters weakened, the options on offer in the colony and the metropole diverged.

ELECTIVE AFFINITIES

The foregoing poses a puzzle: Despite the emergence of a far-right potential, why (apart from Poujadism, a short-lived newcomer) did the traditional far right not exploit it at the time? Even today, the *pieds noirs* distance themselves from the far right of the 1930s, 1940s, and 1950s. They equate the battle for French Algeria with the French Resistance movement. They deplore comments by Jean-Marie Le Pen that hint at anti-Semitism. They show impatience with Holocaust deniers. Instead, Arabs are the problem. In the eyes of most German and Italian voters today, similarly, ties to Nazism or fascism stigmatize and delegitimize the far right. In Spain, fidelity to Francoism penalized Fuerza Nueva during the 1970s and 1980s, Vox after. In Portugal, likewise, nationalism remains suspect due to its association with the authoritarian Salazar regime.[110] Voter perceptions of far-right antecedents matter.[111]

Here are elements for studying the far-right affinity on which this book hinges. The term elective affinity comes to us via Max Weber, who found it in a romance by Goethe, who probably took it from a Swedish treatise on chemistry. Before Weber, elective affinity referred to a mutual attraction whereby two separate elements (chemical substances or human souls) seek and marry each other. In premodern chemistry as in Goethe's novel, an elective affinity results in a transformative union: a new reality—a complex substance or a loving couple—emerges, greater than the sum of its parts. Not so with Weber. The Protestant ethic and the capitalist spirit reinforced each other during the early phase of capitalism's takeoff—but without fusing.[112]

Under the Fifth Republic, by analogy, an elective affinity with the Europeans from Algeria lent a special vigor to the far right. In other postwar European democracies, ties to Nazism, fascism, wartime collaboration, or reactionary authoritarianism kept parties and movements of the far right beyond the fringe. In France, by contrast, the battle against decolonization gave the far right a chance to gain respectability and relevance. Defending French Algeria pushed into the background the far right's ties to royalists, prewar fascistic leagues, Pétainism, and collaboration with Nazi Germany. In addition to dedicated cadres and activists, the defense of French Algeria gave the far right a potential social base. The subculture of the Algerian settlers danced with the far right, as we will see, but never fused with it.[113]

PART II
Ex-colonials in the Metropole

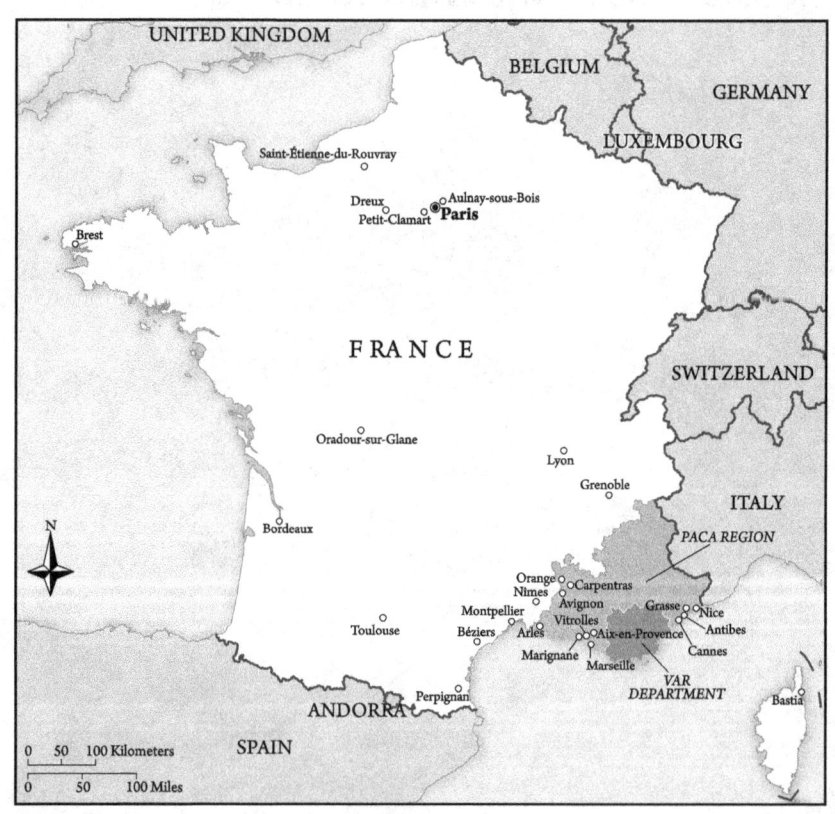

Map 2. France.

CHAPTER 3

From Newcomers to Incipient Constituency

The initial destination for most of the approximately 600,000 Europeans who left Algeria in 1962 was Marseille, where the right-wing press expressed outrage and pity:

> Here is an old man, more than 80 years old, a widower with no family at all. His name is Julien Gandy and he owned a small farm in Guelma. He lost his only son in 1944, during the Italian campaign. The FLN chased him, literally, from his few acres of land. The Red Cross in Bône has sent him to an old people's home in Haute-Garonne. Lost in deafness, in transit in Marseille he resembles an anonymous package. He cries like a child before his grief gives way to anger: "We will never trust those people again! Peace accords? Really? They want to kick us all out until nobody is left." Very gently, a young woman from the welcoming committee calms him and guides him away, just as she did earlier with two sleeping twins born scarcely a month ago on the other side of the sea. At least they still know nothing about the tragedy that has upset their short lives.[1]

During a single day at the peak of the exodus, some 3,000 refugees came aboard steamships from Bône, Oran, and Algiers; 44 flights brought another 3,000 to the city's Marignane airport. Although some four-fifths of those who arrived in Marseille proceeded to other destinations, by June the authorities decided the city had reached its limit. To relieve the pressure, they redirected some refugee ships to Toulon.[2]

The reception of the *pieds noirs* in Toulon is the main subject of this chapter, which emphasizes local activism, social solidarity, and partisan choice. In 1962, as we will see, politicians like the mayor of Toulon had to decide where they stood on Gaullism. Along with the Communists, most *pieds noirs* ruled out the Gaullists; unlike the Communists, the Gaullists enjoyed wide popularity. They held the presidency and dominated the legislature. Still, a mayor who rejected Gaullism and extended patronage to the *pieds noirs* might gain their support. In cities of the south, the repatriates soon formed between 10 and 15 percent of the electorate (roughly the same as the weight of today's African American electorate in the United States). To cite only a few examples, the *pieds noirs* became clients of the right-wing mayor of Montpellier (François Delmas), the center-left mayor of Nice (Jean Médecin), and the Socialist mayor of Marseille (Gaston Deferre). Studying how the mayor of Toulon reacted to the arrival of the repatriates gives a window on how, starting in the 1960s, mayors shunted a far-right potential *away* from the far right. Down the road, the example of these southern cities also suggests, the crisis of an established political machine could unleash support for the far right.

Map 3. The Var Department.

TOULON

Saying that Toulon was reaping what it had sown when the repatriates came from Algeria would be a bit much. Still, the expeditionary force that conquered Algiers in 1830 had set sail from its shore. Founded by the Romans, Toulon occupies a coastal plain wedged between a broad bay and a limestone massif. Medieval Aix, Avignon, and Marseille overshadowed this town, but eventually the monarchy decided to capitalize on its unique geography: a protected harbor with waters deep enough for the largest ships, surrounded by heights that bar invasion from the interior and give command over land and sea approaches for forts and artillery. After 1500, Toulon replaced Marseille as the chief port for the kingdom's Mediterranean fleet. From the era of the galley ship to that of the aircraft carrier, the state built, enlarged, and modified the city's fortifications, shipyards, warehouses, and barracks.

When the *pieds noirs* came, Toulon was the biggest city in the Var, a department of hills and forests with a tradition of rural socialism.[3] In the backcountry, farmers raised sheep, grew olives, and harvested chestnuts. Nearer the coast, products for national and international markets included wine (Côtes de Provence, Vin de Bandol), cut flowers (from greenhouses near Ollioules and Carqueiranne), and fruit and vegetables (especially from market gardens outside Hyères). Crafts like cork production and leather tanning were almost gone, but the Var remained an important source of lumber and bauxite. On the coast, a few communities lived from fishing or mussel farming and—with 400 kilometers of beaches, forested islands, and ports for pleasure craft—the department had become a magnet for mass tourism. Sharing the Côte d'Azur with the Alpes-Maritimes to the east, the Var attracted thousands of vacationers who in a few months spent more than its wage earners did in a year.[4]

Little of this manna fell on Toulon, which could not offer the glamor of Cannes and Saint-Tropez or the architecture of Avignon and Aix-en-Provence. It lacked the beaches of Bandol, Sanary, Le Lavandou, Ramatuelle, Fréjus, and Saint-Raphaël, all in the same department. Its animated market along the Cours Lafayette was a gem of Provençal life; but not Little Chicago, a sailors' quarter of bars, prostitutes, and gangs. Toulon came out of World War II in better shape than other port cities hit by the Allies, but the shells of bombed-out buildings made some quarters seem like Palermo in Sicily. Postwar reconstruction had raised a curtain of concrete buildings that blocked the waterfront from the inner city. Tall cranes and long warehouses filled the docklands. The absence of quality hotels was both result and further cause of Toulon's failure to profit from tourism.

Instead, the city depended on the Navy, the heaviest spender in the Var. Toulon was home to the biggest naval base in the country, a sprawling naval hospital, the largest dry-dock on the Mediterranean, and the main facility for repairs to the fleet. In addition to the 23,000 officers and sailors based there, the Navy and its subcontractors employed 20,000 civilians. Toulon was a center for ship demolition, which employed another thousand in the private sector; a thousand more worked for firms that made steel frames for ship hulls. Across the bay, at La Seyne-sur-Mer, an enterprise that had built the first French battleships relied on 4,000 employees to fill contracts in Europe, Africa, South America, and the Middle East.[5]

As elsewhere in the country, chain stores and shopping malls had yet to come. Toulon supported a petty bourgeoisie of self-employed artisans, café owners, and small shopkeepers who depended on the flow of Navy money. This made the city vulnerable (a problem that persists to this day). The other big component of the local economy was construction. Navy dry docks, warehouses, and wharves bombed in 1943 and 1944 had required repairs and rebuilding. La Seyne-sur-Mer needed facilities for the construction of oil supertankers. The Navy controlled most of the port lands, whose scarcity on the real estate market slowed development; but the coast was growing, with Toulon and its surrounding area accounting for over half the department's population.[6]

Never a center for the colonial trade like Marseille, instead Toulon had been a garrison town as France expanded, consolidated, and then lost its hold over Africa and Southeast Asia.[7] In shops, cafés, theaters, and markets, civilians rubbed shoulders with naval personnel and their families. Navy ships and submarines passed daily through the harbor. The city invited the Naval Prefect and other high-ranking officers to public ceremonies and official meetings. Annual events on the city's calendar included a concert at the municipal theater by the Navy orchestra and a military parade down the main boulevard on Bastille Day. Every few days, the local newspaper devoted a whole page to officer promotions, activities in other naval districts, retired naval officers and their association, and events in Brittany (birthplace of many sailors and home to the other main base in Brest).[8] Just as Toulon mattered for the Navy, the Navy had shaped Toulon.

THE POLITICAL FIGHT FOR L'ALGÉRIE FRANÇAISE IN THE VAR

This military presence had made the region hospitable to French Algeria activism. The Var was home to some 12,000 veterans, mostly from the Navy and living in Toulon.[9] Out of solidarity with the *pieds noirs*, in 1959 a veterans' association promoted the twinning of Toulon with municipalities in Algeria.[10] The founder of the department's most important Algérie française group was a decorated World War II veteran, Jean Reimbold (whose anti-independence activities during the 1950s had led to his expulsion from Morocco). Reimbold and his group recruited among naval officers, former Poujadists, and veterans of the Indochinese war. In 1960–1961, they organized meetings against Algerian independence that attracted up to a thousand people. Such was their success that other anti-Gaullist imperialists (including Jean-Marie Le Pen) saw no need to expand into the Var.[11] Reimbold went underground in 1962, when the police stepped up its anti-OAS campaign. Staying in touch with dissident military officers and others opponents of Algerian independence, he agreed when the OAS asked him to set up a local branch.[12] OAS graffiti sprouted in Toulon, and a dozen bomb attacks targeted Gaullists, Communists, and Algerians.[13] When the bomb they were transporting went off accidentally, three French Algeria activists died outside the home of a Gaullist official.[14] Only a police sweep that resulted in the arrest of 44 French Algeria activists paralyzed the OAS in Toulon.[15]

Ex-colonials from Morocco and Tunisia had formed a national interest group with a problem that would also afflict those from Algeria: some wanted a nonpartisan group, an option others rejected as spineless and unprincipled.[16] Infighting gave birth to a new group that backed De Gaulle in 1958 and included settlers now arriving from Algeria.[17] Although this politicized group grew to 3,000 members in the Toulon area, more infighting bred yet another national group.[18] Its leader in the Var was Colonel Jean-Marie Reymond—a native of Algiers, veteran of both world wars, and go-between for army officers, OAS organizers, and French Algeria activists. By 1962, Reymond's group had branches in Bandol, Fréjus, Hyères, Draguignan, and Toulon (where it attracted up to 800 members).[19]

One speaker at its rallies was Jean-Louis Tixier-Vignancour. Born in 1907, Tixier had studied law in Paris before election to the National Assembly in 1936. After active duty as a second lieutenant early in World War II, Tixier worked for the Vichy civil service but resigned because it was serving Germany. After the war, he earned his reputation as a brilliant lawyer, notably by defending from charges of treason and collaboration the anti-Semite Louis-Ferdinand Destouches (the author Céline). Hopeful when De Gaulle took power in 1958, Tixier became disillusioned and joined with Jean-Marie le Pen in creating their own patriotic group (the Front national pour l'Algérie française). At the trial of *pieds noirs* accused of fomenting the 1960 insurrection in Algiers, moreover, Tixier represented the defense.[20]

Among political parties, the Centre national des indépendants et paysans (CNIP) had opposed the government in the referenda on Algerian self-determination and the Évian Accords. In addition, the CNIP was the only party not to condemn the 1961 putsch in Algiers. Heading it in the Var was Henri Pieroni. While studying law in Aix-en-Provence, he had led an anti-communist group; and during military service in Algeria, he had joined a unit known for its officers' anti-Gaullism. Following his discharge, Pieroni organized a memorial mass in the Toulon Cathedral for two soldiers killed by the FLN (among the 350 people in attendance were the mayor and other anti-Gaullists on the city council). In the spring of 1962, the CNIP's departmental newspaper (*Le National*) explained how readers could listen to radio broadcasts from OAS renegades in Portugal. A few weeks later, at a CNIP rally in Toulon, the audience heard praise for the OAS and charges that De Gaulle was violating the constitution, ruining the country, and helping the Communists.[21]

Many politicians had switched to the party of De Gaulle when he became president, including Maurice Arreckx, mayor of Toulon and future patron of the *pieds noirs*. Born in 1917, Arreckx spent his childhood in Toulouse, joined the wartime Resistance, and then moved to Toulon, where he became a city councilor whose allies included Henri Fabre and Jean Vitel. Catholic and anti-communist, the trio projected an image of pragmatic, competent decision-makers. Fabre and Vitel had won election to parliament after jumping onto the Gaullist bandwagon in 1958; and Arreckx followed them a year later by becoming the Gaullist mayor of Toulon.[22]

In a 1959 interview, though, De Gaulle had hinted that independence was inevitable: "The Algeria of yesterday is finished." He went even further a few months later, as we have seen, by announcing that Algerians had a right to self-determination. Changing its direction, his party expelled members who belonged to anti-independence groups.[23] French Algeria activists in the Var reacted vividly. In an open letter to politicians, Reimbold's group asked, "When you were elected, you were in favor of French Algeria. Today are you in favor or against?" Fabre and Vitel replied that they wanted the French Republic to include Algeria. Backing words with action, Vitel attended public gatherings organized by Reimbold's group; Fabre joined the Comité de Vincennes, a new French Algeria group. Standing firm, they criticized the government's treatment of the insubordinate generals whose putsch had failed.[24] For the referendum on the Évian Accords, they urged a vote against independence: "By voting 'no,' you are expressing your mistrust. You are protesting the hundreds of thousands of francs promised to an Algerian state already friendly with foreign powers. You are resisting the unrestricted delegation of supreme power."[25] Following the referendum, the two men quit the Gaullist Party.[26]

Most French wanted peace, though.

The war punished families like that of Guy Moutardier, a second lieutenant killed in the Department of Oran. A local politician gave the eulogy for this 26-year-old, who had graduated from Sciences Po in Paris and left a wife and child behind:

> A brilliant future lay ahead of him. His brutal death, only three months before his discharge, has affected us all. He was born into a highly respected family from Toulon. Their loss, as well as the loss to society of such a remarkable élite, fills each of us with sadness. In the name of our Mayor, the City Council, the War Memorials Commission, the patriotic associations, and the people of Toulon, it is my painful duty to bid a supreme and final *adieu* to our young fellow citizen.[27]

In addition to the loss of so many like Moutardier, holding onto Algeria had sown moral doubt, OAS terrorism, and anxiety over the fate of the thousands of soldiers still fighting. For the referendum on the Évian Accords, parties across the spectrum—including those of the left—had joined the Gaullists in urging a "yes" vote.[28] They were in tune with the metropole, which voted overwhelmingly in favor of a peace settlement that promised independence. The Var—which belonged among the five departments where support for Algerian self-determination was lowest—was out of tune with the rest of the country.[29]

Already Arreckx had twinned schools in Toulon and Algeria. The city had sent Christmas gifts to soldiers in the colony.[30] At a private dinner when De Gaulle came to Toulon for a visit with his son (a naval officer), Arreckx hardly minced words. The president asked for his thoughts on the Algerian situation. With the flight of the *pieds noirs* underway, Arreckx replied:

> Like many French people in the metropole, Mister President, we received very little information about this tragedy. If we set that aside, nonetheless, for my part a question comes to mind. Why is it that the French army, which was in Algeria at the time, did not intervene more effectively so that the exodus could have taken place under less harsh conditions?[31]

De Gaulle responded: "History will be our judge, *Monsieur le maire*."[32] The Algerian question had permeated into local politics. At a council meeting following the referendum on the Évian Accords, Arreckx backed a resolution that honored soldiers and civilians killed by Algerian nationalists. It also condemned those responsible for acts of terrorism, including the OAS.

Affirming faith in republican liberties and institutions, it called for national reconciliation.[33] However, Socialists on the city council said the resolution should omit the Algerian nationalists:

> We do not condone what the FLN has done. It slit the throats of women and children. Now that 90 percent have voted in favor of the Évian Accords, however, the situation has changed. There is no longer any point in condemning the FLN. Besides, the FLN is not the same as the OAS. The Accords are now a fact, so instead of talking about the exactions of the past we should look to the future.[34]

Indeed, a Communist counter-resolution urged the government to neutralize the OAS assassins. When the council could not agree on a resolution, Arreckx admitted that he was unhappy with the government, the Évian Accords, and the loss of Algeria.[35] He had taken another step away from Gaullism.

THE REPATRIATES ARRIVE IN TOULON

Early that June, the city welcomed some 200 children sent from Algiers for safety.[36] Later that month, fishing boats bearing 10 passengers were the first vessels to arrive directly from Algeria.[37] Once Toulon became an official destination, the flow surged. Between June 30 and July 2, 1962, five ships from Oran, Bougie, Philippeville, and Mostaganem brought 5,000 passengers to the naval docks. Military and civilian officials greeted the new arrivals, who registered as repatriates and proceeded to Navy warehouses for a meal, first aid, and a place to sleep.[38] Families traveled together (not always accompanied by their men who, biding their time until the return of order, did not want to abandon homes, automobiles, and other property). More ships bearing *pieds noirs* (as well as *harkis* and civilians employed by the Navy, and their respective families) arrived throughout the month of July.[39] By the end of the summer, 16,350 repatriates had passed through the port.[40]

More than 20 voluntary associations and trade unions joined the city in welcoming, feeding, and guiding the refugees.[41] The Red Cross set up a voluntary agency to help with lodging, employment, and bureaucratic procedures.[42] The local newspaper started a regular column—"With the Repatriates from North Africa"—with updates on housing, job opportunities, and state programs.[43] City authorities and religious orders solicited billets in private homes as well as donations of food, clothing, and household items.[44] When 575 *harkis* arrived aboard the Phocée, between an official welcome and their onward trip to Paris "meals were served, taking into account, in the choice of dishes and drinks, the precepts of the

Islamic religion."[45] One school became a reception center for 240 people from Oran.[46] To lodge another 233 repatriates, the Count of Pierredon reopened the vacant Tamaris Grand Hotel, with fellow citizens donating furniture.[47] Supported by the mayor and city council, others collected money and distributed food.[48]

Press, television, and radio expressed sympathy. A journalist on board the aircraft carrier La Fayette went below decks and witnessed:

> A painful spectacle whose sad images evoke a scene unfortunately too frequent: an exodus of horror-stricken refugees. Men, women, and children crammed together, squeezed one against the other, some even spread out on the steel deck or collapsed on hastily knotted bundles of clothing. The very image of human suffering! Most striking and astonishing, though, is the silence that hovers in these enormous hangars supplied with air by huge panels connected to the flight deck. Not a shout, not a sigh, words that seem whispered, muffled sounds, moaning from a child, cries from one of many babies. Even the dogs, mostly German Shepherds, with powerful muscles and impressive jaws, lie down and stay quiet. All give the impression of being in shock, as if they had emerged unscathed from a terrible accident. They still cannot grasp what happened.[49]

For the transport of large possessions like furniture, senior civil servants and others with privilege could use shipping containers. Their personal vehicles turned the flight deck of La Fayette into a parking lot.[50] Images of deprivation dominated news reports, though:

> In an unimaginable state of destitution, yesterday morning 700 French from Algeria disembarked from the freighter Le Havre. They were coming from Oran where, of course, they had left everything behind. Their despair is virtually beyond description: people without even a suitcase who, after spending 15 days on the docks in Oran, stormed onto this freighter in unprecedented numbers.[51]

News photos showed mothers and children descending a gangplank; sailors carrying infants in their arms; and a uniformed official comforting a woman with her head buried in her hands.[52] A right-wing Provençal newspaper (*Le Méridional*), pitied the refugees from Oran:

> They have abandoned that accursed city under the mocking gaze and triumphant smile of the new masters, while the *youyous* [ululating female cries] rang out from the large bay windows of the ultra-modern buildings occupied by the citizens of this new state. Nothing, not a single regret, except for having contributed so much to the development of a country that very soon will surely taste the bitter fruit of independence.[53]

A tearful woman described her situation:

> I don't know, I don't know any more. My husband is gone. The fifth of July was a day of horror. The provocation and killing kept getting worse. The fear was driving us crazy. I hid, I fled, I waited eight days before boarding La Fayette. And now, here I am alive, with my baby. But what will become of me? I don't have a family, I no longer have anyone![54]

A reporter for a right-wing newspaper quoted another refugee from Oran:

> It is hell, sir, said an older woman whose grandparents had left Alsace at the request of the French government to go and turn a barren land that was rampant with disease into a country that flourished. It's awful, sir, she added between sobs. We never believed we would have to leave under such awful conditions. You can imagine that those who, like others, believed in official promises have been enlightened in short order. Now it's all over. The *bled* [backcountry] is now empty. Only Oran still has a few thousand French, but not for long, because everything has an end, even an illusion.[55]

A man who left behind a factory with 30 workers doubted an independent Algeria would manage:

> Speaking practically, I am moving here having lost all means. Everything stayed over there and it's impossible to ship our machine tools. They can keep everything. It's all the same to me. They'll always need someone French to show them how. But don't count on me anymore. I won't be there.[56]

Although Toulon received the *pieds noirs* well, most moved on after the press, the mayor, and the Red Cross told them a dearth of jobs and housing meant they should not stay.[57]

Apart from Paris, Lyons, Bordeaux, Toulouse, and Grenoble, the French of Algeria resettled mostly near the Mediterranean (east of Toulon in Nice, Cannes, and Fréjus, for example, and to the west in Marseille, Aix-en-Provence, Avignon, Arles, Nîmes, Montpellier, Béziers, and Perpignan).[58] This confounded the plans of the state, which had tried to direct their resettlement by tying living allowances to staying away from the Mediterranean.[59] Similarities to the climate, culture, and geography of North Africa are often mentioned as reasons why the *pieds noirs* preferred the south of France. As for Toulon, it was home to the Navy—whose vessels had brought many over—and its welcome contrasted with the indifference, if not the hostility, that met the *pieds noirs* elsewhere.[60] A few stayed initially, others returned and, by year's end, some 17,000 *pieds noirs* had moved to Toulon.

THE ENTRENCHMENT OF ANTI-GAULLISM

The repatriates formed a minority in Toulon, but almost nowhere else in France was their share of the population so large—about 15 percent. Forming a unified bloc, they might decide elections. Over the following decades, this would affect not only the calculations and campaigns of local politicians but also the space for the far right.

In the first presidential election of the Fifth Republic, only members of the Electoral College had been eligible to vote.[61] Previously, De Gaulle had stated his preference for a strong executive: a president not beholden to parliament or parties, with authority over the Council of Ministers (whose members, including the prime minister, he could choose). In August 1962—one week after the OAS again tried to kill him as his car traveled through the Parisian suburb of Petit-Clamart—De Gaulle told the government that he wanted a reform: the election of the head of state by all French voters, not just the Electoral College. Cooperating with his wishes, the Parliament dissolved itself and the government announced a national referendum on the proposed reform.[62]

Previously the only directly elected president had been Louis-Napoleon Bonaparte—who turned into an autocrat—and investing supreme power in the head of state contradicted the working principles of the Third and Fourth Republics. De Gaulle associated these principles with government instability and policy inconsistency. Opposition to the "yes" vote combined fear that the new Fifth Republic was moving toward a modern Bonapartism; reservations about the referendum's unconstitutionality (an opinion backed by the Council of State and the president of the Senate); and visceral anti-Gaullism among those angry over the loss of Algeria.[63] De Gaulle turned the referendum into a personal plebiscite. If the "no" vote prevailed, he warned, "his historical task would become immediately unfeasible" and he would resign. He was gambling that a "yes" victory in the referendum followed by a majority in the parliamentary elections would consolidate his power.[64]

The *pieds noirs* of Toulon had yet to organize politically. That would come later. Some 300 had attended a meeting that fall to form an association, but its aims were social and charitable.[65] At this early point, they represented 5,600 out of 94,000 eligible voters (6 percent of the city's electorate).[66] Upon their arrival, a cross-party coalition—its members included not only Arreckx, Fabre, and Vitel but also leading Socialists in the Var—had sponsored a Municipal Settlement Committee.[67] When the ships with repatriates came to Toulon, though, the right-wing press credited one man above all:

Ex-Colonials in the Metropole [57]

> Preaching by example, our first magistrate conquered the *pieds noirs*. For nearly two days they could see him among the refugees, offering words of comfort here, there pointing some distraught persons in the right direction, devoting himself unreservedly to these poor people, who nonetheless expressed, in a humble manner, their keenest gratitude to him.[68]

For the 1962 referendum, Arreckx was ready to break with Gaullism. Others in the Var also opposed the "yes" side of the president: the Socialists, Communists, Radicals, CNIP of Pieroni, and Christian Democrats.[69] Urging a "no" vote, Fabre and Vitel put their parliamentary seats on the line. De Gaulle, they said, was asking the people for permission to do anything he wanted. The president himself—not the party politics he abhorred—was responsible for the faults of the Fifth Republic.[70] They deplored the unconstitutionality of the referendum and asked why the president should have dictatorial powers:

> The nation needs to heal its deep wounds after the Algerian drama, which has left so many nationals in a state of distress. Those who put their faith in France have suffered so much hardship. This is a moment when we should be giving all of our concern to the repatriates from Algeria.[71]

Joining his allies, Arreckx came out openly against De Gaulle. The referendum, he said, divided the French at a time when the Algerian problem remained unresolved.[72]

The result confirmed De Gaulle's intuition that other political parties had lost touch with the French: with 62 percent in favor, the "yes" option prevailed. Still, the Var belonged to a group of southern departments (others were Bouches-du-Rhône, Gard, Haute-Garonne, and Hérault) where the strong "no" vote stood out. With a "no" vote of 48 percent, similarly, Toulon belonged to a set of southern cities (also including Marseille, Nîmes, Toulouse, and Montpellier) less likely to support the government's position. Already there was a new reason to single out the particularity of the south. Apart from its left-republican tradition and the weaker penetration of Gaullist propaganda (the state held a monopoly over broadcasting, but many in the south did not yet own a television set), the south had a stronger "no" vote because of the repatriates.[73]

The outcome of this referendum did not guarantee a Gaullist victory in the parliamentary elections to be held soon after.[74] For each of the Var's four electoral districts, the CNIP endorsed a French Algeria candidate, politicians like Fabre or Vitel.[75] Gauging the climate, the Gaullists avoided the scramble for the repatriate vote.[76] The Socialists assured the Europeans of Algeria that, unlike other politicians, they were not opportunists chasing their vote—and then chased it anyway.⁷⁷ Electorally the opposition performed well enough in the Var, where no candidate won in the first round, but Fabre and Vitel placed only third in their respective districts. To prevent a fragmentation of the anti-Gaullist vote, each withdrew from the run-off round, but the Gaullists prevailed.⁷⁸ In the year the Algerian War ended, De Gaulle was riding high.

SUBCULTURE, PARTISANSHIP, AND PATRONAGE

The extension of the franchise, Max Weber wrote, led to the replacement of the notable by the political entrepreneur. In America, he added, this new type of personality took form as the political boss, a figure in the "system of the plebiscitary party machine" who delivered votes and money to the party. The boss kept a low public profile and rarely sought office (except as senator, for this allowed him to engage in patronage by handing out offices to those who had helped his party). He was also unscrupulous: he did what was necessary to capture votes. The boss system was dying out, Weber concluded, because the increasing professionalization of political life in America left no room for dilettantes.⁷⁹

In democratic politics, it turned out, the boss system did not die out. Nor did bosses avoid political office. Just as important, in unveiling the latent functions of bossism, Robert Merton suggested that bosses and their political machines provide a means by which the "deprived classes" can meet their needs. Unlike government and charitable agencies that dispense assistance in a cold and demeaning manner, the boss and his agents help their clients—and potential voters—in a personalized manner that protects dignity by using the language of friendship.⁸⁰

This chapter has followed the steps taken by a mayor on his way to becoming a political boss. Anti-communism and anti-Gaullism narrowed the repatriates' options. Still, how could the mayor of a southern city be sure of their vote? Would the *pieds noirs* revert to past electoral patterns, thereby spreading their vote across the left and right? The mayor of Toulon had welcomed the first boatloads of refugees. He had mobilized voluntary associations and political authorities. After speaking out against the Évian Accords, he had quit the Gaullist party. He had set the foundations for patron-client relations, but the *pieds noirs* had yet to organize.⁸¹ They would do so after 1962, with two long-term results. They formed a bloc of votes that carried weight in their city and department, and they lay the foundation for the survival of a far-right potential.

CHAPTER 4
New Political Configurations

Between the time De Gaulle decided to abandon Algeria and 1968, the year much of France turned against him, the far-right potential of the *pieds noirs* changed shape. In Algeria, it had manifested itself in mass protests, civil disobedience, OAS solidarity, and support for military over civilian authority. In the metropole, it persisted in the group's acceptance of past crimes in the name of French Algeria. Some parties wanted to grab this potential; none disowned it entirely. As we will see in this chapter on politics and society in Toulon until 1967, much of this potential profited the moderate right.

To see how, we look at efforts by Mayor Arreckx and his team to build on their closeness to this community. Favors from city hall accompanied the rhetoric of sympathy and friendship. In chasing the *pied noir* vote, the moderate right outdid the Socialists and the Nationaux. The purest expression of French Algeria rancor, the Nationaux did not last long, but before disappearing this party challenged the moderate right and sowed dissent among the *pieds noirs*. Thereafter—from the eclipse of the Nationaux until the rise of the National Front—the moderate right channeled the far-right potential of the city's *pied noirs*.

THE *PIEDS NOIRS* RAISE THEIR PROFILE

Not passive, the *pieds noirs* elbowed their way into city politics.[1] They mounted civic events that signaled their electoral potential. Their leaders sounded out political options, then gave instructions on whom to support. Apart from cementing ties to the moderate right, the repatriates were building identity. They formed only one of the city's constituencies; others were its Corsicans, shopkeepers, military personnel, and arsenal workers. Showing capacity for organization, they made themselves influential. In 1962, the local branch of a national association had mounted the Day of the Repatriates, a one-day event at the Municipal Theater (which the city put at their disposal at no cost).[2] *Pied noir* leaders complained about difficulties with housing and red tape: "We wish to be treated as French like the rest, nothing more, with equal rights and responsibilities. After turning us into colonialists, now they want to make us look like gangsters." Political influence, they told the *pieds noirs*, hinged on staying united. Then they introduced Arreckx who, amidst applause and cries of "Long live our mayor," told his audience that being French depends less on blood than on heart.[3]

Building on this success, in early 1964 the repatriates held the Quinzaine des Rapatriés, a fortnight of civic, cultural, sports, and religious events. To line up sponsors and resources, the organizing committee relied on men of experience—one a former mayor of Bab El Oued, another (Louis Boutigny) a former executive secretary to the mayor of Algiers and director of the municipal credit union of Algiers.[4] Officially, the Quinzaine was nonpolitical: its slogan ("Thanks and Solidarity") acknowledged the Var's welcome. Organizers sent press releases to the friendly *Méridional* and *République-Le Provençal*, as well as *Le Petit Varois*, the local communist newspaper. Private donors pitched in: for a lottery prize, Air France donated a round-trip ticket to Corsica; for a sports prize, Paul Ricard, the *pastis* distiller living near Toulon, donated cash.[5] As official patrons, the organizers recruited the minister for repatriates in Paris; the maritime prefect and other naval officers posted in Toulon; a Jewish Rabbi, Catholic archpriest, and Protestant pastor; and heads of voluntary associations. Musical detachments from the Navy and the Foreign Legion agreed to perform.[6]

Lobbying and partisanship crept into ceremonies and receptions, where dignitaries from the armed forces and the political class mixed with leaders of civil society and repatriate groups. Official patrons included the prefect and sub-prefect, as well as two deputies, three mayors, and five senators.[7] To attract funding, the organizers even enlisted Gaullists (with Communists, though, it drew the line).[8] Visitors to the Quinzaine donated money for the *harkis* and French Algeria prisoners.[9] Waiving its usual fees, the city offered the use of sports stadiums, the Municipal Theater, and the Art Museum. The mayor gave a speech that bothered *Le Petit Varois*:

> We have no desire to detract from the appeal or success of an event such as the Quinzaine des Rapatriés, but it seems helpful to clarify its boundaries. These the Mayor failed to respect. In his opening words, he himself said, "I think we can agree on the non-political character of these events." Why, then, his strange comments about "the ideals for which

you fought," "the faith and courage of those who could not accept a surrender," and so on? And why his high-flown call for clemency toward "her children who fought—perhaps a bit immoderately—for what they believed in?" "Perhaps a bit immoderately," he says? What about the assassins from Toulon who killed Locussol; the bombers who disfigured Delphine Renard; the three other activists in Toulon who blew up in their Citroën; those who wounded innocent people and eliminated decent human beings; the Fascist killers "so full of faith and nobility" that they devastated clinics; cowards who sowed death on our soil and in Algeria; who fomented the putsch of 13 May 1958; who perpetrated warfare against the Algerian people while spreading blood, anti-France hatred, and dreams of establishing a pro-Hitler regime? Mr. Arreckx absolves them. Not for a moment does he show any willingness to condemn the crimes of the OAS. He even goes so far as to assert, "There is not a single party or spiritual authority that is not calling for a pardon." He seems to forget that, along with the Communist Party, all republicans and men of the Left deplore the state's clemency toward those Michel Debré refers to as "prodigal children." To Mr. Arreckx, the repatriates of Toulon are an electoral clientele for the upcoming Cantonal elections.[10]

After the Quinzaine, its patrons received a letter of thanks.[11] Printed in *Le Méridional*, Arreckx's letter added a promise that the *pieds noirs* would remember him.[12] A few days later, at the launch of his campaign for the cantonal elections, Arreckx declared himself a non-partisan with few equals in helping the French refugees from North Africa.[13] As a barometer of opinion, these cantonal elections suggested that the Gaullists were stalling.[14] Arreckx won—an outcome the prefect attributed to the repatriates.[15] The Socialists had helped too, because after the first round they withdrew their candidate in favor of Arreckx. So strong was anti-Gaullism that even *Le Petit Varois* broke with the Communist Party, giving Arreckx its second-round endorsement.[16] Left as well as right were indulging the *pieds noirs*.

A few months later in Toulon, the darker side of anti-Gaullism played out. In August 1964, De Gaulle visited to inaugurate the city's Memorial to the Liberation of Provence by the Allies. Not caring about bystanders at the ceremony, OAS diehards hid an explosive meant to kill the president.[17] It failed to detonate, but those still loyal to the fight for French Algeria would resort to violence again.[18]

THE 1965 MUNICIPAL ELECTIONS AND THE SCRAMBLE FOR THE REPATRIATE VOTE

Activism in favor of French Algeria had united disparate forces: Maurrasiens and Pétainists of the old far right; veterans of the Resistance against Nazi Germany; veterans of the Indochinese War; Left-Radicals and Socialists committed to empire; supporters of the Poujadists and the CNIP; and disillusioned Gaullists.[19] After 1962, remnants of these forces flowed into the Nationaux, who placed the fight for Algeria in a narrative of national decline. Modern France was unhealthy, they held, and the fight for Algeria belonged to a project of social, political, and spiritual renewal.[20] A man like Arreckx might be their ally, but he never joined their party.[21] By dividing the repatriate vote in Toulon, then, the Nationaux threatened to serve the Gaullists.

The Socialists wanted to retake city hall in the 1965 elections; Arreckx, who held only a minority on city council, chased a majority.[22] National leaders of the Gaullist party had decided that its local candidates should emphasize expertise and leadership, not partisanship.[23] Accordingly, its ticket in Toulon camouflaged itself as the "Non-partisan Union for a Sound and Efficient Administration of Toulon and Its Future." The repatriates now formed a seventh of the city's voters, and the scramble for their support would dominate these elections.[24] Communists aside, every ticket included repatriates or veterans of the Algerian War: 3 for the Socialists, 3 for the Gaullists, 6 for the Arreckx list, and 16 for the Nationaux.[25] Arreckx opened his campaign with a reminder that his administration had opened its heart to the repatriates. A split in the nationalists' vote, he warned, would help the Communists. Asking why the head of the Gaullist ticket (a Resistance veteran, vice admiral, and exnaval prefect) had done nothing to prevent the transfer of naval activities from Toulon to Brest, Arreckx also accused the Gaullists of callousness toward the refugees from North Africa. At a rally, candidates on the Arreckx slate repeated their opposition to the Évian Accords. Not backing down, the Socialist candidate reminded the repatriates of his fight, in the Senate, for their right to compensation for lost property. His candidacy speech listed many achievements—defending the Arsenal and the shipyards, as well as retirees, naval officers, shopkeepers, and postal workers—but only after mentioning his defense of the repatriates. By the time the campaign closed, half of the candidate statements in local newspapers mentioned the repatriates.[26]

To prevent a split in the anti-Gaullist vote, the Socialists and Nationaux asked for a pact with Arreckx, who gambled and refused both. The Socialists responded by driving a wedge between Arreckx and the party whose fascism they said was barely hidden, the Nationaux. The Gaullists condemned the demagogy of other politicians toward the repatriates—who should worry because they would have to leave this city unless it created jobs. Friction between the Nationaux and Arreckx, they added, made Gaullism the only alternative to the left.[27]

Groups of patriots, anti-Gaullists, and Algerian War veterans endorsed Arreckx.[28] One repatriate leader reminded them that he—a native of Algiers, a decorated war veteran wounded six times in combat, a man imprisoned for anticolonial activism—had joined the Arreckx slate.[29] For advice, Arreckx relied on the director of the municipal credit union, Boutigny, who had founded a *pied noir* group, the Front des Réfugiés d'Afrique du Nord (FRAN).[30] The FRAN took aim at the Gaullists:

> We are victims of disloyalty who must be loyal to those who helped us. We must not forgive those who are responsible for putting the best among us in prison and keeping them there in a spirit of hatred. The time has come to show our gratitude to our allies, those who gave us true compassion, aid, and friendship. These elections are also the time to punish all those who bear the responsibility for our suffering and the suffering of our nation.[31]

In addition to organizers of the Quinzaine, the FRAN's leaders included Georges Dahmar. A priest of Berber origin expelled from Algeria in 1960 for ministering to insurgent *pieds noirs*, now he served as vicar of the cathedral. Titled "Repatriates, My Fellow Citizens," the closing statement of the Arreckx campaign reiterated his support for their grievances and promised to create a social agency for them under Dahmar.[32]

The FRAN got voters out for the first round and the Arreckx list came well ahead, followed by the Communists, Gaullists, and Socialists. Now eliminated, the Nationaux asked its supporters to back Arreckx. The Socialists withdrew but endorsed Arreckx instead of their usual partners, the Communists: "the watchword of the Socialist Party remains unchanged: defeat the Gaullist party and the partisans of personal power."[33] Dahmar reminded the repatriates not to disperse their votes; others urged them to block two tendencies equally harmful to France, Gaullism and communism.[34] The Gaullists responded that "sour, resentful recalcitrants who remain stuck in the past" had supplied more than half the Arreckx vote.[35]

In Toulon (as well as in other cities with *pied noir* communities like Nice, Montpellier, and Toulouse), the incumbent defeated the Gaullists and Communists.[36] Thus, these elections revealed the limits of Gaullism and the sturdiness of anti-Gaullism.[37] They also revealed a break with electoral patterns in Algeria before the war of independence: many *pieds noirs* were not reverting to their old partisanship.[38] In southern cities, these elections solidified ties between local patrons and *pied noir* clients.[39] The Nationaux did not disappear quite yet, as we will see, but better times for them would come only when the National Front became viable.

FROM FRIENDS TO "FRIENDS"

At its first meeting in April 1965, the new city council passed a resolution urging Paris to forgive the hardliners of the OAS and the putschists of Algiers, now wanted men or prisoners.[40] *Pied noir* councilors and leaders joined in a special celebration of the mayor's re-election: "We gave each other our friendship," Arreckx declared, "and I hope that the road we will travel together will be very long."[41] Embracing Dahmar, he then confirmed that the city would set up the promised social agency, the Commission extra-municipale des rapatriés, which a few months later opened its doors.[42] The Commission helped repatriates in need of work, housing, clothing, household items, or guidance in dealing with bureaucracies.[43]

The city provided its staff as well its office in an old building on the Place Paul-Comte (along with furniture, equipment, and supplies).[44] Yet the Commission stood outside the public sector.[45] Its *pied noir* directors, whom the mayor chose, took care of fundraising, press relations, legal issues, and lobbying.[46] The Commission was thus a curious beast. Jacobin France mistrusts bodies between unitary state and citizenry: since the Revolution, the Church; associations from the time of the Le Chapelier law until 1901; Breton, Occitan, and Corsican regionalism since the 1960s; and Islamic and ethno-racial identities since the 1980s. Making membership in the *pied noir* community a condition for help, in effect the city was discriminating among the needy. Giving a discretionary turn to republican fraternity, the Commission served a system of patronage that upheld a community of identity.[47]

At the agency's opening, the mayor reminded his audience that he had kept his electoral promise.[48] Before thanking him, Dahmar made a teensy detour:

> Not one *pied noir* can forget the sinister and terrible hours of the exodus when, together with others, haggard and desperate, like a pitiful flock without a hearth or a home, they landed. It was the height of summer and the holidays were in full swing. The hotels were bursting, and the Côte d'Azur was welcoming its usual fauna. The devil with worries and bothers: a cut-rate peace, nicely cooked up at a hotel in Évian, had bought considerable relief. It was time for people to go to the beach, get a tan, and bury in the sand whatever served as their conscience. We are grateful to you, *Monsieur le Maire*, for the unstinting efforts of you and your associates amidst this indifference, which was guilty, if not criminal.[49]

So far, so good for Mayor Arreckx and his clients.

In December 1965, France held its first direct presidential election since 1848. One of the candidates was Jean-Louis Tixier-Vignancour, whose brilliant court defense had saved General Salan's life. Tixier had also defended other military men and OAS members, including two executed for their crimes: Lieutenant Roger Degueldre (head of the military arm of the OAS in Algiers, the Delta Commandos) and Colonel Jean-Marie Bastien-Thiry (organizer of the failed attempt to assassinate De Gaulle at Petit-Clamart in 1962). When a committee under Jean-Marie Le Pen had asked Tixier to represent the Nationaux in this election, he accepted.[50] Le Pen then became his manager in a campaign that solicited the *pieds noirs*:

> A people that had suffered and was profoundly worried about abandoning the land and cemeteries of its ancestors rose up again with the OAS, which was also the honorable response of French officers obliged by conscience to keep the oaths they had sworn.[51]

In a televised speech, Tixier cited the execution of Claude Piegts (a 27-year-old *pied noir* and OAS member found guilty of assassinating a government official in Algiers) as an example of the fundamental injustice of the Gaullist regime.[52] In the first round, Tixier attracted only 5 percent of the vote (out of anti-Gaullism, he would urge a second round vote for the Socialist, Mitterrand). Still, the Var gave Tixier more support than any other department in the country; and in Toulon (where Arreckx, avoiding a position for or against the Nationaux, endorsed none of the presidential candidates), Tixier attracted 16 percent of the vote.[53]

Clearly, the far-right potential absorbed by Arreckx had survived. Indeed, Tixier's share of the vote exceeded that for the Nationaux in the municipal elections. Were it not for Arreckx, this implied, the far right might do well in Toulon. Staying on track, Arreckx sent a letter to mayors of 39 other municipalities that criticized a clemency law for crimes in the name of French Algeria.[54] His council called for a blanket amnesty for those crimes; and a full rehabilitation of French Algeria activists and military men stripped of honor, rank, or office in the Legion of Honor, the military, or the public service.[55] Strikingly, unanimous support for similar motions came from the departmental council of the Var, a body controlled by Socialists and counting a few Communists. How far would the influence of the *pieds noirs* go?

THE COMITÉ DE DÉFENSE ET D'UNION DES RAPATRIÉS

In towns and cities across the south, the *pieds noirs* were gaining ground. Their national associations lacked unity, however, so local groups in the Var decided to create a federation. This might make them arbiters in local party politics and national *pied noir* affairs. With the 1967 parliamentary elections in mind, the FRAN's leaders created the Comité de Défense et d'Union des Rapatriés (CODUR). Its grievances were familiar: freedom, amnesty, and rehabilitation for French Algeria activists; compensation for property lost in Algeria; and searches for settlers gone without a trace during the turmoil in the colony.[56] The CODUR also reacted to events like the state visit of the president of Algeria, Ahmed Ben Bella, a founder of the FLN:

> Will General de Gaulle welcome to the Élysée Palace the man who slaughtered so many or our compatriots, both Muslim and French? Will he share with him the sumptuous paneling of Versailles or the delicate woodwork of the Trianon? Will he invite this man with bloodstained hands to a show by the new ballet at the Opera? Will he instead offer the sadistic pleasure of allowing him to watch, from above the Champs-Élysées, a ceremonial tilting of the tricolor flags chased out of the thirteen departments of Algeria? Veterans, *nationaux*, will you continue your silent approval of these excesses? Algiers insists on twice the cost of the Algerian War, which our army won but we lost to a pro-Communist government now sacrificing the unity of Western Europe for the sake of a Franco-Soviet alliance.[57]

During 1966, the CODUR held outreach meetings in Hyères, Le Lavandou, Saint-Raphaël, and Saint-Tropez, followed by a bigger assembly with representatives from nine municipalities.[58] The group made plans for ceremonies and monuments in the name of French Algeria and agreed to compose a program for the upcoming parliamentary elections.[59] Before leaving, it elected the Abbé Dahmar as president and Boutigny (the director of the Toulon credit union) as secretary-treasurer.[60]

Reaching out to *pied noir* groups across the Var, the CODUR urged them to increase their political weight by joining. If De Gaulle won another majority, the group warned, the National Assembly would forget the *pieds noirs*. Keeping its options open, the CODUR thanked the leading Socialist in the Var, Le Bellegou, for defending its position on amnesty. In an open letter, the CODUR praised imprisoned leaders of the failed putsch of 1961 (Generals Salan and Jouhaud) and demanded amnesties for "fervent patriots whom History will restore to their proper place among the men of feeling in our nation" (OAS leaders Georges Bidault and Jacques Soustelle, who were wanted men in exile).[61] Blending praise with censure, the CODUR kept alive the French Algeria version of history.

It also quarreled over how to honor the past. Testing the waters, the CODUR asked its members to mark the anniversary of the Rue d'Isly massacre in Algiers by placing wreaths at the Monument to the Dead in Toulon. Seeing a protest in disguise, the sub-prefect imposed a ban and, on March 26, the police barred access to the monument.[62] All this exposed the spiteful essence of the Gaullist regime, the *pieds noirs* must have thought.

Keeping pain fresh, Dahmar dedicated his mass on All Saint's Day, 1966, to the repose of the souls of those now buried in "places to which we will never again return or place flowers."[63] Yet he declined when the mayor of a town northwest of Toulon (Ollioules) invited him to inaugurate a monument in memory of France's former colonies. As president of the CODUR, Dahmar explained, he could not stand beside the same sub-prefect who had banned the ceremony at the Monument to the Dead in Toulon.[64] Likewise, the CODUR objected to plans for a monument to French Algeria in La Garde, near Toulon, because the mayor was a Communist: "It's up to the Communists if they wallow in the mire of denial, of betrayal, of deceitful shame, of hypocrisy."[65] A tad duplicitously, the CODUR commented that exploiting the repatriates' anti-Gaullism for electoral ends was opportunistic and deplorable. Actively making friends, enemies, and trouble, the group was pressing history into the service of interests and identity.[66]

THE 1967 PARLIAMENTARY ELECTIONS

Nationally, the Gaullists and their allies would proceed to win the 1967 parliamentary elections.[67] What concerns us here is how these elections affected relations between the *pieds noirs* and Arreckx. The CODUR aimed to deliver a bloc of votes to each candidate it endorsed; it would succeed only in part. The city straddled two electoral districts of the Var: the east fell into the Third District, the west into the Fourth.[68] There was no problem in the Fourth District, where the preferences of Arreckx and the CODUR aligned. Not so in the Third District, where they would clash. Revealing a margin of unreliability in the *pied noir* vote, these elections curbed their relations with Arreckx. After he would continue to capture much of their support, but these elections set enduring limits on their influence.

As candidates in the Fourth District, then, the mayor and the CODUR agreed on French Algeria activist, Pascal Arrighi, and his running mate, Jean Vitel, the Arreckx ally and city councilor who had broken with the Gaullists.[69] Arrighi was a lawyer, veteran of the Resistance, and former deputy for Corsica. During the *pied noir* rebellion of May 1958, he had traveled to Corsica with the mission of recruiting paratroops for an insurgency. Arrighi had supported the OAS and served as witness for the defense at the trial of General Salan.[70] At an electoral rally in February 1967 at Saint-Mandrier-sur-Mer (across the harbor from Toulon) attended by French Algeria notabilities, he and Vitel talked about jobs, education, and pensions. Heeding local interests, the two promised price floors for wine, funding for wine storage facilities, and restrictions on cheap imports from Spain and North Africa. In addition to amnesty, rehabilitation, and compensation, they spoke about better terms on state loans to repatriates and announced that the CODUR had endorsed them.[71] Arrighi performed respectably in the first round but came well behind the Gaullist and Communist candidates.[72] He withdrew, which boosted the Gaullist's chances among voters averse to an even greater evil, victory by a Communist. The Gaullist candidate reminded voters of state investments in local shipyards; he believed a Gaullist government would sign contracts for the demolition of naval vessels at Toulon and La Seyne-sur-Mer. He and his running mate repeated their support for amnesty and compensation, and had the audacity of calling themselves *candidats nationaux*. The Gaullist lost to the Communist (the popular mayor of working-class La Seyne-sur-Mer).[73] Arreckx could not blame the CODUR for this outcome.

In the Third District, by contrast, the situation would degenerate. Here Arreckx's man was Henri Fabre, vice-mayor of Toulon and vice-president of the departmental council. Like Vitel and Arreckx, he had broken with the Gaullists over the future of Algeria. Initially, Fabre made a deal with CODUR: if the group endorsed him, it could choose his running mate. Fabre and a majority in the CODUR favored a repatriate on city council; Dahmar led a losing minority that favored the director of the municipal credit union, Boutigny, whose battle against corruption in the city did not suit everyone. Beaten, Dahmar resigned from the presidency, which reverted to the group's secretary-general, Boutigny, who, after more squabbling and confusion, quit too. Rudderless and disintegrating, the CODUR lost value for Fabre, who turned around and chose Arreckx as his running mate.[74]

The discord only worsened thanks to Tixier, a surprise candidate in the Third District of the Var. His candidacy pitted one loyalty against another: a CODUR member called the sense of gratitude toward Tixier "visceral."[75] During the 1965 presidential campaign, people now in the CODUR had helped Tixier ("a fervent patriot and ardent defender of those who fought for a French Algeria") by holding rallies for him in Toulon, Hyères, and Sanary.[76] Even Arrighi had campaigned for Tixier; in return, Tixier now endorsed him as his preferred candidate in the Fourth District. Fearing a disastrous split in the *pied noir* vote, twice the CODUR sent delegations to Tixier in Paris and twice he promised to stay out of Toulon.[77]

In late 1966, suddenly, Tixier announced his candidacy in the Third District of the Var.[78] Traveling to Berlin soon after for the launch of an anticommunist group with Soviet Bloc refugees, Tixier declared that France's pullback from the North Atlantic Treaty Organization (NATO) showed the Gaullists' complicity with communism:

> Europe from the Atlantic to the Urals is a soviet France: what the French Communist Party could never achieve, De Gaulle has accomplished. The French Communist Party

betrays the interests of its voters: it sacrifices the standard of living of the French working class to the foreign policy of De Gaulle. Now, in the National Assembly, Communists and Gaullists are voting together against an amnesty.[79]

Tixier won endorsements from national groups of repatriates and French Algeria prisoners, as well as French Algeria notables (Madame Salan, the wife of the imprisoned general, and the Bachaga Boualem—a *harki* leader, former politician, and OAS ally). The CNIP helped too. Deciding not to field a candidate in the Third District, it pitched in by holding a Tixier rally attended by repatriates, French Algeria activists, and "former political prisoners, some of them just out of the Gaullist cells. Fearing that the rival candidacies of Fabre and Tixier would help their opponents, only the reactionary Action française dissented.[80]

Confusion and disunity had eroded the CODUR's influence: some of its leaders backed Tixier; others argued that beating the Communists and Gaullists outweighed personal loyalty. Seeking a withdrawal by one of the rivals, the group tried in vain to arrange a meeting with Fabre and Tixier. A month before the elections, Tixier took a chance and asked Dahmar to be his running mate. Dahmar refused the man who had broken his word and urged him to abandon his candidacy.[81] The disarray among the *pieds noirs* and their past allies drew comments from the Gaullists:

> This illustrates exactly what it is we do not want to see again, extremism, bungling, and ambiguity. It presents no serious alternative to the present parliamentary majority. This election is serious. The stakes are serious. What matters right now is the future of France, Toulon especially, so we can do without all the folklore and bugle calls.[82]

Their opponents wanted to topple the Fifth Republic, warned the Gaullists, who promised efficacy and stability instead.[83]

In a campaign where the dominant issues were taxes, education, state spending, economic growth, and youth unemployment, all parties targeted the *pieds noirs*. Calling for reconciliation and fraternity, the Gaullist candidate in Toulon said he supported compensation and amnesty. Fabre and Arreckx recalled all they had done for the *pieds noirs* and reminded them of the CODUR's call to support the candidate with the best chance of beating the Communists and Gaullists. After acknowledging the repatriates' strong attachment to Tixier—the lawyer for the defense of General Salan—they said the heart must sometimes give way to reason. Two thousand at the Municipal Theater heard Fabre and Arreckx denounce the three Gaullist deputies in the Var. Unable to prevent the transfer of naval operations to Brest or the crisis of the shipyards at La Seyne-sur-Mer, they asked, how could Gaullists fix the city's problems with tourism, transportation, and industry? Fabre ended by accusing Tixer of trying to divide the repatriates.[84] At rallies attended by Madame Salan and the Bachaga Boualem, Tixier turned on Fabre and Arreckx: "Mediocrity and ineptitude have been crushing Toulon for too long."[85]

After the authorized period for electoral campaigning closed, President De Gaulle gave a radio and television speech asking the French to give him a majority in the National Assembly. Tixier decided to reply outside his Toulon headquarters on the Rue de la République. Invoking the official end of the campaign, the sub-prefect prohibited Tixier's impromptu speech and sent in the riot police. Moving to a balcony, Tixier addressed the crowd below (amidst cries of "Liberate Jouhaud!" and "Liberate Salan!") until a tear-gas grenade hit him in the head. A night of disorder ensued, with 30 people arrested in the city streets.[86]

Tixier placed a respectable third in the first round, while Fabre arrived fourth. Their combined support exceeded that for either the Gaullist front-runner or his Communist runner-up, so the CODUR had been right about the danger of vote splitting. Fabre withdrew but endorsed no one for the runoff. The Gaullist urged voters to unite with him in the fight against left and right extremists. The repatriates had given Tixier their "bloc support," in his view, and he understood their sentiments.[87] Tixier, however, was a

> neo-fascist leader who calls himself the defender of the repatriates when he only does them harm: politically because he represents nothing, morally because all he can do is bring back their pain and resentment instead of helping them to better integrate into the French collectivity.[88]

A dissident group of repatriate war veterans backed the Gaullist, a general married to a woman born and raised in colonial Africa. A vote for Tixier, the group said, would be a betrayal of those whose "blood had stained the soil at Bir-Hakeim, Strasbourg, Monte Cassino, and Toulon." Their compatriots must choose the Cross of Lorraine, the veterans added, not the shadow of the swastika.[89]

With the Algerian War still fresh, the Gaullist reminded women "that thanks to General de Gaulle they have no reason to feel fear or worry, or to cry over their loved ones."[90] Tixier countered that women in this city knew what was real: stark unemployment, low wages, and poor pensions. Asking them to thank De Gaulle was an insult: "It implies that they want peace at any cost. A Frenchwoman admires peace when it is a reward for courage, not a payment for desertion and cowardice."[91] How could the Gaullists call themselves republicans and democrats when they monopolized the state media? Accountable to the head of state, not Parliament, why should they keep their promises to voters? They were the extreme right, not him.[92]

Tixier attracted more votes in the runoff than a week earlier but placed only third while the Gaullist won. In all of France only one candidate from Tixier's tiny party was elected (in Nice, another *pied noir* stronghold).[93] Henceforth, the man who had defended Salan and other partisans of French Algeria would lose political relevance.[94]

WHAT COULD ARRECKX CONCLUDE?

Since 1962, Arreckx had nurtured his relations with the *pieds noirs*, who had ensured his reelection as mayor. His city council included a good number of *pieds noirs*. He had followed up on election promises by creating a social agency for them and criticizing the government's failure to enact a full amnesty. The city had provided facilities for the CODUR's meetings. It had offered jobs and public housing. Arreckx had recommended a head of the CODUR, Boutigny, for a top position in the city's administration.[95] His patronage ought to have delivered more. Soon after the parliamentary elections, the mayor dissolved the Commission extra-municipale. With the repatriates now integrated, he announced, they had the same needs as others. For help, they could contact their elected representatives or the city administration, who would be at their service.[96]

Gone were the warm tones of friendship.

Looking ahead, though, Arreckx would rely on the repatriates still. At that time, France offered two routes for political advancement: top-down and bottom-up. Moving top-down, after entering the upper levels of the central administration, graduates of the state schools that produced technocrats (the Grandes Écoles) would seek a nomination in a safe constituency. Instead, Arreckx was following the other route: starting locally, he would cumulate office at different levels of government. This would improve his access to Paris, bringing goodwill, resources, and support for his constituents and himself.[97] While he built his career in this way, the *pieds noirs* would continue to serve the interests of Arreckx.

For now, anyway, Arreckx and his team had derailed the far right. The French Algeria imprint of Tixier and the Nationaux made them popular in cities of the south. By addressing the repatriates, offering them patronage, and capturing their votes, though, politicians like the mayor of Toulon outbid the far right. Only with the founding of the National Front in 1972 would interwar reactionaries and fascists, as well as Nazi collaborators and Pétain supporters, join again with the Nationaux.[98] Even then, though, the far right would stay marginalized from politics for another decade.

PART III
Shift in Opportunities

CHAPTER 5
Gaullism Loses Ground

During the 1970s Arreckx used his relations with the *pieds noirs* to promote their interests. Cementing their support, he suppressed their far-right potential. Similar relations of patronage grew in other cities. Consider Montpellier, where the repatriate's share of the population was about as high as in Toulon.¹ Like Arreckx, its mayor, François Delmas, was a conservative who had sided with French Algeria (members of the Montpellier city council even resigned over his refusal to condemn the OAS). Welcoming the *pieds noirs*, Delmas aided their resettlement. Offering jobs and public housing, he established a clientele that guaranteed his re-election as mayor in 1965 and 1971. Even *pieds noirs* who supported other political tendencies in national elections gave him their vote. Leaders of their community, in turn, served as his go-betweens. Until the mid-1970s, then, Toulon and Montpellier followed similar paths.² Economically and socially, though, the two cities differed. At the time of Algerian independence, Montpellier had attracted many *harkis*. The seat of one of Europe's oldest universities, moreover, it had a large student population. While Toulon relied on the Navy, Montpellier was expanding by attracting firms like IBM. The electoral potential for the Socialists thus differed across the two cities.³

In the early 1970s, a professor of legal history at the University of Montpellier, Georges Frêche, entered electoral politics as a Socialist. His strategy had two prongs: first, to unify the left by forming an alliance with the Communists; second, to compete with Delmas by establishing close relations with minority constituencies. In 1973, Frêche, won a seat in the National Assembly; in 1977, he replaced Delmas at city hall. During the next three decades (when he served as mayor, deputy, and president of the council for the Hérault region), Frêche used grants and other support to firm relations with diverse groups—including the Moroccan community, the Jewish community, and the city's gays and lesbians. As for the *pieds noirs*, Frêche found funding for their association and its urban headquarters. He befriended one of their national leaders, Jacques Roseau, and in the National Assembly supported a bill to oblige teachers and textbooks to recognize the positive role of colonialism, especially in North Africa. Officially, this man of paradox—a former anticolonialist and Maoist—had poor relations with the Socialist headquarters in Paris. Frêche won elections, though, and to this day Montpellier stands out as a southern city of *pieds noirs* with a weak far right.[4]

Comparison with Montpellier suggests that *pied noir* support for Arreckx was not a foregone conclusion: the Socialists, who once held power in Toulon, presented another option. The Socialists still dominated towns in the interior of the department, whose council they controlled. To fight off the leftist competition, Arreckx hitched himself to a right-wing, anti-Gaullist alternative on the rise: the party of Valéry Giscard d'Estaing. The manifest effect of the alliance between Arreckx and Giscard was to end the domination of the Var by the Socialists. At a deeper lever, it had two results. Opening the flow of resources, it gave material and organizational means for perpetuating, over time, the distinctive community of Toulon's *pieds noirs*. In addition, it solidified a political machine whose crisis in the mid-1990s would create an opening for the far right.

THE *PIEDS NOIRS* REACT TO THE ANTI-GAULLISM OF MAY 1968

In 1958, the French hailed De Gaulle as a savior, a strong leader who would rescue them from the instability of the Fourth Republic. A decade later, many believed the Fifth Republic suffered from too much stability. Even those unhappy with his route to power could admire his success in ending the Algerian War, reforming French political institutions, spreading French influence in global affairs, and winning consent for the regime. Agricultural reform was transforming the rural economy. Construction of new housing continued. Ever more households owned an automobile, a telephone, a refrigerator, a television, and a washing machine. Alongside a more trenchant approach to decolonization, European integration, and French participation in NATO, however, the state's response to social inequality, housing shortages, rising unemployment, and problems in higher education lagged.[5] Many now viewed De Gaulle as needlessly authoritarian, a man who should heed the people now that the Algerian crisis was over.[6]

By 1968, the economic integration of the repatriates was well underway. State programs helped initially by giving them special unemployment benefits, housing subsidies, and priority in job hiring. Relative to metropolitans, a bigger share of *pieds noirs* worked in certain occupations (e.g., professionals, engineers, managers, white-collar workers, or police and armed forces). Relatively fewer were farmers, artisans, blue-collar workers, or business owners. Like women who had migrated to the metropole from Spain, Italy, or Portugal, *pied noir* women born before 1939 had rates of labor force participation well below those for metropolitan women. At 4.5 percent, though, *pied noir* unemployment more than doubled the national average. Doing well enough economically, then, they had yet to reach parity.[7]

That year, students in Paris occupied the Sorbonne and set up barricades in the Latin Quarter. Vandalism and violent clashes with the police left hundreds injured and resulted in thousands of arrests. Tension increased when unions called for a general strike on 13 May 1968—by coincidence the 10th anniversary of the *pied noir* insurrection in Algiers. Workers occupied factories and, by 20 May, an estimated 10 million were on strike. Shutting down schools and factories, the protests and strikes also impeded travel by bus, train, or air. As stocks of fuel ran out, pumps went dry at gas stations. Suspension of mail delivery, newspaper distribution, and most state radio and television broadcasts hindered communication.[8] Contestation in the provinces did not reach the same levels as in Paris but did affect schools, banks, grocery stores, and professional services in Toulon.[9]

Protest by the French had boosted De Gaulle into power in 1958. Now it threatened to unseat him. Not sure if the military remained loyal, on 29 May he traveled in secret to the French base in Baden-Baden, West Germany. Believing the crisis might require a deployment of troops, he met with General Massu, who agreed to support De Gaulle in return for a pardon of OAS veterans and military insubordinates from French Algeria (political officials in exile, such as Georges Bidault and Jacques Soustelle, as well as Massu's superior in Algeria, the imprisoned General Salan). Reappearing in Paris the next day, De Gaulle dissolved the legislature, called national elections, and hinted at the use of force unless the situation improved. Thousands in the capital who wanted no more of the strikes or protests showed their support for him by marching in a rally. Who among them saw a connection between the regime's vulnerability and the announcement, one week later, of an official pardon for people who had committed crimes for French Algeria?[10]

The *pieds noirs* reacted to May '68 with ambiguity. Apart from the inconveniences it caused, they could hardly agree with students who admired Che Guevara, Leon Trotsky, and Chairman Mao. Some called this a moment of terror.[11] Yet many shared the protestors' antagonism toward De Gaulle. Exposing the vulnerability of the Gaullist regime, the unrest had opened an opportunity. Three days before De Gaulle went to Baden-Baden, thousands of *pieds noirs* followed the example of the students and workers. In Toulouse, they occupied the Prefecture and presented a list of demands for the Prefect to convey to Paris. They did the same in Toulon, warning that without a prompt response the government would be responsible for "any spontaneous reactions." A month later, the *pieds noirs* received a reply from Prime Minister Pompidou, who promised a bill for a full amnesty for French Algeria activists. The government would consider a moratorium on debts incurred due to resettlement and implement 1961 legislation on compensation.[12]

Pied noir leaders exploited May '68 to expand their networks. In Aix-en-Provence, they created the Fédération du Sud des Rapatriés (FSR), which sought to unify the *pieds noirs* of the Var, the Vaucluse, and the Bouches-du-Rhône.[13] The FSR echoed Tixier's message from the 1965 presidential campaign: Gaullism meant aid to communism both yesterday—when De Gaulle let go of Algeria—and today: "Who was it that allowed communism to achieve nearly all of its objectives, if not the Gaullists themselves? Without the tacit support of the Head of State, its siege of French society would have been less thorough and assured."[14] Commenting on the Soviet invasion of Czechoslovakia that spring, the FSR contrasted the Soviet Union, which "reduced people to slavery," with France, "which had cheerily cut off its most beautiful and promising departments."[15] Presumably the FSR advocated a different approach that kept empires intact but allowed subject peoples more freedom than under communism. One day after the great procession of De Gaulle's supporters through the streets of Paris, the FSR held a counter-rally in Marseille. Speakers told a crowd of some 5,000 *pieds noirs* that the time for action was ripe. Calling for the release of General Salan, the FSR sent a delegation to the Prefect.[16] With fuel for automobiles still scarce, in June the FSR rented buses to transport the *pieds noirs* to a rally in the Var.[17] Former members of the CODUR founded a new FSR section in the Var and held a rally at the municipal stadium in Toulon attended by hundreds of *pieds noirs*.[18]

Winning no fewer than 358 out of 485 seats in the 1968 parliamentary elections, the Gaullist Party recovered. Now the government balked at a full amnesty or the return of rank, honors, and other titles stripped in punishment for French Algeria crimes. During his visit to Algeria at the height of the revolt in 1958, De Gaulle had told the *pieds noirs*: "I understand you." Challenging the prime minister in 1968, the FSR asked the *pieds noirs*: "Did Pompidou not tell the students and workers, 'We understand you'? As repatriates, we know what that means. We must remain vigilant."[19] More *pied noir* associations in the Var joined the FSR.[20] As the regime regained stability and the crisis faded from view, though, the political and organizational opportunities that May '68 seemed to create for the *pieds noirs* passed.

ARRECKX'S PROSPECTS BRIGHTEN

Displeased with the results of a national referendum on decentralization and Senate reform, De Gaulle resigned in April 1969. Georges Pompidou won the presidential election held soon after and kept relations with interest groups the same (favoring shopkeepers, farmers, and big business, but not workers or teachers).[21] During the Pompidou presidency (1969–1974), however, the left grew stronger. In 1972, François Mitterrand and others created a new Socialist Party, which reached an agreement to govern with the Communist Party if they won a national election. The right managed to win the parliamentary elections in 1973, but with its majority much reduced. Within his own bloc, moreover, Pompidou faced challenges from right-wing politicians who wanted to succeed him as president.

In the presidential election held after Pompidou died in 1974, his Minister of Finance and Economic Affairs, Valéry Giscard d'Estaing, prevailed. A non-Gaullist, President Giscard offered a new vision. His government gave young people the right to vote at the age of 18. It created a new secretary of state for the status of women and liberalized contraception, abortion, and divorce laws. Relations between the state and interest groups changed, and the regime reached out to unions.[22] Giscard had once belonged to a group of independent, right-wing deputies who championed French Algeria. After this group disbanded in 1962, some of its members stayed in the right-wing, anti-Gaullist opposition; others—including Giscard—went over to the government side.[23] He had received an important ministerial portfolio in return, but fell out with De Gaulle and created his own party, the Républicains indépendants (RI). As a minister under Pompidou, Giscard kept apart from the Gaullists by presenting himself as a progressive politician of the liberal center.[24] With the left on the rise and the Gaullists still challenging him after he became president, Giscard sought to expand his young party. The Var, crucially, fit into this plan, which involved recruiting Arreckx, winning over the *pieds noirs*, and weakening the Socialists.

Historically a red department of anticlerical peasants, in the first parliamentary elections of the Third Republic (in 1871) the Var had chosen candidates from the Radical Party for all six of its seats. Future Prime Minister Georges Clemenceau (a firm anti-Bonapartist, anticlericalist, and supporter of Dreyfus) became senator for the Var in 1902. While the unions organized in the big shipyards at Toulon and La-Seyne-sur-Mer, in the rural interior the Socialist Party prevailed in centers such as Draguignan and Brignoles.[25] After 1945, the Var came under Édouard Soldani, a Socialist who held simultaneously offices as mayor of Draguignan, senator for the Var, and president of the departmental council. Voters in this department put Giscard behind Mitterrand in the 1974 presidential election, but change in the balance between the rural interior and the urbanized coast was loosening Soldani's grip.[26] The red peasants of the countryside and the Communist workers of the shipyards were disappearing. Partly due to the influx of retirees (who tended to vote for the right) and *pieds noirs*, towns and cities along the coast were expanding.[27] Arreckx, the mayor of the largest city in the Var, belonged to no party, wanted to stay clear of the Gaullists, and harbored political ambitions beyond Toulon.

Giscard dangled bait. In 1790, when an administrative system based on departments replaced the provinces of the Old Regime, the authorities chose Toulon as the administrative center for the Var. Three years later, a royalist faction took control and opened its port to the English and Spanish, who occupied the city. In late 1793, a siege in which Napoleon Bonaparte won notice as an artillery commander allowed the revolutionary government (the Convention) to retake Toulon. As punishment for its betrayal of the Revolution, the city lost the prefecture of the Var—which (after brief relocations in Grasse and Brignoles) in 1797 moved to Draguignan.[28] Almost two centuries later, in September 1974, the French government announced its decision to transfer the prefecture of the Var from Draguignan to Toulon. A few weeks later, Arreckx joined the party of Giscard.[29]

In local politics, the era of the political broker was overtaking—though not replacing entirely—the era of the established notable. With his background in the Resistance, Arreckx belonged to a postwar cohort of local elites whose election owed less to status as a man of independent means than to an image of republican loyalty and administrative effectiveness.[30] Under the presidencies of De Gaulle and Pompidou, anti-Gaullism had penalized Arreckx. Membership in the RI of Giscard when it sought to expand in the Var gave Arreckx new influence; and if he became their broker with Paris, the *pieds noirs* might gain too. As a non-Gaullist, the president could readily court this electorate. During the 1974 presidential campaign, Giscard had promised that if elected he would redress the grievances of the *pieds noirs*. Following through, the government sponsored laws that benefited the *pieds noirs* and the *harkis*.[31]

Giscard's party stood to lose the parliamentary elections scheduled for March 1978. To gain the support of the Gaullists after he became president in 1974, for his Prime Minister he had selected Jacques Chirac, a man with presidential ambitions too. Chirac resigned as Prime Minister in 1976 and reshaped the old Gaullist party into the neo-Gaullist Rassemblement pour la République (RPR). Chirac's successor as Prime Minister, Raymond Barre, wrestled with inflation, unemployment, labor unrest, and Corsican nationalism. Meanwhile, the Socialists, Communists, and Left-Radicals had reached a new electoral accord. Given these problems, Giscard needed to broaden his base, and the *pieds noirs* represented many thousands of potential votes.

Most lived in the south, with the Var alone containing some 100,000 repatriates (fully one-sixth of the department's population).[32] To date, their gains under Giscard overshadowed those under his predecessors, Presidents De Gaulle and Pompidou. Yet they remained aggrieved. The slow pace at which the administration was handling their claims for property left behind in Algeria galled them.[33] At this rate, the state would not settle the final claim before 1981. Further, the state had set a ceiling on full compensation for private property abandoned in Algeria (beyond this ceiling, awards became less generous).[34] Indeed, *pied noir* dissatisfaction with the government contributed to the defeat in the 1977 municipal elections of the mayor of Montpellier, François Delmas, who belonged to the party of Giscard, by Georges Frêche of the Socialist Party.[35]

ARRECKX RISES

Rising to the challenge from the *Midi*, Giscard announced that in July 1977, he would launch his parliamentary campaign from Carpentras, a town whose mayor had joined his party.[36] Fanning the hopes of the *pieds noirs*, Giscard added that the new secretary of state for repatriate affairs would be at his side when he gave his speech in Carpentras:

> As you know, throughout my time in politics I have been acutely aware of the problems of the French from North Africa. Long before the current situation, I made my position clear. On a personal level, I might add, I count many friends among them. I will address the two aspects of their problems: the psychological aspect, which pertains to the fraternal place that the national community must make for them; and the problem of the economic and social consequences of their return.[37]

A new federation in the Var, the Union des Amicales Varoises des Français Rapatriés d'Outre-mer (UAVFROM), reacted by declaring that its constituents would vote against the party of Giscard unless he promised more generous compensation for their property abandoned in Algeria.[38] On the day of Giscard's speech, the UAVROM backed its threat by providing buses to take some 200 repatriates from Toulon to Carpentras. From across the south, indeed, the repatriates mobilized to disrupt the president's speech. After unfurling their protest banners, they planned an angry exit.[39]

In his nationally broadcast speech, Giscard began by attacking the program of the left, warning it would impose brutal social changes not wanted by half the country. Raising the stakes, he issued a challenge to any who might have a coup d'état in mind. After boasting about the government's social achievements and the country's economic prospects, he made an announcement appropriate to Carpentras, whose economy depended on fruit cultivation and wine production: France would pressure Brussels for an agricultural policy more favorable to farmers in the Mediterranean region. Addressing the *pieds noirs* next, the president recalled his meetings with them in Montpellier, Nice, Toulouse, Perpignan, and Toulon:

> I knew these were French who had lost what each one of us cannot replace: homes, family memories, neighbors, and a land—all these were gone. I knew that when they returned with their scars from a land of sun, France, despite its efforts, had seemed unfriendly and uncaring.[40]

Giscard announced he would ask the government to prepare a bill with two new measures: one providing a letter of credit for those awaiting a compensation award; the other expediting the payment of compensation for repatriates who had reached the age of retirement. The president concluded: "May wounds opened by history now heal over and close; and fraternity console those French who left their memories far away."[41] Giscard's announcement caught the repatriates by surprise. Their mood relaxed and some even applauded.[42] The secretary of state for repatriate affairs, Jacques Dominati, took over and provided details about the new bill.[43] Wary of promises not kept, the *pieds noirs* listened with reserve and insisted on further talks with the government.[44]

That summer the president and his party, the RI, lay siege to the Var. The day before Giscard spoke in Carpentras, his son Henri—a leader of the party youth branch—visited Arreckx and other officials in Toulon. From Carpentras, in turn, Giscard and his wife proceeded to the Var, where they hosted Arreckx and his wife at the presidential retreat near Bormes-les-Mimosas. The RI held its national meeting for party officials in Toulon. Seeing an opportunity, repatriate associations in the Var asked Arreckx to arrange for a meeting for them with Dominati.[45] The secretary of state agreed, but with the understanding that his office would arrange his visit to the Var in consultation with Arreckx and the Prefect.[46]

In 1976, a new national federation, the Rassemblement et coordination unitaire des rapatriés et spoliés d'outre-mer (RECOURS), had warned it would call for the defeat of Giscard's candidates in the next elections unless the government did more for the *pieds noirs*. Keeping the pressure on, Boutigny—president of the UAVFROM and representative of the RECOURS in the Var—invited national leaders of the RECOURS to join in meetings with Dominati in Toulon.[47] Boutigny warned Arreckx against ignoring the 100,000 repatriates of the Var. Politicians and parties could not mold them, he said, and a bad decision would compromise their friendship with the mayor.⁴⁸ In Paris, meanwhile, Dominati received the leaders of the RECOURS, who told repatriates across France to stay vigilant.⁴⁹ Before the parliamentary elections, the RECOURS added, the repatriates would increase their influence by keeping to a position of strict neutrality toward all political parties.⁵⁰ When Dominati visited Toulon to confirm the government's intentions, hundreds of *pieds noirs* from the Var packed the meeting hall.⁵¹

Others counter-attacked.⁵² Declaring that the nation should do whatever necessary to "ensure that the repatriates regain their full trust in the community to which they belong," Jacques Chirac proposed an alternative to the promises at Carpentras.⁵³ Giscard fought back: alongside the graves of unknown soldiers from the two world wars at the National War Cemetery, he presided over the internment of a soldier who had died in the Algerian War.⁵⁴ Pitching in, Dominati represented the government at an event that brought figureheads of the fight for French Algeria to Avignon for the inauguration of a monument in honor of those who had died overseas in the name of France.⁵⁵ In late 1977 and early 1978, finally, the government pushed its bill through Parliament. Some national associations gave their reserved approval, but not the RECOURS, which urged other parties—including the Socialists and the Left-Radicals—to best the RI by working with the *pieds noirs*. Analyzing the results from previous parliamentary elections, the group identified 23 districts where the *pied noir* vote could prove decisive in 1978.⁵⁶

THE 1978 PARLIAMENTARY ELECTIONS

With both the compensation law and the parliamentary elections imminent, in October 1977 the *pieds noirs* of the Var had let Dominati know their disappointment when he visited them again. Arreckx responded that he would put the utmost pressure on his party but doubted this would make much difference because he was only a local politician.⁵⁷ His implied message: Arreckx, who planned to run as a RI candidate, could do more for the repatriates if elected to the National Assembly. During a meeting at the Elysée Palace the next month, Arreckx talked to Giscard about his city's needs: creating a new university; avoiding declines in Navy spending; countering threats to the shipbuilding industry; providing housing credits for the construction sector; and, most pressing of all, compensating the repatriates.⁵⁸ Returning to the Var two months later, Giscard accompanied the Prefect and other officials on a visit to new public housing for the *harkis* at Caunes (near Bormes-les-Mimosas) before proceeding to the presidential retreat at the Fort of Brégançon.⁵⁹

Angling for advantage, the UAVFROM invited politicians from other parties to local meetings with the *pieds noirs*.[60] Jacques Chirac visited and, after informing his hosts that his rural circumscription in the Corrèze contained not a single *pied noir*, accepted with good humor when Boutigny offered to send one over. Chirac said he favored a generous compensation plan. The problem was that his constituents—the farmers on the Plateau de Millevaches—had different problems on their mind, such as the price of veal.[61] A veteran of the Algerian War with a sense of bonhomie, Chirac came off well, but visits like his tested *pied noir* unity: the invitation of a guest guilty of being a neo-Gaullist, a Socialist, or an opponent of Arreckx set off quarrels.[62] Not all accepted the approach of the RECOURS, which asked the *pieds noirs* to set their partisanship aside and vote for politicians who would advance their group interests.

For his election as deputy, Arreckx counted on more than his friendship with the *pieds noirs* or their gratitude for lobbying Giscard and Dominati. He could point to favors already done. He had served as honorary president of the organizing committee for a monument in memory of Europeans from colonial North Africa inaugurated at the Lagoubran Cemetery in Toulon.[63] He had ensured the city reacted favorably to repatriate associations when they requested funding for a chapel at Cap Brun (on the coast east of Toulon) dedicated to Notre Dame d'Afrique.[64] Thanks to him, in 1976 the city had provided a locale for their associations: La Maison du Rapatrié. Located in vacant barracks near the Porte d'Italie, La Maison du Rapatrié opened after renovations and furnishing at the city's expense. Under a long-term, renewable agreement, the city then leased it to the associations—with utilities and maintenance included—for the symbolic fee of one franc annually.[65] To please the UAVFROM, in 1977 Arreckx had composed and publicized a more generous alternative to the government's compensation bill.[66] Later that year, *pieds noirs* from Toulon had attended a meeting of the RECOURS in Aix-en-Provence thanks to Arreckx, who provided municipal buses at no cost.[67] Amidst the growing alienation from Giscard and his party during the parliamentary debates around the compensation bill, similarly, Arreckx had approved a request from the UAVFROM for permission to erect, in a public square near the Maison du Rapatrié, a memorial to the Heroes of French Algeria.[68] Other parliamentary candidates courted the *pieds noirs* but the mayor had a record of patronage and an endorsement from five *pieds noirs* on the city council.[69]

Arreckx contested these elections as a candidate for the new party of Giscard, his Union pour la démocratie française (UDF). The right prevailed in the National Assembly, but the Socialists passed the Communists and were gaining. The UDF did well, for its part, but did not surpass the neo-Gaullists.[70] The president could thus be pleased with his party's performance in the Var, long dominated by the left. Despite the rise of the Socialists nationally, the UDF conquered all three districts on the department's coast.[71]

The repatriates did not always get what they asked for. In 1969, Dahmar had approached Arreckx with the idea of creating a home for aged repatriates. Arreckx said the city would make a property available, but the project never materialized.[72] In 1976, the repatriates lost another battle close to their hearts. Careful about losing support to the neo-Gaullists, municipal politicians decided to rename a coastal road after De Gaulle. The ally of the *pieds noirs*, Colonel Reymond, resigned from city council in protest, but the new road name stuck.[73] In 1977, the repatriates asked the city to give space and funding for a center that would house a private collection of historical documents on Algeria. They received only a small building and the collection wound up in the municipal library.[74]

Perhaps some of these requests were excessive. With time, moreover, Arreckx relied less on the *pieds noirs*. Their influence diminished as his career ascended and his base expanded. When he moved into other political arenas, the resources he needed differed from those the *pieds noirs* could offer. All the same, the relations of patron to client that joined the mayor to this community endured long past their honeymoon of the 1960s. More important, his election as deputy would harden the barrier to other parties in the Var—including the National Front.

CHAPTER 6

Building a Base for the National Front

Let us return to the antecedents of Tixier and the Nationaux; and then see what the National Front made of this heritage. The intellectual turn against the Revolution made nineteenth- and twentieth-century France a nursery for reactionaries and proto-fascists. Anti-Enlightenment romantics fantasized about rolling back time and re-establishing the Old Regime. Biological materialists extolled the French race and feared its loss of vitality through miscegenation. Monarchists blamed the decline of their country on Freemasons, Socialists, Protestants, and Jews. Apologists of violence admired the socialist movement for its myths, whose power had moved the masses to action.[1] So much fertility on the plane of ideas fed the diversity, if not always the quality, of French letters and public discourse.[2]

In politics, though, a ton of ideas weighs less than an ounce of shrewdness.[3] Between the two world wars, one dominant organization gained control over the reactionary or revolutionary right in Germany, Spain, Romania, and Italy. In France, by contrast, rival groups crowded the same niche.[4] After 1940, the anti-liberal right fared better under Marshall Pétain, but only to exit from World War II with a lasting stigma. Collaborating with Nazi Germany, persecuting Jews, and harming the Resistance counted among its unforgivable errors. Wartime defeat and postwar purges left a wounded minority of fascist diehards and authoritarian conservatives. When they pulled together and tried to form a party in the early 1950s, it failed.[5]

Later that decade, fears and resentments within the old middle class propelled the flash party of Pierre Poujade, a small business owner. His party lacked organization, contested only one election, and no longer mattered when the Fourth Republic fell. Until the rise of National Front, still, Poujadism gave postwar France the strongest proof of a mass potential for the far right. Poujade exploited the fear that losing Algeria would weaken his country. Married to a *pied noir*, he held his first big political rally in Algiers. A *Time* cover article about Poujade describes his conspiratorial worldview:

> He explains his new theory on Algeria: "Big Wall Street syndicates found incredibly rich oil deposits in the Sahara, but instead of exploiting the discovery they capped the wells and turned the Algerians against us." He discourses on France's alliances: "All this is a great diabolic scheme to dismember France. Already the Saar is gone, and soon the Italians will want Corsica." He adds slyly: "As for those who are against us, I need only say: let them go back to Jerusalem. We'll even be glad to pay their way."[6]

Time queried Poujade about his willingness to recruit cadres with a background in the far right:

> About the collaborators and ex-fascists on his staff, Poujade is abrupt: "I'm tired of people looking for lice in my hair. I fought the Germans and I know what resistance is. I don't need anybody to give me lessons in patriotism."[7]

Anti-tax, anti-parliamentary, anti-Semitic, and anti-communist, his Union de défense des commerçants et artisans (UDCA) won 11.6 percent of the vote in the 1956 elections.[8]

When UDCA deputies addressed the National Assembly, they complained about the "social-communist government" and the excessive power of the central state.[9] UDCA activists also led the May 1958 uprising in Algiers, but by then their party had alienated many *pieds noirs*. Nasser's regime had been helping the FLN, yet Poujade instructed his deputies in the National Assembly to vote against the Suez expedition in 1956 (which did not serve the national interest, he believed). In 1957, moreover, French authorities had arrested UDCA members after a plot gone awry killed the chief of staff of General Salan.[10] Like the *pieds noirs*, initially the UDCA had backed De Gaulle's return to power; but De Gaulle rebuffed Poujade by excluding his party from government. Poujade responded by instructing his 35 deputies to vote against a bill that gave full powers to the new president. Only five obeyed and, when Poujade's weakened party contested the next parliamentary elections a few months later, it received less than 1 percent of the vote.[11]

Those who abandoned Poujade included Jean-Marie Le Pen, who had entered the National Assembly after running as a candidate for the

UDCA. When the Suez crisis erupted, Le Pen put his anti-communism on the line by resigning his seat in Parliament and joining the French paratroops in Egypt. He next served in Algeria and then formed his own nationalist group, the Front national des Combattants (FNC). Initially the speakers at Algérie française rallies of Le Pen's FNC included not only Pétainists and neo-fascists, but also Gaullists. Support for De Gaulle's return to power in 1958 had clouded the line between patriotism, conservatism, and authoritarianism.[12] Learned observers thus wondered about a similarity between Gaullism and Bonapartism.[13] Seymour Martin Lipset noticed that opponents of the Poujadists and Gaullists lumped them together as fascists, but decided that De Gaulle was a conservative in the French tradition.[14] Another political sociologist, Raymond Aron, accepted that De Gaulle respected parliamentary democracy, yet detected an affinity with Boulanger, Maurras, and Pétain in De Gaulle's penchant for a quasi-monarchy.[15] Amalgams of Gaullism with the far right proved flimsy. In the words of Le Pen: "The General resorted to a fantastic act of historical falsification when handling Algeria and returning to power."[16] The Gaullists and the far right parted inexorably once the president made public his vision of an independent Algeria.

The battle for French Algeria reignited a current in French politics made weak and irrelevant by the outcome of World War II. Politically, it bred a front strong enough to override the differences between Pétainists and veterans of the Resistance (who cherished the territorial integrity of France). Socially, mobilization by nationalist groups opposed to decolonization inducted a new generation of youth into the dissident subculture, activism, and networks of the far right. Culturally, the conflict revitalized themes with roots in the country's defeat in the Franco-Prussian War and loss of Alsace-Lorraine. The nationalist movement of General Boulanger and the anti-Dreyfusards at the end of the nineteenth century had deployed these themes: France was humiliated, with its pride wounded and grandeur crumbling.[17]

Allies of the moment more than ideological converts, most *pieds noirs* stayed outside the far right. "To defend French Algeria," a former OAS activist once declared, "was not to practice politics."[18] After independence, the Gaullist regime chipped away at the far right by criminalizing, imprisoning, or co-opting its activists and leaders. Men like Le Pen took refuge in other branches of the non-Gaullist right, especially the CNIP. Recurring problems—interpersonal rivalry, ideological disagreement, low membership, and organizational disarray—would hamper the French far right for another two decades.[19]

FROM TIXIER TO DUPRAT

A test of voter demand for right-wing extremism came in 1965, as we have seen, with the presidential candidacy of Tixier. Relying on former French Algeria activists, his campaign started slowly and then picked up speed in the south, where his rallies attracted sizeable crowds of *pieds noirs*.[20] Tixier called for an abrogation of the Évian Accords, the end of foreign aid to Algeria, and controls on immigration:

> There must be a very strict selection policy toward Algerian emigration to France. We wanted a French Algeria, but we do not want an Algerian France. We wanted Algerian citizens to be French like all the rest of us, but we do not want a France invaded by multitudes of starving people, of troublemakers, of invalids, of people with no technical background, with no civic education, people trained by the FLN and turned against France, which they treat as a sanctuary and a trough.[21]

After De Gaulle's re-election, though, far right leaders and activists withdrew from politics or formed small, fascistic groups.

When the regime seemed to totter in 1968, the far right responded with ambivalence. It disliked the Gaullist regime, but Bolshevism remained the primordial enemy. May '68 fit into the far-right narrative of communist ascendency and Western surrender, a story with the Yalta Conference a turning point and later developments in Yugoslavia, Hungary, Algeria, Belgian Congo, Cuba, Vietnam—and now Prague and Paris—providing tragic confirmation. Antagonism toward the class politics of the workers' movement oriented these anti-egalitarians, who mythicized race, people, or nation. Ideology aside, the far right was allergic to the hedonism of the youth revolution. With their ad-man cleverness, the student graffiti ("Under the paving stones, the beach" or "Workers of all countries, enjoy") did not resonate with a culture of order and sacrifice. Whether one was a fascist who admired martial virtues or a conservative wedded to traditional norms, this plebeian *libertinage* seemed degenerate.[22]

Leftists repaid the favor. In Paris, right-wing extremists who tried "to join the students on the barricades, imprudently brandishing the Celtic cross" quickly found themselves rejected.[23] Others on the far right (including Tixier) chose the lesser evil: swallowing their hostility toward De Gaulle, they joined the thousands in Paris who marched in the pro-government rally for order on 30 May 1968.[24] Recollecting the anti-Gaullist revolts in Algiers a decade earlier, men such as Le Pen felt shock. The protests of May '68 had achieved "what hundreds of thousands of *pieds noirs* could not do, shake the throne."[25]

After the crisis, the regime proceeded to ban left-wing extremist groups; still vulnerable, it abided a few more months' of far-right violence against Maoists, Marxist-Leninists, and Trotskyists. Then it outlawed Occident, a group of university students and former French Algeria activists that "compensated for its numerical weakness with raids launched by commandoes armed with metal bars and axe handles."[26] The loss of Occident opened a void that extremists filled in 1969 with Ordre Nouveau (ON). The new group's founders included François Duprat, an anti-Semite, OAS member already in his youth, and former Occident leader. Duprat would later become the chief strategist and second in command of the National Front.[27]

Seeking to extricate the French far right from its political ghetto in the early 1970s, Duprat looked to Italy for guidance. There the neo-fascist party—the Movimento sociale italiano (MSI)—had adopted a strategy of duplicity: tacit support for extremism combined with the reassuring image of a defender of order. Likewise, ON would contest elections while its activists pursued street violence against leftists. Duprat's first attempts to emulate the MSI failed (ON fielded few candidates in 1970–1971, and they attracted paltry support).[28] When voting for the MSI climbed in 1972, though, Duprat published a history of the far right in France that concluded: "Drawing lessons from the great electoral victory of its fellow party, the MSI in Italy, Ordre Nouveau hopes to perform credibly in the next electoral competition."[29] Duprat still hoped the far right could exploit the post-1968 fears of conservative voters who wanted a government less permissive and more muscular than the center-right now in power.[30]

THE NATIONAL FRONT'S EARLY YEARS

Looking to the next parliamentary elections, in 1972 Duprat and his group decided to found the National Front. To attract voters, the new party should project an image of respectability; to attract activists, it should unify the younger generation with the dispersed veterans of the Vichy regime, the Poujadist movement, the French Algeria fight, and the Tixier campaign. Because Le Pen's connections put him at the crossroads of these different strands of the French far right, ON recruited him to lead the new party.[31]

The influence of Italy's neo-fascists showed itself again, for the National Front copied the MSI's logo: a trapezoid that represents the casket of Mussolini, surmounted by a three-tongued flame that stands for the undying spirit of fascism. In place of the Italian green-white-red, Le Pen's party colored its version of the neo-fascist flame with the blue-white-red of the French tricolor.[32] The MSI, in turn, provided material support (thousands of posters, campaign publications, and party stickers, all printed and transported to France at no cost to the National Front). For the 1973 parliamentary elections, the new party fielded candidates in 101 of the metropole's 473 districts (mostly in the Parisian region and the Mediterranean areas of *pied noir* settlement) but attracted only 1 percent of the vote. After more violence and a failed protest on the Champs-Élysées against French policy toward Algeria, the government banned ON. Its leaders could not retreat into the party of their own creation: thanks to internal maneuvering by Le Pen, he and the Nationaux now controlled the apparatus.[33]

When Le Pen won only 0.7 percent of the vote in the 1974 presidential election, dissidents joined with others to create an alternative, the Parti des forces nouvelles (PFN). Less fractured but now sharing its niche with another party, Le Pen's party floundered.[34] Like the National Front, the PFN adopted illiberal positions on abortion, immigration, and the death penalty, and until the 1980s it would dominate the French far right. With an estimated 4,000 members, its organization was about four times larger than the National Front's. Unlike its rival, moreover, the PFN enjoyed the backing of the major newspaper of the French far right, *Minute*. Italy's neofascists picked the PFN as their partner for the 1978 European elections, with the MSI printing its tracts and posters and helping to organize PFN rallies across France. Between 1979 and 1982, leaders of the PFN and the MSI attended each other's party congresses. The PFN did not field a candidate in the 1981 presidential election, however, and afterward its cadres and members began migrating to the party of Le Pen.[35]

THE NATIONAL FRONT ENTERS THE PARTY SYSTEM

Although the PFN's decline left the National Front with more space, Le Pen's party lacked influence at every level of politics. Unable to collect the 500 signatures from elected officials that a candidate needed, Le Pen could not enter the 1981 presidential election won by Mitterrand, the Socialist candidate. Struggling to recruit candidates for the 1981 parliamentary elections—which the left also won—the National Front contested only 74 out of the 491 districts in France, its poorest showing ever. In the 1982 cantonal elections, similarly, the party managed to field only 65 candidates in the 1,945 cantons across France. At the beginning of the Socialist experiment in 1981, then, the moderate right—not the far right—was profiting from discontent with the left.[36]

The National Front started to emerge in 1983, when it attracted unusual support in a handful of local elections.[37] National media focused on Dreux, an industrial town near Chartres. The secretary-general of the National

Front, Jean-Pierre Stirbois (a veteran of the struggle for l'Algérie française and the 1965 Tixier campaign) had used Dreux as a testing ground for grassroots nativism: one of his posters read "Stop Immigration: Work for All the French." After the far-right slate won 16.7 percent in the first round of a by-election, the neo-Gaullists agreed to an anti-left alliance for the runoff. Their joint slate won and, as part of his deal with the moderate right, Stirbois became associate mayor of Dreux. Other isolated gains attracted attention and concern across France. For the first time since Poujadism, the far right was moving out of the wilderness and into the *polis*.[38]

Le Pen appeared on national television in 1984 and warned that France was undergoing a process of dual colonization by the Soviet Union and the Islamic-Arab world.[39] Three weeks later, in European elections held under a proportional system that favors protest parties, his party collected 11.2 percent of the vote. For the 1985 cantonal elections, it fielded 1,521 candidates (96 percent more than in 1982) who attracted 8.8 percent of the vote. No longer could the other parties ignore this intruder, whose strength "lay more in its capacity to prevent or promote the election of candidates of the mainstream right rather than to have its own candidates elected."[40] Soon this changed entirely, for the far right received a huge gift.

Anticipating the defeat of his Socialist Party in the 1986 parliamentary elections, President Mitterrand surrendered to expediency: he replaced the usual electoral system (two-round, first-past-the-post) with a system of proportional representation. This yielded the expected payoffs. By splitting the right-wing vote between different parties (including the National Front), the proportional system limited the Socialists' defeat. It also robbed the moderate right of a sizeable majority. Mitterrand's decision let the far right enter the National Assembly, with no fewer than 35 deputies.[41] An outsider for over a decade, the party of Le Pen had penetrated the party system. From fewer than 50,000 supporters in the 1981 parliamentary elections, its electorate had swollen to 2.2 million in the 1984 European elections and 2.7 million in the 1986 parliamentary elections.

Certain features of its electorate have remained quite stable. Even today, its support weakens among women, practicing Catholics, rural voters, and those with more education. Opinion polls tell us its supporters agree the country has too many immigrants and one no longer feels at home in France. They are more likely to want the return of capital punishment.[42] The class background of its electorate has evolved, though. Annoyed with the leftist government, initially bourgeois voters were more likely to support the National Front. Without disowning this electorate, afterward the party moved down the class scale. It drew more heavily on self-employed skilled workers as well as the petty bourgeoisie of shopkeepers and small business owners, and then made vast inroads among workers disappointed with the left.[43]

The geography of its support departed from that of Poujadism (primarily a rural vote of farmers and the self-employed in the center-west and center-south of France). Instead, National Front support has always increased in the Mediterranean areas of *pied noir* resettlement that embraced Tixier in 1965. Some Parisian suburbs also provided stronger support. Propelled by the spread of National Front support within the working class, during the twenty-first century the declining industrial and mining areas of the north and east joined the south as bastions of the far right.[44]

By comparison with other French parties, the National Front of the 1980s and 1990s led the way in using innovative means of communication. It set up a pay-per-call telephone number that gave listeners an updated message with party news and propaganda. It produced video and audio cassettes such as "Immigration: Le Pen Explains Himself." Issued while public debate over the Muslim headscarf was raging in 1989, it summarizes the party's message nicely. Listeners to this tape recording hear Le Pen speaking about the problem of French identity. A conquering spirit animates Islam, which mixes religion with the social and the political. He respects the Quran, but the laxity of the political class poses a threat to the neutrality that should prevail in public education (a neutrality violated by Marxist teaching in the schools, he adds). The integration of immigrants is a dream; only aliens marginalized by their community wish to integrate. Immigration has created non-European ghettoes, what Le Pen refers to as "cells of alien colonization." He wants a constitutional reform that would allow a popular referendum on immigration with the question, "Do you agree with further growth in the phenomenon of immigration, or should it be halted completely and should we even instigate its regression?" For each immigrant getting family benefits and public housing, another 10 will follow. After World War II, the Algerian people wished to become French; now, with France in decline, foreigners are prouder of being Muslim than French. "Those who today favor integration," Le Pen affirms, "are the same ones who denied its possibility when we were in French Algeria."[45]

DID ECONOMIC CONDITIONS FAVOR THE FAR RIGHT?

While worsening economic conditions loom in the background of the National Front's breakthrough in the 1980s, a direct influence does not seem obvious. Clearly, a sudden rise in joblessness did not trigger the party's penetration of the party system. The rate of unemployment did worsen during the early 1980s (from 7.9 percent at the end of 1981, by late 1984 it had reached 10.2 percent). This continued a trend already underway, though: the jobless rate been climbing steadily since 1963.[46] No change in this trend either preceded or accompanied the breakthrough of the National Front in the mid-1980s.

Once might wonder, then, if not economic conditions themselves, but peoples' perceptions of these conditions, were worsening. Consumer confidence did fall between 1982 and 1984. As with unemployment, though, this was not new: consumer confidence had been falling since 1973. Moreover, the next two years—when the National Front consolidated its breakthrough in the 1984 European elections and the 1986 parliamentary elections—coincided with a recovery in consumer confidence.[47]

Another possibility is that government policy mediated the economy's effect on far-right support. When the Socialists assumed power in 1981, voters expected an increase in state intervention. Nationalizations did follow, but so did a global economic recession that increased fiscal pressures on the state. By 1983, the Socialist government had taken a U-turn toward austerity. Sacrificing a policy that had aimed to reduce inequality and unemployment, now its policies aimed at monetary stability and improving the balance of payments.[48] Did the National Front thus emerge when it did, then, because the working class felt abandoned by a leftist government that had made its peace with the market?

During the 1980s, the National Front and its leaders appealed above all to an electorate reminiscent of Poujadism. The party had an anti-tax, small government platform. Le Pen admired the neoliberalism of President Ronald Reagan and Prime Minister Margaret Thatcher yet opposed the spread of shopping centers. In 1984 and 1986, he and his party received most support among petty-bourgeois voters (shopkeepers and small business owners). Only later did it perform particularly well among workers. The Socialists' acceptance of the market did not spur unusual support for the far right among workers, in sum. The National Front's metamorphosis into the strongest workers' party in France came only later.[49]

If disenchantment with the Socialist government had triggered the breakthrough of the far right, moreover, former left supporters would form a large share of the National Front electorate. The more a French voter identified with the left, on the contrary, the smaller their likelihood of supporting the far right. Survey data show only 27 percent of those who supported the National Front in the 1984 European elections had supported the Socialist candidate (Mitterrand) in the 1981 presidential election.[50] If concern over the Socialists' U-turn had driven disillusioned voters toward the National Front, economic concerns would have set them apart. Instead, their chief preoccupations were immigration and crime. Issues like unemployment mattered more among supporters of the left as well as the moderate right;

so did inequality and the rising cost of living.⁵¹ The proposition that economic troubles created a sudden surge in far-right voting provides at best a secondary, partial explanation.

PARTISAN DEALIGNMENT, IMMIGRATION POLITICIZATION, AND PARIAH LEGITIMATION

Before the far-right breakthrough, significantly, attachment to the established parties of the left and the right was weaker than voting results suggested. In each of the seven parliamentary elections held between 1958 and 1981, certainly, the main parties commanded between 97 and 99 percent of the vote. From one election year to the next, moreover, change in their collective share of the vote always fell below 3 percent. The marginalization of other alternatives (including the far right) had been an enduring feature of the Fifth Republic. Until the 1978 elections, nonvoting (abstaining or casting a blank or invalid ballot) had exceeded 25 percent only once (in 1962, when the victory of the Gaullist party was a foregone conclusion). Afterward, though, the hold of the established parties loosened.⁵² In the 1981 parliamentary elections, nonvoting rose to 30 percent—the highest level in two decades.⁵³ The National Front, as we have seen, did take some voters away from the left; significantly, it also attracted new voters. About half of its support in 1984 and 1986, still, came from former supporters of the moderate right.⁵⁴ Rather than economic change, a loosening of the established parties' hold on voters provided a precondition for the breakthrough of the far right.

After 1981, currents of the moderate right came out more clearly in favor of the right—a term discredited since World War II and Nazi collaboration.⁵⁵ Some wanted a more neoliberal approach to the economy. Reacting to progressive measures by the Socialist government (abolition of capital punishment, for example, and laws to protect the rights of convicts or homosexuals), some also gave a new emphasis to the problem of law and order. In this context, the National Front's claim to represent the true right lost much of its stigma. Further, attributing crime to immigration provided an answer to an issue promoted by the moderate right.⁵⁶

French society contained a nativist potential long before the rise of the National Front. I have tried to explicate its roots, content, and intensity among the former settlers from Algeria (especially, as we will see in a later chapter, among those with fewer ties to diverse others). Consider now the depth and nature of nativism in France at large. Among those participating in a national poll in 1968, 51 percent said there were too many "immigrants" (e.g., Africans, Spaniards, or Jews) in their country; by 1977, the proportion had climbed to 61 percent. Better accepted were Jews (17 percent said they were too many in 1977), followed by black Africans (25 percent) and Spaniards (27 percent). Well beyond these levels was rejection of North Africans: 63 percent considered there were too many in France.[57] Elements other than nativism (loyalty to the heroes of French Algeria, for example) had certainly entered into the *pied noir* affinity toward the far right. All the same, an antipathy toward *les Arabes* had permeated the rest of society as well. Since the 1980s, clearly, this antipathy has festered.[58] Unlike Vichy and World War I, memories of the Algerian War—and fears that it may repeat itself in France today—continued to resonate.[59]

Hostility toward immigration had been a plank in the National Front's platform from the very beginning. Only after established parties turned immigration into a salient issue in electoral competition did the National Front have a chance to break through. During the 1970s, Communist politicians governed more than half of the cities with concentrations of immigrants. Some municipalities launched initiatives that conceded limited political participation to immigrants. Backed by their party's leaders in Paris, they also supported immigrants on strike or trying to lobby government. Some Communist municipalities complained they were carrying an undue burden, though, and took measures to stop and even destroy public housing for immigrants. Others targeted immigrant criminality. Nationally, the Communist Party balanced a conciliatory approach toward its local leaders with the old message that immigrants belong to a highly exploited fraction of the working class. Originating in Belgium, Italy, Poland, Portugal, and Spain, the migrants the party once defended were predominantly white, European, and Christian. During the 1981 presidential campaign, by contrast, the Communist candidate supported anti-immigrant measures in towns run by his party. He had broken the tacit consensus, among political elites, to exclude from public discourse an issue that preoccupied much of the electorate.[60]

Mitterrand had long courted the *pied noir* vote. After De Gaulle's victory in the 1965 election, he had promoted a bill to reinstate the position, rights, and pension of government officials who had broken the law in the name of French Algeria. In 1974, the Socialists had called for a widened amnesty that pardoned those responsible for the failed putsch of 1961. After the Socialist victory in 1981, finally, the government pushed through a law that reinstated the pension of civil and military officials punished for their political involvement in North Africa. Not only the Communists and the Gaullists opposed this law, but also younger Socialist deputies. They could not pardon those who had tried to bring down the Fifth Republic. Apart from generational change in Socialist perceptions of the colonial past, the party was turning toward the descendants of the colonized. The question of their status had started to simmer in the 1970s. In 1983 and 1984, French youths who were the children of immigrants mobilized.[61] Led by an anti-racist movement, SOS Racisme, they marched in the name of equality and fraternity. The Socialist Party backed this movement, and later co-opted its leaders.[62] In a short period, then, the governing left had downgraded state socialism and upgraded civil rights. This must have heightened the discomfort of those who wanted people of North African ancestry to stick to their old place in society. When President Boumediene visited Paris in 1983, Mitterrand added to their discomfort. For the first time ever on French soil, an official band played the Algerian national anthem. Previously, it had served as the anthem of the FLN, which the *pieds noirs* blamed for their miseries. The Socialists were alienating those with nostalgia for empire.[63]

The moderate right helped pave the way too. In 1981, it had failed to keep the left from power. Divided between rival parties, it lacked an uncontested leader. In 1983, it helped turn the far right into a legitimate option by entering into a pact with the National Front in Dreux. Elements of the moderate right had already wavered over the question of inclusion. France was already a multiracial society, they said, so had proven its ability to assimilate; at the same time, they added, there were limits to what the country could absorb. Exploiting the hedging in this message, the National Front stated bluntly that non-Europeans—North Africans in particular—could or would not assimilate. Expressing what many believed, in 1984–1986 this attracted to the far right a migration of cadres, candidates, and voters from the moderate right.[64]

A favorable sequence of elections did no harm. The proportional voting systems in place for the 1984 Europeans elections (when the National Front won 10 seats) and the 1986 parliamentary elections (when the National Front won 35 seats) ensured a vote for the far right would not be a wasted vote. In the 1985 cantonal elections, though, the party managed to attract almost 9 percent of the vote despite its weak local roots and a non-proportional voting system. Despite its weak organization, by then the party had acquired one of the most loyal electorates in France.

The far right's ascent might have stalled or reversed after the National Front scored 11 percent in the 1984 European elections. Already that year, though, rival politicians and the mass media were complicit in eroding the pariah status of the far-right party and its leader. Twice in early 1984, widely watched interviews on national television let Le Pen reach out to potential voters. He spoke about crime and unemployment, which he blamed on foreigners. Instead of ignoring his definition of the key issues, others gave it the oxygen of publicity.[65] Rival politicians conceded that he was saying the wrong things, but about real problems. On radio and television broadcasts, host after host would ask other politicians for their reaction to Le Pen. As the National Front exited from the political ghetto, it brought new stakes into interparty competition. For three decades since, the cleavage that pits the native against the outsider has shaped party politics in France.[66]

CHAPTER 7

The Far Right Organizes in the Var

After its birth in 1972, the National Front tried to set up local sections and departmental federations in parts of France with concentrations of royalists, Catholic fundamentalists, or neo-fascists.¹ In Mediterranean departments like the Var, moreover, it counted on veterans of the military and political battles against Algerian independence:

> These people possessed a common past, shared memories, and special bonds born of action. All this gave unity to their activism within the National Front. The Algerian war, their war, had given them an education in political engagement. They had learned a conception of political engagement both personal and energetic, one with plenty of references to their trajectory "on the other side of the sea." Their speech code was suggestive. It referred to clearing or occupying the zone, to rat hunting, to sweeping the territory. Their talk was full of metaphors taken from their combat in Algeria.²

The early Var federation shared the party's problems in attracting members, cadres, candidates, and votes. It languished in the shadow of the PFN, also weak electorally but stronger in this department than elsewhere in France. The Var federation commanded so little loyalty that when their mandate ended two secretaries in a row migrated to other parties. At this time, activism mattered less in what was more a private club than a party federation.³

Given the Var's potential, once the party started to rise its central headquarters named Bernard Mamy as departmental secretary. Mamy's pedigree made him a good fit. A former Poujadist and military officer during the Algerian War, Mamy had participated in the *pied noir* insurrections of May 1958 and January 1960, as well as the failed putsch of the generals in 1961. After escaping justice by living in exile, he returned to France and joined the Tixier committee for the 1965 presidential campaign. Next he migrated to the non-Gaullist moderate right, where he became a party official and municipal politician. The paths of Mamy and Le Pen had crossed before, in the Poujadist movement, the FNC of Le Pen, and the Tixier presidential campaign. Mamy joined the National Front in 1983, when the tide was starting to turn in its favor.[4]

Parachuted into the Var in 1984 from Paris, at first the federation's members did not welcome Mamy. He proved himself by establishing street-front offices for the party in Draguignan, Saint-Tropez, and Toulon. The Var, Mamy soon claimed, counted between 700 and 800 National Front members. He fought his election campaigns by adhering to the party line:

> To be French, that is why we are fighting. We want capitalism for the people and we are on the side of the victims, not the assassins. The people of France need better protection, whether against nuclear attack or everyday criminality. Immigrants need to go back to where they came from and make room for French workers.[5]

Nationally, the party won 11 percent of the vote in the 1984 European elections; in the Var, it won 22 percent. In the cantonal elections a year later, its share of the vote in Toulon climbed to 31 percent, the highest in France. However, Mamy's feats turned him into a rival of Le Pen's lieutenant, Stirbois, the party's star politician in Dreux. In the autumn of 1985, the party removed Mamy from his position as departmental secretary.[6] As his successor, it sent Yann Piat, a goddaughter of Le Pen.

Born in French Indochina, raised in Saint-Raphaël, and educated in Toulon, Piat belonged among the losers of decolonization. Her father was a soldier killed at the battle of Dien Ben Phu; after serving as a military nurse in Indochina, her mother served time in prison for helping the OAS in Algeria.[7] Piat felt at home when recruiting among those she described as

> veterans of the war in Indochina, *pieds noirs*, people with nostalgia for *l'Algérie française*, citizens unhappy with the feebleness of the parliamentary right, ardent nationalists who consider themselves the only guardians of moral and patriotic values that they carry in their heart like crusaders.[8]

In her autobiography, Piat recounts an exchange with a *pied noir* wine-grower, Roger, on his land a dozen kilometers outside Hyères. Aiming to recruit him, she talked about family values, moral decline, and patriotic renewal, but Roger cut her off:

> You're wrong. If you dance around immigration, you won't get a single *pied noir* vote. Immigration is a scandal, for two reasons. First, until now we repatriates have received no help at all, except a bare minimum. We had to deal with misery, and the disrespect

of the metropole. Algerians who come to France, illegally, mind you, enjoy the good graces of the government, which gives them housing. Me and my wife, when we arrived we barely survived in pathetic hotels. Them, they get welfare payments, health care, everything. Second: there are going to be more and more of them, and one day before too long they will drown us. The French don't have children anymore. The Arabs are as prolific as rabbits.[9]

Piat agreed with *pieds noirs* like Roger. Knowing this milieu, though, she excluded those who might damage the party by substantiating "enemy propaganda that treats us as dangerous fascists."[10] Confirming her intuition, four activists (one a former National Front candidate) died in Toulon six weeks after she expelled them, when a bomb in their vehicle exploded by accident.[11]

Initially the naming of Piat as secretary for the Var struck members as another imposition by the party headquarters in Paris. Abetted by Mamy, a crisis erupted, and Paris decided it had no choice but to expel Mamy.[12] Piat lost members but more than compensated by attracting former moderate right supporters. One of 35 National Front candidates entering the National Assembly in 1986, Piat credited her team of committed activists and the *pieds noirs* in the department.[13]

Building on what Mamy had accomplished, she worked at recruitment and retention, solidarity and motivation. Activism included leafleting and putting up posters. Apart from meetings and lectures, the federation organized events that combined social life and political activism in ways that appealed to the *pieds noirs*: dinners, celebrations, dances, trips, and *méchouis* (North African style barbeques). In turn, a major *pied noir* association in the department invited Piat as an official guest to its 1987 rally in a village of the interior.[14] The association also invited Le Pen, who reminded an audience of a thousand *pieds noirs* about the state's failure to keep its promises:

> I understand the economic problems that are torturing the members of this community, first betrayed and then treated unfairly. For twenty-five years, you have remained faithful to the wisdom and the heritage that your ancestors transmitted to you. . . . History has proven that we were right. Just look at what shape our country is in today. . . . France for the French! The government has not been able to control immigration for the last twenty-five years. We are not xenophobes or racists, but the French should come first.[15]

Le Pen now faced another challenge. Unlike the 1986 parliamentary elections held under a proportional system (and resulting in the election of 35 National Front deputies), the 1988 elections would revert to a majoritarian system that punishes small parties.

Piat ran as the National Front candidate for Hyères, her district some 20 kilometers east of Toulon. She won re-election, but every other National Front candidate in the country lost. As the party's sole representative in the National Assembly, her importance grew. So did tension with the party leadership in Paris, especially when she disobeyed its instructions for a vote in the National Assembly. The breaking point came when Le Pen uttered the words "*Durafour-crématoire*" (a play on the French word for crematorium and the name of a minister who was a Jew). Le Pen knew how to zigzag between outrage and restraint, so maybe welcomed the outrage his feeble pun provoked. Certainly it tested the loyalty of Piat, who reacted by joining in the public condemnation of her leader.[16] Soon after, in October 1988, the national directorate expelled Piat and replaced her with Jean-Marie Le Chevallier, who would become mayor of Toulon.

THE ARRECKX SYSTEM, THE DECLINE OF THE LEFT, AND THE RISE OF THE FAR RIGHT

The French political system tolerates multiple mandates, a practice now waning but not gone. During the 1970s, the mayor of a big city might also sit as president of their departmental council and as a senator or deputy in Paris. Among the advantages offered, a politician increased their salary as well as their expense, tax, travel, and staff benefits. Having more than one mandate enhanced prestige and broadened networks. It lent influence when a politician sought resources for their overlapping constituencies—say when a mayor who was also a deputy or president of a departmental council wanted ministerial backing for a project in their city.[17]

Mayor Arreckx had won election to the National Assembly in 1978, as we have seen, and he belonged to the departmental council. With more influence, he could do more for his clients. At the request of the *pieds noirs*, Arreckx lobbied the prefect to have Boutigny appointed to a commission studying official policy on loans to repatriates.[18] Arreckx served as a go-between with Paris, where Giscard showed a greater tolerance of OAS admirers. After agreeing in principle to the idea of establishing the city's first mosque and Moslem cemetery, a meeting with the department's *pied noir* leaders in 1978 changed his mind. As one of them said, "The repatriates are still so traumatized that they cannot help but judge severely the fact of giving a mosque to the Arabs."[19]

For the 150th anniversary of the conquest of Algiers, Arreckx granted their request to erect two monuments, which the *pieds noirs* justified with a precedent: "the celebrations of exceptional splendor that France organized in 1930 on the occasion of the centenary of the taking of Algiers."[20] At the mayor's behest, the city council gave 20,000 francs to help pay for the monuments.[21] In asking the city for public space on which to erect their memorials, the *pieds noirs* wrote:

> It is not a question of stirring up nostalgia for a French Algeria—which for the repatriates of our region has disappeared forever—but to highlight the civilizing mission of France, which for example was able to transform in a few years the pestilent marshes of Boufarik into the rich Plain of the Mitidja. Young people of the coming generations need to know they should be proud of all that France brought to the Muslim People of Algeria in the space of 132 years. There is too much of a tendency to make them feel like this is something of which to feel ashamed.[22]

To attract allies and influence, *pieds noirs* in charge of the sesquicentennial of the conquest of Algiers recruited a sponsoring committee. Locally, its members included a bishop, a rabbi, Mayor Arreckx, and François Léotard (the mayor of Fréjus). Others included the directors of national *pied noir* associations; a representative of the *harkis* (Bachagha Saïd Boualem); and leaders of the failed putsch in Algiers (Generals Jouhaud, Juin, Salan, and Zeller).[23]

Many of these people attended the public unveiling in 1980 of a monument that seems out of place amidst the sunbathers on the Mourillon beach because it looks like a gravestone. Its inscription reads like a paean to empire:

> *From this anchorage*
> *on 25 May 1830*
> *by order of King Charles X*
> *a fleet commanded by Admiral Duperré consisting of 103 war vessels*
> *and 500 trading vessels supported by 20,000 sailors,*
> *carrying an expeditionary force of 35,000 men*
> *under the command of General de Bourmont, Minister of War,*
> *set sail for Algiers to bring Liberty back to the Sea and to make of Algeria*
> *a land of progress that more than a century of shared labors and battles*
> *would unite to France with bonds of fraternity.*

These words the *pieds noirs* composed not only to honor great exploits but also to snub those not willing to acknowledge the benefits of empire.

Their second monument near the Porte d'Italie they dedicated to the OAS and other "Resistance fighters who died for French Algeria." Stealing the name of the French patriots who risked their lives in the underground during World War II was a provocation. The response came a week before the inauguration, when an anonymous bomb shattered the monument's bas-relief.²⁴ The inauguration proceeded anyway, with the secretary of state for repatriates, Jacques Dominati, serving as master of ceremonies. Guests in attendance included Bastien-Thiry's daughter; former OAS leaders (such as Pierre Sergent and Colonels Argoud and Garde); and politicians from Giscard's party—not only Arreckx but also the mayors of Fréjus (François Léotard) and Nice (Jacques Médecin). "Under the Gaullist regime," observes a historian of Provence, "the presence of the government at such a ceremony would have been inconceivable."²⁵ Stone carvers repaired this monument, which still stands. Heavy steel chains and a pair of cannon separate it from the vehicles and passers-by that cross this square near the old city ramparts. *Pieds noirs* and veterans of the Algerian War gather here twice each year to commemorate two tragedies: the Rue d'Isly massacre in Algiers on 26 March 1962; and the massacre in Oran on 5 July 1962. The monument's bas-relief depicts a firing squad executing a soldier whom the people of Toulon take to be Roger Degueldre, a member of the French Resistance during World War II and a paratrooper in Indochina. A military court had condemned Degueldre to death by firing squad for leading a group of OAS diehards on a campaign of cold-blooded murder.²⁶

The connection between the *pieds noirs* and Arreckx endured amidst changes in the Var, which had the fastest rate of population growth in France.²⁷ The economy still depended on the Navy, which supported some 100,000 employees and their families. Agriculture (principally for the production of wine, cut flowers, and olive oil) now accounted for only 7.5 percent of employment in this department. Industry accounted for another 29.5 percent of the labor force, so most jobs were in the service sector. The Var had once led the world in bauxite extraction; during the 1980s, the last mines closed. Shipyards in the area were suffering too. The Navy was spending less, and rivals in Japan and South Korea were winning international contracts. After state bailouts, restructuring plans, factory occupations, and labor strikes, in 1989 the old shipbuilding works at La Seyne-sur-Mer folded. Apart from indirect effects on the local economy, an already-trimmed workforce of 5,800 people joined the unemployed. Toulon suspended projects: a new city hall as well as construction of a retail-office complex in the heart of the city, on the Place de la Liberté.²⁸

The moderate right tried to make the far right seem redundant. At a public gathering in 1983, Mayor Arreckx declared that foreigners were overwhelming his city:

> The right to asylum should not be transformed into a welcome for people all over the world who want a job.... The number of immigrant workers in France should be reduced by a million.... We must refuse to be the trashcans of Europe.²⁹

Others from the moderate right joined in. Reacting to the rise of the far right in 1984, a neo-Gaullist politician said:

> Toulon is a border city and the Mediterranean is a weak obstacle. At the end of this century, there will be one hundred million inhabitants in North Africa. All should be aware of the threat this represents. It is urgently necessary to resolve the problem of immigration.... Now is the time to take the firm steps needed to protect the French identity.[30]

In April 1985, hundreds of antiracists reacted to news of attacks on Jews and North Africans in Paris by joining a march through the streets of Toulon.[31] Playing on anxieties, the mayor criticized this march:

> We need to face the facts: we are being invaded. The immigrant population is increasing—especially immigrants who work in the region surrounding Toulon. Politicians will need to accept their responsibilities. For us, the immigrant population means things need to change. Now we are the ones who will invade the center of our city.[32]

Rhetoric aside, Arreckx ensured his slate for the 1985 municipal elections included a few National Front candidates.[33]

The left, meanwhile, continued to slide. For a century after the creation of departmental councils in 1871, Radicals, Socialists, and Communists had dominated the Var thanks to support for left-wing notables in the rural interior and organizing by unions and workers' parties in industries near the coast. As the interior lost inhabitants and the coast lost industry, power had tilted to the right, a trend accelerated by the arrival of *pieds noirs* and elderly retirees. Transferring the Prefecture from Draguignan to Toulon in 1978 had symbolized the end of the left's dominance. The Socialist sweep in 1981 did not spare Arreckx, who lost his seat in the National Assembly. Unlike other parts of France, still, here the left did not renew itself by riding the waves of antiracism and anti-fascism. The Var department was sliding inexorably toward the right.[34]

Arreckx replaced a Socialist in 1985 as president of the departmental council, the first time it came under right-wing control.[35] This came when decentralization under Socialist governments was transferring power to subnational politicians. Gaining new influence and opportunities, Arreckx decided to resign as mayor of Toulon—but without disturbing the system of public-private patronage, elite connections, and popular support that had sustained him. As his successor, Arreckx designated an associate mayor and long-time ally on city council, François Trucy. Concerned about problems that the crumbling old town posed for commerce, business, and housing, the new mayor made a priority of urban renewal.[36] Showing vision, Trucy understood that suburban retailers would suck consumer spending away from cities like Toulon.[37] In response, his administration promoted construction of an indoor shopping mall near the old downtown core.

Like Arreckx, Trucy tried to block the far right by borrowing its rhetoric. "Security, the number one problem" was the theme of his first press conference, which dwelled on immigration from North Africa:

> It has reached a level far beyond what is reasonable, about 5,500 people or fifty percent of the foreign presence, so it modifies fundamentally the appearance and identity of the core of the city. It compromises the conditions for a peaceful coexistence of peoples inasmuch as their customs and ways of living are so vastly different that exceedingly serious problems will inevitably result.[38]

Trucy opposed plans to build a reception center for asylum seekers: "Under the present circumstances this is a risky project that will not contribute to the feeling of safety that we wish to re-establish in Toulon."[39] Yet the National Front continued to rise. In the 1986 parliamentary elections, it attracted 9.9 percent of the vote nationally but 20.3 percent in Toulon. Trucy reacted with a speech that again sounded like the far right: "At this moment there is a race that is chasing away another, it is like the red ants of Argentina, which have chased away the black ants of Provence. I am simply in favor of giving Toulon back to the people of Toulon."[40] Concessions to the language of the far right may have enhanced its appeal, for in the first round of the 1988 presidential election, Le Pen came fourth nationally (after Mitterrand, Chirac, and Barre) but first in six of the Var's seven districts.[41] Observers started to wonder if the National Front was on its way to becoming a front-runner in Toulon.[42] Rather than criticizing Le Pen's success, the mayor of Toulon responded almost obligingly. The results of the presidential election, Trucy said, revealed much about the wishes of "the supporters of the UDF, the RPR, and the National Front with respect to the big problems in our society: family, national identity, security, immigration."[43]

For the 1988 parliamentary elections, France abandoned the proportional system that had allowed the National Front to win 35 seats in 1986. Even if the Var preferred Le Pen, then, these elections would penalize his party. Still, the moderate right did the far right another favor. Arreckx belonged to a party alliance whose leaders in Paris decided to impose a candidate not of his choosing for the district of Hyères. Arreckx retaliated by persuading this candidate (the mayor of Hyères, Léopold Ritondale) to withdraw from the runoff round. Ritondale complied, thereby allowing Piat's re-election as deputy for Hyères. In exchange, Arreckx secured Ritondale's position on the departmental council; and the National Front repaid Arreckx by withdrawing from the runoff in two other districts of the

Var, thereby permitting the election of his protégés.[44] Standing by these deals, Arreckx said he refused

> to ghettoize a quarter of the voters, not all of them Fascists or Nazis.... In my Third District, I would rather see the election of a candidate from the National Front than one from the Socialist Party.... If the National Front leads the forces of the right at the end of the first round, I will ask candidates from my party to withdraw.[45]

After the National Front expelled Piat and sent Le Chevallier to take over as the departmental secretary, more deals between far and moderate right ensued.[46] The 1980s thus ended well for the National Front in the Var, where municipalities of more than 3,500 inhabitants elected 30 National Front candidates (including 7 to the city council in Toulon, 5 in Saint-Raphaël, and 3 in Fréjus). In the 1989 European elections, nationally Le Pen's slate received 11.9 of the vote; in the Var, it attracted 22.9 percent—behind the slate of Giscard (28.3 percent) but ahead of the Socialists (18.0 percent). The National Front closed the decade of its breakthrough by hosting thousands of supporters at a rally in Toulon.[47]

For the left, by contrast, the 1980s ended badly. Unable to set aside their differences, Socialists and Communists could not mount the alliances needed for victory in this department.[48]

From his stronghold in Toulon, Arreckx oversaw a system still accepted by the department's other political heavyweight, François Léotard. Allies of Arreckx held power in 28 of the department's 38 municipalities with a population above 3,500. Apart from controlling the departmental council, the moderate right held all the department's seats in the Senate and National Assembly.[49] When tactics meant a blurring of boundaries with the far right, then, Arreckx operated from a position of strength. In the 1989 municipal elections, the moderate right joined the far right to defeat the Socialist incumbent in Le Luc (a town northeast of Toulon).[50] To outbid the National Front and Arreckx, in turn, a neo-Gaullist politician in Toulon launched a neighborhood petition against a North African couple who wanted to open a shop. His opposition, he said, served a higher purpose:

> To conserve the local, regional, and traditional character of the shops on Louis-Bozzo Avenue. This petition mentions that locating a Maghrebi restaurant (or grocery store and butcher) on this main street would risk creating tensions among the inhabitants. This would upset the tradition of understanding between all the people. It always starts with a shop, and it always ends up looking like some of the streets in old Toulon or some of the main roads in Marseille.[51]

Working this terrain, Le Pen travelled to Fréjus and Saint-Raphaël for public events that included a ceremony to honor the French soldiers who had fallen in Indochina. At another meeting that Le Chevallier organized in Saint-Raphaël, Bruno Mégret (Le Pen's lieutenant) argued against the "disappearance of the human races due to the spread of *métissage*."[52] Invited to give a speech in Tourves, Le Pen spoke about immigration, Europe, and defense.[53]

Opponents of the far right did not sit still. After SOS-Racisme announced a countermarch, the prefect banned a march that Le Pen planned to lead through the streets of Toulon in 1992.[54] That year, likewise, a group of bishops issued a cautionary statement. In politics, they warned, clichés, slogans, and words with hidden meanings lead to muddled thinking about legal refugees, asylum seekers, undocumented migrants, migrant workers and their families, youths whose parents were immigrants, and French citizens in overseas departments and territories. "We urge Catholics to re-read the parable of the Good Samaritan," they continued, "Jesus refuses to answer the question: 'And who is my neighbor?'" Coexistence between diverse communities may raise challenges, the bishops acknowledged, but Catholics in countries that are better off should abide by peace and social inclusion, recognition of fundamental human rights, and aid for poor countries.[55]

The far right was rising, but the dam held. In 1992, indeed, the moderate right crept closer to a monopoly of power in the department council (the number of seats it controlled climbed from 31 to 34 out of 41).[56] This reassured Arreckx, who declared that republican discipline in the Var was containing the far right.[57] That year, though, political strife and factional violence returned to Algeria. As events of terrible brutality beset the former colony, French fears of Islam regained vigor. The attacks of 9/11 as well as their aftermath of stubborn wars and terrorist killings remained a decade or more away. Yet Algeria in the 1990s gave the *pieds noirs* a postcolonial confirmation of what they believed, and thought others refused to believe. Arreckx needed to reckon with the growing loyalty of voters for Le Pen and his party. Apart from gaining a larger share of the vote, fewer of the far right's first-round supporters now transferred their second-round vote to candidates with a realistic chance of winning. If the Var were to turn against Arreckx and his political machine, would republican discipline still hold?

THE PIAT AFFAIR AND THE ARRECKX SCANDAL

As his accomplice in running politics in the Var, Arreckx counted on a man with a similar profile, François Léotard: the mayor of Fréjus, a deputy in the National Assembly, and a senior official in their branch of the UDF (the Parti républicain, or PR). In 1992, a court found Léotard guilty of corruption, influence peddling, and abuse of public office. Another court found the mayor of Saint-Tropez guilty of theft and extortion. These shocks to the political class had a ripple effect on organized crime (which had interests in the department's real estate and drug trafficking). Bombings, arsons, physical assaults, and attempted killings swept the department (notably in Toulon but also in Hyères, Fréjus, Sanary, Le Luc, and Le Pradet). The boss of organized crime in the Var, Jean-Louis Fargette, controlled his operations from just across just the border, in the north of Italy, where he lived as an outlaw. In 1993, assassins found and killed him.[58]

Fargette's death had no immediate effect on party politics in the Var. Amidst high unemployment, uncertainty over naval spending, and mediocre prospects for the tourism sector, instead the 1993 parliamentary elections confirmed the decline of the left. With only 12.4 percent of the vote in the department, the Socialists reached a new low (even failing to progress to the second round in any of the department's districts); the Communists and Greens did even worse. The National Front placed second in six of the department's seven circumscriptions, by contrast, and won 27.0 percent of the vote in Toulon. Still, the moderate right prevailed (not only its incumbent candidates in Toulon and Fréjus, but also its recruit in Hyères, Piat).[59] Then the dam burst.

Piat had confided to friends that probing into links between organized crime, land speculation, and political corruption in the Var was making enemies for her. In a private letter written in 1992, she named Arreckx and Fargette among those who would welcome her death. On 25 February 1994, hired assassins on a hillside road outside Hyères shot and killed Piat.[60] The neo-Gaullists, who stood to gain from a weakening of Arreckx and his system, moved quickly, with the minister of the interior launching an anticorruption campaign in the Var. Within days, the police interviewed three vice-presidents of the departmental council. Arreckx defended the system by which the department had awarded thousands of public works contracts, but police searched his home and took him in for questioning.[61]

Le Pen sped to the Var, where he gave a press conference that alluded to the political bribery scandals (*Tangentopoli*) underway in Italy. This department, he said, needed two brigades of Italian judges. He remarked, quite accurately, that Piat's death "was a revelation of profound corruption in the political fabric. It also reveals an unanticipated consequence of state decentralization, which allows political elements to handle enormous flows of money."[62] The odor of corruption hung over the cantonal elections later that month. Arreckx lost his seat to the candidate from the National Front,

Éliane Guillet de la Brosse, thereby also losing his presidency of the departmental council, which the National Front entered for the first time.

At the request of a state prosecutor assigned to the Piat case, five months later Arreckx lost his parliamentary immunity as a Senator. A wiretap of Fargette's telephone revealed that millions of francs in bribes for public works contracts had flowed to Arreckx and another politician. Authorities arrested Arreckx in August 1994 and charged him with conspiracy, accepting bribes, breach of trust, and possession of stolen goods. Front-page newspaper photos show him a free man one sunny afternoon as he walks with his lawyers toward the Palace of Justice in Toulon; and, later the same day, confined to the back seat of a police car that took him, after night fell, to the Baumettes Penitentiary on the eastern edge of Marseille.[63]

As the lid came off, more signs of corruption and mismanagement in this part of Provence emerged. An audit raised questions about the probity of the mayor of Le Lavandou. The mayor of La Seyne-sur-Mer came under investigation for improprieties in awarding public works contracts. Police arrested the mayor of Salernes for irregularities in awarding public works contracts. Built next to a conference center as part of Toulon's revitalization plan, the Palace Hotel declared bankruptcy.[64] A state review of contracts and expenditures for construction of a high-tech, educational-commercial hub in Toulon raised suspicion that politicians had received bribes or turned a blind eye to graft. "The competition for the contract," an official report read, "was rigged and resulted in inflated over-billing."[65] Trucy reacted by shifting the responsibility for construction of the high-tech hub to the departmental council, not his city.[66] He also turned against his former patron. "Arreckx," he said, "took us for idiots."[67]

Trucy's long association with Arreckx was costing him. A report from the regional accounting office raised concerns about influence peddling, conflict of interest, and improper use of public funds in the mayor's office (Trucy's principal secretary also managed a communications agency that held contracts with the city, allegedly channeling public funds into trips, publicity, and opinion polls for the mayor and his allies).[68] The noose tightened when a court imposed a five-year prison sentence on a friend of Arreckx (the former vice-president of the department's Chamber of Commerce), for extortion, false accounting, and improper use of public funds. Seeing trouble ahead, a neo-Gaullist politician jumped ship by resigning from the city council.[69] His premonition proved accurate.

Pretrial findings against Arreckx revealed that between 1982 and 1994, firms involved in shipbuilding or public works had deposited 6.3 million French francs into his Swiss bank account.[70] His four children appeared in court after it emerged that 4 million francs had flowed from their father's account into accounts opened on their behalf.[71] Although Arreckx announced his resignation from politics in 1995, the legal proceedings against him did not let up until he died from cancer six years later.[72] Death, La Bruyère writes, can bring as much relief to those who go as to those they have left behind.

CHAPTER 8
A City under the Far Right

Some quick math brings out the improbability of the far right's victory in Toulon in 1995. Between 1989 and 2014, France held five municipal elections; and, among all municipal elections held in the 236 cities with more than 30,000 inhabitants across this 25-year period, the National Front won four times. These numbers put the odds of a far-right victory at roughly 5,000 to 1.[1]

Why did the far right beat the odds in Toulon?

Analysis of French municipal elections suggests that a moderate-right politician stands a better chance of re-election if they also hold office at another level of government. Multiple mandates boost visibility, status, and influence. In Toulon, though, the mayor who lost to the far right was also a senator. Two further conditions favor incumbents. Leading a unified political camp (because dissidence harms an incumbent mayor's image and vote share), and entering a two-way runoff (to avoid vote splitting).[2] In Toulon in 1995, dissidence within the moderate right and a three-way runoff worked against the re-election of the mayor. Other factors also mattered, though. Some were of the moment. A corruption scandal had tarred the incumbent and his camp. The left disobeyed its leaders in Paris. Other factors had roots in the past: the years of organizing and mobilizing by the FN; the moderate right's rhetorical and tactical indulgence toward the far right; and the presence of a community, the *pieds noirs*, whose support could tilt the balance.

GRASSROOTS ORGANIZATION CONTINUES

After Yann Piat left the party in 1988, the National Front had named a new head for the Var, Jean-Marie Le Chevallier. A man of experience, he had served on the executive committee of the French Red Cross and had run a section of Giscard's party, the UDF, in Brittany. As chief of staff for Secretary of State Jacques Dominati (1975–1976), he knew the concerns of the *pieds noirs*. As chief of staff for Le Pen (starting in 1983, when the National Front expanded by recruiting from the moderate right), Le Chevallier knew the National Front from the inside.[3] The Var received Le Chevallier as an opportunist imposed by Paris; building on Piat's initiatives, he proved the doubters wrong. Printed at 5,000 copies per month, *National 83*—before his arrival the local party newsletter—had corrected unsympathetic accounts of the far right in the mainstream media. Apart from articles on Le Pen, National Front ideology, and colonial Algeria, it updated members about local issues and party affairs. Le Chevallier replaced it with a periodical, *Le Patriote du Var*, sold cheaply at newsstands to reach a wider readership and putting more emphasis on local politics, notably problems with the Trucy administration.[4]

Le Chevallier deployed his activists in residential areas, whether *populaire* or *bourgeois*, as well as public spaces like the open-air market along the Cours Lafayette. They handed out fliers that drew on the city's love-hate relationship with the state: the presence of the Navy and the Arsenal underwrote both pride in France and dependency on Paris, which was said not to understand or care.[5] One of his goals, Le Chevallier said later, was to soften the image of the far right:

> People would see our militants every Saturday. Starting in 1989, on every Saturday we handed out over 6,000 fliers in the markets. We were the only ones. Taking the time to hand out fliers had two pluses: beside the message the flier conveys, there's the physical presence of the man or woman who gave it to you. People start talking, a dialogue begins, there's almost a kind of bodily contact. There's both the message and the person you see regularly, you run into them where they go to buy cheese or vegetables, so it's alive. All this really suited the Mediterranean mentality, in my view.[6]

Like the old Communist Party, Le Chevallier was using grassroots activism to stake out his political territory.[7]

In addition, he sponsored flanking organizations that recruited from segments of the city's population: its women, *pieds noirs*, military personnel, military veterans, needy, and unemployed. He reached out to Catholic traditionalists and veterans of the Algerian War. To spearhead his campaign for the 1995 municipal elections, he created a civic association, Living Better in Toulon.[8] Exploiting outrage after Arreckx's arrest, Le Chevallier created Clean Hands in the Var. Disguised as a citizen's group, it infiltrated neighborhood associations loyal to Arreckx and Trucy and sorted the good from the bad by asking mayoral candidates to accept its charter of integrity.[9]

Not everything went smoothly, of course. In 1993, Le Chevallier received the resignation of the four National Front representatives on the regional council. Through his tactics, though, the party deepened its penetration of society.[10]

Deep changes in the Var helped. The decline of the left had created a situation ripe for vote splitting. In the 1989 municipal elections, when Le Chevallier was still a new face, his slate attracted 20.3 percent of the first-round vote and 24.2 percent in the second round. After he and six other National Front candidates joined city council, his political apprenticeship advanced.[11] To gain attention, his group turned culture into a point of contention.[12] Calling television programs unhealthy, it called for stronger regulation of their content. It wanted renovations to a neo-Baroque church and a festival devoted to French music. It sponsored a bill to rename the waterfront's Stalingrad Quay:

> We have had a reconciliation between France and Germany. There is no more reason for dwelling on this part of history, which undergoes constant revision. We want anything to do with communism or Marxism removed from our country.[13]

His group decried as fake social-democratic generosity the social programs in housing projects with ethno-racial minorities.[14] Apartments in these projects required renovation, one National Front councilor conceded, but only for the French.[15] Another of Le Chevallier's councilors denounced a milk program for pupils in poor neighborhoods as a form of favoritism and questioned the need for bookmobiles because the suburban poor (a euphemism for minorities) would never develop good reading habits.[16] The law forbids discrimination, yet one far-right councilor wanted to restrict social assistance only to so-called French families.[17]

Remarkably, Le Chevallier noticed a difference between perceptions of his party and Le Pen, a man potential supporters disliked due to his "odious statements" or because he seemed "a real fascist."[18] In response, propaganda from his federation devoted less attention to Le Pen. This worked, apparently. Before Le Chevallier took over, support for the far right in the Var tended to increase with the scale of the election: the National Front (or Le Pen) performed better in European and presidential elections than in parliamentary or municipal elections. After 1989, the pattern reversed itself: in the Var, the far right tended to perform better in parliamentary, departmental, or local elections. Indeed, the 1993 parliamentary elections confirmed that the National Front had replaced the left as the main opposition to the moderate right in Toulon.[19] Le Pen made the city one of his first stops for his 1995 presidential campaign. He talked about the far right's usual issues ("unemployment, immigration, insecurity, taxes, a low birthrate, political corruption, lax morality, the destruction of agriculture, the weakness of national defense, and institutional reform") but also tailored his speech to the 2,000 or more supporters out to cheer for him at the Municipal Theater.[20] The country needed to strengthen its military capacity, which had declined during the past decade. Pensions for veterans aside, the defense budget now stood at some 200 million francs annually; meanwhile, the country spent more than 300 million francs annually on immigration, "a form of aggression as dangerous as a military attack, the most formidable fifth column ever seen on our soil."[21] Other candidates fought back, with conservatives Jacques Chirac and Edmond Balladur appealing to the *pied noir* vote.[22] The Var, though, favored the far right. Ahead of Balladur, Chirac, and Jospin (the Socialist), in the 1995 presidential election this department put Le Pen first.[23]

THE 1995 CITY ELECTIONS

Soon after the presidential election, the 1995 municipal elections asked the citizens of Toulon to choose between no fewer than nine slates. Accusations of political mismanagement as well as connections with the disgraced Arreckx had wounded Trucy. From across the political spectrum, candidates ran an anti-corruption campaign. Anticipating the incumbent's downfall, for the first time in half a century the Socialists, Communists, and Radical Leftists set aside their differences. A victory by their joint slate would raise a barrier to the far right and "end the reign of the corrupt right, whose practices of widespread patronage have kept this city shackled for 36 years."[24] Their mayoral candidate, Christian Goux, could seem stiff and aloof, however, and he hailed not from Toulon but Bandol, where his record as mayor was unimpressive. His slate suffered from a lack of credibility: the newfound unity of the left seemed opportunistic and fragile. It also lacked ties to the electorate, for the left had neglected grassroots activism.[25]

Trucy fought back by presenting himself as responsive and transparent. To project an image of renewal, his slate excluded four veteran city councilors and his campaign spotlighted a youth committee that endorsed him. He overhauled Toulon Communication, the firm accused of violating its arms-length relationship with the mayor's office and misallocating public funds. Dissent within his own camp hurt him nonetheless. A deputy from Toulon, Louis Colombani, belonged to the same party as Arreckx and Trucy. As scandals cascaded, Colombani defied his party by announcing his separate candidacy for mayor.[26] Further splitting the moderate-right vote, the neo-Gaullists fielded a slate.[27] As his chances of defeat mounted, Trucy waited for the Paris headquarters of the moderate-right parties to send national leaders to his campaign events, but they stayed away.[28]

Between the first and second rounds of the 1989 municipal elections, Le Chevallier had asked Trucy for a merger of their slates; in exchange, he wanted the National Front to be a junior partner in city government. Not needing the far right, the mayor had refused; in 1995, by contrast, Le Chevallier opposed a slate uniting the far and moderate right. Despite the resistance of National Front politicians in Hyères, Sanary, and Saint-Raphaël, Le Chevallier imposed his prohibition against alliances on the entire department.[29] In these elections, the far right would stand or fall alone.

Le Chevallier had a public manner more relaxed and familiar than that of Goux or Trucy. Further, he could count on a seasoned campaign director: the chief editor of *Le Patriote du Var*, Jean-Claude Poulet-Dachary, who had five election campaigns behind him.[30] Their strategy would be to steal support from the moderate right by presenting an image of competence and moderation. Reaching out to voters with a military background, the Le Chevallier slate included six military men. An engineering manager and former head of the Arsenal served as president of his sponsoring committee. To reassure moderate-right supporters, his slate included a retired admiral, the wife of a Navy officer, and a former superintendent in the National Police. For help in spreading its message, his party could rely on the state (any slate winning at least 5 percent of the first-round vote could ask the Prefecture to reimburse the printing costs for its platform and posters).[31] Le Chevallier also had the good luck of avoiding serious countermobilization. The Communists organized an antiracist rally in the heart of the city, but no more than 300 people attended.[32] Municipal employees removed or covered National Front election posters, but a court found the city guilty of an offense against freedom of expression.

Like his rivals, Le Chevallier attacked Trucy by tying him to the Arreckx scandal, which had "tainted pretty well every UPR and neo-Gaullist politician in the Var."[33] Toulon had experienced two disasters, he said—once during the war; again under two mayors who lacked good sense—and he promised a financial audit if he won.[34] For shock value, his campaign used slogans like "The French First in Toulon" and "Toulon: French City."[35] To these, Le Chevallier added a five point, right-wing populist platform: (1) improve security by hiring more police; (2) end waste and corruption; (3) end elitism in publicly funded activities and events; (4) end deficits by balancing the budget, with a tax reduction to follow; (5) implement a French-first policy of national preference in education, welfare, and public housing.[36]

A three-way competition between the moderate right, left, and far right afforded the best run-off scenario for Le Chevallier, and he got it. With

31.0 percent of the first-round vote, his slate placed well ahead of those of Trucy (23.2 percent) and Goux (21.7 percent). By comparison with the last municipal elections, the moderate right had suffered only a moderate drop in support (less than 5 percent), but Trucy now competed against others in the same political space. Vote splitting within the moderate right had helped to push the mayor's share of the first-round vote down to half its level in the last city elections. Victory by Le Chevallier would depend on the turnout (in the first round, only 58.2 percent of eligible voters had gone to the polls).[37] It would also depend on transfers of votes from slates eliminated in the first round. Above all, a withdrawal by either Trucy or Goux would prevent a far-right victory.

Trucy stood firm: the left should withdraw because in the first round his list had done better. In exchange for Goux's withdrawal, the mayor let the Socialists know, he would agree to a power-sharing arrangement that gave them important positions and resources at city hall.[38] Supporting Trucy, the national leader of the Socialist Party asked Goux to agree.[39] Crucially, Goux refused: he would do nothing that allowed the re-election of Trucy. Departmental leaders of the UDF and the neo-Gaullists tried to secure endorsements for Trucy from leaders of the eliminated slates, but also in vain.[40] So opposed to Trucy was Colombani (the moderate-right dissident) that he urged his voters to transfer their support to Goux. With three slates to choose from in the second round, the electorate preferred that of Le Chevallier (37.0 percent of the vote) above those of Trucy (34.8 percent) and Goux (28.2 percent). In this way, then, Toulon became the largest city under the far right of any postwar European democracy.[41]

TOULON UNDER THE NATIONAL FRONT

Along with Toulon, that year the National Front triumphed in two smaller municipalities of the south: Orange and Marignane. Some in the party were glad to have these showcases, but Le Pen disliked being in the shadow of others. He also worried about losing control over his party.[42] Le Chevallier resisted, declaring, "The National Front will not run my city."[43] Instead of fighting in public, Le Pen waited for a private meeting with his mayors. He insisted on two policies: suspension of municipal funding for associations deemed unfriendly to the party, and implementation of national preference (pro-French discrimination in the allocation of welfare, housing, and other public services). Confident after his victory—the greatest yet for the National Front—Le Chevallier told his leader not to interfere. In any case, French law forbade a policy of national preference. The mayor of Toulon instead announced that his administration would scrutinize the residence permits of people applying for social assistance (with 43 applicants already refused). Le Pen paid an official visit for Bastille Day in 1995 but afterward avoided this city.[44]

A hermetic seal does not separate associations from politics. Local governments consult with associations that deliver social services or implement educational, charitable, cultural, or sports programs. Associations depend on cities for funding. Parties, in turn, ensure that association leaders are included on electoral slates and sit on municipal councils. Entwined in relations of influence and power, associations thus enter into the calculations and tactics of politicians, parties, and political blocs.[45] A stake in interparty competition in Toulon, the relationship between association funding and political patronage had preceded the National Front's takeover. In 1992, the party had requested an audit of 15 associations funded by the city.[46] A month later, in a heated session at city hall, the Socialists had questioned grants to associations that were "no more than an extension of the Trucy administration."[47] Three years later, while campaigning for election as mayor, Le Chevallier had called for more transparency and accountability in awarding grants: "Patronage is thriving on a grand scale: the associations need to be cleaned up."[48]

Consistent with Le Pen's request, the Le Chevallier administration took a hard line against associations suspected of being "friends of the previous administration" or "allowing immigrants to obtain as many financial and social benefits as possible."[49] In 1995, the city tried to ban an annual street festival that associations held in a poor neighborhood. For justification, Le Chevallier cited public safety: "all gatherings of foreign peoples create a dangerous situation."[50] In 1997, he banned a Bastille Day rally by a national anti-racist association.[51] His administration ejected labor unions from the Labor Exchange, a building in the old city that remained empty for decades after.[52] The city cut grants and other resources to a parent-teacher association, a Protestant charity, and groups that fought poverty, racism, and AIDS.[53]

Like Arreckx and Trucy before him, in turn, Le Chevallier placed party members on the board of directors for public transport, public housing, student housing, a youth agency, a recreational association, and an arts center.[54] The city also increased funding to associations deemed friendly. It named the mayor's wife, Cendrine Le Chevallier, as director of an association that provided social services. Renamed Toulon Youth, it consumed as much as 70 percent of the city's budget for associations. To shift the balance in social services from minorities to whites, the city granted funding and official duties to the local branch of French Fraternity. A leader of this National Front parallel organization explained that "we give priority to French families in need. This does not mean that we ignore others, but we care first for our children and for our families that do not have all their country owes them."[55] In sum, the party that made a myth of unity fostered discord.

Nationally and internationally, the election of the National Front provoked outrage. Toulon already suffered from its image as a squalid city so unlike the Côte d'Azur. Now labeled a fascist city, it became a kind of outcast. The city council of its sister-city in Belgium, Liège, voted to "suspend all relations with a city governed by a party that is racist and xenophobic."[56] To avoid "a banalization of the FN," stage artists cancelled performances in Toulon.[57] On the cultural front, though, Le Chevallier proceeded with more restraint than his counterparts in Orange and Marignane (which prevented municipal libraries from acquiring books written by authors disliked by the far right or dealing too liberally with multiculturalism, Islam, or homosexuality). In Marignane, the public library even ended subscriptions to mainstream periodicals like *Libération*, *Le Monde*, and *La Marseillaise*.[58]

In Toulon, not the municipal library but the annual book fair became a cultural battleground. This was not Le Chevallier's preference, but others on his council wanted a chance to combat left-liberal ideology.[59] In 1995, a first clash over the book fair pitted the far-right administration against local booksellers who had run this event in the past; under a last-minute compromise, an invitation to a left-wing publisher balanced another to a far-right publisher.[60] The city tried to make the fair decidedly right-wing the next year; this backfired when book dealers withdrew to protest the mistreatment of a local publisher of minority origins.[61] Further, the 1996 book fair faced competition: a counter-fair with high-profile patrons at the Châteauvallon cultural center.[62] Amidst national attention, Hubert Falco—who had replaced Arreckx as president of the departmental council—decided to step in. Starting in 1997, Falco announced, the Var would sponsor its own book fair. Adorned by posters of Le Pen, the city's 1997 book fair on the Place de la Liberté attracted a few thousand visitors; on the waterfront, the fair launched by the department attracted some 50,000 visitors.[63] This cultural battle the far right had lost.

Still, the clientelistic model guided Le Chevallier. After the Arsenal, the biggest employer in Toulon was its city hall. With National Front members receiving preference in hiring, a thousand people joined the party in 1998 alone, most of them city employees.[64] In turn, the number of city employees continued to grow.[65] The youth association created by the National Front hired more than 200 people, and nepotism spread (one councilor hired his sister, another his daughter; and a member of the party's executive committee got a fake job for her retired husband).[66] For a position with her youth association, Cendrine Le Chevallier refused to hire a former secretary of Trucy: "Fair is fair: I am an elected official from the National

Front and I am prepared to hire people from the National Front."[67] The city transferred Ahmed Touati, a national anti-racist organizer and ex-chief of staff for a moderate-right politician, to garbage collection duties.[68] Unions fought back as alarm grew over the number of employment contracts not renewed for partisan reasons.[69]

The *pieds noirs* had formed the original core of the National Front in the Var, and they had joined Piat and Le Chevallier in building it. In 1993, Le Chevallier endorsed their request that France implement a national repatriates' day.[70] The National Front's councilors included *pieds noirs*, one of whom said, "In Algeria I started my service on 27 January 1954. I left Algeria without animosity toward those people. But on the other hand I would like it if they were sent back to where they came from."[71] Once again, though, the far right sowed division. Its parallel group for *pieds noirs*—the Front national des rapatriés (FNR)—alienated others. Boutigny raised concern over a degeneration in his group's relations with the Le Chevallier administration. Established *pied noir* associations in the Var would stay non-partisan, he warned.[72]

The tension erupted at an annual ceremony to mark the Rue d'Isly massacre in Algiers. Included in the 1996 ceremony at the mayor's request, the FNR unfurled its banner. Then, contrary to the wishes of Boutigny and other association leaders, a FNR leader gave a speech that praised the election of Le Chevallier, criticized the Human Rights League, and remarked that for National Front members like himself, "What is going on around here with immigration shows that we are right."[73] Requesting that the administration express its disapproval, afterward Boutigny complained to the mayor that the FNR had derailed a commemoration that he and others had launched two decades earlier.[74] A few weeks later, the associations under Boutigny held a second, expiatory ceremony at the Monument for the Dead of French Algeria.[75] Boutigny tried to mend relations, but the following year heard that the mayor, not an association, would oversee the Rue d'Isly ceremony.[76] Le Chevallier tried to avoid taking sides, but his relations with the *pieds noirs* had worsened.

Under the slogan "Heads High, Hands Clean," Le Chevallier's 1995 campaign had promised probity. To justify the city's ban on a street festival in the poor Saint-Musse quarter, Cendrine Le Chevallier said that "here the terrorists feel at home in France."[77] A year later, a court found her guilty of defamation: she had called the leader of a Catholic association that sponsored this festival "a socialist or a communist, an agitator in Islamic circles."[78] In 1998, a court found her guilty of practicing political favoritism by requesting that her association, Toulon Youth, hire party members first.[79] Another court ordered the liquidation of Toulon Youth, thereby adding 6.3 million francs to the city deficit.[80] Other party members on city council came under investigation in 1998: three for accepting bribes in return for school cafeteria contracts; and another for rape, sexual assault, and sexual harassment.[81] Citizens learned that pressure from the mayor and his wife had forced a director of Toulon Youth to create a bogus paid job for a political ally.[82] Instead of cleaning up at city hall, the Le Chevallier administration was playing its own tricks.

For the average French city, the public sector provided 41 percent of total employment; for Toulon, this level was 71 percent—the highest in France. The Var remained the most important military department in the country, with some 72,000 personnel from all branches stationed there (and Navy consolidation increasing their number slightly). With 4 billion francs in annual sales, the Arsenal was the most important industry between Marseille and Nice.[83] Its labor force had dropped considerably, however, and the state was looking at privatization.[84] As naval subcontracting shrank, job cuts loomed at a time of stagnation in the Var's trade, industrial, and service sectors.[85] Trade unions remained vigilant, ready to mount demonstrations and strikes.[86]

To reassure citizens, the city printed posters and leaflets with the slogan "The National Front is working." It launched a newsletter that listed the administration's successes: not lofty and expensive projects, it proclaimed, but services that responded to citizens' needs and requests. Behind the scenes, though, its administration was clumsy and amateurish. Le Chevallier had to contend with a flight of experienced, upper-level bureaucrats. Legislative committees broke down and lost effectiveness. Majority and minority on the city council avoided compromise. Through haste, negligence, and sidetracking, decision-making suffered. Unable to cooperate with nearby municipalities run by the left or the moderate right, his city did not develop forward-thinking strategies. Two months after Le Chevallier's victory, his chief of staff, Jean-Claude Poulet-Dachary, a veteran of the Foreign Legion, died in an apartment stairwell after visiting a gay bar in Toulon. Forgetting its homophobia, the party pulled together (at the funeral, Le Pen even delivered a eulogy). Still, Le Chevallier lost the collaborator who had composed his platforms, managed his activists, and selected his candidates.[87]

The major feats of Le Chevallier's term were more policing and a balanced budget. Financing of projects started before Le Chevallier took office had left a huge debt.[88] In response, his first budget put a hold on investment.[89] This more than offset the increase during Le Chevallier's term in the cost of city employees (whose salaries represented two-thirds of total expenses). Although the region assessed the city's finances as fragile, the debt shrank considerably. As for city contracts, the far right managed some well (with a private firm that operated the Municipal Theater, for example) but mishandled others (collecting garbage, renovating the old city hall, or operating the Oméga Zenith concert hall). To reduce expenses, in 1997 the city halted construction of a new retail and office complex (the Palais Liberté). With excavation already underway, this left an eyesore (an abandoned pit, next to the city's main public square, surrounded by construction hoarding) as well as legal battles and financial settlements so costly the prefect tried to have them annulled. Significantly, other levels of government choked the flow of public funds into the city.[90] Combined with the debt inherited from Trucy, his commitment to balance the books, and the absence of a working consensus at city hall, Le Chevallier lacked means for effecting change.

For room to maneuver, Le Chevallier kept the party's rank and file at a distance. He suspended meetings with local activists and publication of their newsletter. On paper, the organization did not seem to suffer: at some 6,000 members, half of them in Toulon, the Var federation of the National Front was the biggest of *any* party in France (though, as we know, some had joined for a job or other favor). In 1998, likewise, the federation survived a rift between Le Pen and Bruno Mégret that resulted in the birth of a new far-right party (the Mouvement national républicain). Across France, cadres and members migrated to Mégret's party, but the Var federation of the National Front resisted. The loss of a few local cadres when Le Chevallier chose his wife as the party's candidate for the 1998 parliamentary by-election hardly posed a setback either.[91]

Instead, tensions on the city council damaged the far right internally. Promoting his wife after the death of Poulet-Dachary, Cendrine Le Chevallier became the director of Toulon Youth, the National Front candidate in a parliamentary by-election, and the deputy mayor. Internal opposition to her ascent cracked far-right unity in 1997, when the mayor removed two party members from city committees.[92] After his poor performance in the 1998 cantonal elections, other dissidents on city council defected.[93] Politically isolated and lacking a stable majority, Le Chevallier lost the backing of Le Pen (who in 1998 ruined his chance of gaining the presidency of the PACA region by refusing a deal with the RPR). For the first time since 1984, Le Pen kept Le Chevallier off his slate for the European elections.[94] Without resigning as mayor, finally in 1999 Le Chevallier quit the National Front.

His election, then, marked the beginning of a far-right experiment that failed. The dividend accrued to the Socialists first, eventually to the moderate right. Following the Piat assassination, the left had profited from the weakening of the moderate right in the Var. In the 1995 municipal elections, the Socialists won in Draguignan, Brignoles, and La Seyne-sur-Mer. Shocked by the election of Le Chevallier, the Var sections of the Socialist and the

Communist Parties renewed themselves. They co-opted the local anti-racist movement, which became an extension of their own organizations. Aided by the dormancy of National Front activism, temporary divisions within the UDF, and Lionel Jospin's popularity, the Socialists gained influence among local unions and associations.[95] On city commissions charged with oversight of public services, the Socialists formed tactical, anti-National Front alliances with the moderate right.[96] Short-term successes followed: in the 1997 parliamentary elections, the Socialist candidate (who ran under the slogan "Proud Again to be a Toulonnais") won the second circumscription of the Var; and in a 1998 parliamentary by-election, the Socialist candidate defeated Cendrine Le Chevallier.

These successes did not reverse the long-term decline of the left in the Var, though. The Socialists had lost most of their historical base in the rural interior and suffered from low membership (officially 1,600 members in the department, with 200 in Toulon). The Green Party remained electorally weak and ideologically divided (with some on the left side of the political divide, others on the right). By comparison with the Socialists, the Communists could claim more members (2,400 in the Var, with 400 in Toulon) but attracted fewer votes. During the Le Chevallier years, a left alliance had resulted in one small gain: for the first time in two decades, a Communist from Toulon sat on the departmental council. With the loss of heavy industry in the Var, however, the old working class was dwindling. Across the country, in fact, the Communists were losing ground to the National Front in the struggle for votes from workers and unemployed, many of whom preferred welfare chauvinism—equality of rights for the true French—to equality and fraternity for all.[97]

After the assassination of Piat and the collapse of the Arreckx system, the moderate right lost legitimacy, unity, and votes. Its renewal depended on Hubert Falco, head of the department's UDF. Falco waited before announcing his candidacy for the 2001 city elections in Toulon, using his time to overcome the disunity and dispersion of UDF members, activists, and organizers. He took into account the maneuvers of the neo-Gaullists. They had no politician of equal stature in the department, but their distance from the Arreckx system made them seem cleaner. By comparison with the UDF, moreover, the neo-Gaullists had more members (officially, about 4,400 members in the Var as opposed to perhaps 3,000 for the UDF).[98] Backed by President Chirac, the neo-Gaullists hoped to take this department. In 1996, therefore, the minister of the interior selected as prefect for the Var a Corsican who during his youth had belonged to the far right, Jean-Charles Marchiani, who used his position as a base for the capture of Toulon. Marchiani followed a double strategy. He tried to draw Le Chevallier away from the National Front and into the RPR (a route taken by Jacques Peyrat, the mayor of Nice), and he prepared the ground for the next city elections. To appeal to the far-right electorate, Marchiani backed Le Chevallier in his 1996 conflict with the cultural center at Châteauvallon, even banning an anti–far-right concert by a rap group (Nique Ta Mère) under the pretext that it offended Christian values.[99] After the left won the 1997 parliamentary elections, however, a new minister of the interior removed Marchiani from office. During interparty negotiations over the leadership of moderate-right slates for the 1997 regional elections, in turn, the neo-Gaullists conceded the Var to the UDF. Falco and his allies had survived the neo-Gaullists' takeover attempt.[100]

Disunity within the moderate right had helped Le Chevallier become mayor. It helped him again during the 1997 parliamentary elections, when victory in the first circumscription of the Var made him the lone National Front deputy in the National Assembly.[101] His decline started in 1998, when a court decided that a violation of campaign financing laws invalidated his 1997 election as deputy. The court also ruled him ineligible for the ensuing by-election; his wife replaced him and lost.[102] Sticking to the party line, in 1999 Le Chevallier warned:

> The Var and Toulon will experience the biggest demographic explosion in France, with French from the north and Europeans wishing to take advantage of our climate, but another part will arrive from the lands to the south, of the Islamic confession. We know that Islam leads to catastrophe when it becomes revolutionary. We are sure to witness a clash between two cultures, with the risk of creating ever more problems in our neighborhoods, in the housing projects, and in the city centers. We need to stay extremely vigilant![103]

That year, Marchiani had the pleasure of becoming a deputy in the European Assembly precisely when Le Chevallier lost his long-time seat.[104]

Le Chevallier contested the 2001 municipal elections as an independent candidate, but amidst more troubles. A court found his wife and him guilty of breach of trust and misappropriation of funds in connection with Toulon Youth. Le Pen sued him for pocketing 250,000 francs from the party's Var section.[105] Another court found Le Chevallier guilty of suborning witnesses: after National Front cadres had found clues that refuted his public allegation that political motives lay behind the death of Poulet-Dachary, the mayor had asked them to stay away from the police investigation.[106] In 1995, Le Chevallier had campaigned on the need for fiscal austerity; in 2001, he promised not only to reduce the city's debt but also to launch an ambitious program of urban renewal.[107] His record betrayed him: the office complex on the Place de la Liberté and the road tunnel to unclog the city center remained unfinished. Problems a far-right politician should have resolved—crime and unemployment—had not gone away. Just before the 2001 elections, the city council voted to honor the 1961 putsch in Algiers by renaming a crossroads after General Salan.[108] This could not save Le Chevallier, who received only 7.8 percent—the worst performance of any incumbent mayor in France. Le Chevallier did outperform the new National Front candidate for mayor, an ex-colonial from North Africa, but not Marchiani, the Socialist candidate, or the eventual winner, Falco.[109] Electoral support that had boosted the far right to victory in 1995 turned out to be soft. The moderate right was back.

LOSING LOCAL POWER

As we saw at the start of this chapter, three factors (unity in their own camp, entering a two-way run-off, and holding multiple offices) favor the re-election of an incumbent moderate-right mayor in France. Looking at Toulon, we find that dissidence in his own camp did penalize Trucy in 1995. As the general pattern also suggests, Trucy lost in a run off with more than one other competitor. Holding more than one office did not save him, though. Even for nationalistic parties, this suggests, politics close to home can greatly affect electoral support. The success of the far right may depend more on the salience of perceived threats to the locality than to the country. These threats can assume various forms: loss of an industry, for example, or merger with another municipality.[110] Our look at Toulon suggests that voters may treat a serious scandal at city hall as such a threat. The French, who in general place less trust in national politicians than in local officials, believe that corruption lies mostly far away, in Paris.[111] When a local official, party, or machine does lose their trust, then, shock and outrage will be all the greater. Scandal contributed to the far right's victory in 1995; and to its defeat in 2001. Apart from corruption, a look at Toulon brings out the importance of far-right organization, including activism; and the moderate right's verbal and tactical merging with the far right. What still needs more discussion is the role of the *pieds noirs*.

PART IV
The Far Right Endures

CHAPTER 9
Discourse and Politics

Elective affinity: this idea entered sociology thanks to Max Weber's *Protestant Ethic and the Spirit of Capitalism*, where it means more than resemblance, less than fusion. In a dynamic interaction, two elements in the same orbit—an ascetic work ethic and a profit-seeking market mentality, in Weber's classic—energized each other. Proceeding by analogy, in this chapter we try to pin down an elective affinity between the *pieds noirs* and the far right. To do so, I examine discourses. My assumption is that people adapt language to the context of communication. As we will see, front-stage discourse—utterances in a broader public context—gives scant evidence of an affinity between far right and ex-colonials. Instead, back-stage discourse—which addresses a restricted audience—shows an overlap. The first part of this chapter, then, examines the front-stage discourse of party and subculture; and the latter part, their back-stage discourse.[1]

The lesson learned is that public discourse can mask subcultural affinities and political potentials. The National Front's official discourse dealt in impression management. By addressing subjects like taxes, education, employment, and Europe, the National Front tried to correct its image as a single-issue, anti-immigrant party. In so doing, it purged older ideologies and grudges. Entangled in the past, conversely, the official discourse of the ex-colonials filtered out party politics. A closer affinity between party and subculture emerges, by contrast, when we compare the back-stage discourses of the far right and the *pieds noirs*. This chapter thus reveals not only the overlap between speech communities, significantly, but also what remained distinct.

FRONT-STAGE DISCOURSE OF THE NATIONAL FRONT

On the economy, until the 1980s the National Front took a third-way position. Liberals and Marxists alike, it asserted, forget that human happiness is not reducible to material well-being. In foreign affairs, the national interest should take priority over economic interests; and in domestic affairs, social justice should take priority over market values. When it attracted more voters, though, the National Front swung toward laissez-faire. "Class conflict will be buried and true national solidarity reestablished," the party said, "when workers read financial reports instead of racing forms, and try their luck on the stock exchange instead of placing their savings in lotteries or bank accounts."[2] To supplant "the irresponsible and pervasive dogmatism of the state" with private initiative, the party called for popular capitalism.[3] This meant shrinking the state to its vital minimum: defense, policing, diplomacy, and justice. With less public spending, France could abolish the income tax. When tenants in public housing had enough money, the state could let them buy their residence. By privatizing state firms, France could transfer ownership to the people (giving financial shares to the head of each household, proportionate to the number of its children).[4]

As for unemployment, Le Pen told a television audience, "French workers could fill at least two-thirds of the jobs now held by immigrants."[5] France should expel aliens who are unemployed, undocumented, or criminal. His party would restrict social benefits to French nationals, who deserve priority in hiring too. The country could afford decent education, public housing, health care, and child benefits—if reserved for French nationals. Using monetary incentives, the National Front would entice immigrants to return to their country of origin. Aliens of European origin differ from those of the Third World, who refuse to assimilate due to cultural or religious differences and pressures from foreign governments or fundamentalist groups.[6] France welcomes "a Portuguese who wholeheartedly wishes to become French."[7] Not quite as easy to assimilate are Asians,

> a hard-working and calm people, who often share our Christian faith and agricultural background. We thus have a certain number of similarities with these people. While Asians may be quiet, however, their presence in France is not without dangers. Chinese immigrants in our cities tend to form groups that are homogeneous, secret, and even uncontrollable.[8]

Others are less compatible with French society:

> Black Africans pose an even greater difficulty. They are culturally and linguistically diverse, and have difficulty in adapting to the social and professional life of our decidedly

northern latitudes. Thus, they present real difficulties, but less in fact than people from North Africa.⁹

Official immigration ended in 1974, the party laments, yet refugees and illegal immigrants keep coming into France. To make matters worse, immigrants are having too many children and enjoying too many rights: "What was the point of mobilizing France against the Germans in 1914 and 1940, if today we must accept a supposedly peaceful invasion of our national territory?"¹⁰ To deal with immigration, France should end family reunification, limit refugee flows, strengthen border policing, and withdraw from the Schengen group.

In a glossy booklet for the 1988 presidential campaign, the National Front explains Le Pen's candidacy as a "strong belief that the nation is in danger and that the French face the threat of being destroyed, overwhelmed, and subjugated."¹¹ Naturalization is a privilege handed out too easily. The National Front wanted to abolish automatic citizenship; restrict *jus soli*; review naturalizations already granted; institute an oath of allegiance; and forbid dual citizenship. It called for quotas on immigrants in classrooms, and an end to multiculturalism and ethnic neighborhoods. Again the party singles out people from the Maghreb: "The National Front is against the integration of the North African community, whose mores, religion, and ways of thinking are radically different from our own."¹² France should forbid new mosques, and monitor Quranic schools and Islamic cultural centers. To offset the foreign presence, the French birthrate must increase—by raising family allowances, restricting common-law relationships, criminalizing abortion, and restoring family values and patriarchal authority.¹³

Crime, the party declared, has increased due to liberal mores and slack institutions. The National Front wanted the death penalty for murder, terrorism, and major drug trafficking, crimes it called threats to state sovereignty. All other crimes should carry fixed prison sentences, with no possibility of early release. The party called for more prisons with stricter discipline. Drug possession and trafficking should carry stiffer penalties, and a specialized court should deal with organized crime.¹⁴

In sum, France needs institutions that respect the will of the people: "Some say we are condemned to live in an increasingly multiracial society. Let's ask the country what it thinks!"¹⁵ Much of the problem lies with those who control culture, media, religion, politics, bureaucracies, and unions.¹⁶ Insulated in Paris, this self-serving oligarchy is corrupt and uninformed: "Whether the concern is with crime, bureaucracy, immigration, or terrorist blackmail, in every case our people reacts with more good sense than its national leaders."[17] Failed mediating institutions—Parliament, parties, and interest groups—keep the people unheard and powerless.[18] France needs a party of the people, not another party of the establishment.[19] Defending the nation as sacred, then, the National Front splits France into parts healthy (the people), diseased (the elites), or noxious (the foreigners). In statements that laud democracy and the good judgment of the French, the party calls for a radical extension of the referendum.[20] A new constitution would not suffice. The real solution is to put Le Pen, a child of the people, in power: "A true head of State is not the one who offers a few technical solutions, but the one who personifies a total project of French renewal."[21] This would lift the barrier between people and government, a barrier that makes France vulnerable and corrupt. Reconciled to itself, France would be reborn. Otherwise, there might be violence.[22]

The state has a supreme responsibility to "ensure the continuity of the Nation, its security, its unity, its strength."[23] The people who lived, toiled, and suffered on French soil have bequeathed a legacy:

> As the only alternative to socialism, the National Front's mission is to unify the majority who want to ensure France's survival, identity, strength, and prosperity. This majority values our ancestors' age-old traditions, and it wants to pass this legacy on to our children.[24]

Squandering this inheritance—"a community of language, of interests, of race, of memories, of culture in which mankind fulfills itself"—would be foolish and ungrateful.[25] At the end of 1989 the party commented, "In this year marked by the outmoded and nauseating celebration of the great ideals of the French Revolution, we had hoped that France, our People, would experience the beginning of an awakening."[26] Firmly on the right, then, the party has called for the repeal of laws stipulating that a business with more than 50 employees should have workplace committees.[27] These laws, it claims, are responsible for "the dictatorship" and "the monopoly" of French unions.[28] Similarly, employees in the public sector should lose the right to strike.[29] The party blames France's cultural decadence on the "cosmopolitan socialism" of the left, whose attacks on the family, justice, the state, and common sense have spread to the fake right.[30] As Le Pen put it when a Socialist government tried to integrate Catholic schools into the public system: "In France, secular education disappeared a long time ago. What we have are the religious teachings of the Marxist sect."[31]

Le Pen cited with approval Alexander Solzhenitsyn's charge, in his 1978 Harvard address, that moral weakness has made the West its own worst enemy. French traditions remain superior to culture that "comes from everywhere and thus nowhere."[32] Advertising debases the French language by using catchy slogans, incorrect syntax, and foreign expressions. The standardization and poor taste evident in architecture, art, and popular music reflect the Americanization of culture: "by financing the cultural activity of the left, the citizen has become dominated by art so international it is ridiculous. Cosmopolitanism in art has successfully changed the citizen into a rootless globe-trotter, a vagabond."[33] A legacy to protect, culture should serve as raw material for France's future.

The foregoing presents the official side of the National Front before it took power in Toulon. The party kept old schemas fresh after by applying them to new developments. Long before the rise of Vladimir Putin, the party made Russia a substitute for the Soviet Union: a scheming power intent on exploiting weakness and division in the West. In the period since the National Front lost power in Toulon, it has moved from neoliberal attacks on public services to welfare chauvinism: a strong program of social protection, but for natives only.[34] Under Marine Le Pen, moreover, the party has abandoned the anti-Republican rhetoric so evident in its denunciation of the French Revolution.

Before the 9/11 terrorist attacks, though, already Islam was replacing communism as the main nemesis. Anti-Islam grafted easily onto the old obsession with North Africans. Populism remains fundamental too. During her 2012 presidential campaign, Marine Le Pen followed her father (and appropriated the rhetoric of the Occupy movement) in denouncing the establishment: "Their 'system' is not made for us, the people of France. It's made for them, a small elite, a closed oligarchy, one percent of the population."[35] The party has become less critical of abortion and homosexuality, but still defends the traditional family (depending on internal power struggles, moreover, its moral positions could harden again).[36] In any case, women, sexuality, and the family matter less for its voters than immigration and security.

At an anti-communist rally near Paris in September 1982, the biggest yet organized by his party, Jean-Marie Le Pen declared:

> We believe in the primacy of man and his dignity, which reflects a portion of the divine within himself. We also believe in the indisputable existence of a moral order. We believe that their survival, defense, and progress depend above all on natural institutions: the family, the local community, the workplace, the nation.[37]

These words echoed the motto of the Pétainist regime ("Work, Family, Country"); references to empire, by contrast, shined by their absence from the party's public rhetoric.

FRONT-STAGE DISCOURSE OF THE *PIEDS NOIRS*

Traces of an affinity prove just as fleeting in the public discourse of the *pieds noirs*. The *pied noir* press concentrates on folklore, reminiscences, association activities, and notable achievements by community members. Some periodicals are explicit: to ward off controversy and division, they avoid party politics.[38] At times, as we have seen, partisanship has weakened and embarrassed the *pieds noirs*. Their federation in the Var published *L'Écho*, a quarterly that refused "to publish articles displaying a political tendency."[39] From Narbonne, similarly, *L'Algérianiste* aimed "to preserve the sociocultural patrimony of French Algeria" and "to identify and denounce historical falsification" but believed the *pieds noirs* "belong to a large family that must not disappear."[40] In neither case, though, did this rule out articles against De Gaulle or the FLN.

A typical issue of one of these periodicals contained articles about Muslim units serving in the French Army from Napoleon's conquest of Egypt until the Algerian conflict; the precolonial architecture of Jewish and Muslim dwellings in the remote M'zab region of the Sahara; and the Faculty of Medicine and Pharmacy at the University of Algiers, founded in 1859.[41] On the 40th anniversary of the flight from Algeria in 1962, another magazine addressed similar themes: the colonial village (in this case Bordj-Bou-Arreridj); the rural settler family (one living in the forest of Baïnem, near Bouzaréah); and the folkways of the *pieds noirs* (specifically the *fouguerra*, a neighborhood celebration in Oran). Illustrations accompany articles: historical photos of homes, forests, towns, landscapes, and artifacts; or paintings of these subjects in Academic, Orientalist, or Impressionist style. The colonial past feeds a curiosity eccentric and learned, yet averse to the grievances of Muslims or analysis of the colony's sociopolitical structure. Apart from cherishing the folkways of Muslim, Jew, and Christian, *L'Algérianiste* dwells on feats in the agriculture, engineering, technology, medicine, and public works of French Algeria. Presumably, this reassures a people others have treated as filthy colonizers. It proves their presence in North Africa did more good than harm. Reading minutiae about colonial railways, tramways, dams, ports, and hospitals gives reason not to feel humiliated.[42]

Keeping collective victimhood alive, *L'Algérianiste* devotes much of one issue to *pied noir* accounts of 1962: the flight from the colony, crossing of the Mediterranean, arrival in the metropole, and struggle with unforeseen difficulties. A book excerpt says the metropolitans treated the *pieds noirs* as "undesirables, people who were not true compatriots, most of whom fully deserved their fate."[43] In the same tone, an editorial from the president of the Cercle algérianiste recalls the European victims of the Oran and Rue d'Isly massacres:

> Thanks to their example, the *pieds noirs*, in their struggle for justice and truth, have adopted the maxim of Charette, the commander-in-chief of the armies of the Vendée: "Always opposed; often defeated; never extinguished." Yes, the martyrs of March 26th as well as those of July 5th are indisputably the anchors of our scarred community.[44]

At stake, he adds, is national reconciliation. Until France identifies those responsible for these crimes, the *pieds noirs* cannot forgive and forget.[45]

Pieds Noirs d'Hier et d'Aujourd'hui has hinted that its readers should support the far right; otherwise, this monthly devotes little space to partisan politics. Like *L'Algérianiste*, instead it deals with the history and geography of the colony, the Orientalist school of painting, and Christian and Jewish traditions. It publishes amateur poetry by readers, recipes from the cross-cultural cuisine of French Algeria, old photos of sports teams and public schools in the colony, and biographies of noteworthy *pieds noirs* of yesterday and today.[46] Still, sometimes its cultural commentary becomes acrid. The Cannes Film Festival reflects the decadence of contemporary France, one columnist writes. After attacking the distortion of history in the movie *Indigène* (and belittling the World War II contribution of Muslim combatants), his article concludes:

> The French government prohibits us from singing Les Africains, and finds specious reasons to prohibit us from laying wreaths at the monuments to our dead. In the *banlieues*, meanwhile, French youths have shown a tendency to celebrate in an unacceptable manner. This film now tells them that their ancestors suffered the worst of ignominies, and France is to blame. To prevent them from setting fire to our cities of France and spilling blood, the government ought to prohibit this perverse, ill-intentioned film of fiction.[47]

In another issue of this publication, a national association president repeats a *pied noir* view of history. French Algeria, she writes, had no place for racism. Jews, Muslims, and Christians lived in harmony. Racism only started in 1962, when the French in the metropole received their compatriots from North Africa with "hostility, incomprehension, hatred, and disgust."[48] *Pieds Noirs d'Hier et d'Aujourd'hui* might accuse a mainstream politician of offending the *pieds noirs*.[49] In addition, articles that exalt the people—as opposed to parties and governments, which usurp power—imply how readers should vote.[50] Still, this is about as far as party politics goes.[51] Evidence of a far-right affinity is slim indeed.

National hebdo, a weekly the National Front launched in 1984, was open to "the different shades of the family of the nationalist right."[52] Initially tagged "The newspaper of Jean-Marie Le Pen" and later "The newspaper of the National Front," by 1988 it no longer depended on the party for funding.[53] This conferred an advantage: if articles revealed too much unseemliness—Holocaust negation, for example—the party could deny responsibility.[54] Along with parallel publications (*Présent, Minute, Rivarol,* and *Le Choc du mois*), *National hebdo* advanced the party's quest for hegemony over the far right.[55] At one National Front congress, indeed, a vast majority (83 percent) of the delegates said they read *National hebdo*—the greatest share of any publication.[56]

In its pages, what visions of politics, history, and society did readers find?

They encountered the heritage of the counter-revolutionary right, including a long view of history that shrinks democracy down to size. France becomes "4,000 years of European culture, 20 centuries of Christianity, 40 monarchs, and two centuries of the Republic."[57] On the light side, an ad for National Front Reserve Vintage proclaims this Burgundy the favorite of King Henry the Fourth. More solemnly, a book review reminds readers that French national consciousness grew out of medieval, monarchical, and Christian roots.[58] These roots are celebrated each year in May, when party supporters rally in Paris to remember Joan of Arc. As Jean-Marie Le Pen once said, "Let's kick the foreigners out of France'—those who will not accept this country as theirs, do not wish to assimilate, and cannot understand the France of Joan of Arc." When her judges asked if she disliked the English, the weekly reminds its readers, Joan of Arc replied, "No, as long as they stay home!"[59]

In the same vein, *National hebdo* prints a positive review of a polemical book about the counter-revolutionary uprising in the Vendée:

> Left-wing republicans as well as Marxists have done everything possible to impose, little by little, their vision of history on French youth. We hear much about the revocation of the Edict of Nantes and the persecution of the Huguenots by the dragoons of Louis XIV, but a polite silence surrounds the Vendée. People condemn the massacre of the Jews by Hitler, but are silent about the Cristeros, Biafra, or Lebanon. We should take this seriously. An analysis of the genocide in the Vendée is of fundamental importance because it shatters two particularly terrible taboos: the history of the Revolution, and that of genocide. With the patience of an ant, Reynald Sécher establishes both the extent of the killings and the will to eliminate a people, to clear a region from the map. This will was steady, official, and justified by ideology: we have here the very definition of genocide. In this respect, the Revolutionaries went further than the Nazis, who for their part always

refused to state clearly the meaning of the Final Solution. We may add, of course, that these massacres took place in the name of the grand ideals of 1789. This discredits the founding myths of left-wing thought and it should trouble those who are the unconditional worshippers of human rights.[60]

An article about Generalissimo Francisco Franco and José Antonio Primo de Rivera (founder of the Falange Party) contrasts their class and panache with the outrages that Republicans committed against the Church during the Spanish Civil War.[61] A besieged Catholicism must find the means to resist. An article on Catholic fundamentalism denounces French bishops as "christomarxists" and approves of a recent group pilgrimage to Chartres in support of the Christians in Lebanon.[62]

National hebdo keeps alive the anti-Semitism that seeped into politics during the Third Republic. One columnist's list of essential readings includes a book by Édouard Drumont, author of *La France juive* (1886).[63] The Russian Revolution, an editor writes, fit into a plan of international control: Jewish banks supported Russian Bolshevism (itself heavily Jewish) "to make even the most powerful states think twice, back away, or give in."[64] *National hebdo* refers admiringly to the works of Robert Faurisson, a former professor whose revisionism doubts that Anne Frank wrote her *Diary*; denies that gas chambers operated in Nazi concentration camps; and absolves Hitler of direct responsibility for the Final Solution.[65] When the National Front underperformed in an election, *National hebdo* printed a fussy cartoon in which a pivoted barrier blocks entry into the National Assembly. This barrier, it turns out, consists of an absurdly elongated nose attached to the head of President Chirac. Behind the pivot on which this nose-barrier swings is a big counterweight with "Weight of B'nai B'rith" written on its side.[66] Elsewhere, allusions to a powerful Jewish lobby uphold the older, counter-revolutionary obsession with an anti-French conspiracy led by secret groups like the Freemasons.

Combined with the vilification of pluralism, parties, and Parliament, the worship of Le Pen recalls Bonapartism.[67] Yet *National hebdo* mentions neither Napoleon Bonaparte (a product of the Revolution, after all) nor his nephew, Louis-Napoleon (an emperor, yes, but illegitimate from the royalist point of view). Articles against the taxman come straight out of Poujadism but without mentioning Poujade.[68] Nor does *National hebdo* give much attention to others in the far-right galaxy (such as Georges Boulanger, Henri Rochefort, Maurice Barrès, Charles Maurras, Georges Valois, Pierre Drieu La Rochelle, and François de La Rocque). This discretion about people, parties, and movements associated with the far-right tradition makes two exceptions stand out.

National hebdo defends Marshall Pétain and those who rallied to the Vichy regime. From its point of view, Pétain in Vichy—not De Gaulle in London—represented continuity with the nation's past. Pétain was a benevolent protector, a shield who saved a defeated France from pointless suffering.[69] The newspaper transmits the mythic image of a leader followed and trusted because he incarnated the nation: France and Pétain were one.[70] Another article reminds readers that even François Mitterrand served in Pétain's civil service.[71] The postwar purges, in turn, spread injustice: "All around there was talk about liberation, about resistance to the occupier, about pulling out the roots of Nazism, about universal fraternity in a world of mutual trust, but fear reigned over all."[72] In courts after the liberation, writes *National hebdo*, former collaborators judged others for collaborating with the enemy. Meanwhile, the Communists claimed a monopoly over patriotism:

> Sending their hatred and false witnesses in pursuit of those who had escaped the summary executions, purge committees, people's tribunals, and other profitable forms of blackmail, they began accusing the Americans, the English, and even De Gaulle himself of being more or less the accomplices of Hitler.[73]

The veterans of Vichy agree that De Gaulle and the Allies served evil. Not because they were the accomplices of Hitler, but because they refused to join Germany in crushing the real enemy: Stalinism.[74]

To a greater degree than Vichy or the postwar purges, however, *National hebdo* dwelt on the collapse of the French empire.[75] Here is its portrait of the party leader:

> In the beginning, Le Pen was an imperialist. He believed in a France of empire, a France across the seas—a France of Africa, a France of Asia, a France of America, a France of the antipodes, in pink on world maps. His perspective did not permit racism. For him, just as yesterday's France could not play a major role without its Empire, today's France cannot play one without Europe.[76]

Among the pivotal developments in French history after 1945, the newspaper selects the battle of Dien Bien Phu. Seen in retrospect, it elicits a mixed reaction: admiration for the patriotism and courage of the French parachutists and legionnaires, who were isolated and outnumbered; resentment toward the United States, which could have provided air support; and bitterness over the loss of French lives and grandeur.[77]

Dien Bien Phu prefigures French Algeria: again, *National hebdo* celebrates the valor of those who fought for the empire. Against dominant opinion, which holds that the soldiers and officers who backed the failed putsch in Algeria (1961) dishonored themselves, the reviewer of a book about a parachute unit that joined in the insubordination praises these elite fighters, who had shown courage and combat spirit. He adds that gathering testimonies among those left "wounded and broken" by "the events in Algeria" would not have made this an easy book to write.[78] The author of another book with a flattering review in *National hebdo* is a veteran of the Indochinese and Algerian Wars who joined the 1961 putsch and ran OAS operations in the metropole. Now he was a National Front deputy in the National Assembly. His book on the history of the OAS is eye-opening, a reviewer asserts, because its members risked their life for the honor of France. With the defeat of the OAS, France succumbed to a new system of betrayal and repression. Many in this country failed to see this at the time, and many still have not.[79] Similarly, *National hebdo* ran admiring articles about figures who stood by the *pieds noirs*, even at the price of their professional career, personal freedom, or very survival.[80] It also printed denunciations of De Gaulle, his regime, and his followers.[81]

To keep the dust off its framing of history, *National hebdo* applied it to current affairs. An article that condemns the bigotry suffered by the son of a *harki* who wanted to volunteer as a firefighter in the Var praises men like his father, who made sacrifices for the French in Algeria; this article chastises anti-racists for not coming to the son's defense.[82] Elsewhere, a supporter of French Algeria says the idea of nationalism had made him enthusiastic about Israeli statehood. After a visit to Gaza disabused him, a new parallel came to mind:

> Before I had been indifferent to the tragedy of the Palestinians. Were they not being chased from their own land? What about the *pieds noirs*? Were they not chased from the land they had conquered and enriched through their work, willpower, and wisdom, and by establishing (especially in the interior) rich and adaptable human relations with the Arab and the Kabyle? Yet, who in the Muslim world (to which they had contributed so much) or in our own world (to which they had also contributed so much) came to their aid? Nobody. I have no tears left to shed for the Israelis.[83]

After deploring the plight of a people robbed of its own land, the article ends with a cheap shot. The Israeli Army, this columnist writes, is using gas against its enemies, just as Adolf Hitler did.[84]

To explain the rise in working-class support for the far right, again *National hebdo* relies on French Algeria. Due to immigration and deindustrialization, the newspaper says, workers are losing their jobs and class-consciousness. Wanting a better future, they are deserting the Communists and Socialists for the National Front. This recalls a precedent:

Bab El Oued and Oran were both bastions of French Algerian resistance. One was a working-class neighborhood, the other a large working-class city. Very often their inhabitants who took up arms were of foreign origin: Spaniards, Italians. Some were veterans of the International Brigades. In Algeria, when their back was up against the wall, their only recourse was the Nation.[85]

When French workers are on the defensive, in sum, national identity overrides class politics. Another article used French Algeria to defend the party in 1990, when the profanation of a Jewish cemetery in Carpentras provoked disgust across the country. Eventually the police arrested most of the perpetrators, young men associated with neo-Nazi groups. At the time of their crime, though, accusations of the National Front burst forth. To shift suspicion, a journalist from *National hebdo* reacted with an insinuating question: Who in Algeria had been responsible, he asked readers, for the profanation in 1962 of thousands of Jewish and Christian tombs?[86]

National hebdo did not frame all current affairs through the lens of empire, obviously. Its treatment of the First Gulf War (1990–1991)—when Le Pen argued for French non-intervention against Iraq—avoided parallels with French Algeria. Yet French Algeria remained central. Jean-Pierre Stirbois spearheaded the rise of the National Front in Dreux and for seven years served as Le Pen's lieutenant. When he died in 1988, an old friend composed his eulogy for *National hebdo*. It mentions the battle of Dien Bien Phu, the 1956 Soviet repression in Budapest, and the loss of French Algeria as shared sources of their anti-communism and frustration with the decline of France. "Ever since our adolescence," the eulogy says, "Jean-Pierre and I each had the same photo in our wallet, right next to our heart: that of Jean-Marie Bastien-Thiry."[87] Nostalgia for French Algeria and admiration for those who fought for empire provided the party's different families with a rallying point.[88]

BACK-STAGE DISCOURSE OF THE *PIEDS NOIRS*

During the summer and winter of 2002, I interviewed two dozen *pieds noirs* living in the Toulon area. Equal numbers of men and women participated, all of whom treated me with courtesy as we sat and talked in their living or dining room. After offering refreshments, they would patiently answer my questions. My Québécois background seemed to help. Like them, some reminded me, I come from a land conquered and colonized by France.[89] When I probed their past, some would break down and weep. When I pressed for details, all would elaborate on matters an outsider might miss or dislike. I needed the words of these people, so did not want them to clam up. One couple told me that during the 1960s, the *pieds noirs* received a worse welcome in Marseille than in Toulon, where the Arreckx administration gave them public housing. "Unfortunately," added the husband, "today it's occupied by North Africans."[90] I could have asked what this meant. Did North Africans not treat public housing with proper respect? Did they not deserve, or appreciate, what had been good enough for the *pieds noirs* in the 1960s? At moments like this, I backed off.

In that year's elections, Monsieur Jobert had cast blank ballots. Politicians played games that exasperated him. This he had seen with De Gaulle: "When it came to Algeria, he lied to us from the very start. He said that Algeria was French and would remain French, yet he knew very well that he would let it go."[91] I asked if other politicians were worse:

> Oh, I put them all in the same basket! Because Communists and Trotskyists, Communists and Socialists, they all helped the FLN. You can't forget that. I knew somebody who passed away not too long ago, a lieutenant in the 4th *Wilaya* [province]. A Frenchman, an Alsatian. He was involved in the murders, the deaths, of 17 *Français d'Algérie* from the village where I lived. He was a union man, a member of the CGT [the communist trade union], so now do you see what I mean?[92]

Listening to Monsieur Riba made it hard to tell who was worse, Gaullists or Communists:

> In Algeria, soldiers who were communist would steal their platoon's weapons and give them to the Arabs. That's what made us anti-communist. There was no way we could be Gaullists. Quite frankly the only one on our side was Le Pen. And since we don't really know much about politics, we vote for Le Pen.[93]

Le Pen had lost the presidential run-off in 2002 to Jacques Chirac. Madame Eugène recalled that Chirac had volunteered to fight in Algeria.[94] Monsieur Moreno showed indulgence:

> He's a Gaullist, okay, but when we lived in Algeria we had no political sense. We had a sense of work. We had a sense of family. We had a sense of patriotism. But we had no political sense. And that's what hurt us. Today, forty years later, a sense of politics is starting to come to us. So that's why even if De Gaulle is the father of Chirac, we realize that at a certain point you have to choose sides. So it's not that Chirac gets our blatant support. But when you're dealing with the cholera and the plague, you choose the lesser of two evils. You choose.[95]

Trying to make me understand, next he asked, "Have you ever heard about troops from a Nazi division, *Das Reich*, who stopped at Oradour-sur-Glane?"

Me: Yes, I have.
Monsieur Moreno:

> How can expect someone who suffered from the massacre that was committed at Oradour-sur-Glane to forgive those people? How can you expect them to say, "Okay, Hitler was a nice person?" Well, we aren't able to say that De Gaulle was a nice person, above all because he knew perfectly well that in the end his solution would be to let Algeria go. Abandoning Algeria was his very clear intention. Out of a kind of racism, he hated the idea of France becoming a Muslim country. Setting aside whatever he believed, that man incited people like the *harkis*, the Europeans, or the young soldiers from the metropole, to engage in activities that some paid for with their life.

Madame Eugène agreed:

> All for nothing. De Gaulle was paranoid. And what's paradoxical is that he was Catholic, you know. He has people shot, which is what he had done in Algeria, and he goes to mass every Sunday, and takes Communion—I could never get over that. When he had the referendum on Algeria—the one to find out if Algeria would be French or Muslim—the French were not allowed to vote. Only the Muslims could vote.[96]

For Monsieur Davin, though, Chirac's military service does not count:

> Plenty of people in French politics never served France like Le Pen did. He did his military service, not for long, okay, but he went to the *djebel* [mountainous regions] of Algeria and he went to Indochina. Ask certain bigshots in French politics what they did. You won't get much of an answer. Right after they were drafted, maybe they stuck their ass in some office chair in some staff headquarters. What really grabs my attention are those who got involved, who fought, who did something for France, who really did, so France could defend its prestige. I'm a nationalist, that's what I am, what can you do? And in the National Front there are plenty of people like me, right, because it's a mix. It doesn't even matter if their name is Spanish or Italian, plenty of them are more French than the *français de France*.[97]

Monsieur Davin tells me that *pieds noirs* who vote for Chirac are confused. In Algeria, he says, charisma and interests—not the left/right opposition—shaped how Europeans made choices in politics. The same with De Gaulle:

> Among those who loved De Gaulle, well, there were French people who loved Pétain. So let me tell you something about De Gaulle. People say he was the first member of the French Resistance. No, the people who resisted were in France, the people who resisted were not over there, in London, you know. They weren't in danger over there, they talked,

they talked, they didn't take any risks. What about those poor guys who got parachuted in, who came here, who put networks together, right, and then they were shot or sent to concentration camps, now there you have the Resistance. Not like the people in London. Let's just say that's an aspect of De Gaulle that does not make me exactly adore him. I'm telling you, the French have a very short memory. Besides, a long time ago in one of his speeches De Gaulle said the French are like calves, the trick is to know how to lead them.[98]

Le Pen's enemies have tried to discredit him by labelling him a Nazi. He has made their job easier by insulting Jews and minimizing the Holocaust. No far-right supporter with whom I spoke agreed with this part of his rhetoric.

MADAME RUBIO: To me, he stands for France. I mean, he's a patriot above all. At times he may be extreme, you know, but I believe in him, I don't know, I think he'd change many things—and we need changes.
MONSIEUR RUBIO: You know, I think he'd be better off if he made himself a bit more moderate.
MADAME RUBIO: A bit more moderate, yes, sometimes he goes a little too far.
ME: You mean when he said "*Durafour-Crématoire*," for example?
MONSIEUR RUBIO: That's it, that's it. In the end, people were right, those aren't the kind of things . . . but okay, people sure made a big deal out of it, huh? He should have been more careful there, because French people are proper, they don't really like that stuff. I'll tell you honestly, I did not appreciate what he said. But Le Pen's general approach is something else, he speaks the truth.[99]

Madame Davin and her husband bring friends to Le Pen rallies, yet she too feels he can go overboard:

My only criticism of Le Pen is that once in a while he slips into language that's a bit harsh, you know. He's a real speaker. He gives fine speeches. But sometimes he lets his eloquence get the best of him.[100]

Monsieur and Madame Rubio insist that Nazism came from Germany and belongs in the past.

MONSIEUR RUBIO: With Hitler, with the Nazis, the country was in the hands of the military.
MADAME RUBIO: I really have to say that if Le Pen really were a Nazi, then we wouldn't vote for him. Don't forget that, all else aside, in Algeria we suffered during World War II. We can't stand Nazism.[101]

Still, one should stick by the people who defended French Algeria:

> Deep down in my heart, I am really on the right. Okay, today that means Le Pen, but there's more to it than that. Previously in France there was Tixier-Vignancour in 1965. That was the only time I ever joined a party. I was quite young, and I campaigned for Tixier-Vignancour because I saw him as someone who had always defended my country. He had defended certain people, people who were on the same side, like Maître Isorni. The military had plenty of people who sacrificed their career for their ideals. They stood by us even when they didn't have to, they could have had terrific careers and they paid a price for what they did. So, in my heart I have always remained loyal to this way of seeing things. I believe that if a man like Tixier-Vignancour were around today, he would have been President of the Republic. He was such a speaker. Oh! He was exceptional! So there you have it, seeing things the way I do, I vote for the right, I vote for Le Pen.[102]

Madame Rigal sees no contradiction between democracy and voting for the far right.

> Oh yes, I always vote, I always vote unless I'm sick, but I avoid abstaining, you know. We—not me, but women—had to fight very hard to get the right to vote. Just think, it only came in '45 or '46, it took a world war, you know, and I think it only came into effect in 1947.[103]

When I remarked that female suffrage came to France relatively late, she expressed disbelief. Women fought hard for the right to vote, and this means they should vote—even by casting a blank ballot. Non-voters, she says, have no right to complain.[104]

I asked everyone if they believed that humanity consists of races with different capacities. National Front supporters replied that differences between people have non-biological causes. Madame Pochard: "It depends on their exposure to civilization. Some are not less talented, they just received less education."[105] Madame Romieu voted for Le Pen, she reminded me, but disliked his lapses into racial prejudice. Maybe he only said these things to attract attention, but for her:

> It's obvious a child who is born in Brazil will not have similar opportunities, unfortunately. But if you give them an education, if you give them the same chance, well, great. Some children are smarter than others, but it's like that everywhere, if they could start early, if all children in the world had the same base.... The way I see things, we are all very similar. Definitely it's the way you are brought up, your education, where you live, all that. It's society that molds you, it's society that makes the difference.[106]

Monsieur Davin said some races are more capable, but his logic was convoluted:

> Me, *négritude* [black consciousness] and all that, I think those people on the African continent depend on help from others. Things will never change, because others are above them and they're right at the bottom. Their families are run by their leaders, not by great people, so the people always get help. They really are not advancing. See? But the Asian races, I think them, yes. Okay, the Japanese are falling back a bit. But look at the Koreans who we hardly even knew before, and you have to admit their industries are doing pretty well. You can see they really are smart, because on one side there's North Korea where people are starving, then there's South Korea where people are not exactly living in luxury but still doing alright. I'm just telling you how I see things. There's no point beating around the bush.[107]

Like other National Front supporters with whom I spoke, in the end Monsieur Davin agrees that environment makes the difference. He ranks societies—not races—when comparing people by ability. Race does not fully explain character and moral worth either. I asked a couple and their friend if they enjoyed good relations with Muslims.

MADAME RIBA: It depends on which ones, right, not the ones in the projects.
MADAME RIZZA: You know, there's a difference between those who are really proper...
MADAME RIBA: — who behave the right way —
MADAME RIZZA: ... who behave completely decently and all that, obviously. What matters is not if they're Arabs or Muslims. Some really want to think they really are French, they want rights and justice, and then there are the ones who act like idiots.[108]

Signs of status insecurity popped up. Madame Eugène told me that in 1962, when she stayed with distant relatives in Alsace, they were surprised to find that she could play their card games.[109] Returning to the present, she discussed the minister of the interior's policy of chartering planes to extradite refugees:

> Sarkozy is not getting to the root of the problem. What he's doing is fine, it's right, but essentially the problem is that our European countries are too attractive. They've just arrived here, and they get family allowance, when their children are born on French soil, right away they're French, right, even when they have a bit of work they get a minimum subsistence income, they get social workers, they're allowed to have more than one wife,

The Far Right Endures [149]

they have nineteen children, and all that, it's attractive. And on top of everything else the European Union makes it impossible to do anything, right, we can't send back illegal immigrants. We can't even send back those on welfare. So it would not surprise me if the dam bursts again, next time maybe not with the National Front, no, but it would not surprise me. Politicians don't know what's going on. They don't see what's going on every day. So elections are safety valves, know what I mean? They give people a chance to let off steam. You get to speak up, you get to protest, you get to fill in your ballot—there you have it. Look, there are no more racists in France than in other countries. Actually, it's the opposite. At the gym where I work out, if you talk to the other members, you'll find out racism is not just about skin color.[110]

When I asked if this is because the French were racist toward the *pieds noirs*, Madame Eugène laughs:

I am not black, not gray, so racism is not necessarily about skin color. Just look at Austria, they had Haider, right, three years have gone by and we haven't heard anything about him. He's gone, and the funny thing is they couldn't change things. What really scares us are these waves of foreigners. Opening up so Turkey can enter the European Union, can you imagine? We've got to keep our identity, what's wrong with that? Look, everyone coming here has only one goal. They're like us when we came here. They want their family back together again, the place they came from, their culture, their religion. Fine, okay, but you tell me, what are we supposed to do when they don't integrate?[111]

A controversy was swirling around General Paul Aussaresses, who admitted to permitting torture during the Battle of Algiers. Aussaresses defended himself as a patriot who accepted full responsibility for his acts. His political masters had not intervened, he added, even though they knew about his methods. My interviewees sided with Aussaresses. In a moment of self-revelation, though, Monsieur Bertou admitted that in French Algeria a feeling of hatred toward Muslims had made him welcome the use of torture.[112] When I asked Monsieur Riba about General Aussaresses, he wondered how many metropolitans ever paused to consider the many *pieds noirs* whom the Algerians had tortured and killed. From this example of unfair treatment, he went straight on to another. Recently the media had overlooked a *pied noir* rally in Paris, but "when a hundred Arabs do the same thing, it's all over the TV."[113]

Yesterday as well as today, *pieds noirs* have often noticed—or been reminded of—their difference from metropolitans. This makes them akin to true immigrants, oddly, for their non-metropolitan identity jars with a republican ideology of unhyphenated assimilation.[114] Speculating, we can imagine that being French, but not like the others, drives a compensatory nativism and hyper-patriotism. If self-worth relies so much on membership in the national community, then intercultural contact, hybridity, and equality become threatening. Without knowing the answer, I wonder if this kind of status insecurity might also make the far right more attractive among French voters of Belgian, Italian, Portuguese, or Spanish descent.

THE AFFINITY BETWEEN THE FAR RIGHT AND THE *PIEDS NOIRS*

Except for a shared hostility toward Gaullism, the front-stage discourses of the National Front and the *pieds noirs* offer little clue of an affinity. Public statements by the party pass in silence over the folkways, Orientalism, and collective memory of the *pieds noirs*. The *pied noir* press, which tends toward nonpartisanship, avoids the National Front's platform. Clues of an affinity emerge more clearly in interviews with the *pieds noirs*. They never mention the party's economic program but many share its nativism, populism, anti-communism, and suspicion of Islam. In an imaginary conversation between a far-right activist and a *pied noir*, they would agree that the Fifth Republic had betrayed French Algeria. The Europeans of Algeria paid too dearly for their patriotism. The fate of the *harkis* was shameful, a stain on the honor of France; the place of Islam and Arabs in the West is another matter altogether. The conversation might turn to military men and OAS members who fought the Gaullist regime: all virtuous heroes, not traitorous outlaws. The French defeat at Dien Bien Phu was a warning. It should have hardened the country's resolve. Instead, thanks to De Gaulle and the Communists, France missed a chance to arrest its historical decline. Words exorcise hurts with roots in the fight for French Algeria.

Just as important are topics a tactful far-right activist might avoid in this conversation. Many *pieds noirs* lack enthusiasm toward the Fifth Republic, but this does not make them anti-republicans. They are not monarchists. They seem as remote as most French from the counterrevolutionaries' mistrust of 1789 or Catholic traditionalists' concerns with religious dogma, institutions, and practice. Pétain gets credit as De Gaulle's rival during the World War II, but *pieds noirs* identify with the Resistance. Most admire the colonial troops who fought alongside the Allies. In our conversations, anti-Semitism, admiration for the Waffen-SS, or sympathy toward Nazism never showed.[115] Though significant, therefore, the elective affinity between *pieds noirs* and far right does not amount to a fusion.[116] The *pieds noirs* seem oblivious to much of the far-right tradition on which the National Front draws. The counterrevolution, Boulangism, opposition to Dreyfus, the leagues of Maurras, the interwar fascists, Vichy, and the postwar purges: these hardly seem to belong in the mental landscape of the *pieds noirs*. Empire and decolonization afford the common terrain.

CHAPTER 10

Transmitting a Far-Right Affinity

While some milieus dampen far-right support, others sustain it. In the 2012 presidential election, in most of France the level of Le Pen support among *pieds noirs* equaled that for other voters. With its greater density of *pieds noirs*, by contrast, the south provided a better environment for their far-right potential: support for Le Pen nearly doubled among *pieds noirs* who lived in Languedoc-Roussillon or Provence-Alpes-Côte d'Azur.[1] Without a *pied noir* community of sufficient density, the foregoing suggests, the aggregate electoral choices of *pieds noirs* lack distinctiveness. This chapter explores the effect on far-right support of belonging to a particular type of milieu that, as we have seen, sustained *pied noir* community: the voluntary association, whose relation to politics fascinated Alexis de Tocqueville.

Worried about the atomization of society after the feudal status group, extended intergenerational family, and paternalistic relations between upper and lower orders lost their integrative force, the author of *Democracy in America* praised the voluntary associations he discovered during his 1831 trip to the United Sates. The population of European stock in America, he wrote, was no less selfish than were the French. Yet a zeal for self-interest properly understood set them apart. Voluntary association fostered a kind of enlightened egoism. Rich or poor, Americans obeyed the dictum that one serves oneself well by behaving morally and serving others.[2] In France, the government undertook public projects; in England, the holders of great estates took the initiative. In the United States, similarly, associations made up for the weakness of isolated individuals: people "of all ages, all stations of life, and all types of disposition are forever forming associations."[3] Apart from combating personal selfishness and social atomization, the American propensity toward association set limits on political tyranny. Voluntary association therefore offered modern democracies a powerful means of curtailing the state.[4]

Later political philosophers and social scientists have joined Tocqueville in lauding voluntary associations. They believe associations engage citizens in joint action that produces collective goods. Associations help maintain a robust citizenry, a civil society not under the tutelage of the state. A related argument holds that associational life fosters democratic political sentiments and participation: associations are schools for democracy. This chapter has two aims, then. Asking if associations in France and Toulon breed autonomy from the state, first it shows that official funding and unofficial patronage can create ties of dependency to parties, politicians, and government. Asking if membership in associations promotes liberal politics, in addition this chapter shows the reverse is possible. Some associations provide a social setting that boosts support for the far right.

ASSOCIATION FUNDING AND PATRONAGE IN TOULON

Despite the Third Republic's initial mistrust of intermediate bodies between citizen and state, mutual aid societies as well as religious and professional confraternities survived in Toulon until the late nineteenth century. By the early twentieth century, when cultural associations of various kinds (scientific, musical, or historical, for example) had started to form, thousands of workers belonged to the city's trade unions.[5] Later, in the 1960s, mobilization on behalf of the *pieds noirs* belied the image of a society of nonjoiners. The Boy Scouts; the Federation of Hoteliers; the Junior Chamber of Commerce; a veterans' association; and Jewish, Protestant, and Catholic charities joined the trade unions and the city to welcome, feed, and guide the refugees as they arrived by ship from Algeria. They also coordinated the teams of volunteers who solicited donations or helped the *pieds noirs* in their quest for housing and work. Today, similarly, the city supports dozens of associations. Many devote themselves to culture: dance, folklore, film, music, choral song, visual arts, historical preservation, cultural festivals, foreign languages, and so on. Others bring together the practitioners of a wide variety of sports. A handful work for animal protection, foreign aid, suicide protection, or civil safety.[6] Tocqueville would be pleased.

Looking some more, though, associations' lack of autonomy would bother him. State funding for associations is a French norm that extends from municipal to national institutions, with every level of government involved. Some things have changed. After President Macron's fledgling party won the 2017 elections and gained control over the National Assembly, it passed a bill that abolished the parliamentary reserve: a sum from the state for a deputy or senator to donate, at their discretion, to associations or public entities. Customarily—but not always—the recipient would be in the politician's district. In 2015, for example, one of Toulon's moderate-right deputies had sprinkled her parliamentary reserve (€130,000) among 55 of the city's cultural, sports, and charitable associations.[7] Decades old, this practice enjoyed a cross-partisan consensus. Before the parliamentary vote to abolish the reserve in 2017, even a deputy from the National Front spoke against the change. Before entering the National Assembly, he said, like other people he had objected to the reserve. After becoming a deputy, however, "I told myself that I had been an idiot to believe in these prejudices, because the parliamentary reserve makes it possible to bring help where it was missing."[8] Illustrating the cross-party consensus, a deputy from the left also argued against the bill (in cities run by the National Front, like Toulon, the parliamentary reserve had ensured the survival of associations that lost funding). Although the National Assembly passed the bill, state funding for associations still persists in France.[9]

Opponents of the parliamentary reserve had cited concerns about political corruption and patronage. Between 1998 and 2004, when a Socialist was serving his first term as president of the PACA region, for example, the amount of funding that his council approved tripled. In 2007, moreover, his region approved 86 percent of the 24,000 funding requests it received from associations.[10] In 2016, the Court of Cassation found a former vice-president of his regional council guilty of channeling some €700,000 in public funds to fictitious associations. In a quid pro quo arrangement, between 2005 and 2007 the beneficiaries of her largesse were to reciprocate by contributing to her re-election The Court declared the accused—a Socialist from Marseille—guilty of misappropriating public funds. She received a fine of €100,000, a suspended sentence of one year in prison, and five years' ineligibility for public office.[11]

Association funding is thus a fixture of politics in Toulon. In 1975, the city council budgeted 1.4 million francs in funding for seven groups that organized cultural events; another 1.2 million francs for 114 amateur and professional sports clubs; 515,250 francs for 102 youth groups; and 159,500 for 133 charitable and social groups.[12] The practice remains entrenched. In 2017, the city provided 137 associations with over €1.4 million in total funding. The smallest grant (€300) went to a riding club, the biggest (€505,452, over one-third of the total) to the Festival and Sports Commission, which organizes a jazz and blues festival. The city sprinkled grants between €1,000 and €10,000 among more than 100 other associations.[13] Whether the sum was small or large, association funding undercut the arms-length relationship between government and civil society.

For a Tocquevillean, patron-client relations of this kind run counter to the sort of civic community expected when citizens become active in voluntary associations.[14] In Toulon, as we have seen, the *pied noir* associations entered into the Arreckx system of favors. As their go-between with Paris, Arreckx advanced their cause by lobbying. Playing along with influence peddling upheld a system of municipal administration less responsive to those without the right connections. Grants listed in the city budget and free use of city property were public forms of patronage in favor of the *pieds noirs*. Another consisted of a donation to an association's campaign to help elderly repatriates.[15] Other exchanges took place at a greater remove from public scrutiny. When the repatriates mounted festivities, meetings, or sports activities, the city waived its rental fee or tax on public events.[16] The 30,000 francs that Mayor Arreckx secured for an association of repatriates before one election far exceeded any amount it had ever requested.[17] Some two decades later, when membership in this association was dwindling due to death and old age, its president decided to spend the remainder of Arreckx's donation on a banquet.[18] No longer able to give Arreckx their vote, perhaps they still remembered their former patron with indulgence.

Corruption and patronage wafted around association funding after Arreckx's exit from politics. During the 1995 mayoral campaign, when his scandals tarnished his protégé, Mayor Trucy, mismanagement and overspending by public works associations were the problem. Opponents decried a lack of oversight under the Trucy administration. The Socialists promised to "eliminate, as soon as we enter city hall, these associations. A high degree of patronage is rife in these associations, which need to be cleaned up."[19] During the same campaign, associations that provided social services for ethno-racial minorities—such as an agency that helped youths in poorer neighborhoods with job qualifications and employment searches—feared a change at city hall:

> Obviously, most of our clients are of North African origin, and under a National Front administration we could suffer indirectly and see our longer-term survival threatened. In the event they tried to make us disappear, though, how could they avoid the social explosion that is bound to happen once this associative network disappears?[20]

After the National Front took office, it strove to reduce the city's deficit, yet its 1998 budget allocated 67 million francs to associations. At 3.7 percent of the total budget, this represented five times more than the city spent on meals in schools and not much less than the service on its debt (4.9 percent).[21]

When Falco became mayor, he cut off funding to Fraternité française, a charity affiliated with the National Front and previously favored by the

Le Chevallier administration.[22] During the next 12 years, on the other hand, the city's funding to associations increased by more than €3 million, reaching €7.4 million in 2013.[23] For some associations, moreover, the city paid the salaries of personnel. Under 180 agreements with associations, the city made property, offices, meeting rooms, and other facilities available for a nominal fee or even without cost. An outside audit found scarce tracking of this support, with annual association reports either incomplete or missing.[24] Yet a Communist criticized the city for not giving its associations even more money. All expected municipal generosity toward associations.[25]

If one examines past city budgets, funding for repatriates' associations pales by comparison with many others. In 1970, the city gave 2,500 francs to a group lobbying Paris for a compensation law for property lost in Algeria. Hundreds of other groups (such as the Federation of Pétanque and Provencal Sports, the Family Planning Association, the Little Sisters of the Poor, the Girl and Boy Scouts Association of France, and the Association for Handicapped Youths) also received grants—some as much as 5,000 francs or more.[26] By the late 1970s, the repatriates of Toulon had formed two dozen associations.[27] Through this decade and the next, city budgets show that only two received grants.[28] In 1976, for example, the Var branch of the FNR received 250 francs from the city—not much considering that 350 other associations (from charities and cultural associations to veterans' groups and sports clubs) received grants between a hundred francs and tens of thousands of francs.[29]

Through other channels, still, patronage did reach the repatriates. The city bought an abandoned barracks and turned it into the headquarters for their associations (the Maison du Rapatrié). This converted building also held offices and meeting rooms for the Scouts, the Catholic Relief Service, the Force Ouvrière trade union, and a folklore group, the Ambassade de Provence.[30] When the city founded the Maison du Rapatrié, in fact, it owned no fewer than 34 buildings occupied by associations.[31] Although Arreckx created the Maison du Rapatrié to advance his career (by binding the *pieds noirs* to himself and the party he had just joined, the UDF of Giscard), his successors continued this cozy arrangement. In 1986, the city council allocated 230,000 francs for renovations to the Maison du Rapatrié.[32] The Trucy administration renewed a lease that gave the repatriates the cost-free use of their headquarters for another decade.[33] These decisions received unanimous support from the city council, and after the National Front took over it upheld them.[34] In 1997, National Front councilors approved a grant of 350,000 francs to an association that planned to mark the 35th anniversary of the repatriates' arrival with a two-day event (later the city provided an additional 115,496 francs to meet the event's deficit).[35] Similar practices have continued since.[36] Critics sometimes disagree about the worthiness of a grant recipient or the amount awarded. From what I have seen, though, nobody in Toulon has ever said that the city should stop giving money or space to associations like repatriate groups. This would bother Alexis de Tocqueville.

THE *PIEDS NOIRS* AND THE NATIONAL ELECTIONS OF 2002, 2007, AND 2012

Every five years, the French elect a president in late spring; a few weeks later, they choose their members of Parliament. Curious about the politics of the *pied noir* population in the Toulon area, I conducted surveys of their voting in the national elections of 2002, 2007, and 2012.[37] I found a robust far-right propensity. *Pied noir* support for a Le Pen (Jean-Marie Le Pen in 2002 and 2007; Marine Le Pen in 2012) reached 50 percent in the 2002 presidential election, 43 percent in 2007, and 45 percent in 2012—twice the levels for Toulon, and two to four times the levels for France.[38] In the three parliamentary elections, likewise, far-right support among the *pieds noirs* reached 32, 34, and 51 percent respectively—two to four times the levels for Toulon, and three to nine times those for France.[39] In weighing these finding, two considerations matter. First, they likely underestimate far-right support among the *pieds noirs*. Keenly aware that many abhor the far right, National Front voters hide their politics from reporters, pollsters, and others who make a living from prying.[40] Second, these findings came after six years of far-right power in Toulon. Despite this eye-opening experience, the far-right vote of the *pieds noirs* remained high.[41]

The single best predictor of far-right voting among the *pieds noirs* was when they agreed with this statement: "Among the races that make up humanity, some races are more talented than others." Past research had used this question to construct an index of ethnocentrism.[42] I found that *pieds noirs* who disagreed with this statement were more likely to vote for the left or the moderate right.

The next best predictor of far-right voting was association membership. Sociologists take as given the interpersonal nature of collective identity. Without ongoing social interaction—regular conversation, common readings, favors exchanged, or joint activities such as meetings and ceremonies—group understandings of "them" and "us" weaken.[43] My interviews provided a few tantalizing hints. One far-right supporter, Madame Eugène, told me that in 1962 some in the metropole did not know that *pieds noirs* were white:

> Now look at things today, you have Africans arriving from Africa, blacks, Ethiopians, whatever, and it's "Come right up." No one even asks them for anything. Listen, last week

the president of our repatriates' association, he tells me, "You really want to hear something?" He has this friend who was taking a plane to go away on holidays. They take one look at his i.d. card that says "Born in Algeria," and they say, "Monsieur, go to the back of the plane and sit with the Algerians." So he says, "But, monsieur, I am French, you know." So they tell him, "No, no, no, born in Algeria, with the Algerians, over there." Last week![44]

Monsieur Ollières voted Socialist, by contrast, and he told me a *pied noir* association would be a deadly bore:

> I left the country at a specific time, when it was at a specific stage. Today, the land I knew is gone. So why would I want to go back to the way things were fifty or sixty years ago? It serves no purpose, absolutely none. Not for me, anyway. If others want to belong to an association, so be it.[45]

Other interviews suggested the link between association membership and partisan choice might be less direct. Monsieur Bertou said his impressions during a return visit to Algeria clashed with his memories: "It was my land, it was still my land, I was not disappointed, but I also found a place that was smaller, streets that were smaller, than I had remembered."[46] This trip made him feel more distant from his *pied noir* association, he told me, yet he voted for the far right. So, did associations provide a setting that sustained a collective affinity for the far right?

My three surveys asked *pied noirs* not only how many associations they belonged to, but also what kind. There were patriotic associations, and there were all the rest. Patriotic meant groups specifically for *pieds noirs* or military veterans. From what I had seen, these held a positive evaluation of empire and colonialism, values much of France dismisses as outmoded, if not suspect. Non-patriotic associations made up the rest that people in Toulon could belong to, such as choir ensembles, seniors' groups, charitable groups, sport clubs, cultural groups, parent-teacher associations, environmental groups, and cross-cultural associations. My hunch was that patriotic associations insulated their members from cross-cutting influences (thus that the *pieds noirs* who belonged to them had less contact with other kinds of people). Talk with roots in colonial Algeria made them feel connected. Hopes, fears, and hurts implanted in Algeria set them apart. Difficulties, resentments, and struggles after migration to the metropole after 1962 give them a stock of shared experience.[47] Consistent with this hunch, *pieds noirs* in patriotic associations turned out to be much more likely to support the far right. *Pieds noirs* outside an association for veterans or ex-colonials—hence, mixing less with people holding an anachronistic view of empire and colonialism—were much less likely to vote for the far right.[48] Beyond a belief in racial differences, in sum, subcultural separation explains far-right support too.

ASSOCIATIONS AND DEMOCRACY

In 1954–1955, American political scientist Edward Banfield and his Italian-speaking wife spent nine months dissecting an agricultural village in the south of Italy.[49] The baseline for their study was the United States as seen by Tocqueville. In a rural town in Utah, writes Banfield, the number and variety of projects freely undertaken by local groups—the Red Cross, the Business and Professional Women's Club, the Future Farmers of America, the Chamber of Commerce—created the impression that public spiritedness was alive and well.[50] The southern Italian village he studied, by contrast, squashed this spirit. It did have one voluntary association: 25 upper-class men whose clubroom provided a space for card games and private conversation. Not even charity could stir the public spirit:

> An order of nuns struggles to maintain an orphanage for little girls in the remains of an ancient monastery, but this is not a local undertaking. The people of Montegrano contribute nothing to the support of it, although the children come from local families. The monastery is crumbling, but none of the many half-employed masons has ever given a day's work to its repair. There is not enough food for the children, but no peasant or landed proprietor has ever given a young pig to the orphanage.[51]

Not feudal remnants, Italian unification, or uneven capitalism explained the problems of this southern Italian village, but an inability to pull together by transcending their narrow, short-term interests for the sake of the public good. Above all, Banfield concluded, these people acted for the sake of their immediate family.[52]

Making the mental trip from Italy to France in the late 1950s and early 1960s requires only a few short steps. The two countries share a Latin and Catholic heritage, after all, and they had the strongest Communist Parties in Western Europe.[53] Postwar observers of French society thus tended to make its associational life seem like that of southern Italy: underdeveloped. The image prevailed of a weak civil society unable to complement the state in promoting the public good.[54] Southern France, however, is not southern Italy. By forming associations and joining in their activities, the people of Toulon have transcended what Tocqueville would have called self-interest improperly understood. Sports, cultural, charitable, and other associations build social networks. In this manner, they counter the disintegrative potential of modern society. Public goods—such as trust—can survive the transition from a hierarchical society to another with more equal opportunity.

Not all voluntary associations confer Tocquevillean benefits, though. Rather than countering tutelage, associations perpetuate the dependency of citizens if they expect governments, parties, or politicians to provide them with funding, facilities, or other favors. The origins of this contemporary form of patron-client relations remain opaque. In some places, it may have roots in older patterns of patronage that linked notable to peasant or artisan. Elsewhere it may have originated in mass party strategy: colonize civil society by tying associations to some mix of partisan newspapers, religious affiliations, grassroots activism, and public hiring. The appeal of patronage to association members not worried about self-interest properly understood seems obvious. Where connections make it easier to deal with a public bureaucracy that is slow, nepotistic, or inefficient, association patronage may belong to a consensus: for help in getting things done, only a fool would not turn to an influential friend.

Still, voluntary associations can discourage the pluralistic tolerance that defines liberalism. Providing an institutional setting for communities that perpetuate a discourse of exclusion, they may direct voters toward—not away from—the far right.[55] For associations to breed tolerance and trust, they must put members in contact with diverse others. Cleavages of class, religion, race, and ethnicity divide societies. Instead of stretching people as they broaden their horizons, associations that recruit on one side of a societal cleavage can reinforce the sense of us against them. Associations must cross cleavages—not reproduce them—if they are to steer members away from the far right.[56] The foregoing assumes members have outlooks amenable to modification. For people with rigid outlooks, contact with diversity may have the opposite effect. Instead of making them reconsider and moderate their opinions, it could make them more entrenched yet.

Membership in patriotic associations insulated the *pieds noirs* of Toulon from contact with people different from themselves. It protected a community of discourse whose shared understandings created an affinity for the far right. When a *pied noir* stayed outside of patriotic associations, their likelihood of supporting the far right weakened. When they belonged to both patriotic and other associations, moreover, the diverging effects did not cancel each other out. Consistent with the idea that social or political rigidity makes people dig in their heels when confronted with views different from their own, *pieds noirs* in both kinds of associations also showed a strong tendency to support the far right.

Enthusiasm about associational life thus requires qualification.[57] During the 1990s, once again, Italy set the stage for claims about voluntary association and the public good. In *Making Democracy Work*, Robert Putnam compared the Italian north with the south. Political institutions in Italy perform better—they are more responsive and more effective—where cooperation for mutual benefit transcends the inequalities of status and power that divide.[58] Like Tocqueville's "self-interest properly understood," civic community places restraints on opportunism and malfeasance. According to this view, norms of trust and generalized reciprocity form a complex with horizontal social networks: these norms do not arise without proper networks, and vice versa. Voluntary associations, the claim goes, belong to the rich fabric of active citizenship and joint action that makes states—as well as markets—more efficient.[59] All this may be true, but only under conditions specified above. Unexpectedly, what we can deduce—given political patronage for associations in Toulon, and higher far-right support among members of some of these associations—is that democratic states can help sustain a milieu receptive to illiberal politics.

CHAPTER 11
Holding Off the National Front

When the far right broke through in the 1980s, its core support came from southern regions that had favored Tixier in 1965; the Parisian area; and zones toward the country's northern and eastern borders. The rural France of farmers, churchgoers, and notables resisted. Since then, we find moderate change in the geography of far-right support. It remains weak where the conservative right has resisted (Britanny, Poitou, Pyrénées, Alps, and Massif Central). Perhaps due to white flight, the big cities (including Paris) now give less support than do the suburbs. The far right is gaining in the countryside, though, and more support now comes from the Garonne Valley as well working-class areas near Paris. Parts of Normandy, Burgundy, Charente, and the upper Loire have also tilted toward the party of Marine Le Pen.[1] Seen from above, then, change in the geography of support since the 1980s seems piecemeal and gradual.[2]

In the southeast, the big cities—Aix-en-Provence, Marseille, Nice, and Toulon—belong to the moderate right. Even so, the Provence-Alpes-Côte d'Azur (PACA) region remains a hotbed of far-right politics. In the 2014 municipal elections, fully one-fifth of 1,544 National Front candidates across France who won election to a city council came from this region alone. That year, when the National Front entered the National Senate for the first time, moreover, its two new senators hailed from Marseille and Fréjus. Elections to the PACA regional assembly tell the same story: between 2010 and 2015, support for the National Front doubled (from 20.3 to 40.6 percent).[3] Having replaced the left as the main opposition to the moderate right in this part of France, the far right is entering different levels of government. Apart from resources and experience, it is gaining status and connections. Depending on its performance and its opponents' response, perceptions the far right is unfit to govern will keep melting; its protest vote will keep changing into an identity vote.

We find similar developments in the Var. In 2014, no fewer than 3 of the 11 municipalities that the National Front won in all of France were in this department: Cogolin, Fréjus, and Le Luc. In the European elections that year, far-right support in this department equaled the *combined* support for the Socialists and moderate right.[4] In the first round of the latest departmental elections, likewise, most of the Var's cantons put the National Front ahead of all the rest. Recruiting more candidates than in the past—and outdoing the Communists in recruiting candidates from the lower classes—the National Front has grown among the unemployed, contract workers, and employees with low-paying or threatened jobs in the service sector. The National Front won only three seats in the 2015 elections to the departmental council, but the left won none.[5]

Putting these pieces together, Toulon stands out. In 2014, the National Front won three municipalities in the Var, but did poorly in Toulon. With almost 60 percent of the first-round vote, instead the man who succeeded Le Chevallier as mayor won re-election. In some ways, the three towns that elected the National Front differed. The new mayor of Fréjus had grown up there; his counterparts in Cogolin and Le Luc were transplants. Infighting and vote splitting had weakened the far right's opponents in Fréjus, but not in Cogolin or Le Luc. Voter turnout was high in Fréjus and Le Luc, but low in Cogolin. Controversy around construction of a mosque helped the National Front in Fréjus; no such issue stirred voters in Cogolin or Le Luc. What the three towns had in common was an incumbent mayor with a poor record. A road project defended by the mayor of Cogolin, who suffered from a do-nothing image, angered property owners. In the run-off, the unpopular mayor of Le Luc received a measly 0.6 percent. The mayor of Fréjus had bungled his town's finances, and before the elections a court found him guilty of conflict of interest.[6]

In this chapter, then, we turn to Toulon for insight into how to keep the far right at bay. Some argue that populists like the far right "collapse under the weight of their unrealistic promises and political inexperience."[7] Given a chance to govern, this suggests, they will deflate. Toulon does and does not fit this scenario: the Le Chevallier years had a terrible effect on the far right's share in municipal elections only. Judging by the results of other elections, though, the city's far-right potential has remained strong.[8] In addition, poor administration does not guarantee that better will follow. Since 2001, when he replaced Le Chevallier, Hubert Falco has twice won re-election as mayor.[9] When France holds its municipal elections in 2020, the Fifth Republic will be 62 years old; during 55 of those years, Toulon will have been under the moderate right. The years when the far right held office were not a mere interlude, still, for politics has not reverted to its older ways. Looking at four factors—partisan control, institutional resources, scandal-free government, and policy achievements—shows what has changed.

PARTISAN CONTROL

Winning election in the 1970s to the municipal council in Pignans, a village northeast of Toulon, Hubert Falco started on the center left. Moving toward the right, he cultivated relations with Arreckx and Léotard, joined their party, and won election to the departmental council (1985). Skilled and connected, Falco rose: election and re-election as deputy in the National Assembly (1988 and 1993); election as mayor of Pignans (1989); and promotion to vice-president of the departmental council (1992). When a tainted Arreckx lost the 1994 cantonal elections to the National Front, Falco succeeded him as president of the departmental council. A year later, he became a senator, a position that requires wide backing within a department's political class (because the electors are themselves elected officials). After the far right made a mess in Toulon, Falco was ready to step in. Like Arreckx, Falco's position as mayor of the biggest city in the department has helped as he navigates between party and state. Unlike Arreckx, Falco need not worry about competition from another moderate-right party: in 2002, the neo-Gaullist and non-Gaullist moderate right fused into a single party. Arreckx had to coexist with Léotard's fiefdom in the eastern Var, moreover. A divided sphere of influence has not hampered Falco, already on the rise before he won election as mayor of Toulon. In a region where the barrier between moderate and far-right electorates is porous, he can block political careers.

Surrounding Falco is a network of politicians whose ascent meshed with his. Geneviève Levy is a lawyer who responded to the National Front's victory in 1995 by forming a local section of the International League against Racism and Anti-Semitism. Falco put her onto his slate for the 2001 municipal elections.[10] Currently the first deputy mayor of Toulon, in addition Levy is serving her fourth term as deputy for Toulon in the National Assembly. Further to the right than Levy, another Falco ally—Philippe Vitel—represented the city as deputy in the National Assembly until 2017. Vitel was also president of the Var section of the party that served Chirac and Sarkozy (Union pour un mouvement populaire, or UMP) and is currently a vice-president of the PACA region. Like Vitel, another Falco ally, Georges Ginesta has been president of the UMP's Var section; like Vitel and Levy, he has served as a deputy in the National Assembly (between 2002 and 2017). Ginesta is also the mayor of Saint-Raphaël. Falco's successor as president of the departmental council was Horace Lanfranchi, a member of the UMP and former mayor of Saint-Maximin-la-Sainte-Baume. Lanfranchi's successor as president of the departmental council since 2015 has been Marc Giraud, former mayor of Carqueiranne. All of these politicians belong to the conservative party that replaced the UMP, Les Républicains (LR).

After Levy, Vitel, and Ginesta entered the National Assembly in 2002, the moderate right rewarded Falco with ministerial positions (initially as Secretary of State for Seniors, later as Minister Responsible for Seniors—appropriate posts, given the high proportion of retirees in the Var). After the 2007 elections that brought Sarkozy to power, Falco again entered government (first as Secretary of State for Regional Planning, then as Secretary of State for Defense and Veterans' Affairs—another appropriate post, given the military presence in the Var). When Jacques Chirac founded the UMP in 2002, Falco became president of its Var section; later, he became national vice-president of the party. When the LR formed in 2015, Falco was its president in the Var, and Sarkozy chose him to lead the party's national committee of mayors.

Falco avoids the anti-immigrant discourse of the far right, and backs this up by treating the far right as a pariah. This he can do because he has the final say in candidate selection for his party in this department.[11] He vetoes former National Front members who wish to run as moderate-right candidates. At the risk of handing a victory to the left, moreover, he blocks alliances between moderates and the far right. When needed, he activates a front against the far right: if a strong first-round performance makes the far right a serious contender for final victory, to avoid vote splitting the left and moderate right agree that the partner with fewer votes in the first round will withdraw. At the expense of the far right, usually this paves the way for victory by the remaining partner. Depending so much on Falco, this system has a weakness: it taxes his limits. Only members of the Electoral College (deputies and senators; and regional, departmental, and municipal councilors) vote in senate elections. In 2014, when National Front candidate David Rachline from Fréjus won a seat in the Senate, a politician relayed a complaint to me. Some among the thousands of elected officials in the Var felt that Falco might have done more to solicit their support: they expected a personal visit from him. This is the standard practice for bigwigs like Falco, but it seems he was overstretched.[12]

INSTITUTIONAL RESOURCES

Falco's story is not only about how a small-town business owner whose grandfather had migrated from Italy rose to the summit of politics in this department. Holding more than one office at a time, Falco learned the game of politics at a time when the rules were changing.[13] Starting in 1999, the central state had encouraged the creation, by municipalities, of inter-municipal federations with their own budget and responsibilities. By coordinating the administration of neighboring towns and cities, the goal was to increase efficiency and economies of scale. Before this decentralizing reform, mayors operated within a system of vertical relations inherited from the Third Republic. To get things done, their partners would be the central state, sub-prefect or prefect, as well as departmental experts from ministries such as public works. Coordinated from above, this system atomized French municipalities. Vertical relations protected the political notables of towns and villages, whose nodal position between citizen and state underwrote cronyism.[14] Nowadays, mayors are more dependent on other mayors: projects without support from their inter-municipal federation can run into trouble. Given these federations' responsibilities—for economic development, zoning regulation, road construction, waterworks, garbage collection, transportation services, public housing, recreational facilities, and environmental protection— much is at stake.[15]

Here France fits into a wider trend. Their budgets under pressure since the 1970s, central states have devolved responsibilities. In the name of rationality and accountability, regions, provinces, and cities now have more to manage. Meanwhile, erosion in barriers between markets means that attracting investments, businesses, and workers places cities in a global competition with each other. Some countries have responded with the stick: in Greece, the government forced municipalities to fuse; in Great Britain, the government created business-led organizations able to bypass local elected officials. Elsewhere (not only in France, but also in Austria, Belgium, Germany, Italy, the Netherlands, and Spain), governments have provided incentives to encourage cooperation between municipalities; sometimes the carrots are fiscal, other times political.[16]

By 2001, Le Chevallier's last year in office, some 100 inter-municipal federations had formed across France; today there are over 2,000.[17] Le Chevallier and his councilors were isolationists. We do not know if the far right saw partnering with nearby municipalities as a risk or a liability, but the possibility of leveraging new resources by taking a broader view of their city and its place in the world did not sway them. Until the end of his term, then, Le Chevallier opposed the creation of a new conurbation anchored by Toulon.[18] Falco led the way by forming a new inter-municipal government with ten nearby municipalities. Since its founding in 2001, the Communauté d'agglomération Toulon Provence Méditerranée (TPM) has always had the same president: Hubert Falco.[19] Operating from a dominant position as mayor of the biggest city gives Falco partners, alliances, and influence unavailable to his predecessors at city hall.

While decentralization has given municipalities, departments, and regions more autonomy from Paris, it has also made politics more complicated. A mayor must deal with added levels of authority in elected office (not just appointed office, as in the past). Apart from horizontal partners (other mayors in the inter-urban federation), an effective mayor will seek vertical alignments—support for a city's projects and interests across the different, nested levels of government above the municipality—to say nothing of the European Union. Between Toulon and Paris, the PACA regional council long provided the weakest link for Falco. The left dominated this council between 1998 and 2015; as the most populous department in the PACA region, moreover, the Bouches-du-Rhône enjoys nearly as much representation (47 out of 123 seats on the council) as the Var and the Alpes-Maritimes combined. Reflecting the weight of the Bouches-du-Rhône, since 1974 Marseille has supplied four of the region's six presidents. In the regional council, therefore, the Var counted as a middleweight.

In the council's politics, still, politicians on the left have combined with the moderate right in a republican front to weaken or block the National Front. Since 2015, moreover, the moderate right has formed the majority on this council, which has not neglected Falco's city. In support of four current projects in Toulon, the PACA region gave €211,598 (with another €1.1 million coming from the European Union). Institutions located in Toulon (its prison, university, research and development institute, and port authority) have received funds from the region and European Union as well. These support joint projects with cities both in France (including Avignon, Bastia, and Marseille) and abroad (notably port cities in Italy such as Genoa and Livorno). The composition of funding for a 2015–2018 project to encourage new digital firms illustrates the multilevel game of the 2000s. Out of a total package of €1.4 million, half came from the European Union while the remainder came from (1) the PACA region, which the LR now controls; (2) the Var department, which Falco allies in the LR control; (3) the TPM inter-municipal federation, which Falco presides; and (4) the research and development institute in Toulon that will manage the project.[20]

When the far right governed in Toulon, this multilevel game proved brutal. Shunned and isolated, the National Front lacked access and allies at other levels of government. Controlling institutions at higher levels, left- and right-wing parties opposed to the far right choked the flow of resources into Le Chevallier's city. In 1997, all other levels of government gave the far-right city €2.9 million in funding; by 2000, this had dwindled to €2.0 million. When Falco took over, the lean years ended: from €6 million already in 2001, by 2005, the level of outside support had climbed to €16.4 million. In 1997, when Le Chevallier was mayor, the department gave the city €407,000; in 2004, it gave fifteen times more (€6.0 million).[21] The far right could never do much when it ran Toulon because players at other levels of government cut off the necessary means.

SCANDAL-FREE GOVERNMENT

As the demise of Arreckx and Le Chevallier show, scandals around corruption can ruin political careers. Falco, to his credit, has kept his name clean. Never has the local press published a serious accusation of criminal malfeasance on his part, but politicians associated with him have raised suspicions. As Trucy learned, public perceptions that a politician has cooperated with dishonest people can create trouble: no court ever found Trucy guilty of a civil offense; even so, his previous ties to a disgraced Arreckx hampered his re-election as mayor in 1995. Accordingly, Falco's party ejected a politician who became a liability. In 2013, a court found the mayor of Fréjus guilty of collusion (he had granted a beach concession to an acquaintance). Falco's party responded by deciding he would not be one of its candidates in the 2014 municipal elections.[22] He ran anyway, and the vote splitting that resulted—as well as his criminal record—contributed to the National Front's victory in Fréjus. A year later, the president of the department's council, Marc Giraud, appeared before a judge who was looking into a potential misappropriation of public funds while Giraud was mayor of Carqueiranne. This ally of Falco remained innocent, but the left and far right reacted immediately, saying his case was emblematic of political impropriety in the department.[23] In 2017, the LR in Saint-Raphaël split after an external audit raised concerns about the town's finances and spending. The mayor chose not to run in the parliamentary elections, but his protégé did and finished third (behind candidates from the National Front and President Macron's new party). Scandal thus caused the moderate right to lose a district it had held for more than half a century.[24] That year an allegation circulated that Falco was among 117 right-wing senators who had pocketed money from a slush fund in Paris, but it did not stick.[25]

At worst, the Falco system seems to involve patronage. An audit of the city has lauded its rigor in awarding public works contracts (an area ripe for bribery, kickbacks, extortion, and bid rigging). In its hiring, though, the city has not followed proper procedure: temporary employees have benefited from preferential hiring and inflated pay.[26] An audit of the department has also deplored nepotistic practices.[27] Among residents who expect that an officeholder should help their friends, however, patronage may not be perceived as a character flaw. In sunny Provence, not practicing patronage could suggest a politician is unfamiliar with the ways of this world. Falco's city council has always included *pied noir* representation. The Maison des Rapatriés remains funded. The city continues to support *pied noir* events.

One bright afternoon in December 2004, a man struck up a conversation with me while we waited at a bus stop near the municipal archives on the edge of Toulon. We ended up talking about the package of delicacies that the city offers its senior citizens at Christmas. This year's gift box had let him down, he informed me: it contained a tin of pâté prepared not from the liver of goose, but of duck. His complaint did not quite make my heart bleed, but it gave me pause. This gift from city hall was a private good for his own, individual consumption—not a collective good like a city park, public beach, or transit system. Although I never found out precisely to whom this gentleman credited his Christmas package—to the administration, a city councilor, or the mayor—he felt entitled to it. I surmised that this kind of patronage becomes acceptable where people do not draw a rigid line between political rights and private entitlements.

POLICY ACHIEVEMENTS

After the UMP won all seven of the Var's districts in the 2002 parliamentary elections, Falco reacted to fears that he would forget Toulon when he accepted his reward of a ministry in Paris:

> I will make my decision in the interest of Toulon. I feel more committed than ever to my task: changing this city, this living space, tackling the issues. The people of Toulon should know that if their mayor enters the government it will be an opportunity for their city. Marseille only took off once Gaudin became a minister.[28]

During its first years in power, the National Front had tried to reduce expenditures by holding off on new projects. Although this did reduce the city's debt, its finances remained fragile due to a lack of funding from other levels of government and the burden of public service employment (which represented two-thirds of the city's expenses).[29] Under the moderate right, by contrast, Toulon has invested heavily in infrastructure, civic amenities, and urban renewal.[30] Le Chevallier had suspended the construction of an office and cinema complex near the main square. For years this created an eyesore, an abandoned site at the intersection of two busy boulevards near the central train station. Falco found new public-private financing, work resumed, and the complex opened.[31] After completion of the first, long-delayed road tunnel in 2002, the city began a parallel tunnel that opened in 2014. More traffic now flows beneath the city instead of clogging and polluting its boulevards, and the city has introduced measures to dampen road noise.[32]

Toulon has a new bus terminal next to the train station, itself expanded and renovated.[33] It refurbished the municipal opera house and the sports stadium, home to one of the best rugby teams in Europe. After the Ministry of Justice decided Nice should no longer handle the Var's administrative cases, it converted a Haussmanian building near the opera into a new courthouse. Nearby, on the main square, the city transformed a historic cinema into a three-theater complex that can hold nearly 1,000 spectators. Other projects underway include the renewal of public squares and commercial streets. A new hospital was constructed—the most expensive public works project ever in the Var.[34] A large building in the old town, the old labor exchange, had stood vacant for decades. Following a major restoration, now it contains offices as well as a Monoprix department and grocery store. Elsewhere in the city center, by 2022 a multimedia library, student residence, and high-tech education facility will rise on the site of the former general hospital. The city hopes such projects will bring new life and business into the old city.

Multiple levels of government have funded these projects. To finance the new hospital, support from Deputies Levy and Vitel as well as the minister of health was instrumental.[35] All levels of government (including the TPM inter-municipal federation) paid for construction of the second road tunnel.[36] Money to buy the empty cinema and convert it into the Théâtre Liberté came from Paris, the region, the department, and the TPM.[37] The same authorities—as well as the city of Toulon and the French rail network—paid for the renovation and expansion of the train station.[38] Thanks to the configuration of power in which Falco has inserted himself, Toulon seems to be catching up.[39] The city's debt is under control and taxes remain relatively low. A 2014 evaluation of mayors by a business newspaper ranked Falco among the very best in the country.[40]

CHALLENGES FACING THE FAR RIGHT AND TOULON

When the far right broke through during the 1980s, it embraced the free market. Under Marine Le Pen, the party has flirted with a program better suited to the depressed north: welfare chauvinism, anti-globalization, and defense of state intervention. Her party faces a tough choice usually associated with the left. To advance, the far right must expand beyond the working class.[41] If economic issues lack salience in interparty competition, the party can expand by sticking to the identity politics that unify its supporters. If its opponents keep economic issues central, however, the far right will face a dilemma: keep silent on the economy, but risk irrelevance; or take a strong stand, and alienate part of its electorate. Going forward, a muddled economic platform may be the best strategy.

Who knows how such a platform would register in Toulon? Clearly, Falco and his administration have improved the city's prospects. As elsewhere in France, though, for decades the spread of suburban shopping malls with commercial chains like Ikea and H&M has been pulling customers away from the city center. Despite a tax holiday for small businesses, parts of the old city are decaying or abandoned.[42] Left-wing critics decry the paucity of new and affordable housing (although a project started in 2015 should help by renovating or replacing dozens of decrepit buildings).[43] Geography sets limits too: wedged between the sea, Navy yards, railroad lines, and limestone massif, Toulon lacks space. Despite the tunnels that entered service in 2000s, problems with traffic and parking continue; and despite high hopes when Falco took office, a tramway to lessen congestion and pollution never materialized. If it takes the shortest route through the interior, a future high-speed railway line between Nice and Marseille will bypass Toulon entirely.[44]

A 2017 study of the economic vitality of 113 French cities with more than 50,000 inhabitants puts most of the cities in the coastal arc that extends from Perpignan to Nice toward the bottom of its ranking, with Toulon 98th.[45] Apart from encouraging new business in the digital sector, Falco has tried to diversify the city's economic base by promoting its university, which has added a Faculty of Information and Communication Studies. The University of Toulon is a latecomer, though: founded in 1979, it lacks the prestige and visibility of other institutions. Also, it has suffered from a corruption scandal. The city lacks research and development synergies (despite the major hospital just built in Toulon, for example, the university lacks a medical school).[46] Unlike Aix-en-Provence and Montpellier, it also lacks an animated student quarter.[47] Students in higher education consign Toulon to the lower half of French cities in which to live and study.[48] Outside of Paris, satellites of Sciences-Po operate in six cities; when Falco lobbied to have a branch for Toulon, his connections proved insufficient.[49]

On the positive side, Toulon now attracts more tourists. The Tall Ships' Race came to the city in 2007 and 2013. Cruise ships bring a quarter-million passengers to the city each year, and ferry lines use its port for the connection with Corsica.[50] Instead of lingering and spending, though, most ferry passengers drive directly to their embarkation.[51] Cruise-ship passengers tend to confine their onshore excursions to a few hours of sightseeing in the National Museum of the Navy or among the market stalls along the picturesque Cours Lafayette before taking their next meal onboard. Ever since the 2008 economic crisis, passenger traffic at the nearby Hyères airport has dropped. Given the transience of its tourists, the city misses the sector-related jobs and opportunities for suppliers of goods and services that climate, landscape, and beaches have brought to other municipalities in the region.[52] Business dynamism remains mediocre, with the city ranking around the middle of French cities (65 out of 113) in the creation of new firms.[53]

Some argue that populist parties target the losers of globalization: white working-class workers in cities that have lost relatively well-paid, secure jobs in heavy industry.[54] Home to the largest naval base in Europe, though, Toulon's dependence on the budget and priorities of the Defense Ministry—not big business—continues.[55] Even more important than the Navy for the local economy are retirement pensions and spending by owners and renters of holiday residences.[56] Putting the different elements of the economy together, production carries so little weight that a 2012 study of valued added in the 62 largest municipalities in France relegated Toulon to the second-last position.[57] Unlike cities reliant on production for capitalist markets, the unique profile of Toulon's economy (its reliance on spending by retirees, vacationers, public servants, and military personnel) insulates it from the pressures and vagaries not only of the national economy but also of economic globalization—just as when the National Front won in 1995.[58] In a series of elections to different levels of government since 2012, candidates from the National Front have won 21 percent or more of the vote in Toulon. Despite its insulated economy and the Falco system, this city still has a far-right potential.

Conclusion

Every year in Toulon, a crowd of *pieds noirs* gathers to commemorate the anniversary of the Rue d'Isly massacre. Walking along the edge of a square beyond the old city walls, participants reach the Monument to the Martyrs for French Algeria. Some have done well for themselves, judging by appearances, but others less so. Most are elderly, some of them veterans with their military beret and war medals. The French tricolor flies, the honor guard stands at attention, and all join in singing "Le Chant des Africains," the *pied noir* anthem. To scratch at old wounds, at one ceremony the organizers play a recording made on the spot, in the streets of Algiers on 26 March 1962. From large loudspeakers issue the sounds of guns firing and people screaming. After this ghastly reminder, a *pied noir* leader gives his revanchist speech: "You did not want Algeria to be French," he says, "We do not want France to become Algerian."[1] More than half a century after they quit their homeland, *pieds noirs* still join in the collective making of meaning. In the following pages, I reflect on what this teaches about the origins, nature, transmission, and activation of political potential. In light of economic analyses of the far right, past and present, I also weigh the lessons learned from this study. Closing the circle, finally, I consider how the foregoing fits with the view of history set forth in this book's introduction.

POLITICAL POTENTIAL

This book began with a riddle: When the French far right exited from the political wilderness, from where had its support come? Resource poor, the party lacked local branches, viable candidates, activist networks, and elected representatives. Polls soon after its breakthrough revealed the age, gender, work, and religious profile of its voters. Polls also showed strong concern about immigration, crime, and unemployment set this electorate apart, as did its relative lack of concern about social inequality, living costs, and European integration. Historians, sociologists, and political scientists contributed by unearthing the party's ideological and organizational lineages. Media studies showed how television and newspapers had pushed the far right and its all-purpose issue, immigration, into the center of public attention and political debate. These analyses were valuable, and *Empire's Legacy* draws on them. Still, there was more to say about the far right's social origins.

In trying to advance, I found it handy to apply the idea of political potential. The everyday definition of potential applies here: possessing the possibility of realization. It means that something has a capacity not yet actualized. In addition to latency and fulfillment, potential connotes contingency: absent proper conditions, qualitative change is suspended.

I also found it handy to move between narrow and broad conceptions of politics. More institutional and conventional, the narrow conception separates the political from the social; under the broad conception, politics saturates society. Consistent with the broad conception, chapters of this book show that inequality permeates social relations (even shaping intimate relations in the private sphere). The broad conception smuggles in a blind spot, though. It edits out, or plays down, variance—across time, situation, and place—in the distance between political organization, narrowly defined, and social life. A broad conception binds the two spheres too tightly together. Ranging from closeness to distance, instead the political incorporation of social groups varies significantly. Not all social potentials, then, translate into actual support for a political option (which can be a social movement, pressure group, political party, armed militia, civil faction, ideological sect, or governing regime). Some potentials remain untapped. The distinction between politics and society used here is semantic, of course, not descriptive. In history, as the preceding pages make clear, the two often overlap considerably. Through a process of selection, still, sometimes what is latent never reaches realization. To engage with the problem of translation means studying the origins, nature, and transmission of potentials; as well as the conditions under which potentials do, or do not, mature into recognizable support for an option.

Every beginning has its antecedents, which in turn have their own beginning. Avoiding infinite regress means deciding when the rewards from looking backward start to dry up. In choosing a beginning for *Empire's Legacy*, I heeded the salience of immigration for the far right in contemporary France. Among its electorate's preoccupations, immigration—a code word for the presence of nonnatives, especially Muslims, whatever their citizenship or legal status—consistently outweighs other issues or concerns. Polls show that the belief that race determines aptitude is a good predictor of far-right support. Consider as well this electorate's preoccupation with Islam and North Africans; the crucial weight of the *pieds noirs* in the rise of the far right; the formative role, for the post-1962 far right, of the Algerian conflict; and its lasting effect on the metropole. Complementing other historical studies, this shifted attention from intellectuals, ideologues, and organizations to social milieus. The evidence also suggested that other factors (such as psychological authoritarianism, moral conservatism, or economic insecurity) had weaker and less consistent effects than immigration. These effects are worth studying. So are other milieus with an affinity toward the far right (including Catholic traditionalism and anti-republican royalism). The latter are largely beyond the scope of this book, for which the conquest of Algeria was the best place to start.

When people travel far to build a new life, even without a suitcase they bring baggage. Not fleeing the state of nature, they bear the imprint of the society from which they came. But what exactly is this imprint that forms a political potential? At different times in this research, I wondered if the *pieds noirs* were carriers, perhaps, of a distinct mentality. Other possibilities were a worldview, disposition, or schema of perception. Concepts such as these seemed too pared down, though. They play down the relational side. Belonging and exclusion, as we have seen, arise in concrete situations in which social distance varies. Inner-group boundaries as well as boundaries with other groups wax and wane. Better, for this analysis anyway, to envision people as carriers of cultural repertoires. Repertoires come out in practice. They imply codes for talk and other symbolic action that people learn and draw on, with more or less competence, as each situation calls for and allows.[2]

Movements of peoples perform a kind of cultural jamming, this book suggests, because they pull repertoires out of context. Mutual adaptation can be slight or profound. After Rome conquered Greece, Greece conquered Rome. The fit between codes of outsider and host varies widely. Even without moving, people become cultural misfits if they belong to the losing side after a conquest, partition, annexation, civil war, or regime change. While I wrote this book, the years after, respectively, the Civil War in the United States, World War II in Europe, and the fall of the Berlin Wall came to mind. Seemingly different from postwar decolonization, all bred subcultures—among whites in Jim Crow America, neo-fascists in postwar Italy, and losers of German unification—perhaps hidden from outsiders, yet still alive and susceptible to the far right.

Submerged networks, halfway houses, free spaces, protected spaces, sequestered social sites, and parallel public spaces: terms like these denote social settings far enough from power to harbor a culture of dissent. Whether in a plural democracy or an authoritarian regime, these settings sustain alternatives either reformist (compatible with the institutions in place) or radical (implying a rejection of some part of the system). The left, as we have seen, enjoys no monopoly over dissident subcultures. When conditions turn favorable, a culture of dissent can break barriers that once kept it marginalized. It may win resources, influence, and power. Even if it fails, it can win voice. Dissidents may be the hidden interlocutors of the powerful. By going beyond the mainstream, then, we find external pressures against which hegemonic discourses resist and respond.[3]

The chief subcultural setting studied in this book was the voluntary association. Other locales, groups, or institutions in society can also segment people: families, neighborhoods, schools, workplaces, sports clubs, religious groups, publishing houses, intellectual networks, and Internet echo chambers. Political actors, in turn, act upon these subcultures. During the Algerian conflict, the military and the OAS organized settler protest. By way of legal measures, public agencies, and official procedures, interaction with the central state reaffirmed group identity and interests. Pressure groups, in turn, mobilized the repatriates for loan forgiveness, official rehabilitation, and property compensation. Politicians sought the *pied noir* vote. Prefects, mayors, and councilors upheld the specificity of the *pieds noirs* by attending to their grievances, transacting with their leaders, and acceding to their requests. Lending legitimacy, influence, and resources, they increased its weight. Acknowledging a subculture in these ways, political actors gave it a meaningful presence. They also affect its inner balance of power.

Engaging in conversation, listening to speeches, reading niche books and newspapers, joining in community pilgrimages, and attending banquets, conferences, rallies, masses, and memorials—practices like these keep subcultural bonds and codes alive. Transmission, as we have seen, requires a degree of social segmentation. Absent a cloistered setting, *pieds noirs* mellowed politically. Cross-cutting ties have a dual effect: they complicate identities and hybridize repertoires. Exposure to diversity helped *pieds noirs* see their community from the outside. They still understood it, but from a distance. Their lives—their interests, their values, their practices—intertwined with those of people outside this community. Their old identity did not vanish. Having other ties and learning other codes, though, their far-right affinity waned. To sustain its alternative codes, then, a potential needs barriers from dissonant milieus.

The same logic, I expect, applies to residential patterns, which shape peoples' opportunity to socialize. In the first half of the twentieth century, migrants from southern and eastern Europe fed much of the growth on the edge of French cities; their integration into French society lent hope that non-European migrants would also blend in. Apart from the class barrier, though, non-Europeans faced the barriers of religion and race. Already in the interwar period, metropolitan stereotypes treated neighborhoods inhabited by colonial subjects as not-yet-civilized intrusions.[4] Starting with the Algerian War, modernist planning of public housing in France created urban peripheries strictly for North Africans.[5] In addition to breeding mistrust on both sides, this has reinforced ethno-spatial identities with colonial roots among blacks and *beurs* of the *cités* and *banlieus*.[6] Structures of society that inhibit sustained, friendly contact across peoples can duplicate the insulating effect of associations.

NATIVIST POLITICS

Chiseled into a 1939 essay on Nazism is this injunction: "He who does not wish to speak of capitalism should also be silent about fascism."[7] Eventually the neo-Marxist who wrote these words would disown the essay in which they appear. Still, he issued a challenge that outlasted its time: his era has passed, but not the idea that capitalism is responsible for the far right. In *The Great Transformation*, to cite a later example, Karl Polanyi wrote that fascism arose in response to the conversion of land and labor into market commodities. Fascism was a bogus way of recreating belonging and solidarity, Polanyi held, because organic relations between work, community, and nature unravel when social relations no longer constrain economic relations. In Germany, Italy, and Japan, then, fascism provided the wrong solution to a real problem. According to Polanyi, the liberal economy had subordinated the social bond to the anarchy of self-interest. Warmongering and authoritarian, fascism furthered the breakdown of freedom and civilization. After the 1929 crash, still, it provided an alternative to class conflict and free trade. Other political alternatives of the day, namely socialism and the New Deal, resembled fascism in one important way: they wanted the economy to be a servant of society, not its solvent. Fascism, for Polanyi, was a reflex of societal self-preservation in the face of corrosive market relations.[8]

Similar arguments from the 1990s blamed the shift from industrial to postindustrial society. They held that workers with less education or few skills faced joblessness in a labor market increasingly oriented toward services and high technology. Fast capitalism—rationalized production and flexible hiring—split society into winners and losers: full-time workers versus those without job security. The anxiety of the vulnerable and marginalized—youths, pensioners, low-income workers, and farmers fearing downward mobility—was pushing them toward the far right.[9]

Today, we are more tempted to believe that failed capitalism—not fast capitalism—explains far right support. Populism seems to be flowering in urban areas once booming with industry. Right-wing populists pander to nostalgia for a golden age of stable jobs and friendly neighborhoods, a time of working-class pride and electoral influence. Promising economic protectionism and nativist patriotism, the current explanation goes, right-wing populism offers hope to a segment of the electorate that feels itself unheard.[10] Journalistic accounts like "Nine Charts That Help Explain Donald Trump's Win" distill the foregoing.[11] The first five charts display social traits said to explain the outcome of the 2016 presidential election. The typical Trump voter was older, white, male, poorer, and racist. He was likely to be an Evangelical Christian who believed that life is worse today than it was 50 years ago. Informative as they are, these features do not explain why a far-right candidate won the US presidential election in 2016 instead of in 2012, 2008, or 2004. The burden of explanation falls on the last four charts, which present trends in the economy. These suggest Trump rose amidst multiple declines—in industrial manufacturing, labor market returns from a high school degree, and working- and middle-class incomes. Plausible as all this seems, it gets the timing wrong. Four or five decades before Trump's victory, these trends were already underway.

The woes of capitalism matter, a look at France suggests, but in ways neither simple nor consistent. Class affects people's propensity to support the far right, yes, but the pattern has changed. Initially, the strongest likelihood of support came from the propertied middle class; afterward, the working class took the lead. The troubled industrial and mining areas of the north and east have always ranked among regions with strong support; but so has the south, more dependent on agriculture and services. The party took off in the 1980s, but unemployment started to rise in the 1960s. In presidential elections, Jean-Marie Le Pen's best performance came in 2002, when unemployment approached its lowest level in two decades. Economic issues like unemployment, inflation, and the cost of living have not ranked among this electorate's chief concerns.[12] For those who decide the party's program, this has permitted a vacillation between laissez-faire, trade protectionism, and welfare chauvinism. Voter surveys, party ideology, and this book instead emphasize a preoccupation with nonwhites, particularly those from North Africa. Far-right supporters blame immigrants for unemployment, but also a host of non-economic problems. Blunting the blows of capitalism, all this implies, will not make the far right disappear.

Strong far-right support among the *pieds noirs* crossed classes. Studying them, we learn that immersion in milieus that inhibit contact with diverse others sustains fear, prejudice, and shunning. We also learn that such settings can foster discourse compatible with the far right. Other politicians may not resonate within these milieus, we learn, because they do not talk about honor, dignity, and duty; or Western civilization, national decline, and personal sacrifice. Singly, of course, each of these terms works its way into political language of different kinds. Communists urge workers and intellectuals to fulfill their duty to the movement. Honoring those who made sacrifices in World War II sanctifies democracy. Even anarchists have asked followers to make sacrifices for the greater cause. It seems to me, though, that putting terms like duty, dignity, and sacrifice together gives them a special coloring, especially when nativism enters the mix.

The far right's victory in Toulon had little to do with capitalism. This city relies heavily on spending by the state, not the private sector. The crisis that brought down the conservative right had its origins in crime, mismanagement, and corruption, not unemployment, inflation, or deindustrialization. When neither of the far right's biggest opponents withdrew from the run-off, politics—not economics—decided the outcome. Times and places change. To the extent that social conditions sustain the ethos dissected in this book, though, I believe a far-right potential will persist. Apart from the economy, explanation should attend to proximate causes: social ties, subcultural milieus, and partisan dynamics.

HISTORICAL CONSCIOUSNESS

Twelve days after the Bastille Day attack of 2016—when a truck driven by an unhinged Tunisian killed dozens and injured hundreds more on the seafront boulevard in Nice—two jihadists stabbed and killed an 86-year-old priest in the small Norman church of Saint-Étienne-du-Rouvray. Amidst the outrage that followed, a former National Front leader tweeted, "We need to get ready for another 'Algerian War' on our French soil. And not stay morally and physically defenseless." Others on Twitter agreed that this was 1957 all over again, when the paratroops under Massu won the Battle of Algiers; or 1962, when European settlers could either leave the colony or die. On television, a *Le Figaro* columnist with *pied noir* origins declared, "We're experiencing revenge for the Algerian War."[13] The temptation of reading today through the lens of yesterday persists: evoking feelings of fear and desire for revenge, images of the immigrant and the *fellagha* merge.[14]

An abiding vision of modernity treats it like a pair of machines: both a steamroller that crushes the remnants of the past, and a bulldozer that clears away the detritus. A relentless process of disintegration is producing new configurations of belonging, this vision suggests. It is undermining traditional patterns of ownership, knowledge, and identity. Modernity means unceasing disintegration and renewal.[15] As Marx and Engels declare in their *Manifesto*, capitalism differs from all previous modes of production. By revolutionizing production, they write, the bourgeoisie turns uncertainty and agitation into constants: "All fixed, fast-frozen relations, with their train of ancient and venerable prejudices and opinions, are swept away, all new-formed ones become antiquated before they can ossify. All that is solid melts into air."[16] Gramsci used a similar image to explain fascism: it filled a void that opens when the masses lose their beliefs and traditions. During the wait before new certainties, a "great variety of morbid symptoms" arises.[17]

While Gramsci withered in a fascist prison, Ernst Bloch was wondering which course of action the German left should take. This question he asked to guide action against the Nazis. Answering it required no less than a rethinking of historical time. From a steamroller or a bulldozer, we might say, he reframed modernity as a tiller or harrow. The present grabs and turns over a great deal, certainly; yet much remains that escapes or resists this churning. Bloch discerned in Weimer Germany a similarity between the proletariat, poor peasants, and battered middle class: each stood opposed to capitalism.[18] Which political force would triumph in harnessing the fear and pent-up anger of these classes remained uncertain. When Bloch wrote in 1932, what he called the Hitler movement was on the rise; still, he wrote, the present contained multiple futures. Apart from regaining its leadership over the proletariat, the left must try to align that class with the discontented peasantry and middle classes. This it might do by appealing not only to economic interests but also, crucially, to subversive and utopian understandings. The left, in sum, must outdo the Nazis in mobilizing dreams of community, justice, and fulfillment.[19]

So much for practice. What about Bloch's vision of time? To reveal the tenacity of utopian visions, Bloch recalled their remote origins. The idealized yesterdays to which the immiserated peasantry and middle classes yearned descended from pre-capitalist times. Its imagery came from biblical stories, Nordic myths, and Gothic tales. It was anachronistic because out of sync with urbanism, capitalism, and parliamentary democracy. People living at the same time do not all live in the same now.[20] Some have made their peace with the present; others miss the past. Among those out of joint with the present, moreover, the historical referents vary. These are important insights for socialists, Bloch argued. They imply that holdovers from the past contain a contradictory potential: they can feed reaction or progress. Capitalism had left a political opening because it failed to co-opt and dissolve these potentials.[21] The past provided alternatives that appeal to the moral imagination. Bloch chastised the left for failing to recognize this critical potential, for not harnessing it before the Nazis did. Yet he still hoped for its reappropriation by the left.

During my interviews, I had mentioned to Madame Eugène a detail that struck me. Every time I asked, a *pied noir* could tell me the exact date of their departure from Algeria. She explained:

> It all goes to show you that we still live with the past. Sometimes, instead of saying, "I'm going into Toulon," we'll say, "I'm going into Algiers," because over there we lived in a suburb. It shows we always have one foot here, another foot over there. It means that just the tiniest little scratch can make everything come back all at once. We never say this, but none of that is buried and over with.[22]

The *pieds noirs* and their political allies inhabit a landscape of imagined time not shared with others. Some argue that the contemporary far right is thriving due to a failure of representation: political institutions (parliaments) and groups (parties, press, movements, and interest groups) that once mediated between citizen and state are no longer doing their job. This leaves people feeling unheard and frustrated.[23] Consider, however, that *not* representing citizen attitudes toward immigration may take oxygen away from the far right (for it to thrive, this study suggests, immigration must become salient in politics). Apart from organizing politically and commanding resources, moreover, opponents of nativism and populist anti-elitism must avoid scandals, govern well, and touch imaginations. Nostalgia for empire belongs to a syndrome out of step with much of Europe, where the ideal of the nation has lost some of its romantic pathos. Still, part of the failure of those who oppose the far right may consist in their inability to take seriously the dreams and desires of those with one foot still in the past. These dreams and desires, this book has shown, include mythical ideas about belonging as opposed to deracination.[24]

For Bloch, the carriers of anachronism in modern societies are economic classes. In this book, by contrast, I examine a status group that transcends class: the *pieds noirs* include managers, professionals, owners of small business, and blue- and white-collar workers. Within this group, far right support depends on membership in associations and belief in a hierarchy of races. Anachronism requires not shared class, the foregoing suggests, but ongoing interaction. Absent such interaction, a shared anachronism will wither. In counselling the left to attune itself to the historical imaginary behind the fears and pent-up anger of Nazi supporters, Bloch neglected the ancillary need of pulling people into cross-class *organizations* (such as unions, clubs, association, and parties) that would sustain an anti-Nazi ideology and fight off competing messages.

ELECTIVE AFFINITY REVISITED

In arguing that the Protestant ethic had spurred capitalist activity, Weber hedged his claim. Today capitalism is victorious, he stated, "it no longer needs asceticism as a supporting pillar."[25] During the 1980s and 1990s, the *pieds noirs* helped the National Front take off. Their political affinity aided the National Front's survival during the lean years before its breakthrough. This affinity helps explain why the National Front remains obsessed with Islam, North Africans, insecurity, honor, and national decline. It is a big part of why the far right conquered Toulon and other cities of the south.[26]

Nowadays, moreover, not only *pieds noirs* but also their descendants give above average support to the far right.[27] In four southern regions (Languedoc-Roussillon, Provence-Alpes-Côte d'Azur, Midi-Pyrénées, and Aquitaine), in turn, voters with a minimum of one *pied noir* parent or grandparent make up 10 to 15 percent of the electorate.[28] The potential that forms the subject of this book thus persists. Nature is taking its course, evidently. The number of *pieds noirs* continues to dwindle. Losing members, *pied noir* associations are shrinking. Avoiding the path of hybridity, some among the younger generations have shouldered nostalgia, resentment, and xenophobia, but others say they are French and Mediterranean or French and Provençal. Looking back to ancestors who migrated to Algeria, a minority consider themselves Franco-Italian, Franco-Spanish, or Franco-Maltese.[29] Now sturdily embedded in party politics, anyway the far right no longer needs the *pieds noirs* as a supporting pillar.

Thanks to politicians who keep immigration on the agenda, however, the cleavage over nativism continues to shape party politics. Since 1962, popular films (such as *The Battle of Algiers*, *Élise ou la Vraie Vie*, and *Le Coup de sirocco*), television programs, newspaper articles, and books by the thousands have dealt with the subject of French Algeria. Some look at the torture by the French military or the deadly repression of Algerian protestors by the police in Paris in 1961. Under domestic as well as diplomatic pressure, successive French presidents on official visits to Algiers have made declarations about the colonial past. The idea of a kind of unhealthy repression into the national subconscious of a history not faced seems untenable.[30]

Yet controversies and evasions persist. Some cherish the civilizing mission. Others reduce colonialism to racism. The Ministry of Education put the Algerian War on the *lycée* curriculum only in 1983. In 2005, the moderate right sponsored a bill with a section so unacceptable that the government later repealed it:

> School curricula shall recognize in particular the positive role of the French overseas presence, especially in North Africa, and attribute to the history and the sacrifices of the

combatants of the French army who originated from these territories their rightful and eminent position.[31]

Not so long ago, the apparatus of the French state—as well as the left- and right-wing parties—endorsed empire overseas. In addition to soldiers and settlers, imperialism drew in countless teachers, missionaries, merchants, and civil servants. Among the people of the metropole, colonial exhibitions, mass advertising, cultural media, and public education purveyed a triumphalist view of the subject races and the civilizing mission. Moving ruler and ruled to sacrifice, resistance, and violence, empire exacted costs that France is still paying.

Appendix

Table 1 NATIONAL FRONT IN TOULON, MUNICIPAL ELECTIONS

Year	Percent of eligible votes, first round
1989	20.3
1995	31.0
2001	5.6
2008	6.6
2014	20.5
Mean	16.8

Note: Comparable national data not available.

Table 2 NATIONAL FRONT IN FRANCE AND TOULON, PARLIAMENTARY ELECTIONS

Year	Percent of eligible votes, first round	
	France	Toulon
1986	9.7	20.3
1988	9.8	24.2
1993	12.4	27.0
1997	14.9	31.2
1998	—	39.7
2002	11.1	20.3
2007	4.3	7.4
2012	13.6	22.2
2017	13.2	22.8
Mean	11.1	23.9

Note: Toulon data based on combined results for Toulon-Sud and Toulon-Nord electoral districts. The 1998 result is for a by-election in Toulon-Sud.

Table 3 JEAN-MARIE LE PEN/MARINE LE PEN IN FRANCE AND TOULON, PRESIDENTIAL ELECTIONS

Year	Percent of eligible votes, first round	
	France	Toulon
1988	14.4	27.0
1995	15.0	24.0
2002	16.9	20.8
2007	10.5	13.5
2012	17.9	23.4
2017	21.3	27.3
Mean	16.0	22.7

Table 4 NATIONAL FRONT/LE PEN LIST IN FRANCE AND TOULON, EUROPEAN ELECTIONS

Year	Percent of eligible votes	
	France	Toulon
1984	11.2	22.3
1989	11.9	28.3
1994	10.5	24.6
1999	5.7	10.7
2004	9.8	15.1
2009	6.3	11.2
2014	24.9	31.0
Mean	11.5	20.5

Table 5 AVERAGE NATIONAL FRONT VOTE, BY ELECTION TYPE

	Parliamentary	Presidential	European
(a) Toulon	23.9	22.7	20.5
(b) France	11.1	16.0	11.5
Ratio of (b) to (a)	1:2.2	1:1.4	1:1.8

Table 6 VOTE FOR NATIONAL FRONT IN 14 CITIES WITH REPATRIATE COMMUNITIES, PARLIAMENTARY ELECTIONS

	2002	2007	2012	2017	Mean
Marseille	19.7	7.0	20.9	18.2	16.5
Toulouse	9.0	3.3	8.9	6.8	7.0
Nice	23.1	6.7	19.6	17.5	16.7
Montpellier	13.0	4.2	12.8	10.0	10.0
Toulon	20.3	7.4	22.2	22.8	18.2
Nîmes	17.9	6.2	21.5	18.6	16.1
Aix-en-Provence	11.2	4.0	13.4	10.8	9.9
Perpignan	19.6	7.1	24.4	21.0	18.0
Avignon	18.3	7.5	22.1	19.1	16.8
Béziers	20.9	8.0	21.3	36.2	21.6
Antibes	20.4	6.1	16.9	16.2	14.9
Cannes	19.6	6.7	22.2	19.3	17.0
La Seyne-sur-Mer	19.9	7.4	23.5	24.3	18.8
Fréjus	25.2	9.0	28.0	30.3	23.1
(a) Mean National Front vote, 14 cities	18.4	6.5	19.8	19.4	16.0
(b) National Front vote, France	11.1	4.3	13.6	13.2	10.6
Ratio of *(b)* to *(a)*	1:1.7	1:1.5	1:1.5	1:1.5	1:1.5

Note: Cities listed from largest to smallest. Percentages for larger cities with multiple electoral districts (Marseille down to Perpignan) based on total share of eligible vote for all city districts.
Source: Calculated from data at www.interieur.gouv.fr/Elections/.

Table 7 PREVIOUSLY VICTORIOUS PARTIES IN DISTRICTS THE NATIONAL FRONT WON IN 2017

Location	Electoral District	Year of Parliamentary Elections			
		2002	2007	2012	2017
Northern France	Nord 19	PS	PS	PS	FN
	Pas-de-Calais 3	PS	PS	PS	FN
	Pas-de-Calais 10	PS	PS	PS	FN
	Pas-de-Calais 11	PS	PS	PS	FN
	Pas-de-Calais 12	PS	PS	PS	FN
Southern France	Gard 2	UMP	UMP	FN	FN
	Pyrénées-Orientales 2	UMP	UMP	UMP	FN
	Hérault 6	UMP	UMP	PS	FN

Source: Calculated from data at www.interieur.gouv.fr/Elections/.

NOTES

ABBREVIATIONS
Archival Sources
AMT   Archives Municipales de Toulon (Toulon)
BP   Louis Boutigny Papers (Toulon and Aix-en-Provence)

Periodical
NH   *National hebdo*

INTRODUCTION
1. Instead of assuming cleavages replace each other over time, cleavage theory examines how later cleavages interact with earlier ones; see Liesbet Hooghe and Gary Marks, "Cleavage Theory Meets Europe's Crises: Lipset, Rokkan, and the Transnational Cleavage," *Journal of European Public Policy* 25/1 (2018), p. 113.
2. Franco Ferraresi, *Threats to Democracy: The Radical Right in Italy after the War* (Princeton, NJ: Princeton University Press, 1996), p. 8.
3. Roger Eatwell, "Introduction," in Roger Eatwell and Cas Mudde (eds.), *Western Democracies and the New Extreme Right Challenge* (London: Routledge, 2004), pp. 8–11.
4. The antidemocratic (or extreme) far right belongs to what Linz calls disloyal or semi-loyal opposition; see Juan J. Linz, "Crisis, Breakdown and Reequilibration," Part 1 of Juan J. Linz and Alfred Stepan, *The Breakdown of Democratic Regimes* (Baltimore, MD: Johns Hopkins University Press, 1978).
5. The far right includes both the extreme right (which rejects parliamentary democracy) and the radical right (which accepts popular sovereignty and majority rule but rejects pluralism and minority rights); see Cas Mudde, "The Far Right and the European Elections," *Current History* 113 (2014), pp. 98–103.
6. Jan-Werner Müller, *What Is Populism?* (Philadelphia: University of Pennsylvania Press, 2016).
7. Given the waves of migrants from elsewhere in Europe during the nineteenth and twentieth centuries, equating immigrants with those descended from former colonial subjects "stigmatizes the most recent arrivals and obscures the history of immigration to France"; Joshua Cole, "Understanding the French Riots of 2005: What Historical Context for the'*crise des banlieus*'?" *Francophone Postcolonial Studies* 5/2 (2007), pp. 78–79.
8. Kai Arzheimer, "Explaining Electoral Support for the Radical Right," in Jens Rydgren (ed.), *The Oxford Handbook of the Radical Right* (New York: Oxford University Press, 2018), p. 147.
9. Mudde, "The Far Right and the European Elections," pp. 100–101.

10. OECD (2016), *International Migration Outlook 2016* (Paris: OECD), pp. 259 and 303.
11. Carmen González-Enríquez, "The Spanish Exception: Unemployment, Inequality and Immigration, but No Right-Wing Populist Parties," Elcano Royal Institute, Working Paper 3, 2017, online at http://www.realinstitutoelcano.org (accessed 6 June 2017).
12. Ibid., p. 37. In 2018, the Vox Party gained 12 seats in Andalucia (where a corruption scandal tainted the once-dominant Socialist Party), the first time since the Franco era that a far-right party has entered a regional assembly.
13. This is the freezing hypothesis of Seymour Martin Lipset and Stein Rokkan, "Cleavage Structures, Party Systems, and Voter Alignments: An Introduction," in their *Party Systems and Voter Alignments: Cross-National Perspectives* (New York: Free Press, 1967), pp. 1–64.
14. Denmark, Finland, France, Germany, the Netherlands, Norway, Sweden, the United Kingdom; see Herbert Kitschelt (in collaboration with Anthony J. McGann), *The Radical Right in Western Europe: A Comparative Analysis* (Ann Arbor: University of Michigan Press, 1997), pp. 146–147.
15. Hooghe and Marks, "Cleavage Theory Meets Europe's Crises," pp. 121–122.
16. This transformation has many implications for cleavage politics; see Simon Bornschier, "Globalization, Cleavages, and the Radical Right," in Jens Rydgren (ed.), *The Oxford Handbook of the Radical Right* (New York: Oxford University Press, 2018), pp. 212–238.
17. Jan-Werner Müller, "Protecting Popular Self-Government from the People? New Normative Perspectives on Militant Democracy," *Annual Review of Political Science* 19 (2016), pp. 249–265.
18. Jens Rydgren, "The Sociology of the Radical Right," *Annual Review of Sociology* 33 (2007), pp. 241–262; and Matt Golder, "Far Right Parties in Europe," *Annual Review of Political Science* 19 (2016), pp. 477–497. The value of applying the language of markets to study politics depends on the heuristic payoff; this does not make markets and politics identical.
19. Rydgren, "The Sociology of the Radical Right," p. 252.
20. Without altering other personal information (such as how respondents voted, where they were born, or in what decade they were born), I use pseudonyms for all interviews in this book. I conducted and recorded these interviews in the Toulon area between June and December 2002. Unless otherwise indicated, all translations from the French in this book are my own.
21. The OAS (Organisation armée secrète) was a paramilitary group that resorted to violence in the metropole as well as the colony in its fight against independence. It enjoyed wide support among settlers and other nationalists who wanted France to remain in Algeria.
22. Daring to disobey and threaten the political regime in Paris, in 1961 the putschists of Algiers crossed the boundary that divides legitimate authority from illegitimacy in liberal and republican ideals of civil-military relations. By supporting the putsch; disobeying military units loyal to Paris; hatching attempts to kill De Gaulle; and resorting to a scorched-earth policy of arson, intimidation, and assassination, the OAS had sponsored crimes. For the *pieds noirs*, bygones should be bygones where the putschists and the OAS are concerned.
23. On variation in *pied noir* voting, see Emmanuelle Comtat, *Les pieds-noirs et la politique: Quarante ans après le retour* (Paris: Presses de la Fondation nationale des sciences politiques, 2009). On this people's internal diversity, shifting boundaries, and changing labels before and after 1962, see Éric Savarese, *L'invention des Pieds-Noirs* (Paris: Séguier, 2002). On their affinity for the far right, see Éric Savarese. "Un regard compréhensif sur le 'traumatisme historique': À propos du vote Front national chez les pieds-noirs," *Pôle Sud* 34/1 (2011), pp. 91–104.

24. Between 1958 and 1984, support for the far right surged in the 1962 referendum on the Évian Accords and the 1965 presidential election; see Pascal Perrineau, "La surprise lepéniste et sa suite législative," in Pascal Perrineau and Colette Ysmal (eds.), *Le vote de tous les refus* (Paris: Presses de la Fondation nationale des sciences politiques, 2003), p. 202.
25. Although it predated the Third Republic, the penetration of the metropole by colonial representations took off in the 1870s. Lasting nearly a century, its vectors included textbooks, newspapers, exhibitions, sports, advertising, literature, theater, and cinema; for a comprehensive treatment, see Pascal Blanchard et al. (eds.), *Culture coloniale en France: De la Révolution française à nos jours* (Paris: Centre national de la recherche scientifique, 2008). For an overview of French research on the after-effects of empire, see Nicolas Bancel et al. (eds.), *Ruptures postcoloniales: Les nouveaux visages de la société française* (Paris: La Découverte, 2010).
26. Narrowness of vision also resulted from concentrating on official memories—with the state a central actor—at the expense of social memories; see Claire Eldridge, *From Empire to Exile: History and Memory within the Pied-Noir and Harki Communities, 1962–2012* (Manchester: Manchester University Press, 2016), pp. 7–10.
27. Examples of legacy research include Andrea L. Smith, *Colonial Memory and Postcolonial Europe: Maltese Settlers in Algeria and France* (Bloomington and Indianapolis: Indiana University Press, 2006); Mary Fulbrook, *Dissonant Lives: Generations and Violence through German Dictatorships* (Oxford: Oxford University Press, 2011); and Donatella della Porta et al., *Legacies and Memories in Movements: Justice and Democracy in Southern Europe* (New York: Oxford University Press, 2018).
28. Ernst Bloch, "Nonsynchronism and the Obligation to Its Dialectics," *New German Critique* 11 (Spring 1977), p. 29.
29. Ibid., p. 30.
30. See Eldridge, *From Empire to Exile*; and Cas Mudde and Cristóbal Rovira Kaltwasser, *Populism: A Very Short Introduction* (Oxford: Oxford University Press, 2017).

CHAPTER 1

1. Gouvernement-Général de l'Algérie, *L'Algérie du demi-siècle vue par les autorités locales* (Algiers: January 1954), p. 261.
2. Cas Mudde, *The Relationship between Immigration and Nativism in Europe and North America* (Washington, DC: Migration Policy Institute, 2012), pp. 9–13.
3. Michel Winock, "Le retour du national-populisme," in his *Nationalisme, antisémitisme et fascisme en France* (Paris: Le Seuil, 1990), pp. 41–49.
4. Against Manichean apology or denunciation, see Emmanuelle Saada, "The Empire of Law: Dignity, Prestige, and Domination in the Colonial Situation," *French Politics, Culture and Society* 20/2 (2002), p. 102.
5. Quoted in Victoria Thompson, "'I Went Pale with Pleasure': The Body, Sexuality, and National Identity among French Travelers to Algiers in the Nineteenth Century," in Patricia M.E. Lorcin (ed.), *Algeria and France, 1800–2000: Identity, Memory, Nostalgia* (Syracuse, NY: Syracuse University Press, 2006), p. 25.
6. Jonathan K. Gosnell, *The Politics of Frenchness in Colonial Algeria, 1930–1954* (Rochester, NY: University of Rochester Press, 2002), p. 12.
7. Rupert Brown, "Social Identity Theory: Past Achievements, Current Problems and Future Challenges," *European Journal of Social Psychology* 30/6 (2002), pp. 745–778; and Esra Cuhadar and Bruce Dayton, "The Social Psychology of Identity and Inter-Group Conflict: From Theory to Practice," *International Studies Perspectives* 12/3 (2011), pp. 273–293.

8. Alexis de Tocqueville, "Rapport fait par M. de Tocqueville sur le projet de loi relatif aux crédits extraordinaires demandés pour l'Algérie," in his *Œuvres,* vol. 1 (Paris: Gallimard, 1991), p. 813.
9. Douglas Porch, "Bugeaud, Galliéni, Lyautey: The Development of French Colonial Warfare," in Peter Paret (ed.), *Makers of Modern Strategy from Machiavelli to the Nuclear Age* (Princeton, NJ: Princeton University Press, 1986), pp. 378–381; Guy Pervillé, *De l'Empire française à la décolonisation* (Paris: Hachette, 1991), pp. 35–36; and Abderrahmane Bouchène et al., "Chronologie 1830–1880," in their *Histoire de l'Algérie à la période coloniale 1830–1962* (Paris and Algiers: La Découverte and Barzakh, 2012), pp. 45–51.
10. Often transmitted by women, this folklore was adapted to the mobilization for independence and then the resistance to modern, standard, literary Arabic as a national language; see Susan Slyomovics, "Algerian Women's *Būqālah* Poetry: Oral Literature, Cultural Politics, and Anti-Colonial Resistance," *Journal of Arabic Literature* 45 (2014), pp. 145–168.
11. Jennifer E. Sessions, *By Sword and Plow: France and the Conquest of Algeria* (Ithaca, NY: Cornell University Press, 2011).
12. From 7,812 Europeans in 1833, their number rose to 35,727 in 1841, 131,283 in 1851, and 192,746 in 1861; see Kamel Kateb, *Européens, 'indigènes' et juifs en Algérie 1830–1962* (Paris: Institut national d'études démographiques, 2001), p. 29.
13. Pervillé, *De l'Empire française à la décolonisation,* pp. 40–41; and Robert Aldrich, *Greater France: A History of French Overseas Expansion* (Houndmills, UK: Macmillan, 1996), p. 144; Owen White, "Roll Out the Barrel: French and Algerian Ports and the Birth of the Wine Tanker," *French Politics, Culture and Society* 35/2 (2017), pp. 111–132.
14. Jeannine Verdès-Leroux, *Les français d'Algérie de 1830 à aujourd'hui: Une page d'histoire déchirée* (Paris: Fayard, 2001), pp. 194–204.
15. Calculated from data in Kateb, *Européens, 'indigènes' et juifs en Algérie,* p. 176. By this time, the official category of "European" inconsistently included Jews with French citizenship. Ultimately, the colony may have cost more to the metropole than it ever returned; see David Todd, "Review of By Sword and Plow: France and the Conquest of Algeria by Jennifer E. Sessions," *Revue d'Histoire moderne et contemporaine* 60/3 (2012), pp. 201–203.
16. Apart from Alsace-Lorraine, the metropole's most important sending region was the south (including Corsica).
17. Maurice Wahl (1882), quoted in Verdès-Leroux, *Les français d'Algérie de 1830 à aujourd'hui,* p. 205.
18. Especially Murcia, Alicante, Malaga, and Valencia; see Charles-Robert Ageron, *Histoire de l'Algérie contemporaine 1830–1999* (Paris: Presses Universitaires de France, 1999), p. 23.
19. Kateb, *Européens, 'indigènes' et juifs en Algérie,* pp. 28–29.
20. Jacques Bouveresse, *Un parlement colonial? Les délégations financières algériennes 1898–1945* (Mont-Saint-Aignan: Publications des Universités de Rouen et Du Havre, 2008), p. 93.
21. Aldrich, *Greater France,* p. 144; and Martin Evans and John Phillips, *Algeria: Anger of the Dispossessed* (New Haven, CT: Yale University Press, 2007), p. 34.
22. Between 1891 and 1921, the non-French share of the European population fell from 40.6 percent to 23.9 percent; see Kateb, *Européens, 'indigènes' et juifs en Algérie,* p. 189.
23. Verdès-Leroux, *Les français d'Algérie de 1830 à aujourd'hui,* pp. 204–212; and Patricia M. E. Lorcin, *Imperial Identities: Stereotyping, Prejudice and Race in Colonial Algeria* (London: I.B. Tauris, 1995), p. 186.
24. Lorcin, *Imperial Identities,* p. 252.

25. Lizabeth Zack, "Who Fought the Algerian War? Political Identity and Conflict in French-ruled Algeria," *International Journal of Politics* 16/1 (2002), p. 65. On the multiplicity of belonging and World War I as a turning point in making the Neos more French, see Hugo Vermeren, *Les Italiens à Bône (1865–1940): Migrations méditérranéennes et colonisation de peuplement en Algérie* (Rome: École française de Rome, 2017), pp. 520–521.
26. In marriages between 1831 and 1915, over 80 percent of the French chose a French spouse; and over 70 percent of other Europeans chose another non-French European; see Claudine Robert-Guiard, *Des Européennes en situation coloniale: Algérie 1830–1939* (Aix-en-Provence: Presses de l'Université de Provence, 2009), pp. 119–127.
27. Lorcin, *Imperial Identities*, p. 186.
28. Women of non-French background were three times more likely to find a French partner than were men in the same category; see Robert-Guiard, *Des Européennes en situation coloniale*, pp. 119–127.
29. Knowledgeable people made finer distinctions: the Tuaregs were the nomadic Berbers of the Sahara, for example, while the Kouloughlis were the offspring of unions between indigenous women and Turkish soldiers. An official publication from 1837 lists three categories of Berbers, two of Schellouk (or Schellouch), and two of Jews. It also lists Arabs (*Arabes homeyrites ou conquérants*), Moors (*Maures*), Kouloughlis (*Koulouglis et enfants de Turcs*), and enslaved and free blacks (*Noirs du Soudan esclaves ou affranchis*); see Kateb, *Européens, 'indigènes' et juifs en Algérie*, p. 196.
30. Emigrants went to Morocco, Tunisia, Egypt, Palestine, Syria, and Turkey; see ibid., pp. 49–58.
31. Ibid., p. 3.
32. Eric R. Wolf, *Peasant Wars of the Twentieth Century* (New York: Harper, 1969), pp. 213–220; Ageron, *Histoire de l'Algérie contemporaine*, p. 24.
33. Before World War I, an estimated 6.4 percent of Muslim households were polygamous. Affording a dowry made polygamy more prevalent among male notables, wealthy landowners, and wage earners than among peasants. Between 1901 and 1914, estimates of the annual divorce rate ranged between 29 and 41 per 100 marriages; see Kateb, *Européens, 'indigènes' et juifs en Algérie*, p. 150.
34. Quoted in Robert-Guiard, *Des Européennes en situation coloniale*, p. 117.
35. Kateb, *Européens, 'indigènes' et juifs en Algérie*, p. 204.
36. Lorcin, *Imperial Identities*, p. 112.
37. Berber society came closer to French civilizational ideals, allegedly, because it was less imbued with religion; sedentary rather than nomadic; egalitarian rather than feudalistic; monogamous rather than polygamous; dynamic rather than static; an incipient nation rather than a hodgepodge of tribes; see ibid., pp. 241–249.
38. Bouveresse, *Un parlement colonial*, pp. 378–379.
39. Lorcin, *Imperial Identities*, p. 207. Their author was Auguste Robinet (1862–1930), a public official in Algiers.
40. David Prochaska, "History as Literature, Literature as History: Cagayous of Algiers," *American Historical Review* 101/3 (1996), p. 705.
41. Jeanne Duclos, *Dictionnaire du français d'Algérie* (Paris: Editions Bonneton, 1992), pp. 8–9.
42. Emanuel Sivan, "Colonialism and Popular Culture in Algeria," *Journal of Contemporary History* 14/1 (1979), p. 34.
43. Ibid., pp. 21–53.
44. Emmanuelle Saada, *Empire's Children: Race, Filiation, and Citizenship in the French Colonies* (Chicago: University of Chicago Press, 2012), pp. 25–30.
45. Unlike the metropole, where a preponderance of small agricultural holdings still prevailed, in Algeria a landholding elite often succeeded in representing its own interest

as the general interest. Among this elite, moreover, interlocking memberships helped to manage conflict (*colons* served on municipal councils and financial boards); see André Nouschi, *Algérie amère 1914–1994* (Paris: Maison des sciences de l'homme, 1995).

46. Bouveresse, *Un parlement colonial*, p. 144. By the 1930s, moreover, like European delegates most of the delegation's *indigènes* were owners of great agricultural estates; ibid., p. 427.
47. Laure Blévis, "La citoyenneté française au miroir de la colonisation," *Genèses* 53/4 (2003), pp. 25–47.
48. Sarah Abrevaya Stein, "Dividing South From North: French Colonialism, Jews, and the Algerian Sahara," *Journal of North African Studies* 17/5 (2012), p. 775. Jews came to Algeria after the sacking of Jerusalem under Titus; and from Castile and Aragon after the expulsion of non-Christians in 1492. An 1856 census puts their number at 21,408 (as opposed to 92,738 French nationals; 66,544 mainly Spanish, Italian, and Maltese aliens; and 2,307,349 *indigènes*). By 1872 the Jewish population had increased to 34,574 (as opposed to 164,175 people of French descent; 115,516 non-French Europeans; and 2,125,052 *indigènes*, whose number had declined due to war, disease, famine, and migration); see Kateb, *Européens, 'indigènes' et juifs en Algérie*, pp. 29–30.
49. Geneviève Dermenjian and Benjamin Stora, "Les juifs d'Algérie dans le regard des militaires et des juifs de France à l'époque de la conquête (1830–1855)," *Revue Historique* 284/2 (1990), pp. 333–339.
50. A Muslim song about the takeover of old Algiers by the French military denounces both the Christians who occupy this neighborhood and the rejoicing of the Jews, see Zeynep Çelik, *Urban Forms and Colonial Confrontations: Algiers under French Rule* (Berkeley and Los Angeles: University of California Press, 1997), p. 27.
51. Joshua Schreier, "Napoléon's Long Shadow: Morality, Civilization, and Jews in France and Algeria, 1808–1870," *French Historical Studies* 30/1 (2002), pp. 77–103.
52. Ultimately, detaching Jew from Muslim brought a part of the native population into the French sphere (however, the Crémieux Decree did not apply to the few thousand M'Zabite Jews living in the Sahara, a military territory); see Zack, "Who Fought the Algerian War," p. 64.
53. The original name of Max Régis, the president of the Ligue antijuive, was Massimiliano Milano. Like many of his followers in the Spanish and Italian neighborhoods of Algiers, he was a naturalized Frenchman; see Zack, "Who Fought the Algerian War," p. 93.
54. Rioting in Algiers resulted in looting, two deaths, and the synagogue's destruction; see Didier Guignard, "Les crises en trompe l'oeil de l'Algérie française des années 1890," in Abderrahmane Bouchène et al. (eds.), *Histoire de l'Algérie à la période coloniale 1830–1962* (Paris and Algiers: La Découverte and Barzakh), pp. 218–223; and Winock, *Nationalisme, antisémitisme et fascisme*, p. 200.
55. Quoted in ibid., p. 129.
56. Zack, "Who Fought the Algerian War," pp. 66–67.
57. Ibid., p. 70.
58. Robert-Guiard, *Des Européennes en situation coloniale*, p. 118.
59. Zack, "Who Fought the Algerian War," p. 76.
60. Gilbert Meynier, "Les Algériens et la guerre de 1914–1918," in Abderrahmane Bouchène et al. (eds.), *Histoire de l'Algérie à la période coloniale 1830–1962* (Paris and Algiers: La Découverte and Barzakh), p. 231.
61. Ibid., pp. 229–234; Benjamin Stora, *Histoire de l'Algérie coloniale 1830–1954* (Paris: La Découverte, 2004), pp. 40–42.
62. From 5,568 departures (and 17,497 returns) in 1919, within six years the annual flow between colony and metropole had swollen to 71,028 departures (and 57,467 returns); see ibid., p. 47.

63. Rabah Aissaoui, *Immigration and National Identity: North African Political Movements in Colonial and Postcolonial France* (London: Tauris, 2009).
64. Bouveresse, *Un parlement colonial*, p. 103.
65. Joshua Cole, "Constantine before the Riots of August 1934: Civil Status, anti-Semitism, and the Politics of Assimilation in Interwar French Algeria," *Journal of North African Studies* 17/5 (2012), p. 842.
66. Kateb, *Européens, 'indigènes' et juifs en Algérie*, pp. 182–184.
67. Jacques Cantier, *L'Algérie sous le régime de Vichy* (Paris: Odile Jacob, 2002), p. 62.
68. Quoted in Nouschi, *Algérie amère*, p. 59.
69. Ibid., pp. 64–69.
70. Cole, "Constantine before the Riots of August 1934."
71. Cantier, *L'Algérie sous le régime de Vichy*, pp. 19–21. The main exception was Oran; see Nouschi, *Algérie amère*, p. 68.
72. Between the two world wars, residential segregation decreased between Europeans of different backgrounds but increased between Europeans and non-Europeans; see Vermeren, *Les Italiens à Bône*, pp. 413–414.
73. Out of nearly 1 million Muslim children, fewer than 70,000 attended schools; see Cantier, *L'Algérie sous le régime de Vichy*, p. 22.
74. Evans and Phillips, *Anger of the Dispossessed*, pp. 38–39.
75. Ibid.; Cole, "Constantine before the Riots of August 1934," p. 854. A contest for control over territory triggers the crime in *L'Étranger* by Albert Camus, who makes the setting for Meursault's murder of the *Arabe* a public beach.
76. Cantier, *L'Algérie sous le régime de Vichy*, p. 62.
77. Quoted in Robert-Guiard, *Des Européennes en situation coloniale*, p. 118.
78. Ibid., p. 277.
79. In 1936 the labor force participation rate for European women over 14 years was 22.3 percent—more than double by comparison with 1911 but still less than half the comparable rate for the metropole; ibid., p. 154.
80. Ageron, *Histoire de l'Algérie contemporaine*, pp. 25–26.
81. Initially Muslims and European foreigners also received the right to elect representatives, but at the request of the French Algerians this reform was rescinded; see ibid., p. 26; and Pervillé, *De l'Empire française à la décolonisation*, p. 37.
82. Cantier, *L'Algérie sous le régime de Vichy*, p. 18.
83. Eugène Audinet et al., (1911), quoted in Kateb, *Européens, 'indigènes' et juifs en Algérie*, p. 200.
84. Cantier, *L'Algérie sous le régime de Vichy*, p. 21.
85. William B. Cohen, "The Colonial Policy of the Popular Front," *French Historical Studies* 7/3 (1972), p. 381.
86. Fernand Braudel, "A propos de L'Histoire de l'Afrique du Nord de Charles-André Julien," in his *Autour de la Méditerranée* (Paris: De Fallois Fernand, 1996), p. 164.
87. Jean-Robert Henry, "Le centenaire de l'Algérie, triomphe éphémère de la pensée algérianiste," in Abderrahmane Bouchène et al. (eds.), *Histoire de l'Algérie à la période coloniale 1830–1962* (Paris and Algiers: La Découverte and Barzakh), pp. 369–375
88. Pervillé, *De l'Empire française à la décolonisation*, p. 158.
89. Ibid., p. 159.
90. The idea of intersecting social circles is Georg Simmel's, of course; see Mario Diani, *The Cement of Civil Society: Studying Networks in Localities* (Cambridge: Cambridge University Press, 2015), pp. 82–83.
91. On the limits to hybridity, see Emmanuelle Saada, "Race and Sociological Reason in the Republic: Inquiries on the *Métis* in the French Empire (1908–37)," *International Sociology* 17/3 (2002), pp. 361–391.
92. Bouveresse, *Un parlement colonial*, pp. 174–178.

CHAPTER 2

1. The new schema reserved a place apart for *harkis* and other French loyalists among the Muslims.
2. Communists supported independence but formed a tiny minority; their voice—the *Alger Républicain* (which authorities later banned)—denounced inequalities between Muslim peasants and large landholders; see *Alger Républicain*, 16 and 18 August 1955. After 1956, the French Communist Party supported independence; see Allison Drew, *We Are No Longer in France: Communists in Colonial Algeria* (Manchester: Manchester University Press, 2014), pp. 192–218.
3. Whenever the metropole resisted them, of course, the settlers would cease, temporarily, to consider Algeria a part of France; see Gosnell, *The Politics of Frenchness*, p. 221.
4. Bouveresse, *Un parlement colonial*, pp. 755–762.
5. Cantier, *L'Algérie sous le régime de Vichy*, pp. 33–41. On opportunities for revolution created by state weakening, see Theda Skocpol, *States and Social Revolutions: A Comparative Analysis of France, Russia, and China* (Cambridge: Cambridge University Press, 1979), especially pp. 47–51 (and p. 287 on cases like Algeria).
6. Gouvernement-Général de l'Algérie, *L'Algérie du demi-siècle vue par les autorités locales* (Algiers: January 1954), p. 265.
7. BP, Préfecture d'Alger, Direction des service économiques (Cuirs et textiles), Circulaire no. 682 (28 January 1944); and BP, letter from Luc Monot, Chef de Groupe, Services de Rationnement, Mairie de la Ville d'Algers, to the Mayor of Algiers, N. 810SE/1/2B, 26 September 1945.
8. Cantier, *L'Algérie sous le régime de Vichy*, p. 180.
9. Ibid., pp. 315–336.
10. Ibid., pp. 185–192.
11. Belkacem Recham, "La participation des Maghrébiens à la Seconde Guerre mondiale," in Abderrahmane Bouchène et al. (eds.), *Histoire de l'Algérie à la période coloniale 1830–1962* (Paris and Algiers: La Découverte and Barzakh), pp. 457–462.
12. Cantier, *L'Algérie sous le régime de Vichy*, pp. 176–180.
13. BP, Préfecture d'Alger, Cabinet du Préfet, n. 3647, 4 July 1944.
14. BP, Gouvernement Provisoire de la République Française, "Appel en faveur de l'Association nationale pour l'Indochine Française," undated (but late 1944 or early 1945).
15. Evans and Phillips, *Anger of the Dispossessed*, p. 40.
16. Nouschi, *Algérie amère*, p. 177.
17. Pervillé, *De l'Empire française à la décolonisation*, pp. 93–102.
18. Annie Rey-Goldzeiguer, *Aux origines de la guerre d'Algérie 1940–1945: de Mers El-Kébir aux massacres du Nord-Constantinois* (Paris: La Découverte, 2001).
19. Stora, *Histoire de l'Algérie coloniale*, p. 85.
20. The Marshall Plan did help Algeria, but only marginally; see Pervillé, *De l'Empire française à la décolonisation*, p. 167.
21. Ibid., pp. 161–175.
22. Ethan B. Katz, *The Burdens of Brotherhood: Jews and Muslims from North Africa to France* (Cambridge, MA: Harvard University Press, 2015).
23. Between 1948 and 1954, the growth of shantytowns on the edge of Algiers furthered ethnic segregation. After 1954, urban development to improve the social condition of Muslims as well as anti-rebel resettlement policies in the countryside again segregated; Çelik, *Urban Forms and Colonial Confrontations*, pp. 81–86, 123–129.
24. Of the 3,971 marriages, intra-Muslim marriages accounted for 47 percent, intra-European marriages for 45 percent, and intra-Jewish marriages for 5 percent; of the mixed marriages, 5 united Christian with Jew; and 26 united Christian with Muslim; see BP, Alger, *Bulletin municipal official de la ville d'Alger*, number 4, February 1949, p. 105.

25. Bertrand Le Gendre, *Guerre d'Algérie: Le choc des mémoires* (Paris: Le Monde, 2013), p. 7.
26. Gouvernement-Général de l'Algérie, *L'Algérie du demi-siècle*, p. 260.
27. Ibid., p. 262.
28. Ibid., p. 243.
29. Ibid., p. 117.
30. Evans and Phillips, *Anger of the Dispossessed*, p. 39.
31. Gouvernement-Général de l'Algérie, *L'Algérie du demi-siècle*, p. 113.
32. Ibid., pp. 45, 95.
33. Ibid., p. 265.
34. Ibid., pp. 249–250.
35. Ibid., p. 250.
36. Ibid., p. 269.
37. Ibid., p. 258.
38. Le Gendre, *Guerre d'Algérie*, pp. 8, 39–41.
39. *Le Figaro*, 13–14 November 1954.
40. Pervillé, *De l'Empire française à la décolonisation*, pp. 169–183.
41. Jeannine Verdès-Leroux, *Les Français d'Algérie de 1830 à aujourd'hui: Une page d'histoire déchirée* (Paris: Fayard, 2001), p. 252.
42. Pervillé, *De l'Empire française à la décolonisation*, pp. 172–181.
43. BP, letter dated 15 December 1955. Presumably the enclosed photos showed corpses of people subjected to rebel atrocities. "*Melons*" was a derogatory term for "Arabs." The "foreign power" referred to could have been the United States or the USSR.
44. Pervillé, *De l'Empire française à la décolonisation*, p. 174.
45. Raphaël Delpard, *L'Histoire des pieds noirs d'Algérie 1830–1962* (Neuilly-sur-Seine: Michel Lafon, 2002), pp. 211–220.
46. BP, Caisse de Crédit Municipal d'Alger (Conseil d'administration), "Séance du 17 Décembre 1955."
47. Delpard, *L'Histoire des pieds noirs*, p. 220.
48. Ibid., p. 224.
49. Ibid., p. 220.
50. Ibid., p. 226.
51. Aldrich, *Greater France*, p. 297.
52. Stora, *Histoire de l'Algérie coloniale*, p. 55; and Pervillé, *De l'Empire française à la décolonisation*, pp. 174–183.
53. David Thomson, *Democracy in France since 1870* (Oxford: Oxford University Press, 1969), pp. 250–253.
54. Neil MacMaster, *Burning the Veil: The Algerian War and the "Emancipation" of Algerian Women, 1954–62* (Manchester: Manchester University Press, 2009), pp. 118–121.
55. *Le Livre Tricolore du 13 mai au 4 juin 1958* (Algiers: Éditions Œdipe, 1959), p. 30.
56. MacMaster, *Burning the Veil*, p. 7. Going against past tolerance of gender inequality in the colony, reforms proposed in the wake of May 1958 included equal educational opportunity for Muslim men and women and bans on the veil, polygamy, arranged marriage, and unilateral divorce; see "De Dunkerque à Tamanrasset: 55 millions de français à part entière," *L'Édile Algérien* 117 (September 1958), pp. 10–22.
57. Neil MacMaster, "L'enjeu des femmes dans la guerre," in Abderrahmane Bouchène et al. (eds.), *Histoire de l'Algérie à la période coloniale 1830–1962* (Paris and Algiers: La Découverte and Barzakh), p. 540.
58. Robert-Guiard, *Des Européennes en situation colonial*, p. 314. "Like the domestic space, women represented the unconquered part of the colony"; Çelik, *Urban Forms and Colonial Confrontations*, p. 88. On "ungovernable" religious, social, and political spaces in the colony, see James McDougall, "The Secular State's Islamic Empire: Muslim Spaces

and Subjects of Jurisdiction in Paris and Algiers, 1905–1957," *Comparative Studies in Society and History* 52/3 (2010), pp. 553–580.
59. Its emotional power may also have come from magically resolving a tension between core values of republicanism, namely official secularism and individual freedom of religious choice; see Mayanthi L. Fernando, *The Republic Unsettled: Muslim French and the Contradictions of Secularism* (Durham, NC: Duke University Press, 2014).
60. *Le Livre Tricolore*, p. 55.
61. BP, letter from Algiers to Lyon, 2 June 1958.
62. *L'Édile Algérien*, 115–116 (July–August 1958), p. 9.
63. Ibid. 113–114 (May–June 1958), p. 35.
64. Ibid., p. 11.
65. Ibid. 123 (March 1959), p. 13.
66. Ibid.
67. Le Monde, *La Cinquième République 1958–1995* (Paris: Le Monde, 1995), pp. 19–20. Programs in agriculture, housing, health, industry, and training dealt with problems with earlier roots in population growth and economic stagnation; see Nouschi, *Algérie amère*, pp. 200–201.
68. *L'Édile Algérien* 121 (December 1959), p. 14.
69. Ibid. 122 (February 1959), p. 22.
70. Ibid. 120 (December 1958), pp. 7, 20.
71. Ibid. 124 (March 1959), p. 9. The deputy was Ahmed Djebbour.
72. Todd Shepard, *The Invention of Decolonization: The Algerian War and the Remaking of France* (Ithaca: Cornell University Press, 2006), pp. 78–81.
73. In a September 1959 national survey, 66 percent of respondents chose Algeria as the most important social or political problem (with prices and the cost of living second, at 12 percent). In February 1960, 78 percent put Algeria first (with prices and the cost of living second, at 5 percent); see Nicolas Lebourg and Jérôme Fourquet, *La nouvelle guerre d'Algérie n'aura pas lieu* (Paris: Fondation Jean-Jaurès, 2017), p. 21.
74. Le Monde, *La Cinquième République*, pp. 21–25.
75. Ibid., p. 26. Some putschists made their way to Franco's Spain; and after Algerian independence, many *pieds noirs* made their way to Alicante.
76. Shepard, *Invention of Decolonization*, p. 91.
77. BP, Organisation Armée Secrète, "Officiers, sous-officiers, caporaux et soldats," undated, but from 1961.
78. Between May and October 1961, the OAS committed more than 700 bomb attacks and assassination attempts; see Le Monde, *La Cinquième République*, p. 28.
79. BP, Organisation Armée Secrète, "Le racisme Gaulliste" (communiqué no. 60), undated (but circa 1961–1962).
80. BP, Organisation Armée Secrète, "Informations" (communiqué no. 59), undated (but from 1961). The OAS also drew blood by purging itself of so-called traitors within the organization.
81. Shepard, *Invention of Decolonization*, pp. 162–166.
82. *L'Édile Algérien* 148–149 (April–May 1961), p. 5; and 154 (October 1961), pp. 6–8.
83. The *pieds noirs* had more cause for bitterness: this referendum opened the final door to Algerian independence, yet the government ruled that *pieds noirs* were ineligible to participate; see Le Monde, *La Cinquième République*, p. 29; and Shepard, *Invention of Decolonization*, pp. 117–124.
84. Shepard, *Invention of Decolonization*, pp. 107–108.
85. *L'Aurore*, 21 May 1962.
86. Ibid., 23 May 1962.
87. Delpard, *L'Histoire des pieds noirs*, pp. 252–261.

88. *L'Aurore*, 11 June 1962.
89. Evans and Phillips, *Anger of the Dispossessed*, p. 69.
90. *L'Aurore*, 6 July 1962.
91. Ibid., 2 July 1962 and 7–8 July 1962; and Evans and Phillips, *Anger of the Dispossessed*, p. 69. An article about the first camp for *harkis* in the metropole (at Larzac) mentions that, on board the ship taking them from Algeria, it was explained to Berber women "that wearing the veil would compromise their assimilation" and that all complied by removing it; see *L'Aurore* 21 June 1962.
92. Shepard, *Invention of Decolonization*, pp. 142–143.
93. *L'Aurore*, 20 June 1962.
94. Shepard, *Invention of Decolonization*, pp. 144–155, 177–182.
95. *L'Aurore*, 7–8 July 1962. Those wishing to leave included most of the Jewish population, whose differences with Algeria's Muslims had been hardening since the birth of Israel; see Maud S. Mandel, *Muslims and Jews in France: History of a Conflict* (Princeton, NJ: Princeton University Press, 2014).
96. "In Algeria electoral fraud has always been a traditional sport with its own champions and a vast public always ready to appreciate its techniques and motives," *Le Figaro*, 2 December 1958. On widespread electoral fraud, see Cantier, *L'Algérie sous le régime de Vichy*, pp. 28–32; Stora, *Histoire de l'Algérie coloniale*, p. 66; and David Prochaska, *Making Algeria French: Colonialism in Bône, 1870–1920* (Cambridge: Cambridge University Press, 2004).
97. Political refugees included "anarchists, socialists, utopians, republicans, antifascists, communists, and opponents of the Franco regime"; see Emmanuelle Comtat, "La question du vote Pied-Noir," *Pôle Sud* 24 (2006), p. 77.
98. Nouschi, *Algérie amère*, p. 72.
99. Ibid., p. 108; and Emmanuelle Comtat, *Les pieds-noirs et la politique: Quarante ans après le retour* (Paris: Presses de la Fondation nationale des sciences politiques, 2009), p. 57.
100. Bouveresse, *Un parlement colonial*, pp. 438–446 and 537–586.
101. Nouschi, *Algérie amère*, pp. 182–185; *Le Figaro*, 12 November 1946.
102. *Le Figaro*, 19 June 1951.
103. Nouschi, *Algérie amère*, p. 192. Because political participation tended to increase with education and income, voter registration and electoral turnouts were slightly lower than in the metropole. Outside the big cities, though—in towns and villages where politics mixed with patron-client relations—the turnout could climb. To maximize votes, some Algerian politicians blunted the left-right cleavage. The moderate right attracted voters who were better off, while the left won elections in big cities like Algiers, Oran, Constantine, and Bône; see Comtat, *Les pieds-noirs et la politique*, pp. 41–70.
104. Ibid., pp. 70–74.
105. Reduced to a few hundred members, what remained of the Algerian Communist Party engaged in clandestine, pro-independence activism; see ibid., p. 73.
106. These tickets included *Liste Algérie française* and *Liste Comité de Salut public*.
107. The Socialist Party managed to field a slate in only 1 of the colony's 18 electoral districts (the Bougie district) while the Communists fielded none; see *Le Figaro*, 2 December 1958.
108. Le Monde, *La Cinquième République*, pp. 12–14.
109. BP, Marc Lauriol and Philippe Marçais, "Lettre Paris-Alger" (number 12), 4 February 1961. Deputies from Algeria elected to the National Assembly in November 1958 agreed to vote as a bloc; see *L'Édile Algérien* 119 (November 1958), pp. 7–8.
110. Portugal—another colonial power that received a sizeable influx of settlers from former colonies—provides an illuminating comparison. After the fall of Marcelo Caetano in 1974, the far right attempted to mobilize the *retornados*, the one-half million Portuguese newly

arrived from Angola and Mozambique. The *retornados* joined in the protests against the new left-wing regime in 1975. As in France, moreover, they formed their own associations, but these soon disappeared. Unlike the *pieds noirs* (of whom the vast majority were born in Algeria), most of the *retornados* were born in Portugal and had migrated to the colonies as recently as a decade or two earlier. With their social networks more open to others in the metropole, the political system reintegrated the *retornados*; see John Veugelers, "Ex-Colonials, Voluntary Associations, and Electoral Support for the Contemporary Far Right," *Comparative European Politics* 3/4 (2005), pp. 426–427. In Britain, the League of Empire Loyalists linked Anglo-centrism and defense of empire with opposition to the European Community. In 1967, moreover, its leader (Arthur K. Chesterton) became the first chairman of the far-right National Front. A pressure group on the edge of the Conservative Party, however, the League lacked a mass base and avoided electoral politics; see Roger Eatwell, *Fascism: A History* (London: Vintage, 1996), p. 265.
111. Former communist countries can embrace far-right nationalism more easily, by contrast, because it offers an antidote to a now discredited internationalism.
112. Michael Löwy, "Le concept d'affinité élective chez Max Weber," *Archives de sciences sociales des religions* 127 (2004), pp. 93–103.
113. Bloch also discerned limits to the affinity between pre-capitalist outlooks and Nazism; see p. 28 of his "Nonsynchronism and the Obligation to Its Dialectics."

CHAPTER 3

1. *L'Aurore*, 20 June 1962. On differences in news reporting, see Jean-Jacques Jordi, "The Creation of the Pieds-Noirs: Arrival and Settlement in Marseilles, 1962," in Andrea L. Smith (ed.), *Europe's Invisible Migrants* (Amsterdam: Amsterdam University Press, 2003), pp. 71–72.
2. *République-Le Provençal*, 26 June 1962; *Le Méridional*, 30 June 1962; and Jean-Jacques Jordi, *De l'exode à l'exil: Rapatriés et Pieds-Noirs en France* (Paris: Harmattan, 1993), p. 93.
3. The Socialists broke through in the Var in 1898, in low-lying areas of specialized agricultural and artisanal production (e.g., wine, cork, and barrels) between the coast (itself divided between anticlerical radicalism and conservative nationalism) and the isolated Alpine foothills (more Catholic and conservative). Traversed by long-distance roads, areas where Socialism took hold communicated more directly with outside markets and political radicalism; see Tony Judt, *Socialism in Provence 1871–1914* (Cambridge: Cambridge University Press, 1979).
4. Dominique Legenne, *Var, terre d'histoire* (Arles: Actes Sud, 1999), pp. 162–164, 240.
5. *République-Le Provençal*, 14 February 1963; and *Livre d'or Toulon-Var* (Toulon: Clayton Publicité, 1960), pp. 83–86, 186–189.
6. Ibid., pp. 83–86, 186–189.
7. In addition to Algiers (1830), it was from Toulon that French troops set sail for Egypt (1798), Indochina (1855), Mexico (1862), Tunisia (1881), Madagascar (1883), Tonkin (1884), and Dahomey (1892).
8. *République-Le Provençal*, 20 April 1962.
9. Ibid., 14 February 1963.
10. Marc Bayle, "Les droites à Toulon (1958–1994): De l'Algérie française au Front national," PhD diss., Aix-en-Provence and Marseille: Université Aix-Marseille I, 2001, p. 149.
11. Ibid., pp. 42–63.
12. Reimbold became OAS regional head at the request of Pierre Sergent, who in 1986 won election to the National Assembly as a candidate for the FN.
13. Ibid., 97–100; and Anne-Marie Duranton-Crabol, *Le temps de l'OAS* (Brussels: Complexe, 1995), p. 97.

14. *République-Le Provençal*, 9 July 1962; *Le Monde*, 13 July 1962, 14 July 1962.
15. Authorities charged them with OAS recruiting; holding OAS meetings; providing liaison between OAS units; printing, storing, and distributing OAS tracts; and transporting OAS leaders and army renegades between France and Algeria; see *Le Monde*, 12 April 1962 and 14 April 1962; and Jean-Baptiste Gaignebet, "A la recherche de nouveaux rôles," in Maurice Agulhon (ed.), *Histoire de Toulon* (Toulouse: Privat, 1988), p. 364.
16. This group was the Association des Français d'Afrique du Nord et d'Outre Mer et de leurs Amis. On the history, politics, and diversity of these associations, see Claire Eldridge, "Unity above All? Relationships and Rivalries within the Pied-Noir Community," in Manuel Borutta and Jan C. Jansen (eds.), *Vertriebene and Pieds-Noirs in Postwar Germany and France* (London: Palgrave Macmillan, 2016), 133–150.
17. This second group was the Association nationale des Français d'Outre-Mer et de leurs Amis.
18. This third group was the Rassemblement national des Français d'Afrique du Nord.
19. Bayle, "Les droites à Toulon," pp. 163–172.
20. Thierry Bouclier, *Tixier-Vignancour* (Paris: Rémi Perrin, 2003); *Le Monde*, 1–2 October 1989.
21. Bayle, "Les droites à Toulon," pp. 109–143.
22. Ibid., pp. 30–36; Gaignebet, "A la recherche de nouveaux rôles," p. 363.
23. Le Monde, *La Cinquième République*, p. 20. This organization was the Rassemblement pour l'Algérie française, led by Georges Bidault; Pascal Arrighi was a founder.
24. Bayle, "Les droites à Toulon," pp. 66–67.
25. *République-Le Provençal*, 6 April 1962.
26. The founders of the Comité de Vincennes were Georges Bidault and Jacques Soustelle; see Bayle, "Les droites à Toulon," pp. 66–67. In the national referendum of January 1961, the vote against Algerian self-determination was 25 percent in France, 34 percent in Toulon; see Gaignebet, "A la recherche de nouveaux rôles," p. 364.
27. *République-Le Provençal*, 8 May 1962.
28. Le Monde, *La Cinquième République*, p. 29.
29. Support for Algerian independence was 84 percent in Toulon, 87 percent in the Var, and 91 in France; see *République-Le Provençal*, 9 April 1962. The five departments with the strongest "no" vote also had the highest shares of *pieds noirs*; see ibid., 10 April 1962.
30. Bayle, "Les droites à Toulon," pp. 149–150.
31. Maurice Arreckx, *Ca suffit* (Toulon: Presses du Midi, 1998), p. 22.
32. Ibid., p. 22.
33. *République-Le Provençal*, 12 April 1962.
34. The Socialist representative was the previous mayor, Édouard Le Bellegou; see ibid.
35. Ibid.
36. Ibid., 6 June 1962, 18 June 1962, and 26 June 1962.
37. Ibid., 19 June 1962.
38. Ibid., 3 July 1962.
39. Among the 1,870 on board the carrier on 22 July were "7 Muslims, 12 *harkis*, and their respective families"; see ibid., 23 July 1962.
40. Count based on all pertinent news reports in *République-Le Provençal*.
41. *République-Le Provençal*, 26 June 1962.
42. Ibid., 30 June 1962.
43. In late 1961, the National Assembly passed a comprehensive bill that spelled out the legal status of France's ex-colonials. In the name of national solidarity, a cross-party majority in the National Assembly supported this legislation. The government feared that without suitable measures, the new arrivals would cause trouble. Provisions included

living allowances and housing allocations, as well as equal access to schooling and help finding jobs. Upon arrival in the metropole, the head of each household would register with authorities at a regional center for repatriates in Paris, Bordeaux, Lyon, Marseille, or Toulouse (or the nearest Prefecture or Sub-prefecture). To administer this legislation, the government created the State Secretariat for Repatriates (under the authority of the Ministry of the Interior). This legislation also established the right to indemnification for property lost in French colonies; see Yann Scioldo-Zürcher, *Devenir métropolitain. Politique d'intégration et parcours de rapatriés d'Algérie en métropole 1954–2005* (Paris: École des Hautes Études en Sciences Sociales, 2010), pp.111–114.

44. Associations that helped included the Boy Scouts; the Federation of Hoteliers; the Junior Chamber of Commerce; a teachers' association; veterans' associations; two labour unions (Force Ouvrière and the Confédération française des travailleurs chrétiens); and Jewish, Protestant and Catholic charitable organisations; see *Le Méridional*, 18 June 1962; and *République-Le Provençal*, ongoing between 20 April 1962 and 29 July 1962.
45. *République-Le Provençal*, 8 July 1962.
46. Ibid., 20 July 1962.
47. Ibid., 25 July 1962.
48. Ibid., 2 June 1962.
49. Ibid., 19 July 1962.
50. Ibid., 9 July 1962, 19 July 1962, and 23 July 1962.
51. *Le Méridional*, 6 July 1962.
52. *République-Le Provençal*, 1 July 1962.
53. *Le Méridional*, 26 July 1962.
54. *République-Le Provençal*, 19 July 1962.
55. *Le Méridional*, 18 July 1962.
56. Ibid., 26 July 1962.
57. *République-Le Provençal*, 19 July 1962. Between 1962 and 1968, the repatriates' entry into the labor market did reduce wages and increase unemployment in the Var; see Jennifer Hunt, "The Impact of the 1962 Repatriates from Algeria on the French Labor Market," *Industrial and Labor Relations Review* 45/3, 1992, pp. 556–572.
58. Only 10 percent of *pieds noirs* who migrated to the metropole settled in rural areas; see Christiane Lees, "L'établissement des *Pieds noirs* dans le Midi méditerranéen français," in Jean-Jacques Jordi and Emile Temime (eds.), *Marseille et le choc des décolonisations: Les rapatriements 1954–1964* (Aix-en-Provence: Edisud, 1996), p. 111.
59. Jordi, *De l'exode à l'exil*, p. 104.
60. Verdès-Leroux, *Les Français d'Algérie*, pp. 381–387.
61. The College consisted of the 81,761 holders of elected political office; see Le Monde, *La Cinquième République*, p. 14.
62. Ibid., pp. 32–35.
63. The new constitution stipulated that amendments required the approval of parliament, not citizenry.
64. Ibid., pp. 32–35.
65. The association was called the Amicale Varoise des Rapatriés d'Afrique du Nord; see *République-Le Provençal*, 14 October 1962 and 27 October 1962.
66. Calculations based on data in ibid., 11 October 1962 and 29 October 1962.
67. The Socialists were Édouard Le Bellegou and Édouard Soldani, and funding for the welcoming committee came from the city and the department; see ibid., 2 June 1962, 4 June 1962, and 26 June 1962.
68. *Le Méridional*, 2 July 1962.
69. *République-Le Provençal*, 13 October 1962, 14 October 1962, and 24 October 1962.
70. Ibid., 19 October 1962.

71. Ibid., 23 October 1962.
72. Ibid., 20 October 1962.
73. François Goguel, "Le référendum du 28 octobre et les élections des 18–25 novembre 1962," *Revue française de science politique* 13/2 (1963), pp. 289–314.
74. Ibid., p. 299. In the 1962 elections, some Gaullist candidates belonged to the Union démocratique du travail, a center-left party that would fuse with the Gaullists in 1967; or the Républicains indépendants, a liberal, pro-Europe group led by the minister of finance, Valéry Giscard d'Estaing.
75. *République-Le Provençal*, 3 November 1962 and 4 November 1962. The department's electoral districts were then Brignoles-Draguignan (First District), Hyères-Saint-Raphaël (Second District), Toulon-La Garde (Third District), and Toulon-La Seyne (Fourth District).
76. *République-Le Provençal*, 4 November 1962, 8 November 1962, 9 November 1962, 14 November 1962, and 16 November 1962.
77. Ibid., 5 November 1962, 10 November 1962, 16 November 1962, and 17 November 1962.
78. Ibid., 19 November 1962 and 26 November 1962.
79. Max Weber, "Politics as a Vocation," in H. H. Gerth and C. Wright Mills (eds.), *From Max Weber: Essays in Sociology* (New York: Oxford University Press, 1946), pp. 102–111.
80. Robert Merton, "Manifest and Latent Functions," in *Social Theory and Social Structure: Toward the Codification of Theory and Research* (Glencoe, IL: Free Press, 1949), pp. 71–74.
81. Patron-client relations denote an unequal system of exchange: the patron provides significant resources in return for political support or allegiance. It is distinct from (1) quid pro quo (nothing given without something given in return, an arrangement that lays bare the resource and power differences of the parties involved); and (2) the precise calculation of values (the "price" of what is given or returned). Instead, patron-client relations belong to the realm of generalized exchange, with exchanges akin to gifts. When patron-client relations become ingrained, they uphold trust and solidarity (willingly foregoing immediate and exactly equivalent compensation because the other party in the relationship should reciprocate later on). See Shmuel N. Eisenstadt and Luis Roniger, *Patrons, Clients and Friends: Interpersonal Relations and the Structure of Trust in Society* (Cambridge: Cambridge University Press, 1984), pp. 33–37; and Andrés Villarreal, "Political Competition and Violence in Mexico: Hierarchical Social Control in Local Patronage Structures," *American Sociological Review* 67/4 (2002), p. 480.

CHAPTER 4

1. Research on the politics of immigrants has moved from an actor-oriented to an institutionalist paradigm. Actor-oriented paradigms treat not only political outcomes (such as voting and naturalization) but also a host of others associated with immigration (such as the decision to migrate, the location of settlement, or language acquisition) as results of cost-benefit analysis by individual immigrants, or background characteristics of immigrants. Institutionalists treat the structure of opportunity as the most significant determinant of political activity. Drawing on social movement theory, political mobilization of immigrants thus is likely to depend on contact with other mobilized immigrants (including leaders and activists). Such contact is more likely to occur at local rather than regional or national levels. This makes cities excellent sites for studying immigrant politics; see Irene Bloemraad, "Becoming a Citizen in the United States and Canada: Structured Mobilization and Immigrant Political Incorporation," *Social Forces* 85/2 (2006), pp. 667–695.

2. The sponsoring group was the Association Nationale des Français d'Afrique du Nord, d'Outre-Mer et de leurs Amis.
3. *République-Le Provençal*, 4 February 1963.
4. BP, letter 158 from Mayor Arreckx to the Prefect of the Var, 12 October 1962; and BP, minutes of meeting of Comité directeur de la Quinzaine des Rapatriés, 5 December 1963.
5. BP, minutes of meetings of Comité directeur de la Quinzaine des Rapatriés, 31 October 1963, 19 November 1963, and 3 January 1964.
6. *République-Le Provençal*, 18 January 1964; *Le Méridional*, 27 January 1964.
7. BP, *Quinzaine des Rapatriés* (Toulon: 1964). Born in Toulon, the minister for repatriates (François Missoffe) was the son of a Navy admiral and a Gaullist since 1949.
8. BP, minutes of meeting of Comité directeur de la Quinzaine des Rapatriés, 5 December 1963. The committee received funding from the city, the departmental council, and the Ministry for Repatriates; see BP, letter from Ministère des Rapatriés to Nicolas Loffredo, 19 December 1963; BP, minutes of meetings of Comité directeur de la Quinzaine des Rapatriés, 19 November 1963, 5 December 1963, and 7 January 1964; and *République-Le Provençal*, 14 January 1964.
9. BP, letter from N. Loffredo to Minister François Missoffe, 7 February 1964. The prisoners in question were former OAS members and other detainees accused of crimes in support of French Algeria.
10. *Le Petit Varois*, 17 January 1964. The OAS assassinated Alfred Locussol, a communist activist who supported Algerian independence, in Alençon in January 1962. Delphine Renard was the child blinded by an OAS bomb meant for André Malraux. Michel Debré served as the Gaullist prime minister between 1959 and 1962.
11. BP, letters dated 7 February to 27 February 1964.
12. BP, letter from N. Loffredo to M. Arreckx, 13 Feburary 1964.
13. *République-Le Provençal*, 22 February 1964 and 2 March 1964; and *Le Méridional*, 5 March 1964.
14. François Goguel, "Les élections cantonales des 8 et 15 mars 1964," *Revue française de science politique* 14/3 (1964), pp. 556–562.
15. "Rapport du 16 mars 1964 du préfet du Var—L'élection cantonale," quoted in Bayle, "Les droites à Toulon," p. 275.
16. In Aix-en-Provence, another city with a sizeable *pied noir* electorate, the withdrawal of a centrist candidate allowed a Socialist victory; see Bayle, "Les droites à Toulon," pp. 269–276.
17. Gaignebet, "A la recherche de nouveaux rôles," p. 364. Found guilty of orchestrating the plot but pardoned in 1968, former OAS leader Jean-Jacques Susini would be a FN candidate in Marseille in 1997.
18. In 1993, notably, in Montpellier three OAS veterans murdered Jacques Roseau, a *pied noir* leader "guilty" of urging his community to vote strategically (hence, at the expense of the FN).
19. *Le Méridional*, 16 June 1964; and Raoul Girardet, *L'idée coloniale en France de 1871 à 1962* (Paris: La Table Ronde, 1972), pp. 348–349.
20. Girardet, *L'idée coloniale en France*, pp. 353, 359.
21. Communiqué from Unité des Rapatriés d'Outre-Mer in *République-Le Provençal*, 26 February 1965.
22. A recent change in the electoral system made it easier for mayors of cities like Toulon to gain a majority.
23. François Goguel "La signification de la consultation," *Revue française de science politique* 15/5 (1965), pp. 911–914.

24. The repatriates represented an estimated 12,000 to 13,000 of the 95,789 registered voters in Toulon; see *République-Le Provençal*, 7 January 1965, 15 January 1965, 25 January 1965, 7 February 1965, 11 March 1965, and 22 March 1965.
25. I draw on Bayle, "Les droites à Toulon," p. 284, but with revised numbers for the Le Bellegou and Arreckx slates based on information in *République-Le Provençal*, 1 March 1965 and 4 March 1965.
26. *République-Le Provençal*, 16 January 1965, 17 February 1965, 26 February 1965, 27 February 1965, 3 March 1965, and 13 March 1965. In candidates' statements, the term repatriates alternates with refugees from North Africa and *pieds noirs*.
27. Ibid., 12 February 1965, 18 February 1965, 24 February 1965, 26 February 1965, 1 March 1965, 3 March 1965, and 5 March 1965.
28. The three groups were: L'association des combattants d'Algérie; L'Association nationale des anciens détenus et internés politiques de la Ve République—Section du Var; and Le comité de coordination des associations de rapatriés et refugiés; see *République-Le Provençal*, 22 February 1965 and 25 February 1965; and *Le Méridional*, 9 March 1965 and 12 March 1965.
29. *Le Méridional*, 12 March 1965.
30. BP, letter from Maurice Arreckx to Louis Boutigny, 24 February 1965.
31. *Le Méridional*, 11 March 1965.
32. Ibid., 12 March 1965 and 14 March 1965.
33. Ibid., 11 March 1965; *République-Le Provençal*, 15 March 1965, 16 March 1965, 18 March 1965, and 19 March 1965.
34. Ibid., 16 March 1965.
35. *Le Méridional*, 17 March 1965 and 21 March 1965.
36. Goguel, "La signification de la consultation," p. 915. The incumbent in Nice was Jean Médecin of the anti-Gaullist right; in Montpellier, François Delmas of the anti-Gaullist right; in Toulouse, Louis Bazerque of the Socialists. In Toulon, the Arreckx list attracted 54 percent of the second-round vote, the Communists 27 percent, and the Gaullists 19 percent; see *République-Le Provençal*, 22 March 1965.
37. They also confirmed the strength of rural communism; see Goguel, "La signification de la consultation," pp. 914–916.
38. Right-wing voters in Algeria seem to have maintained most continuity in the metropole: 93 percent who supported the right in Algeria did the same in 2002. For both left-wing and centrist voters in Algeria, by contrast, continuity with voting in the metropole fell to 59 percent; see Comtat, *Les pieds-noirs et la politique*, p. 267.
39. In Toulon, the beneficiary was Arreckx; in Marseille, the incumbent mayor and his council were Socialist. In both cities, an alliance between Socialists and non-Gaullist right wingers had controlled the city council. In both cities, moreover, a sizeable body of repatriates had to choose between the incumbent, Gaullists, Communists, and Nationaux. In both cities, finally, incumbents cultivated their relations with the repatriates, and repatriate associations directed and mobilized the vote of their constituencies; see Marcel Roncayolo, "L'élection de Gaston Defferre à Marseille," *Revue française de science politique* 15/5 (1965), pp. 930–946; and Jordi, *De l'exode à l'exil*, 168–170.
40. Dated 21 April 1965, this resolution is referred to in BP, "Voeu exprimé par le Conseil Municipal de Toulon au cours de sa séance publique du mercredi 19 Janvier 1966."
41. *Le Méridional*, 5 April 1965.
42. Ibid., 5 April 1965; *République-Le Provençal*, 4 June 1965; and BP, letter from Maurice Arreckx to Louis Boutigny, 1 October 1965.
43. *Le Méridional*, 8 October 1965.

44. BP, Commission Extra Municipale des Rapatriés, list of materials requested from the municipality, undated (circa June 1967).
45. BP, Charter of the Commission extra-municipale des rapatriés, 1965.
46. *Le Méridional*, 8 October 1965; BP, Charter of the Commission extra-municipale des rapatriés, 1965; BP, letter dated 18 November 1965 from Louis Boutigny to the president of the Commission Extra-municipale des rapatriés; and BP, agenda for meetings of the central committee of the Commission Extra-municipale des rapatriés, 12 November 1965 and 29 November 1965.
47. Like the Commission extra-municipale, by the 1990s associations formed under the initiative of local authorities throughout France were "helping to coordinate relations between the town hall and prominent local interests"; see Henri Mendras with Alistair Cole, *Social Change in Modern France: Towards a Cultural Anthropology of the Fifth Republic* (Cambridge: Cambridge University Press, 1991), p. 140.
48. *Le Méridional*, 8 October 1965.
49. Ibid., 12 October 1965.
50. *Le Monde*, 1–2 October 1989; and Bouclier, *Tixier-Vignancour*.
51. Bouclier, *Tixier-Vignancour*, p. 216.
52. Television broadcast of 19 November 1965; see *République-Le Provençal*, 20 November 1965.
53. Ibid., 4 December 1965 and 6 December 1965. Tixier-Vignancour urged his supporters to give their second-round support to Mitterrand, who courted the *pieds noirs* in a television broadcast that reiterated his support for compensation and amnesty. Others urging the *pieds noirs* to support Mitterrand in the second round were the RANFRAN, the ANFANOMA, and Jacques Soustelle; see *République-Le Provençal*, 12 December 1965, 16 December 1965, and 18 December 1965. Mitterrand lost the second round with 45.4 percent of the vote, but in the Var outdid De Gaulle with 52.6 percent of the vote; see *République-Le Provençal*, 20 December 1965.
54. BP, letter from Maurice Arreckx to "Monsieur le Maire et cher Collègue," 27 January 1966.
55. BP, "Voeu exprimé par le Conseil Municipal de Toulon au cours de sa séance publique du mercredi 19 Janvier 1966." The prefect annulled this resolution.
56. BP, document signed by Abbé Georges Dahmar, undated (circa early 1966); *Recueil des actes administratifs de la Préfecture du Var*, No. 128, May 1966; and *Journal Officiel de la République Française*, 19 November 1965. After De Gaulle won re-election in 1965, his government took small steps to reconcile the partisans of French Algeria: the National Assembly passed a bill for a partial amnesty, and the president pardoned 12 out of 203 French Algeria criminals, including General Zeller. The government no longer had a minister for repatriates, however.
57. *Le Méridional*, 19 June 1965. Shortly thereafter, the vice-president, Houari Boumedienne, deposed Ben Bella.
58. BP, "Constitution du Comité d'Union du Département du Var—visites jeudi 30 juin 1966"; and BP, letter from Abbé Georges Dahmar, 10 August 1966.
59. *Actualités Varoises*, 1 November 1966; and BP, CODUR, "Réunion du 20 mai 1966."
60. Attending on August 27 were 7 representatives from Toulon; 3 from La Seyne-sur-Mer; 2 from each of Hyères, Saint-Cyr, Le Lavandou, Saint-Raphaël, Sanary and Bandol; and 1 from La Valette; see BP, CODUR, "Réunion du 27 Août 1966." After expanding rapidly, the federation modified its system of representation, with municipalities represented on the executive in proportion to their share of the total *pied noir* population in the Var. Of 30 delegates on the executive, there were now 10 from Toulon; 3 from La Seyne-sur-Mer; 2 from each of Draguignan, Hyères, La Valette, Fréjus-Saint-Raphaël, Les Issembres-Sainte Maxime, and La Garde-Le Pradet; and 1 from each of Bandol,

61. BP, Communiqué dated 8 October 1966 from Abbé Georges Dahmar; BP, CODUR, "Au sujet du projet de loi d'amnistie," undated (1966); *République-Le Provençal*, 13 October 1966; and *Le Méridional*, 1 January 1967.
62. BP, CODUR (Toulon section), "Séance du 12 mars 1966"; BP, CODUR, 25 March 1966; and BP, letter from Abbé Georges Dahmar to the Mayor of Ollioules (Var), 20 October 1966.
63. *République-Le Provençal*, 4 November 1966; see also 27 October 1966.
64. BP, letter from Abbé Georges Dahmar to the Mayor of Ollioules (Var), 20 October 1966.
65. BP, letter from Abbé Georges Dahmar to the mayor of La Garde (Var), 15 November 1966. This letter refers to Henri Maillot, a *pied noir* and a Communist who diverted weapons and ammunition to the Algerian nationalists when he deserted his infantry unit in 1956.
66. *Le Méridional*, 17 November 1966; and Eldridge, *From Empire to Exile*, pp. 14–16.
67. With 244 out of the 486 seats in the National Assembly, the Gaullists and their allies (the Républicains-Indépendants) won a narrow majority; see *Le Monde*, 14 March 1967.
68. The other districts were Draguignan/Brignoles (First District) and Hyères/Fréjus (Second District).
69. If the titular candidate became ineligible for office after election as a deputy, their running mate replaced them in the National Assembly.
70. Arrighi would later join the FN.
71. *République-Le Provençal*, 23 February 1967 and 3 March 1967.
72. Results for the Fourth District: Merle (Communist), 33.9 percent; Bayle (Gaullist), 33.8 percent; Arrighi (Centre Républicain), 16.3 percent; Basse (Fédération de la Gauche Démocratique et Socialiste), (10.4 percent); and Schotte (Centre Départemental des Indépendants et Paysans) 5.6 percent; see *République-Le Provençal*, 7 March 1967.
73. Ibid., 7 March 1967, 8 March 1967, 9 March 1967, 10 March 1967, and 11 March 1967. Results for the Third District: Pouyade (Gaullist), 44.5 percent; Delplace (Communist), 33.4 percent; and Tixer-Vignancour (Alliance Républicaine pour les Libertés et le Progrès), 24.7 percent. Results for the Fourth District: Merle (Communist), 51.1 percent; Bayle (Gaullist), 48.6 percent; see *République-Le Provençal*, 13 March 1967.
74. BP, "Protocole" between CODUR and Henri Fabre, undated (circa November 1966); BP, letter from Henri Fabre to Abbé Dahmar, 24 November 1966; BP, minutes of CODUR meeting held on 19 January 1967; BP, letter from Louis Boutigny to the directors of CODUR, 25 January 1967; BP, letter dated 7 February 1967 from Abbé Georges Dahmar to Jean-Louis Tixier-Vignancour; *République-Le Provençal*, 23 January 1967; and *Le Méridional*, 24 January 1967.
75. BP, CODUR, extract from minutes of meeting on 24 November 1966.
76. *Le Méridional*, 11 May 1965; and *République-Le Provençal*, 12 May 1965 and 18 November 1965.
77. *République-Le Provençal*, 2 March 1967; *Le Méridional*, 11 May 1965; and BP, CODUR, "Séance du 5 novembre 1966 (Compte, rendu)."
78. BP, undated letter from ARLP, the party of Tixier.
79. Electoral tract, ARLP, in Bouclier, *Tixier-Vignancour*, p. 260. The postwar European far right disagreed over NATO. For the Atlanticists among them, the Soviet Union was the great enemy; others, who wanted an autonomous Europe, put the Soviet Union and the United States in the same basket.

80. The French Algeria group was the Association nationale des anciens détenus et internés politiques de la Cinquième République; see *République-Le Provençal*, 23 February 1967, 24 February 1967, 25 February 1967, 1 March 1967, and 2 March 1967.
81. BP, CODUR, "Séance du 5 novembre 1966"; BP, letter dated 29 November 1966 from Abbé Georges Dahmar to CODUR members; BP, letter dated 2 December 1966 from G. Clément (Sainte-Maxime-sur-Mer, Var) to Abbé Dahmar; BP, letter dated 8 December 1966 from Pascal Arrighi to Abbé Dahmar; BP, letter dated 8 December 1966 from François Garcia (for Jean Lecanuet) to Abbé Dahmar; BP, letter dated 7 February 1967 from Abbé Georges Dahmar to Jean-Louis Tixier-Vignancour; *République-Le Provençal*, 8 November 1966; and *Le Méridional*, 10 December 1966 and 27 January 1967.
82. *République-Le Provençal*, 1 March 1967.
83. Ibid., 2 March 1967.
84. Ibid., 4 March 1967.
85. Ibid., 24 February 1967 and 2 March 1967. A rally on February 26 at the Cinéma Comédia in the Mourillon quarter attracted 2,050 supporters; another at the Municipal Theater the next night attracted more than 1,800 supporters; see Bouclier, *Tixier-Vignancour*, p. 259; and *République-Le Provençal*, 25 February 1967, 28 February 1967, and 1 March 1967.
86. *République-Le Provençal*, 5 March 1967; and Bouclier, *Tixier-Vignancour*, p. 259.
87. *République-Le Provençal*, 7 March 1967, 8 March 1967, and 10 March 1967.
88. Ibid., 11 March 1967.
89. Ibid.
90. Ibid., 9 March 1967.
91. Ibid., 10 March 1967.
92. Ibid., 8 March 1967.
93. The candidate was Jacques Médecin, the mayor of Nice, another *pied noir* stronghold; Bouclier, *Tixier-Vignancour*, pp. 260–261.
94. Ibid., p. 256.
95. BP, CODUR, "Réunion du Comité d'Union de Toulon: Vendredi 14 Octobre 1966 à 21 H."; BP, letter dated 22 October 1966 from Louis Boutigny to Joseph Valverde; BP, letter dated 27 October 1966 from Abbé Georges Dahmar (President of CODUR); BP, letter dated 21 November 1966 from Abbé Georges Dahmar (President of CODUR); and BP, announcement dated 28 December 1966 from Abbé Georges Dahmar.
96. BP, letter dated 15 March 1967 from Maurice Arreckx to the CODUR.
97. Following either route, a politician became a broker better able to lean on, offset, or circumvent the prefect; see Sidney Tarrow, *Between Center and Periphery: Grassroots Politicians in Italy and France* (New Haven, CT: Yale University Press, 1977); Ezra N. Suleiman, *Elites in French Society: The Politics of Survival* (Princeton, NJ: Princeton University Press, 1978; and Marcus Kreuzer and Ina Stephan, "France: Enduring Notables, Weak Parties, and Powerful Technocrats," in Jens Borchert and Jürgen Zeiss (eds.), *The Political Class in Advanced Democracies* (Oxford: Oxford University Press, 2002), 124–141.
98. Jean-Yves Camus, "Origine et formation du Front national (1972–1981)," in Nonna Mayer and Pascal Perrineau (eds.), *Le Front national à découvert* (Paris: Presses de la Fondation nationale des sciences politiques, 1989), pp. 17–20; and Valérie Igounet, *Le Front national de 1972 à nos jours: Le parti, les hommes, les idées* (Paris: Le Seuil, 2014), pp. 23–51.

CHAPTER 5

1. Pierre Baillet, "L'intégration des rapatriés d'Algérie en France," *Population* 30/2 (1975), p. 312.
2. Emile Chabal, "Managing the Postcolony: Minority Politics in Montpellier, c. 1960–c. 2010," *Contemporary European History* 23/2 (2014), pp. 240–245.
3. Ibid.
4. Ibid., pp. 246–257. The Frêche influence endured: between 2002 and 2017, far-right support in Montpellier was lower than in most other cities with concentrations of *pieds noirs* (see Table 6 in the Appendix).
5. Le Monde, *La Cinquième République*, p. 59.
6. *Le Monde*, 14 March 1967.
7. Hunt, "Impact of the 1962 Repatriates," pp. 557–558. By comparison with metropolitans, despite a narrowing of the difference over time the unemployment rate for *pieds noirs* has usually been higher, especially for women; see Marie-Paule Couto, "L'intégration socio-économique des pieds-noirs en France métropolitaine: le lien de citoyenneté à l'épreuve," *Revue Européenne des Migrations Internationales* 29/3 (2013), pp. 105–118.
8. Le Monde, *La Cinquième République*, pp. 61–62.
9. Gaignebet, "A la recherche de nouveaux rôles," p. 366.
10. Richard Vinen, *A History in Fragments: Europe in the Twentieth Century* (Cambridge, MA: Da Capo, 2000), p. 333; and Le Monde, *La Cinquième République*, pp. 62–63.
11. *Le Méridional*, 5 July 1968.
12. BP, communiqué dated 3 June 1968; *Le Méridional*, 29 May 1968; and *République-Le Provençal*, 14 June 1968.
13. *Le Méridional*, 20 May 1968.
14. Ibid., 5 July 1968.
15. Ibid., and 23 July 1968.
16. Communiqué signed by Abbé G. Dahmar and published in *République-Le Provençal*, 31 May 1968.
17. The rally took place near Saint-Maximin. A rival organization—the Front national des rapatriés (FNR)—tried to outflank the FSR. Recent events, the FNR argued, showed protests led to government concessions. The *pieds noirs*, it said, would add to the strife caused by the students and workers unless the state took a more positive attitude. The president of the FNR had applied pressure on the authorities in the Rhône-Alpes region and hoped to meet very soon with the prime minister; see *Le Méridional*, 29 May 1968.
18. Ibid., 21 June 1968.
19. Ibid., 13 July 1968 and 14 July 1968.
20. By September the FSR claimed to have branched out into the Vaucluse, Gard, Hérault, Drôme, Ardèche, and Lozère departments; see *Le Méridional*, 26 September 1968 and 24 October 1968.
21. John T. S. Keeler, "Situating France on the Pluralism-Corporatism Continuum: A Critique of and Alternative to the Wilson Perspective," *Comparative Politics* 17/2 (1985), pp. 238–239; and David S. Bell, *French Politics Today* (Manchester: Manchester University Press, 2002), pp. 133–137.
22. Keeler, "Situating France," pp. 241–245; Bell, *French Politics Today*, p. 138; and Le Monde, *La Cinquième République*, p. 108.
23. The right-wing opposition included the CNIP.
24. *Le Monde*, 9 April 1974.
25. Dominique Legenne, *Var, terre d'histoire* (Arles: Actes Sud, 1999), pp. 136–137.
26. Ibid., pp. 233–242.

27. In 1977, most of the 100,000 repatriates of the Var lived in towns and cities on the coast (with farming occupying only 250 repatriate households); see BP, speech by Paul Feuilloley, prefect for the Var, on the occasion of a meeting between secretary of state Jacques Dominati and repatriate associations of the Var, Préfecture du Var, Toulon, 22 July 1977.
28. Michel Vovelle, "Un champ de bataille de la Révolution (1789–1815)," in Maurice Agulhon (ed.), *Histoire de Toulon* (Toulouse: Privat, 1988), pp. 179–190.
29. *République-Le Provençal*, 5 October 1975. Another politician the RI recruited from a part of the Var with a high concentration of *pieds noirs* was François Léotard, who joined the RI in 1974, became mayor of Fréjus in 1977, and entered the National Assembly in 1978. The RI's predecessor (the Fédération nationale des républicains indépendants) held the May 1977, national meeting at which it renamed itself the Parti républicain in Fréjus; see Le Monde, *La Cinquième République*, p.104.
30. Tarrow, *Between Center and Periphery*.
31. One law provided for a fuller amnesty than in June 1968 (it reinstated civic rights stripped for illegal action on behalf of French Algeria). Others made the *harkis* eligible for veterans' pensions, special housing, and education grants; extended benefits to those wounded in action or imprisoned by the new Algerian state; and harmonized pension contributions in the colony with those in the metropole. Within months of Giscard's election, the government raised the threshold for full compensation and added price indexation; see Pierre Goinard, "Dossier: Les rapatriés d'Algérie," *L'Informateur*, May 1977.
32. BP, speech by Paul Feuilloley, Préfecture du Var, Toulon, 22 July 1977.
33. Claims for compensation totaled 190,000 (170,000 for property lost in Algeria, the rest for property lost in Morocco and Tunisia); see Goinard, "Dossier: Les rapatriés d'Algérie." By 1987, when the issue became largely closed, four indemnification laws had been voted; see William B. Cohen, "Pied-Noir Memory, History, and the Algerian War," in Andrea L. Smith (ed.), *Europe's Invisible Migrants* (Amsterdam: Amsterdam University Press, 2003), p. 131.
34. In addition, the *pieds noirs* awaited a full rehabilitation.
35. The Socialist winner in Montpellier was Georges Frêche.
36. Elected to the National Assembly in 1978 as a candidate for the RI, a year later the mayor of Carpentras received an appointment as a minister.
37. *L'Aurore*, 8 July 1977.
38. Comuniqué from L'UAVFROM in *Var-Matin République*, 6 July 1977.
39. *Var-Matin République*, 14 July 1977.
40. *Le Figaro*, 9–10 July 1977.
41. Ibid., 9–10 July 1977.
42. *Var-Matin République*, 14 July 1977.
43. Dominati, who had belonged to the Resistance, was also an old friend of Le Pen.
44. *Le Monde*, 10–11 July 1977.
45. *Var-Matin République*, 8 July 1977. The retreat is at the Fort of Brégançon.
46. BP, letter dated 8 July 1977 from Patrick-Olivier Picourt (Chef de Cabinet, Secrétariat d'Etat) to Maurice Arreckx; and BP, letter dated 12 July 1977 from Maurice Arreckx to Paul Feuilloley, Préfet du Var.
47. BP, letter dated 8 July 1977 from Louis Boutigny to Professor Goinard. Other RECOURS leaders attending were Claude Laquière, Jacques Roseau, and Guy Forzy.
48. BP, letter dated 12 July 1977 from Louis Boutigny to Maurice Arreckx.
49. *Le Monde*, 22 July 1977.
50. *Var-Matin République*, 23 July 1977.
51. In addition to Dominati and his chief of staff, politicians on hand included the mayor, the prefect and his chief of staff, two members of the Var departmental council, and seven

members from the Toulon city council; see *Var-Matin République*, 24 July 1977; and *L'Aurore*, 25 July 1977.
52. In government (apart from the RI): the neo-Gaullist RPR of Chirac and the Centre des démocrates sociaux of Jean Lecanuet); and in opposition: the Socialists of Mitterrand and the Communists of Georges Marchais.
53. BP, letter from Jacques Chirac, 20 September 1977.
54. *L'Aurore*, 17 October 1977.
55. Raphaëlle Branche, *La guerre d'Algérie: Une histoire apaisée?* (Paris: Le Seuil, 2005), p. 27.
56. *Le Figaro*, 19 December 1977; *Le Méridional*, 19 December 1977; Valérie Esclangon-Morin, *Les rapatriés d'Afrique du Nord de 1956 à nos jours* (Paris: Harmattan, 2007), pp. 242–259; and BP, letter from Boutigny to presidents of the repatriate associations of the Var, 10 August 1977.
57. BP, letter from Louis Boutigny to Jacques Dominati, 29 October 1977; and BP, letter from Maurice Arreckx to Louis Boutigny, 10 November 1977.
58. *Var-Matin République*, 31 December 1977.
59. Ibid., 27 February 1978.
60. BP, letter from Louis Boutigny to Maurice Arreckx, 17 November 1977; BP, "Procès-verbal de la réception de messieurs Arreckx, Fabre et Colombani," 22 November 1977; and BP, meeting with Parti des Forces Nouvelles, undated (circa December 1977).
61. BP, "Visite de Monsieur Jacques Chirac à la Maison du Rapatrié, le mercredi 22 février 1978."
62. BP, letter from Louis Boutigny to Councillor Slama, 16 November 1977; BP, letters from UAVFROM to Monsieur Gomez, 12 December 1977, 23 December 1977, and 10 January 1978.
63. The inauguration took place in 1973; see *République-Le Provençal*, 21 March 1973.
64. This chapel joined other churches with *pied noir* devotees, the Sacré-Cœur in Antibes and Notre-Dame de Santa Cruz in Nîmes; see Branche, *La guerre d'Algérie*, p. 18.
65. BP, Amicale des Anciens de la Province d'Alger (Toulon), 19 November 1976.
66. BP, Mairie de Toulon, "Projet de loi relatif à l'indemnisation des Français rapatriés d'outre-mer," 29 November 1977.
67. BP, letter from Maurice Arreckx to Louis Boutigny, 12 December 1977. Some 500 repatriates from the south of France attended the RECOURS meeting in Aix-en-Provence; *Le Monde* 19 December 1977.
68. BP, letter from Maurice Arreckx to Louis Boutigny, 20 December 1977; and BP, letter from Louis Boutigny to Maurice Arreckx, 17 January 1978.
69. *Var-Matin République*, 9 March 1978.
70. The UDF won 120 seats in the National Assembly, the RPR 145; see Nicolas Denis, "Les élections législatives de mars 1978 en métropole," *Revue française de science politique* 28/6 (1978), pp. 977–1005. Over the next two decades, still, Giscard and the UDF remained magnets for the *pied noir* vote; see Comte, *Les pieds-noirs et la politique*, pp. 245–247.
71. Apart from Arreckx, other UDF candidates winning election in the Var were François Léotard in the Second District and Arthur Paecht in the Fourth District.
72. BP, letter dated 24 November 1969 from Maurice Arreckx to Abbé Georges Dahmar. In a veiled homage to the OAS, Dahmar proposed to call this residence The Oasis.
73. BP, Amicale des Anciens de la Province d'Alger, "Comptes-rendus des Réunions du Bureau," 21 May 1974 to 11 April 1979; and BP, Amicale des Anciens de la Province d'Alger, untitled, 9 July 1976.
74. BP, "Note sur le projet de création d'un Centre municipal d'études, de documentation et de recherches maghrébines (Fonds donation Philibert)," 12 May 1975; BP, letter from Louis Boutigny to Valverde, Adjoint au Maire, Toulon, 26 May 1977; BP, letter from Louis Boutigny to Maurice Arreckx, 11 June 1977; and BP, letter from Louis Boutigny to François Trucy, 2 July 1986.

CHAPTER 6

1. Winock, *Nationalisme, antisémitisme et fascisme en France*; and Gabriel Goodliffe, *The Resurgence of the Radical Right in France: From Boulangisme to the Front National* (Cambridge: Cambridge University Press, 2012).
2. Antoine Compagnon, *Les antimodernes: De Joseph de Maistre à Roland Barthes* (Paris: Gallimard, 2016) evokes this richness in his survey of writers whose skepticism about historical progress, triumphant liberty, and human perfectibility has placed them occasionally within the French far-right camp.
3. I steal here from Baltasar Gracián, *The Art of Worldly Wisdom* (Boston: Shambhala, 2006), p. 51.
4. These included the Faisceau, the Action française, the Croix-de-feu, the Parti social français, and the Parti populaire français.
5. Winock, *Nationalisme, antisémitisme et fascisme en France*, pp. 248–271; and Juan J. Linz, "Political Space and Fascism as a Late-Comer: Conditions Conducive to the Success or Failure of Fascism as a Mass Movement in Inter-War Europe," in Stein Ugelvik Larsen et al. (eds.), *Who Were the Fascists: Social Roots of European Fascism* (Bergen: Universitetsforlaget, 1980), pp. 153–189. The CNIP absorbed the postwar Pétainist Party (*Union des nationaux indépendants et républicains*).
6. *Time*, 19 March 1956.
7. Ibid.
8. Possibly to avoid alienating Muslim shopkeepers who supported him, Poujade disapproved of Algérie française protests when Prime Minister Guy Mollet visited Algiers in February 1956; see François Duprat, *Les mouvements d'extrême-droite en France depuis 1944* (Paris: Albatros, 1972), p. 76.
9. Romain Souillac, *Le mouvement Poujade: De la défense professionnelle au populisme nationaliste 1953–1962* (Paris: Presses de Sciences Po, 2007), pp. 189–191.
10. The assassins had targeted Salan because he seemed too liberal toward the Algerians; see ibid., p. 320.
11. Ibid., pp. 317–338.
12. Pierre Milza, *Fascisme français: Passé et présent* (Paris: Flammarion, 1987), pp. 294–315.
13. On the pedigree of Gaullism; see David Thompson, *Democracy in France since 1870* (Oxford: Oxford University Press, 1969), pp. 274–285.
14. Seymour Martin Lipset, *Political Man: The Social Bases of Politics* (Baltimore, MD: Johns Hopkins University Press, 1981), pp. 154–165.
15. Raymond Aron, *Mémoires* (Paris: Julliard, 1983), pp. 526–529.
16. *L'Aurore*, 11 June 1962.
17. Girardet, *L'idée coloniale en France*, p. 348.
18. Duprat, *Les mouvements d'extrême-droite*, p. 66.
19. Ibid., pp. 119–127.
20. Ibid., pp. 247–248.
21. *Minute*, 24 April 1964, quoted in Joseph Algazy, *L'extrême droite en France 1965 à 1984* (Paris: Harmattan, 1989), p. 22.
22. Duprat, *Les mouvements d'extrême-droite*, p. 158.
23. Harvey G. Simmons, *The French National Front: The Extremist Challenge to Democracy* (Boulder, CO: Westview, 1996), p. 57.
24. Duprat, *Les mouvements d'extrême-droite*, pp. 158–163.
25. Simmons, *French National Front*, p. 58.
26. Algazy, *L'extrême droite en France*, p. 60.
27. Ibid., pp. 160–170.
28. Ibid., pp. 8–105.

29. Duprat, *Les mouvements d'extrême-droite*, p. 207.
30. René Chiroux, *L'extrême-droite sous la Cinquième République* (Paris: Librairie générale de droit et de jurisprudence, 1974), Table 8.
31. Camus, "Origine et formation du Front national (1972–1981)," pp. 17–21.
32. The FN would modify its logo a few times during the decades before it became the National Rally, but without eliminating the neo-fascist flame.
33. Igounet, *Le Front national de 1972 à nos jours*, pp. 39–42; and Chiroux, *L'extrême-droite sous la Cinquième République*, Table 8.
34. Camus, "Origine et formation du Front national," pp. 20–24; and Algazy, *L'extrême droite en France*, pp. 88–115.
35. Algazy, *L'extrême droite en France*, pp. 194–210; René Monzat, *Enquêtes sur la droite extreme* (Paris: Le Monde-Editions, 1992), pp. 272–291; *Il Secolo d'Italia*, 28 January 1978, 6 February 1978, 4 April 1978, 13 November 1979, 29 January 1980, 24 June 1981, and 22 February 1982.
36. Pascal Perrineau, "Les étapes d'une implantation électorale (1972–1988)," in Nonna Mayer and Pascal Perrineau (eds.), *Le Front national à découvert* (Paris: Presses de la Fondation nationale des sciences politiques, 1989), p. 41.
37. The local elections took place in Dreux, Aulnay-sous-Bois, Morbihan, and Paris's 20th arrondissement.
38. Milza, *Fascisme français*, pp. 398–400.
39. The television program was *L'Heure de vérité*.
40. Perrineau, "Les étapes d'une implantation électorale," p. 47.
41. Ibid., pp. 41–49.
42. Nonna Mayer, *Ces français qui votent FN* (Paris: Flammarion, 1999); and Igounet, *Le Front national de 1972 à nos jours*.
43. Nonna Mayer, "Comment Nicolas Sarkozy a rétréci l'électorat Le Pen," *Revue française de science politique* 57/3 (2007), pp. 429–445. Possibly the only significant change since the ascent of Marine Le Pen to leadership of the National Front is a rise in female support; see Nonna Mayer, "From Jean-Marie to Marine Le Pen: Electoral Change on the Far Right," *Parliamentary Affairs* 66/1 (2013), pp. 160–178.
44. Joël Gombin, "'Nouveau' FN, vieille carte électorale? Les territoires du vote pour le Front national de 1995 à 2002," paper presented at the Congrès de l'Association française de science politique, Paris, 2013.
45. *Immigration: Le Pen s'explique*, audio recording (Paris: Front national, 1989). The cover of this cassette explains Le Pen's program in more detail:
    (1) expulsion (tighter border controls, promotion of a European immigration policy, severe penalties for immigration traffickers, and expulsion of foreigners who are illegal or criminal;
    (2) French first (no voting rights for immigrants, and national preference—priority to those who are French in public employment, housing, and welfare);
    (3) repatriate immigrants (end abuses of the right to political asylum, limit new or renewed residence permits, end family unification, and repatriate foreigners whose residence permit or unemployment benefits have lapsed); and
    (4) end automatic acquisition of French citizenship.
46. Mendras with Cole, *Social Change in Modern France*, p. 9.
47. INSEE, "Monthly Consumer Confidence Survey," online at https://www.insee.fr (accessed 2 March 2018).
48. Bell, *French Politics Today*, p. 61.
49. Data for the 1984 European, 1986 parliamentary, and 1988 presidential elections. Although still below the level for shopkeepers and small business owners, in 1988

workers' support for Le Pen exceeded the mean; see Perrineau, "Les étapes d'une implantation," Table 4.
50. In 1981, 55 percent had supported Giscard while the other 18 percent had not voted (either because they abstained or did not have the right to vote); see Colette Ysmal, "Le RPR et l'UDF face au Front national: concurrence et connivences," *Revue Politique et Parlementaire* 913 (1984), p. 8.
51. Gérard Le Gall, "Une élection sans enjeu, avec conséquences" *Revue Politique et Parlementaire* 910 (1984), p. 44.
52. Rejection of the left was stronger (around 57 percent in 1979), yet some 43 percent in turn rejected the right; see Martin A. Schain, "The National Front in France and the Construction of Political Legitimacy," *West European Politics* 1/2 (1987), pp. 233–234.
53. Colette Ysmal, *Le comportement électoral des Français* (Paris: La Découverte, 1990), Table 1.
54. In FN voting in 1984 and 1986, about one-quarter of support came from former left supporters, an equal share from new voters, and the remaining half from former supporters of the right (author's calculations from data in Schain, "The National Front in France and the Construction of Political Legitimacy," p. 234). On inter-election voter flows, see John Veugelers, "Social Cleavage and the Revival of Far Right Parties: The Case of France's National Front," *Acta Sociologica* 40/1 (1997), pp. 31–49.
55. The proportion of French identifying with the right rose from 31 to 37 percent between 1981 and 1986 while the proportion identifying with the left fell from 42 to 36 percent; see Piero Ignazi, "Un nouvel acteur politique," in Nonna Mayer and Pascal Perrineau (eds.), *Le Front national à découvert* (Paris: Presses de la Fondation nationale des sciences politiques, 1989), p. 67.
56. Documentation française, "Taux de chômage, 1967–2005." Online at www.ladocumentationfrancaise.fr (accessed 2 March 2018); Jean Baudouin, "Le 'Moment néo-libéral' du RPR: Essai d'interprétation," *Revue française de science politique* 40/6 (1990), pp. 830–844; and Mathias Bernard, "L'opposition de droite après l'alternance de mai–juin 1981," *Histoire@Politique* 28/1 (2016), pp. 97–107.
57. A 1977 poll found that attitudes toward North Africans had hardly changed from 1968, when 62 percent said they were too many; see Schain, "The National Front in France and the Construction of Political Legitimacy," Table 4.
58. This has been due to developments such as controversy over the Islamic headscarf, veil, or burkini; crime and rioting by ethno-racial minorities; opposition to the construction of mosques; deadly attacks, in France and abroad, by Islamic terrorists; ongoing immigration from the southern shores of the Mediterranean; and fear that conflicts in the Arab world are spilling over into Europe.
59. Benjamin Stora, *Le transfert d'une mémoire: De l'"Algérie française" au racisme anti-arabe* (Paris: La Découverte, 1999); and Jérôme Fourquet and Nicolas Lebourg, *La nouvelle guerre d'Algérie n'aura pas lieu* (Paris: Fondation Jean Jaurès, 2017).
60. Martin A. Schain, "Immigration and Changes in the French Party System," *European Journal of Political Research* 16/6 (1988), pp. 597–621; and Patrick R. Ireland, "Race, Immigration and the Politics of Hate," in Anthony Daley (ed.), *The Mitterrand Era: Policy Alternatives and Political Mobilization in France* (London: Palgrave Macmillan, 1996), pp. 258–278.
61. Branche, *La guerre d'Algérie*, pp. 31–35.
62. John Veugelers and Michèle Lamont, "France: Alternative Locations for Public Debate," in Robert Wuthnow (ed.), *Between States and Markets: The Voluntary Sector in Comparative Perspective* (Princeton, NJ: Princeton University Press, 1991), pp. 125–151.
63. Branche, *La guerre d'Algérie*, p. 28.
64. Ysmal, "Le RPR et l'UDF face au Front national," pp. 6–20.

65. The expression is Margaret Thatcher's, applied to Sinn Fein.
66. Schain, "The National Front in France," pp. 229–252; and Monica Charlot, "L'émergence du Front national," *Revue française de science politique* 36/1 (1986), pp. 30–45.

CHAPTER 7

1. Guy Birenbaum and Bastien François, "Unité et diversité des dirigeants frontistes," in Nonna Mayer and Pascal Perrineau (eds.), *Le Front national à découvert* (Paris: Presses de la Fondation nationale des sciences politiques, 1989), pp. 83–106; and Jean-Philippe Roy, *Le Front national en région centre 1984–1992* (Paris: Harmattan, 1993).
2. Frédéric Delmonte, "Le Front national à Toulon: De la sous-société des débuts à la contre société de juin 1995," *Recherches Régionales—Alpes-Maritimes et contrées limitrophes* 148 (1999), pp. 51–83.
3. The leaders migrated to the PFN in the late 1970s and the CNIP in the mid-1980s. The first three secretaries were Jacques Aubanel, Jean Rabuel, and René Communal; see ibid., pp. 53–54, 60–63; and Bayle, "Les droites à Toulon," pp. 604–605.
4. Delmonte, "Le Front national à Toulon."
5. *Var-Matin République*, 15 June 1984.
6. Ibid., 24 October 1985; Delmonte, "Le Front national à Toulon," pp. 55–66; and Bayle "Les droites à Toulon," p. 607. Mamy quit the National Front and launched a lawsuit over the right to use the party's name in the Var (*Var-Matin République*, 5 February 1986).
7. Yann Piat, *Seule, tout en haut à droite* (Paris: Fixot, 1991), p. 88.
8. Ibid., p. 79.
9. Ibid., pp. 94–95.
10. Ibid., p. 98.
11. Ibid., p. 126. The expelled activists belonged to the far-right group SOS France. Based in Toulon and headed by a *pied noir*, it planted bombs at businesses in Toulon and Marseille patronized by people of North African background. In July 1986, 60 to 80 activists from this group and the Maison du Para (a Toulon veterans' association) traveled to Cogolin (a town between Sainte-Maxime and Saint-Tropez) to disrupt a concert organized by SOS Racisme; see *Le Nouvel Observateur*, 29 August, 1986; and *Var Matin-République*, 30 January 1987, 31 January 1987, and 1 February 1987.
12. After Mamy's dissident list (Fédération Nationaliste du Var) did poorly in the 1986 regional and parliamentary elections, he withdrew from politics.
13. Piat, *Seule, tout en haut à droite*, p. 32. With Piat's agreement, Henri Pieroni (the Algérie française activist and former CNIP leader in the Var) contested the 1986 cantonal elections as a candidate for the FN in La Seyne-sur-Mer; he left the section when Le Chevallier took over; see *Var Matin-République*, 10 June 1989.
14. The village was Tourves, some 50 kilometers from Toulon, and the host was the Union des syndicats de défense des intérêts des Français rapatriés d'Algérie; Delmonte, "Le Front national à Toulon," pp. 74–83.
15. *Var Matin-République*, 15 June 1987.
16. In 1989, another FN politician in the Var, Henri Arion (elected in 1985 to the departmental council) quit the National Front because he was disturbed by its anti-Semitism and joined the RPR. In 1990, Robert Michel (vice-president of the regional council and formerly a town councilor in Sanary) quit the party. In 1991, other elected officials quit, including Edgard Chaix (Saint-Raphaël) and Christian Ricard and Marie-Claude Barrier-Gallou (Toulon); see Piat, *Seule, tout en haut à droite*, pp. 152–213; and *Var Matin-République*, 12 October 1988, 14 September 1989, 20 November 1990, and 29 December 1991.
17. Mendras with Cole, *Social Change in Modern France*, pp. 132–140; and Kreuzer and Stephan, "France: Enduring Notables, Weak Parties, and Powerful Technocrats," pp. 134–138.

18. BP, letters from Louis Boutigny to Maurice Arreckx, 16 November 1978 and 15 December 1978; BP, letter from Maurice Arreckx to Louis Boutigny, 12 January 1979; BP, letter from Maurice Arreckx to Pierre Manière (prefect of the Var), 2 January 1978; and BP, letter from Pierre Manière to Maurice Arreckx, 19 January 1979.
19. BP, Procès-verbal de la réunion du bureau du 22 mai 1978, UAVFROM.
20. BP, letter from Mr. Lucien Chaillon ("Ancien Délégué à l'Assemblée Algérienne, Ancien Maire de Georges Clemenceau") to Louis Boutigny, 13 April 1978. The group lobbied Arreckx using the *pieds noirs* on the city council as their intermediaries; see BP, letter from Louis Boutigny to Joseph Valverde, deputy-mayor, 22 April 1978.
21. BP, Comité d'Honneur, Comité du Cent Cinquantenaire de l'Expédition d'Alger (Toulon, 1979).
22. BP, letter from Louis Boutigny to Monsieur Deferre (executive director of *Var Matin-République*), 18 May 1978; and *Var-Matin République*, 22 June 1978.
23. BP, Comité d'Honneur, Comité du Cent Cinquantenaire de l'Expédition d'Alger (Toulon, 1979).
24. That year another *pied noir* monument, the statue of the Virgin of the Cap Falcon east of Toulon, also suffered damage; see *Var-Matin République*, 26 November 1980.
25. Jean-Marie Guillon, "Inauguration d'un monument à l'Algérie Française à Toulon (14 juin 1980)—Éclairage," online at https://fresques.ina.fr/reperes-mediterraneens/fiche-media/Repmed00433/inauguration-d-un-monument-a-l-algerie-francaise-a-toulon.html (accessed 14 June 2019). Dominati's presence at the 1980 inauguration ceremony sparked a reaction among neo-Gaullist deputies so strong that Prime Minister Raymond Barre intervened.
26. Degueldre held the rank of lieutenant in a paratroop regiment. The plans for this monument describe its bas-relief as "a paratrooper who has just fallen and is living his final moments, with his lieutenant's shoulder tabs showing signs of clumsy ripping—the greatest insult, inflicted on those condemned to death"; see *L'Écho* 12 (September 1979), p. 17. Under the patronage of Mayor Jacques Médecin, in 1973 Nice had erected a similar memorial with the words "Roger Degueldre, symbol of French Algeria" inscribed on one side; see Branche, *La guerre d'Algérie*, p. 25. Other OAS monuments were inaugurated in Perpignan in 2003 and Marignane in 2005 (with FN cadres attendance); see Romain Bertrand, *Mémoires d'empire: Controverses autour du "fait colonial"* (Bellecombe-en-Bauges: Le Croquant, 2006), pp. 50–52.
27. Most migration went to the coast rather than the interior of the Var; see Legenne, *Var, terre d'histoire*, p. 253.
28. Ibid., pp. 206–208; and *Var Matin-République*, 12 January 1978, 29 December 1985, 30 December 1986, 1 January 1989, 29 December 1992, and 29 April 1995.
29. *Le Monde*, 20 November 1984. An anti-racist group (Mouvement contre le racisme et pour l'amitié entre les peoples) launched a suit against Arreckx but a court found him not guilty of inciting racial discrimination, hatred, or violence.
30. The neo-Gaullist was Louis Bernardi; see *Var Matin-République*, 8 April 1990.
31. Ibid., 29 December 1985.
32. Ibid., 12 July 1985.
33. Virginie Martin, *Toulon la noire: Le Front national au pouvoir* (Paris: Denoël, 1996), pp. 91–92
34. The left (Communist and Socialist votes combined) last dominated the Var in the 1981 presidential and parliamentary elections; the right (RPR, UDF, and FN votes combined) prevailed in the department starting with the 1984 European elections; see *Var Matin-République*, 23 April 1995; and Legenne, *Var, terre d'histoire*, p. 242.
35. Even La-Seyne-sur-Mer—a bastion of the Communist Party—switched to the moderate right; see *Var Matin-République*, 29 December 1985.
36. Ibid., 7 November 1985.

37. Across France, construction of commercial projects in city centers has continued to decline and today represents no more than 6 percent of the national total, with construction in suburbs accounting for most of the rest; see *Le Figaro*, 15 December 2017.
38. In addition to immigration, Trucy attributed crime to deindustrialization, unemployment, and homelessness; see *Var Matin-République*, 27 March 1986.
39. Ibid.
40. *Le Monde*, 2 April 1986.
41. Among the larger municipalities, voters gave least support to Le Pen in Saint-Tropez (18.3 percent) and most in Le Luc (31.1 percent). Average support came from Draguignan (22.6 percent), Hyères (25.2 percent), La Seyne-sur-Mer (25.5 percent), Toulon (27.0 percent), and Fréjus (28.13 percent). In the district where Le Pen came second, only 0.05 percent of the vote separated him from the front-runner; see *Var Matin-République*, 26 April 1988. In the runoff, the Var preferred Chirac (56.3 percent of the vote) over the winner, Mitterrand; see ibid., 10 May 1988).
42. Ibid.
43. Ibid.
44. The allies of Arreckx were François Léotard and Daniel Colin, who five months later succeeded Arreckx as president of the departmental section of the UDF; see ibid., 31 May 1988; and *Le Monde*, 15 March 1989.
45. *Var Matin-République*, 31 May 1988.
46. A few FN candidates thus joined anti-left slates put together for the 1989 municipal elections by the moderate right (UDF and RPR); see *Var Matin-République*, 22 February 1989; and *Le Monde*, 15 March 1989.
47. *Var Matin-République*, 31 December 1989.
48. Disunity afflicted the Socialists in some towns (Saint-Maximim and Aups), the RPR and UDF in others (Saint-Tropez, Saint-Cyr, and Sanary); see *Var Matin-République*, 31 December 1989.
49. *Le Monde*, 15 March 1989; *Var Matin-République*, 31 December 1989.
50. *Var Matin-République*, 1 January 1991.
51. This RPR politician, Louis Bernardi, was the same who in 1984 had said that North Africans posed a threat to Toulon; see *Var Matin-République*, 8 April 1990.
52. Igounet, *Le Front national*, p. 253.
53. *Var Matin-République*, 8 April 1990. At the invitation of the UAVFROM, this was Le Pen's third visit to Tourves since 1987.
54. *Var Matin-République*, 29 December 1992.
55. Ibid., 3 February 1992.
56. Arreckx's majority consisted of 14 politicians from the UDF, 12 from the RPR, and 8 independents (mostly from the left); see ibid., 31 March 1992.
57. Ibid., 30 March 1992 and 31 March 1992.
58. Ibid., 29 December 1992 and 29 December 1993.
59. Ibid., 23 March 1993. When Léotard was able to put the corruption scandal in Fréjus behind him, the prime minister named him minister of defense.
60. Police arrested Piat's killers in June 1994. Previously, Édouard Soldani had survived an assassination attempt (in February 1984). Daniel Perrin (a PR member and influential city councilor in La Seyne-sur-Mer who was probing into bribery for public works contracts) was murdered in August 1986. In March 1991, two men ambushed and beat up the mayor of Hyères, Léopold Ritondale; see *Var Matin-République*, 29 December 1991 and 21 February 1995; and *Libération*, 25 October 1997.
61. Police also questioned another moderate-right politician (Guy Liautaud) as well as the vice-president of the chamber of commerce (Jean-François Barraud); see *Var Matin-République*, 7 March 1994.

62. Ibid., 16 March 1994. On corruption among local officials after decentralization, see Kreuzer and Stephan, "France: Enduring Notables," p. 137.
63. *Var Matin-République*, 2 August 1994.
64. Ibid., 31 December 1994, 26 January 1995, 1 April 1995, and 12 April 1995.
65. This hub was the Maison des Technologies; see ibid., 1 February 1995, 2 February 1995, and 6 May 1995.
66. Ibid., 7 February 1995.
67. Ibid., 8 February 1995.
68. This agency was Toulon Communication.
69. The RPR politician was Louis Bernardi; see ibid., 4 February 1995, 24 March 1995, 21 April 1995, and 20 May 1995.
70. An amount equivalent to about US$1.5 million today; see ibid., 6 May 1995 and 11 May 1995.
71. Ibid., 1 June 1995.
72. Ibid., 2 June 1995. Upholding a previous verdict, in 1997 an appeals court found Arreckx guilty of accepting 2 million francs in bribes in return for contracts to build the Maison des Technologies in Toulon.

CHAPTER 8

1. Calculated from Richard Nadeau et al., *Villes de gauche, villes de droite* (Paris: Presses de la Fondation nationale des sciences politiques, 2018), p. 14, Table 7.
2. When the FN does compete in the runoff, significantly, on average the moderate right loses nearly 8 percent. Only in the 2014 municipal elections did the presence of the far right in the runoff hurt the left more than the moderate right; see ibid., pp. 125–127 and 156–161.
3. Delmonte, "Le Front national à Toulon," pp. 58–60; and *Le Monde*, 20 June 1995. As a member of Le Pen's slate, in 1984 Le Chevallier won election to the European Parliament, where until 1989 he served as treasurer for the Euro-right group (which also included Italian and Greek far-right parties). Sharp differences over party strategy with Jean-Pierre Stirbois, Le Pen's lieutenant, may explain the transfer of Le Chevallier from Paris to Toulon (like Piat, Le Chevallier favored more openness toward the moderate right); see Igounet, *Le Front national de 1972 à nos jours*, pp. 157–206.
4. Delmonte, "Le Front national à Toulon," pp. 68–79.
5. Ibid., p. 94.
6. Quoted in Stéphan Di Iorio, "D'un 'système' à l'autre: les facteurs explicatifs du vote Front national à Toulon," mémoire de DEA (Paris: Institut d'études politiques, 1998), pp. 90–91.
7. Ibid., p. 91.
8. *Var Matin-République*, 22 March 1994.
9. Ibid., 27 February 1995.
10. Ibid., 29 December 1993; and Delmonte, "Le Front national à Toulon," p. 74.
11. Di Iorio, "D'un 'système' à l'autre," pp. 46–47.
12. Peter Davies, *The National Front in France: Discourse, Ideology and Power* (London: Routledge, 1999), pp. 171–187.
13. *Var Matin-République*, 22 June 1995.
14. Ibid.
15. This councilor was Jean-Claude Lunardelli; see ibid.
16. This councilor was Louis Soccoja; see ibid.
17. This politician was Éliane de La Brosse; see ibid.
18. Di Iorio, "D'un 'système' à l'autre," p. 95.
19. Ibid., p. 48.

20. *Var Matin-République*, 22 January 1995.
21. Some 50 demonstrators (referred to as "anarchists and punks" by the press) harassed Le Pen supporters as they arrived at his political rally at the Municipal Theater and were eventually dispersed by state police who used tear gas and arrested 10 of them, one armed with a knife; see ibid., 22 January 1995.
22. At a campaign meeting near Montpellier attended by some 600 *pieds noirs*, Chirac spoke of the country's need to speed up programs aimed at them (including compensation and settlement credits) and "to uncover and showcase the enormous enterprise of civilization that the French empire was able to achieve in barely a century" (ibid., 11 March 1995). At a campaign rally in Fréjus (attended by François Léotard, François Trucy, and Hubert Falco), Prime Minister Balladur told a crowd of 4,000 supporters that if elected the state would speed compensation for the *pieds noirs*. He also commended their achievements as colonizers; see ibid., 19 March 1995.
23. Le Pen received 15.1 percent of the vote nationally but 22.4 percent in the Var (which gave 21.1 percent of the vote to Balladur, 19.1 percent to Chirac, and 17.3 percent to Jospin). Trucy hoped a split among local neo-Gaullists due to Balladur's rivalry with Chirac would help his re-election as mayor a few weeks later; despite Chirac's better chances, he thus backed Balladur. In parts of Toulon, Le Pen won as much as 35 percent of the vote; after his elimination, hard core supporters refused to transfer their second-round support to Chirac; see ibid., 19 April 1995, 24 April 1995, and 10 May 1995.
24. Ibid., 16 March 1995.
25. Di Iorio, "D'un 'système' à l'autre," pp. 68–69.
26. The Var sections of the UDF and the PR reacted to the Colombani candidacy by excluding him; see *Var Matin-République*, 11 April 1995 and 14 April 1995.
27. Vote splitting would have hurt the moderate right even more if one of its candidates (Marc Bayle) had not desisted in obedience to the interim president of the RPR (the mayor of Bordeaux, Alain Juppé), who backed Trucy; see ibid., 23 May 1995.
28. Di Iorio, "D'un 'système' à l'autre," pp. 62–63.
29. *Var Matin-République*, 27 February 1995. Le Pen defused the problem by asking Le Chevallier's chief adversary (Colonel of the Gendarmerie Jean-Jacques Gérardin, commander of the Presidential Guard under Giscard, now FN chief in the Var's Seventh District) to join the staff for his presidential campaign. Others in the party raised doubts about Le Chevallier's commitment to French Algeria because he had deserted from his unit in 1956; they also circulated accusations about excessive professionalization, absence of financial transparency, and the homosexuality of his campaign director; see ibid., 1 March 1995, 25 May 1995, 26 May 1995, and 13 November 1995.
30. Ibid., 9 June 1995.
31. Ibid., pp. 87–88; and *Var Matin-République*, 13 May 1995 and 1 June 1995.
32. Ibid., 28 February 1995.
33. Ibid., 3 February 1995.
34. Ibid., 24 February 1995.
35. Di Iorio, "D'un 'système' à l'autre," p. 89.
36. Ibid.
37. In much of the Var the moderate right declined at the expense of either the left or the FN, which survived to the second round in 18 of the department's municipalities; see *Var Matin-République*, 12 June 1995 and 13 June 1995.
38. The national headquarters of the Socialist Party snubbed Trucy's offer; see ibid., 14 June 1995.
39. This national leader was Laurent Fabius.
40. Staunchly opposed to Trucy, Colombani crossed party lines and endorsed the Goux list; see ibid., 13 June 1995.

41. With a 67.8 percent turnout, the second round mobilized more voters. The Le Chevallier list received 28,879 votes, 9,408 more than in the first round, but more voters supported the Trucy and Goux lists too; see ibid., 19 June 1995.
42. Igounet, *Le Front national*, pp. 207–208 and 268–270.
43. *Var Matin-République*, 22 June 1995.
44. Ibid., 4 November 1995, 7 November 1995, and 13 November 1995; and Di Iorio, "D'un 'système' à l'autre," p. 97.
45. Yohei Nakayama, "Associations, Party Models and Party System: Changing Patterns of Party Networks in Twentieth Century France," *French Politics* 7/2 (2009), pp. 96–122.
46. *Var Matin-République*, 31 October 1992.
47. Ibid., 7 November 1992.
48. Ibid., 28 April 1995.
49. Ibid., 7 November 1995.
50. The festival (which included minorities of North African descent) proceeded nonetheless; see ibid., 5 November 1995, 6 November 1995, and 7 November 1995.
51. This association was SOS Racisme, close to the Socialists; see ibid., 14 July 1997.
52. The city neither relocated the evicted unions nor found another use for the Labor Exchange, which Le Chevallier said might be transformed into "an Italian-style opera house"; see ibid., 8 November 1995.
53. Associations losing funding included Aides Provence; Secours Populaire; Fédération des Œuvres Laïques; Français musulmans; l'Entraide protestante; Secours populaire; Fédération des conseils de parents d'élèves; and Ligue de l'enseignement: see ibid., 17 November 1996; and *Le Monde Diplomatique*, July 1996.
54. The arts center at Châteauvallon and a theater in the Mourillon neighborhood reacted to the FN victory by rejecting city funding; *Var Matin-République*, 22 June 1995.
55. Virginie Martin et al., "Le Front national entre clientélisme et recherche d'un enracinement social," *Critique internationale* 3/4 (1999), p. 177.
56. *Var Matin-République*, 21 June 1995.
57. Ibid.
58. Jo Kibee, "Aux armes citoyens! Les bibliothèques publiques françaises face à l'extrême droite," *Bulletin des bibliothèques de France* 49/6 (2004), pp. 10–19.
59. *Var Matin-République*, 7 November 1995
60. The left-wing publisher was *Plein Sud*; that of the far right was *Présent*; see ibid., 4 November 1995.
61. The publisher, Mourad Boudjellal, was of mixed Algerian and Armenian background (a decade later, he became president of the city's championship rugby team); see ibid., 24 November 1996.
62. In attendance at Châteauvallon were Marek Halter (a founder of SOS Racisme excluded from the city's fair); François Léotard (UDF); and two former ministers of culture, Jack Lang (PS) and Philippe Douste-Blazy (UDF); see ibid., 23 November 1996.
63. Ibid., 23 November 1996 and 31 December 1997.
64. Martin et al., "Le Front national entre clientélisme et recherche d'un enracinement social," pp. 169–182.
65. From 2,987 in 1996, their number rose to 3,297 in 2001; see *Var-Matin*, 31 December 2002; and *Les Échos*, 27 March 2014.
66. *Les Échos*, 27 March 2014; and *Le Monde*, 10 January 1998.
67. *Libération*, 23 January 1998.
68. Touati was a former member of the national executive for SOS-Racisme; see *Libération*, 23 January 1998.

69. These unions were the Confédération Générale du Travail, Confédération française démocratique du travail, Confédération française des travailleurs chrétiens, and Force ouvrière; see *Var Matin-Republique*, 7 November 1995, 8 November 1995, and 31 December 1995.
70. BP, letter from Jean-Marie Le Chevallier to Louis Boutigny, 2 March 1993.
71. Michel Samson, *Le Front national aux affaires: Deux ans d'enquête sur la vie municipale à Toulon* (Paris: Calmann-Lévy, 1997), p. 64.
72. The umbrella group was the UAVFROM; see BP, letter from Louis Boutigny to Louis Soccoja, 18 September 1995.
73. *Var Matin-République*, 28 March 1996.
74. BP, letter from Louis Boutigny to Jean-Marie Le Chevallier, 2 April 1996.
75. *Var Matin-République*, 17 April 1996.
76. BP, letters from Louis Boutigny to Louis Soccoja, 21 October, 1996, 18 February 1997, 25 February 1997, and 20 March 1997; BP, letters from Louis Boutigny to Jean-Marie Le Chevallier, 5 March 1997, 20 March 1997, and 3 April 1997; and BP, letters from Louis Soccoja to Louis Boutigny, 13 March 1997 and 25 March 1997.
77. *Var Matin-Republique*, 7 November 1995.
78. Ibid., 7 November 1995 and 3 December 1996.
79. *Libération*, 19 February 1998.
80. *Les Échos*, 27 March 2014.
81. *Le Monde*, 1 November 1998.
82. Martin et al., "Le Front national entre clientélisme et recherche d'un enracinement social," pp. 169–182.
83. The Arsenal remained busy with maintenance, repairs, and overhauls to vessels from the French and American navies; see *Var-Matin République*, 22 January 1995, 7 November 1995, and 31 December 1995; and *Libération*, 19 May 2000.
84. Paris eventually shrank the fleet but did not privatize the Arsenal or reduce the number of military personnel in Toulon; see ibid., 3 November 1995 and 31 December 1996.
85. Repairs to the carrier Foch at the Arsenal dry docks in 1996–1997 accounted for 900,000 hours of work alone; see ibid., 27 September 1997.
86. Fearing cuts in the defense budget, in September 1997 the major trade unions organized a large rally in Toulon; see ibid., 24 September 1997 and 27 September 1997.
87. Di Iorio, "D'un 'système' à l'autre," p. 97; Samson, *Le Front national aux affaires*, pp. 17–33; *Le Monde Diplomatique*, July 1996; and *Var Matin-Republique*, 8 November 1995.
88. These big projects included the Centre Zénith-Oméga, the Centre Mayol, the Stade Mayol, the Palais des Congrès, and the Palais Liberté.
89. Commuter, regional, and long-distance traffic flowed directly through the city center. Design modifications that resulted in cost overruns and collapse of a section under construction delayed completion for years. Le Chevallier spoke about putting a hold on the tunnel, but co-financing (by the central state, the PACA region, and the department) meant Toulon could not act unilaterally; see *Le Monde Diplomatique*, July 1996; and *Var Matin-Republique*, 23 September 1997.
90. Chambre régionale des comptes de Provence-Alpes-Côte d'Azur, *Rapport d'observations définitives sur la gestion de la commune de Toulon (Département du Var), Années 1995 à 2005* (Marseille: Chambre régionale des comptes de Provence-Alpes-Cote d'Azur, 2006), p. 10.
91. *Var-Matin*, 26 December 1998; and *Libération*, 25 April 1998.
92. *Var Matin-République*, 26 September 1997.
93. De La Brosse and Admiral Guy Nachin (the city's associate mayor) also denounced the nepotism of the Le Chevallier couple in city employment; see Martin et al., "Le Front national entre clientélisme et recherche d'un enracinement social," pp. 169–182.

94. In exchange for presidency of the PACA region, the deal would have required that the FN back Édouard Balladur for presidency of the Île-de-France region; see Igounet, *Le Front national*, pp. 295 and 340.
95. *Var-Matin*, 28 December 1998. The Socialist candidate in the 1995 presidential elections, Lionel Jospin, became prime minister in a cohabitation government under President Chirac in 1997.
96. *Var Matin-Republique*, 31 December 1995.
97. *Var-Matin*, 28 December 1998, 30 December 1998, and 31 December 1998.
98. Ibid., 27 December and 29 December 1998.
99. By backing Le Chevallier, the prefect snubbed François Léotard, a rival for moderate-right control over the department who had sided with the director of the Châteauvallon arts center.
100. *Le Monde Diplomatique*, July 1996; *Var Matin-Republique*, 26 September 1997; *L'Express*, 24 June 1999; and *Libération*, 21 February 2000. Found guilty of influence peddling and condemned to a three-year prison sentence in 2008, Marchiani received a pardon from President Sarkozy in December 2008; see *Var-Matin*, 24 December 2008.
101. Le Chevallier attracted 53.2 percent of the vote in second round.
102. Di Iorio, "D'un 'système' à l'autre," p. 67.
103. *Var-Matin*, 10 January 1999.
104. *L'Express*, 24 June 1999.
105. *Libération*, 20–21 January 2001.
106. Ibid., 16 December 2005.
107. *Var-Matin*, 3 March 2001.
108. Ibid., 1 March 2001, 4 March 2001, and 9 March 2001.
109. The 7,586 voters (13.3 percent of the electorate) who voted for Bouguereau or Le Chevallier thus formed the hard core of far-right support in Toulon.
110. Jennifer Fitzgerald, *Close to Home: Local Ties and Voting Radical Right in Europe* (Cambridge: Cambridge University Press, 2018), p. 14.
111. Kreuzer and Stephan, "France: Enduring Notables, Weak Parties, and Powerful Technocrats," p. 137.

CHAPTER 9

1. Back-stage discourse can involve as much preparation and performance as front stage. Like Erving Goffman, who coined the distinction, I do not propose that back-stage selves or interactions are more authentic.
2. Front national, *Pour la France: Programme du Front national* (Paris: Albatros, 1985), p. 13.
3. Jean-Marie Le Pen, interview in *Valeurs actuelles*, 23 February 1985, quoted in Désiré Calderon, *La Droite française: Formation et projet* (Paris: Messidor, 1985), p. 203.
4. Front national, *Pour la France*.
5. *Le Monde*, 12 June 1984.
6. Front national, *Pour la France*, p. 112.
7. Jean-Marie Le Pen, *L'espoir* (Paris: Albatros, 1989), p. 29.
8. Ibid.
9. Ibid.
10. Front national, *Pour la France*. p. 113.
11. Front national, *Le Front national c'est vous* (Paris: Front national, 1990), p. 1.
12. *Le Monde*, 14 September 1983.
13. Le Pen, *L'espoir*, pp. 126–137; Deborah R. Levy, "Women of the French National Front," *Parliamentary Affairs* 42/1 (1989), p. 107; and Pierre-André Taguieff, "La métaphysique de Jean-Marie Le Pen," in Nonna Mayer and Pascal Perrineau (eds.),

Le Front national à découvert (Paris: Presses de la Fondation nationale des sciences politiques, 1989), p. 176.
14. Front national, Pour la France, pp. 98–109; Front national, La lettre de Jean-Marie Le Pen, 15 November 1990.
15. Le Monde, 14 September 1983.
16. Le Pen, L'espoir, p. 5.
17. Front national, "Le Pen Président," in La Lettre de Jean-Marie Le Pen (April 1987), p. 11.
18. Ibid., p. i.
19. Front national, Le programme du Front national: Défendre les français (Paris: Front national, 1984), p. 8.
20. Front national, "Le Pen Président," p. 23; and Front national, Le Front national c'est vous, p. 11. Still, the FN opposed the 1988 referendum on independence for New Caledonia on grounds it was unconstitutional; see Le Monde, 11 November 1988.
21. Front national, "Le Pen Président," pp. 1 and 15.
22. Le Monde, 16 September 1986.
23. Front national, "Le Pen Président," p. 7.
24. Front national, Le Front national c'est vous, p. 5.
25. Front national, Pour la France, p. 1.
26. Front national (Paris), "Radio Le Pen—Emission du 24 décembre 1989" (author's transcription of recorded telephone message of 24 December 1989).
27. These laws cover the civil service as well as firms in the private and public sectors; see Mendras with Cole, Social Change in Modern France, pp. 87–90.
28. Front national, Défendre les français, p. 6.
29. Le Monde, 22 June 1984.
30. Le Pen, L'espoir, pp. 163–170.
31. Le Monde, 9 June 1984.
32. Le Pen, L'espoir, p. 168.
33. Ibid., p. 166.
34. Sarah L. de Lange, "A New Winning Formula? The Programmatic Appeal of the Radical Right," Party Politics 13/4 (2007), pp. 411–435.
35. Reuters (France), 7 April 2012, "2012-Marine Le Pen lance une charge contre Goldman Sachs," online at http://fr.reuters.com/article/companyNews/idFRL6E8F707020120407 (accessed 7 November 2017).
36. Developments include defections from the party by its vice-president, Florian Philippot, who is openly gay; and by Marine Le Pen's niece, Marion Maréchal-Le Pen, a successful politician with a base in the PACA region who defends traditional values and criticizes her aunt's leadership.
37. Le Monde, 21 September 1982.
38. On the 30th anniversary of the Cercle algérianiste, its founder wrote that nonpartisanship both defined this association and explained its success; see Maurice Calmein, "1er novembre 1973–1er novembre 2003," L'Algérianiste 104 (December 2003), p. 4.
39. Marcel Gori, "Présentation de L'Écho," L'Écho 7 (April 1978), p. 3.
40. Association Culturelle des Français d'Afrique du Nord, Le Cercle algérianiste (Narbonne: Cercle Algérianiste, n.d. [circa 2003], p. 1.
41. L'Algérianiste 97 (March 2002), number 97, pp. 4–10, 38–47, and 67–75. The same themes proliferate in L'Écho (from Saint-Raphaël), Aux Échos d'Alger (from Nîmes), and L'Écho de l'Oranie (from Nice).
42. L'Algérianiste 98 (June 2002), pp. 56–69.
43. Excerpt from Pierre Dimech, "Le Grand Dérangement," quoted in L'Algérianiste 98 (June 2002), p. 3.

44. Editorial by Thierry Rolando, president of the Cercle algérianiste, in *L'Algérianiste* 98 (June 2002), p. 2. Rolando has supported François Fillon, the conservative politician; and Robert Ménard, a *pied noir* allied with the FN and since 2014 the mayor of Béziers; see "Pays de la Loire: La garde rapprochée de Bruno Retailleau," in *L'Express* 6 June, 2016, online at https://www.lexpress.fr/ (accessed 15 November 2017).
45. Editorial by Thierry Rolando, *L'Algérianiste* 98 (June 2002), p. 2.
46. The personalities include Daniel Auteuil (actor), Patrick Bruel (singer), Bernard Attali (administrator), Alain Afflelou (entrepreneur), Jean-Claude Beton (founder of Orangina soft drinks), Yves Saint Laurent (fashion designer), Albert Camus (writer), Jacques Derrida (philosopher), Marcel Cerdan (boxer), Jean Daniel (founder of *Nouvel Observateur*), and Alain Savary and Julien Dray (PS politicians); see *Pieds Noirs d'Hier et d'Aujourd'hui* 100 (April 1999).
47. Fred Artz, "Grandeur et décadence," *Pieds Noirs d'Hier et d'Aujourd'hui* 186 (June 2010), p. 5.
48. Francette Mendosa, "Le racisme a commencé à Marseille avec l'arrivée des Pieds noirs en 1962," *Pieds Noirs d'Hier et d'Aujourd'hui* 43 (February 1999), p. 9.
49. Claude Saëz, "Mon billet d'humeur," *Pieds Noirs d'Hier et d'Aujourd'hui* 205 (May 2012), p. 41.
50. Clovis, "Mensonges, illusions et réalités de la campagne présidentielle," *Pieds Noirs d'Hier et d'Aujourd'hui* 204 (March 2012), pp. 4–5.
51. One issue denounces the Évian Accords; calls for a new compensation law; recalls Gaullist opposition to amnesty for a leader of the 1961 putsch; reports a lawsuit by families of victims of the Oran massacre; and announces a committee to represent *pied noir* grievances in the next European elections; see *L'Écho de l'Oranie* 261 (March–April 1999).
52. Guy Birenbaum, *Le Front national en politique* (Paris: Balland, 1992), p. 263. Major families included the monarchist, traditionalist Catholic, Poujadist, French Algeria, New Right (GRECE), and neo-liberal (Club de l'horloge); see Peter Davies, *The National Front in France: Ideology, Discourse and Power* (London: Routledge, 1999), pp. 27–35.
53. Birenbaum, *Le Front national en politique*, pp. 258–262. *National hebdo* lasted until 2008 (an online version not aligned with the FN continues at www.national-hebdo.net).
54. Jonathan Marcus, *The National Front and French Politics: The Resistable Rise of Jean-Marie Le Pen* (New York: New York University Press, 1995), p. 125. Among its journalists and shareholders, the newspaper counted members of the FN's central committee; see ibid., pp. 125–126; and Birenbaum, *Le Front national en politique*, p. 260.
55. *National hebdo* had a circulation of 15,000 in 1991; see Birenbaum, *Le Front national en politique*, pp. 252–254. On the different families (e.g., monarchist, Catholic traditionalist, Pétainist, and New Right) represented in the pro-FN press, see Harvey J. Simmons, *The French National Front: The Extremist Challenge to Democracy* (Boulder, CO: Westview, 1996), pp. 197–198; and James G. Shields, *The Extreme Right in France: From Pétain to Le Pen* (London: Routledge, 2007), p. 245.
56. *Présent* came next among the delegates, with its readership at 76 percent; see Birenbaum, *Le Front national en politique*, p. 254.
57. NH 62 (1985), p. 3.
58. NH 87 (1986), pp. 14–15.
59. NH 95 (1986), pp. 11–12.
60. NH 97 (1986), p. 12.
61. NH 244 (1989), p. 28.
62. NH 96 (1986), p. 11. On the polemical side of this work, see Jean-Clément Martin, "Review of Vendée: Du Génocide au mémoricide. Mécanique d'un crime légal, by Reynald Sécher," *Annales de la Révolution française* 368 (2012), pp. 194–196.

63. NH 164 (1987). The anti-Semitism of Drumont (1844–1917) drew from multiple sources: a Catholic counterrevolutionary tradition that denounced the plotting of Jews and Freemasons; a Socialist, anticapitalist current that denounced the usurious Jewish plutocracy; and scientific racial theories. Initially, the anticapitalist element in Drumont's mix of ideas slowed its adoption by conservatives, but this changed with the Dreyfus Affair; see Winock, *Nationalisme, antisémitisme et fascisme en France*, pp. 117–144.
64. NH 274 (1989), pp. 4–5.
65. NH 270 (1989), p. 9.
66. NH 204 (1988), p. 28.
67. René Rémond, *Les Droites en France*, revised edition (Paris: Aubier, 1982). On Bonapartism and De Gaulle, see Aron, *Mémoires*, pp. 254–257.
68. NH 74 (1985), p. 1 of supplement.
69. NH 303 (1990), pp. 5–6.
70. NH 277 (1989), p. 4, and NH 255 (1989), p. 13.
71. NH 294 (1990), p. 2.
72. NH 251 (1989), p. 19.
73. NH 251 (1989), p. 19.
74. NH 155 (1987), p. 6.
75. This modifies claims that Vichy remains the most important reference for the French far right; see Shields, *The Extreme Right in France*, p. 307.
76. NH 166 (1987), p. 4.
77. NH 203 (1988), p. 27; and NH 243 (1989), p. 24.
78. NH 124 (1986), p. 12.
79. The book's author was Pierre Sergent; see NH 202 (1988), p. 24.
80. On Jean Bastien-Thiry (executed in 1963 for organizing a failed attempt to assassinate De Gaulle), see NH 87 (1986), p. 3 of supplement. On Hélie de Saint Marc (court-martialed and imprisoned for his participation in the 1961 putsch), see NH 242 (1989), p. 24. On Jean-Louis Tixier-Vignancour, see NH 120 (1986), p. 3 and NH 272 (1989), p. 7. On Roger Holeindre (former OAS activist and FN deputy, afterward party vice-president), see NH 244 (1989), pp. 14–15.
81. For anti-Gaullism, see NH 154 (1987), p. 4; NH 194 (1988), p. 3; NH 241 (1989), p. 20; NH 244 (1989), p. 25; NH 274 (1989), p. 17; NH 287 (1989), p. 4; and NH 311 (1990), p. 18.
82. The anti-racist vilified in this article is Harlem Désir, leader of SOS-Racisme; see NH 100 (1986), p. 2.
83. NH 182 (1988), p. 5.
84. Ibid.
85. NH 196 (1988), p. 8.
86. NH 304 (1990), p. 7.
87. NH 225 (1988), p. 4.
88. Géraud Durand, *Enquête au coeur du Front national* (Paris: Jacques Grancher, 1996), p. 149.
89. To test the survey described in Chapter 10, in 2002 I had interviewed 24 *pieds noirs* residing in the Toulon area (these were the only people asked to participate in the interviews, with all agreeing). The possibility of analyzing their words—and not just their survey responses—occurred to me only later. An interview would last an hour or two. In addition to taking notes, I had people's permission to make an audio recording. The translations of their words into English are mine. While I cannot claim that this sample was statistically representative, my field observations, the primary literature, and the academic literature suggest that what I heard was discursively representative. Consisting of 12 men and 12 women, the sample has no gender bias and, because it includes supporters and non-supporters of the far right, there is no sampling on the dependent variable. To protect the anonymity of respondents, I use pseudonyms.

90. FN supporters, born 1920s in Koléa.
91. Usually casts a blank vote, born 1920s in the metropole, in Algeria lived in Maison-Carrée.
92. Ibid.
93. FN supporter, born 1920s in Affreville.
94. FN supporters, born 1920s in Algiers and 1930s in Bône.
95. Ibid.
96. Ibid.
97. FN supporter, born 1920s in Koléa.
98. Ibid.
99. FN supporters, born 1920s in Algiers.
100. Ibid.
101. Ibid.
102. FN supporter, born 1940s in Blida. Jacques Isorni was a famous lawyer who during the 1940s and 1950s had defended Marshall Pétain and Robert Brasillach, both accused of crimes including consorting with the enemy. During the 1960s, like Tixier he defended military men and OAS veterans accused of breaking the law in the name of French Algeria.
103. FN supporter, born 1940s in Blida.
104. Ibid.
105. FN supporter, born 1920s in Algiers.
106. FN supporter, born 1940s in Blida.
107. FN supporter, born 1920s in Koléa.
108. FN supporters, born 1920s in Algiers and Affreville.
109. FN supporter, born 1930s in Bône.
110. Ibid.
111. Ibid.
112. FN supporter, born 1940s in Algiers.
113. FN supporter, born 1920s in Affreville.
114. Nicolas Bancel et al., *La République coloniale: Essai sur une utopie* (Paris: Albin Michel, 2003), p. 32.
115. Anti-Semitism helped set apart the electorate of Jean-Marie Le Pen (20 percent of his second-round supporters in 2002 agreed that "Jews have too much power in France," compared with 7 percent of those who supported Chirac). Immigration mattered even more, still, with 70 percent of Le Pen's supporters agreeing that "there are too many immigrants in France" (compared with 22 percent of Chirac's supporters); see Jean Chiche and Élisabeth Dupoirier, "De Chirac à l'UMP: Mutations et reconquête," in Pascal Perrineau (ed.), *Le vote de tous les refus: Les élections présidentielle et législatives de 2002* (Paris: Presses de la Fondation nationale des sciences politiques, 2003), p. 184.
116. This agrees with findings about the FN and the *pieds noirs* in other parts of France; see Comtat, "La question du vote Pied-Noir," p. 84.

CHAPTER 10

1. In Languedoc-Roussillon and Provence-Alpes-Côte d'Azur, Le Pen received 29.5 percent of the vote from *pieds noirs* (defined here to include younger voters with at least one parent born in French Algeria). In the rest of France, by contrast, she received only 17 percent among *pied noir* voters, the same level as for other voters; see IFOP (2014), "Le vote pied-noir: mythe ou réalité?"
2. Alexis de Tocqueville, *Democracy in America* (New York: Harper and Row, 1969), p. 526. Tocqueville drew on Michel de Montaigne here.

3. Ibid., p. 513.
4. Ibid., pp. 513–517.
5. Paul Gonnet, "Toulon dans les premiers drames du XXe siècle (1904–1929)," in Maurice Agulhon (ed.), *Histoire de Toulon* (Toulouse: Privat, 1988), pp. 317–341.
6. *Var-Matin*, 27 February 2017.
7. Recipients included Alzheimer Var, Trisomie 21 Var, and Planning Familial de Toulon; see information for Geneviève Levy at Assemblée nationale, Répartition de la réserve parlementaire en 2015, online at *assemblee-nationale.fr* (accessed 5 October 2017).
8. *Le Monde*, 29 July 2017.
9. Ibid.
10. *Var-Matin*, 27 December 2007.
11. *Le Monde*, 10 November 2016.
12. AMT, carton 51W1, "Budget primitif 1975, Etat de répartition des subventions," pp. 1–8.
13. *Var-Matin*, 27 February 2017.
14. Robert D. Putnam, *Making Democracy Work: Civic Traditions in Modern Italy* (Princeton, NJ: Princeton University Press, 1993), p. 99.
15. AMT, carton 4W87, "Délibérations du Conseil Municipal de Toulon, Séance du 29 Juillet 1970, Attribution d'une subvention au Front National des Rapatriés pour ses Œuvres Sociales."
16. AMT, carton 4W121, "Délibérations du conseil municipal de la commune de Toulon, séance du 22 février 1974, Exonération des Droits de Location et Taxes sur les Spectacles à l'occasion de la Rencontre de Football organisée par le Front National des Rapatriés le 10 mars 1974 à Bon-Rencontre."
17. BP, letter dated 31 January 1983 from Maurice Arreckx to Louis Boutigny.
18. Author's interview with Georges Boutigny, La Valette-du-Var, 17 December 2004.
19. *Var-Matin*, 28 April 1995.
20. Ibid., 16 June 1995.
21. AMT, carton 70W28, "Commune de Toulon, Registre des délibérations du conseil municipal, Séance du 30 janvier 1998, Budget primitif pour 1998."
22. *Var-Matin*, 17 May 2001. On Fraternité française and the National Front in Toulon, see Martin et al., "Le Front national entre clientélisme et recherche d'un enracinement social," pp. 169–182.
23. Ville de Toulon, "Aide aux associations." Online at http://toulon.fr/sites/new.toulon.fr/files/aidesauxassociations2013.pdf (accessed 8 April 2015; no longer online).
24. Chambre régionale des comptes de Provence-Alpes-Cote d'Azur, *Rapport d'observations définitives sur la gestion de la commune de Toulon (Département du Var), Années 1995 à 2005*, pp. 18–19 and 36.
25. *Var-Matin*, 24 December 2003.
26. This group was the Association Nationale Villes et Rapatriés; see AMT, carton 4W85, "Délibérations du Conseil Municipal de Toulon, séance du 3 avril 1970."
27. AMT, carton 49W9, "Associations et Amicales de Rapatriés," undated (circa 1978).
28. These were the departmental branches of the Cercle algérianiste and the FNR (before its takeover by the FN); see AMT, carton 51W7, "Etat de répartition des subventions et participations accordées. Exercice 1982"; and AMT, carton 49W9, Marie de Toulon, "Budget primitif 1984. Subventions."
29. AMT, carton 51W1, "Budget primitif 1975. Etat de répartition des subventions"; and AMT, "Budget primitif 1976. Etat de répartition des subventions."
30. The city purchased the empty barracks in 1974; see AMT, carton 49W9, "Caserne Truguet, dossier no. 771 AC," undated (circa 1978).
31. AMT, carton 49W9, Mairie de Toulon, "Immeubles communaux affectés à des associations et organismes diverses," undated (circa 1980).

32. AMT, 45W65, "Registre des délibérations du Conseil municipal, séance du 7 mai, 1986, délibération no. 86/00267/5."
33. AMT, 45W77, "Registre des délibérations du Conseil municipal, séance du 29 avril 1987, délibération no. 87/00230/5)."
34. On city funding for repatriate associations, see *Var-Matin,* 14 April 2007, 21 May 2007, and 26 December 2007.
35. AMT, 70W28, "Commune de Toulon, Registre des délibérations du conseil municipal, Séance du 30 janvier 1998."
36. In the city's 2013 budget, for instance, the Cercle Algérianiste de Toulon received €900 while the Fédération Nationale des Anciens en Algérie, Maroc et Tunisie received €300; see Ville de Toulon, "Aide aux associations," online at http://toulon.fr/sites/new.toulon.fr/files/aidesauxassociations2013.pdf (accessed 8 April 2015; no longer online).
37. To launch the survey, I mailed the questionnaire to all members of a *pied noir* association whose president had provided me with a membership list as well as a cover letter that encouraged participation. To enlarge the sample beyond the first wave, the questionnaire asked respondents to provide the name and address of other *pieds noirs* to whom I could also send the questionnaire. The 2002 survey had 158 respondents ($n = 61$ for the first wave, $n = 97$ for waves two through seven) and a response rate of 58.7 percent. The 2007 survey ($n = 81$) had two waves (the first consisting of potential respondents to the 2002 survey, the second consisting of new respondents) and had a response rate of 25.0 percent. The 2012 survey ($n = 50$) had a response rate of 22.1 percent among the 226 potential respondents to the 2007 survey. I attribute decline in the response rate between 2002 and 2012 to mortality and decreased capacity (in 2012 the average age of respondents was 77 years). To check for sampling bias, I compared responses in each of the six subsequent waves of the 2002 survey with responses in the first wave. This failed to uncover patterns of similarity between the electoral choice of respondents in later waves and that of the original respondent who provided their name and address. I also checked for self-selection bias and found that almost none of the respondents had chosen to join an association close to the FN although this option was available. Colleagues and I analyzed the data using a combination of exploratory bi-variate analysis and confirmatory regression analysis; see John Veugelers et al., "Colonial Past, Voluntary Association and Far-Right Voting in France," *Ethnic and Racial Studies* 38/5 (2015), pp. 775–791.
38. Percent voting for the far right, first round of presidential elections:

Election year	France	Toulon	*Pieds noirs*
2002	19	24	50
2007	12	21	43
2012	18	23	45
mean	16	23	46

39. Percent voting for the far right, first round of parliamentary elections:

Election year	France	Toulon	*Pieds noirs*
2002	10	14	32
2007	4	8	34
2012	14	22	51
mean	9	15	39

40. In the first round of the 2002 presidential election, for example, Le Pen won 17 percent of the vote; yet 8 opinion polls during the previous four weeks (the last three days before the election) had set his support between 10 and 13 percent; see Pascal Perrineau, "La surprise lepéniste et sa suite legislative," in Pascal Perrineau and Colette Ysmal (eds.), *Le vote de tous les refus* (Paris: Presses de la Fondation nationale des sciences politiques, 2003), p. 201.
41. Consistent with the 2002 levels for presidential and parliamentary elections in Toulon, a 2002 survey of *pied noir* voting in other parts of France found that 44 percent of those born before 1947 had voted for the National Front in at least one election; see Comtat, *Les pieds-noirs et la politique*, p. 221.
42. Mayer, *Ces français qui votent FN*, pp. 50–57 and 356–357.
43. The annual pilgrimage of *pieds noirs* to Notre-Dame de Santa Cruz in Nîmes provides another example of ritual; on its history and meaning, see Michèle Baussant, *Pieds-noirs: Mémoires d'exils* (Paris: Stock, 2002), pp. 240–314.
44. FN supporter, born 1930s in Bône.
45. PS supporter, born 1940s in Algiers.
46. FN supporter, born 1940s in Algiers.
47. Other research suggests that *pieds noirs* find refuge in associations that counter deracination with a nostalgic and closed solidarity that views France with ambivalence; see Smith, *Colonial Memory and Postcolonial Europe*, pp. 202–209.
48. The effect is robust. Even after factoring in respondents' social background and response to the race question, regression analysis confirms that association membership has a significant effect on voting.
49. Banfield's father-in-law was a village landowner; see Sidney Tarrow, "Comparison, Triangulation, and Embedding Research in History: A Methodological Self-Analysis," *Bulletin de Méthodologie Sociologique* 141 (2019), p. 24.
50. Edward C. Banfield, *The Moral Basis of a Backward Society* (Glencoe, IL: Free Press, 1958), p. 15.
51. Ibid., p. 17 ("Montegrano" was Chiaromonte in the province of Potenza).
52. Against Banfield, who attributes the narrowness of interests to short life expectancy, scarce land tenure, and isolated family structure, see Sydel F. Silverman, "Agricultural Organization, Social Structure, and Values in Italy: Amoral Familism Reconsidered," *American Anthropologist* 70/1 (1968), pp. 1–20.
53. Alongside these parallels, however, old cleavages (between Church power and anticlericalism, for example) distinguished one region or city from that of another; see Mattei Dogan, "Political Cleavage and Social Stratification in France and Italy," in Stein Rokkan and Seymour Martin Lipset (eds.), *Party Systems and Voter Alignments: Cross-National Perspectives* (New York: Free Press, 1967), pp. 129–195.
54. Veugelers and Lamont, "France: Alternative Locations for Public Debate," p. 135.
55. On culture as action, interaction, and production, see Robert Wuthnow, *Communities of Discourse: Ideology and Social Structure in the Reformation, the Enlightenment, and European Socialism* (Cambridge, MA: Harvard University Press, 1989).
56. Whether from Indonesia to the Netherlands, Kenya to Britain, or Mozambique to Portugal, the postwar migration of settlers from colony to metropole differs from other migratory movements. These migrants were "living embodiments of a history repudiated around the world"; see Frederick Cooper, "Postcolonial Peoples: A Commentary," in Andrea L. Smith (ed.), *Europe's Invisible Migrants* (Amsterdam: Amsterdam University Press, 2003), p. 172. Nonetheless, research on transplanted settlers can benefit from, and contribute to, immigrant studies. The present chapter works within the same theoretical framework as Laura Morales and Katia Pilati, "The Role of Social Capital in Migrants' Engagement in Local Politics in European Cities," in Laura Morales and Marco Giugni

(eds.), *Social Capital, Political Participation and Migration in Europe: Making Multicultural Democracy Work* (Houndmills, UK: Palgrave Macmillan, 2011), pp. 88–91.
57. Analysis of the Gironde finds that Le Pen did worse in the 2002 presidential election in municipalities that gave residents more associational opportunities; see Fitzgerald, *Close to Home*, p. 132. These associations crossed cleavages, presumably.
58. Putnam, *Making Democracy Work*, p. 173.
59. Ibid., pp. 63–76, 89–93, and 171–181.

CHAPTER 11

1. Joël Gombin, "2015, Les trois visages du vote FN," *Le Monde Diplomatique* (December 2015), pp. 1–6; Joël Gombin, "Le changement dans la continuité: Géographies électorales du Front national depuis 1992" in Sylvain Crépon et al. (eds.), *Les faux-semblants du Front national: Sociologie d'un parti politique* (Paris: Presses de la Fondation nationale des sciences politique, 2015), pp. 403–414; and Nonna Mayer, "Le plafond de verre électoral: Entamé, mais pas brisé," in Sylvain Crépon et al. (eds.), *Les faux-semblants du Front national: Sociologie d'un parti politique* (Paris: Presses de la Fondation nationale des sciences politique, 2015), pp. 299–321 In the 2017 presidential election, 20 departments in metropolitan France that had given below 20 percent of their vote to Le Pen in 2012 now exceeded this threshold. The geographical contiguity of these 20 departments with those already above the 20 percent threshold in 2012 is remarkably consistent and suggests a contagion effect. Contagion could be due to party organizational strategy (e.g., organizing outward from stronger departments); expansion of activist networks; or a bandwagon effect among voters. Paris and its adjacent departments remain notably aloof from these national trends; see maps and analysis in *Le Figaro*, 24 April 2017, "Comment le vote des Français a évolué entre 2012 et 2017," online at http://www.lefigaro.fr/elections/presidentielles/2017 (accessed 14 August 2017).
2. In the 2017 parliamentary elections, sharp regional differences showed when National Front deputies won at the expense of the left in the north but the moderate right in the south (see Appendix, Table 7).
3. Between the 2010 and 2015 elections, in PACA the moderate right stayed at 29 percent; paying for the unpopularity of the Socialist government in Paris, the left's share fell from 42 to 24 percent; see Gilles Ivaldi and Christine Pina, "PACA, une victoire à la Pyrrhus pour la droite?" *Revue Politique et Parlementaire* 1078 (2016), pp. 139–150.
4. The FN won 35.0 percent, as opposed to 9.5 percent for the Socialists and 25.2 percent for the UMP.
5. Martial Foucault and Elisabeth Dupoirier, "Nouvelles régions, nouveaux élus?" *Revue Politique et Parlementaire* 1878 (2016), pp. 85–101; and *Var-Matin*, 31 March 2015.
6. *Var-Matin*, 24 March 2014.
7. David Art, "Party Organizations and the Radical Right," in Jens Rydgren (ed.), *The Oxford Handbook of the Radical Right* (New York: Oxford University Press, 2018), p. 245.
8. Compare the results for elections starting in 2001 in Table 1 vs. Tables 2, 3, and 4 of the Appendix.
9. In 2008 and 2014, unusually for a big city, the Falco list attracted a majority vote in the first round, thereby making a runoff unnecessary.
10. *Var-Matin*, 19 June 2002 and 11 June 2007.
11. Ibid., 30 December 2007.
12. Author's interview with LR politician, Toulon, 24 July 2015.
13. People assume that politics and Freemasonry overlap in the Var. The secrecy of the Freemasons makes this assumption difficult to assess. One report describes a 2009 intervention with President Sarkozy in support of Falco by the head of the Grande Loge nationale française; see *Le Nouvel Observateur*, 18 August 2011. Another alleges that

members of the Grande Loge nationale française in the Var include many elected officials and business leaders; see *Var-Matin*, 9 January 2014.
14. Gilles Pinson, "Le maire et ses partenaires: Du schéma centre-périphérie à la gouvernance multi-niveaux," *Pouvoirs* 148 (2014), p. 106.
15. Bernard Jouve, "From Government to Urban Governance in Western Europe: A Critical Analysis," *Public Administration and Development* 25/4 (2005), pp. 285–294.
16. Governments justify change in local administration using the rhetoric of public accountability and consultation, but these reforms may give more power to non-elected officials (who derive authority from their specialized expertise on technical questions and their comprehensive grasp of complex issues); see Jouve, "From Government to Urban Governance in Western Europe."
17. The French call these federations *intercommunalités, communautés de communes,* or *communautés d'agglomération*. Data from *Le Monde*, 19 July 2017; see also Jouve, "From Government to Urban Governance in Western Europe," pp. 289–290; and Fitzgerald, *Close to Home*, pp. 112–115.
18. *Var-Matin*, 19 March 2001. In the 2002 presidential election, municipalities that had recently federated with others also gave higher support to Le Pen; maybe Le Chevallier judged that federating Toulon with other municipalities would offend his supporters' sense of local attachment; see Fitzgerald, *Close to Home*, pp. 110–111.
19. Forty-three percent of the Var's population lives within the TPM (Carqueiranne, La Crau, La Garde, Hyères, Ollioules, Le Pradet, Le Revest-les-Eaux, Saint-Mandrier-sur-Mer, Six-Fours-les-Plages, La Seyne-sur-Mer, Toulon, and La Valette-du-Var).
20. Région Provence-Alpes-Côte d'Azur (2017), "Projets soutenus par des financements européens en région Provence-Alpes-Côte d'Azur" (Marseille: Région Provence-Alpes-Côte d'Azur). Online at http://www.europarl.europa.eu/france/resource/static/files/bureau-marseille/europe-concret/projets_soutenus_par_des_financements_europeens_en_region_provence-alpes-cotes_d_azur-avril-2017.pdf (accessed 14 July 2017).
21. Chambre régionale des comptes de Provence-Alpes-Cote d'Azur, *Rapport d'observations définitives sur la gestion de la commune de Toulon (Département du Var), Années 1995 à 2005*, p. 11.
22. *Le Figaro*, 30 January 2014.
23. *Le Monde*, 23 July 2015.
24. *Le Point*, 3 March 2017.
25. Ibid., 13 October 2017.
26. Chambre régionale des comptes—Provence-Alpes-Côte d'Azur, *Rapport d'observations définitives sur la gestion de la commune de Toulon, Exercices 2009 à 2013*.
27. (1) Thirty-six percent of the civil servants in the public administration for the Var had the same surname as another; (2) about one-fifth shared their surname with two others; and (3) three sons of former presidents of the Var (Arreckx, Falco, and Lanfranchi) held full-time positions in the department's administration; see *Le Monde*, 30 June 2016.
28. *Var-Matin*, 18 June 2002.
29. Chambre régionale des comptes de Provence-Alpes-Cote d'Azur, *Rapport d'observations définitives sur la gestion de la commune de Toulon (Département du Var), Années 1995 à 2005*, p. 35.
30. Each year between 1997 and 2001 (so, during the Le Chevallier administration), the city's investment budget was below €24 million; between 2001 and 2005 (after the Le Chevallier years), it climbed steadily and reached €45.4 million; see Chambre régionale des comptes de Provence-Alpes-Cote d'Azur, *Rapport d'observations définitives sur la gestion de la commune de Toulon (Département du Var), Années 1995 à 2005*, p. 10.

31. While the original plan called for the city's first multimedia library, the final project consisted of stores, offices, and a commercial cinema; Chambre régionale des comptes de Provence-Alpes-Cote d'Azur, *Rapport d'observations définitives sur la gestion de la commune de Toulon (Département du Var), Années 1995 à 2005*, p. 38.
32. *Var-Matin*, 29 April 2007.
33. Nouvelle gare SNCF: une réalisation exemplaire, Toulon actualités, 28 Novembre 2013, online at http://toulon.fr/actualites/ (accessed 9 April 2015; no longer online).
34. *Var-Matin*, 31 December 2005, 30 December 2008, 31 December 2008, 27 December 2011, and 28 December 2011; and Centre Hospitalier Intercommunal Toulon-La Seyne sur Mer, "Nouvel Hôpital Sainte Musse," online at http://www.ch-toulon.fr/ (accessed 9 April 2015; no longer online).
35. *Var-Matin*, 8 May 2008.
36. Région Provence-Alpes-Côte d'Azur, Direction Régionale de l'Environnement, de l'Aménagement et du Logemenet, "Tunnel de Toulon," (2013), online at http://www.paca.developpement-durable.gouv.fr/ (accessed 8 April 2015).
37. Communauté d'agglomération Toulon Provence Méditerranée, "Le Théâtre Liberté—Origines" (2011), online at http://m.tpm-agglo.fr (accessed 8 April 2015).
38. Toulon actualités, "Nouvelle gare SNCF: une réalisation exemplaire," online at http://toulon.fr/actualites/ (accessed 9 April 2015; no longer online).
39. One index of municipal financial management between 1983 and 2014 gives the following rankings for Toulon among 236 cities with a population above 30,000: 102nd in 1983, 156th in 1989, 223rd in 1995, 194th in 2001, 136th in 2008, and 84th in 2014. These suggest a worsening (relative to other municipalities) of the city's finances under Arreckx and Trucy; a small improvement under the National Front; and a great improvement under Falco; see Nadeau et al., *Villes de gauche, villes de droite*, pp. 187–196.
40. Laurent Verdier, "Qui sont les maires qui gèrent le mieux leur ville?" *Challenges*, 20 March 2014, online at http://www.challenges.fr/ (accessed 8 May 2015).
41. Florent Gougou, "Les ouvriers et le Front national: Les logiques d'un réalignement électoral," in Sylvain Crépon et al. (ed.), *Les faux-semblants du Front national: Sociologie d'un parti politique* (Paris: Presses de la Fondation nationale des sciences politique, 2015), pp. 323–343.
42. *Var-Matin*, 13 April 2007.
43. Funding for this urban renewal project in the Ilot Beaudin quarter comes from the central state, PACA region, Var department, and TPM inter-urban federation; see https://toulon.fr/avenir-se-construit/dossier/ilot-baudin (accessed 18 July 2017; no longer online).
44. *Var-Matin*, 31 December 2008.
45. *Le Figaro*, 24 August 2017.
46. Among municipalities, Toulon ranks only 84th in France for the number of patents per 10,000 inhabitants; see ibid., 24 August 2017.
47. With its high share of retirees, among cities Toulon ranks 105th in the country for the ratio of younger to older inhabitants; see Laurent Davezies, "Fort développement et faible croissance," in Jean Viard (ed.,) *Toulon, ville discrète* (La Tour d'Aigues: L'Aube, 2014), pp. 109–110.
48. *Var-Matin*, 28 December 2009; and http://www.letudiant.fr/educpros/actualite/le-palmares-2014-des-villes-ou-il-fait-bon-etudier.html (accessed 9 April 2015).
49. *Var-Matin*, 21 December 2008.
50. Ibid., 3 December 2001, 1 June 2002, 16 May 2007, 28 December 2010, and 29 December 2010.
51. Site officielle de la ville de Toulon. "Tourisme—un atout," online at toulon.fr/ (accessed 20 May 2015).
52. *Var-Matin*, 16 May 2007 and 28 December 2011. The 19 hotels in the city contain a total of 795 rooms, small numbers next to the Var's 472 hotels and 13,138 rooms; see INSEE,

Commune de Toulon/Département du Var, Chiffres clés at http://www.insee.fr/ (accessed 20 May 2015).
53. *Le Figaro*, 24 August 2017.
54. On the social and political effects of deindustrialization in East London, Britain, and Youngstown, Ohio, see Justin Gest, *The New Minority: White Working Class Politics in an Age of Immigration and Inequality* (New York: Oxford University Press, 2016).
55. *Var-Matin*, 29 December 2003.
56. Davezies, "Fort développement et faible croissance," p. 98.
57. Association des Maires de Grandes Villes de Frances, *Rôle économique des grandes villes et grandes agglomérations* (Paris: Association des Maires de Grandes Villes de Frances, 2012), online at http://franceurbaine.org/ (accessed 18 July 2017), p. 5.
58. Davezies, "Fort développement et faible croissance," pp. 100–102.

CONCLUSION

1. Author's observations, Toulon, 26 March 2008. Nowhere at this ceremony did I see signs of political parties, let alone the FN. A city councilor attended, but she was also president of the department's federation of *pied noir* associations (the UAVFROM).
2. My understanding of repertoires was more research product than starting point; see Ann Swidler, "Culture in Action: Symbols and Strategies," *American Sociological Review* 51/2 (1986), pp. 273–286.
3. Raymond Williams, *Marxism and Literature* (Oxford: Oxford University Press, 1977), pp. 112–114; and William C. Dowling, *Jameson, Althusser, Marx: An Introduction to the Political Unconscious* (Ithaca, NY: Cornell University Press, 1984), p. 131.
4. Joshua Cole, "Understanding the French Riots of 2005: What Historical Context for the 'crise des banlieus'?" *Francophone Postcolonial Studies* 5/2 (2007), pp. 90–91.
5. Françoise de Barros, "Des 'Français musulmans d'Algérie' aux 'immigrés': L'importation de classifications coloniales dans les politiques du logement en France (1950–1970)," *Actes de la recherche en sciences sociales* 159 (2005), pp. 26–53.
6. Sylvie Tissot, "The Role of Race and Class in Urban Marginality," *City* 11/3 (2007), pp. 364–369.
7. The words are Max Horkheimer's; see Martin Jay, "The Jews and the Frankfurt School: Critical Theory's Analysis of Anti-Semitism," New German Critique 19/1 (1980), p. 138.
8. Karl Polanyi, *The Great Transformation: The Political and Economic Origins of our Time* (Boston: Beacon Press, 1957 [1944]).
9. Hans-Georg Betz, "Politics of Resentment: Right-Wing Radicalism in West Germany," *Comparative Politics* 23/1 (1990), pp. 45–60; Hans-Georg Betz, "The New Politics of Resentment: Radical Right-Wing Populist Countries in Western Europe," *Comparative Politics* 25/4 (1993), pp. 413–427; and Herbert Kitschelt with Anthony J. McGann, *The Radical Right in Western Europe: A Comparative Analysis* (Ann Arbor: University of Michigan Press, 1995). As we have seen, the FN moved between pro- and anti-market policies. By comparison with other right-wing parties, moreover, some of its electorate is less—not more—in favor of laissez-faire. Among supporters of presidential candidates in 2002, those who supported Jean-Marie Le Pen or Bruno Mégret were at the French average on economic liberalism or opposing globalization; and close to supporters of moderate-right candidates on privatizing the national railway sector. Instead, disliking immigrants and supporting repressive measures against crime set them apart; see Gérard Grunberg and Étienne Schweisguth, "La tripartition de l'espace politique," in Pascal Perrineau and Colette Ysmal (eds.) *Le vote de tous les refus: Les élections présidentielles et législatives de 2002* (Paris: Presses de la Fondation nationale des sciences politiques, 2003), pp. 348–354.

10. Studies that embed politics in locality include Gest, *The New Minority*; Arlie Russell Hochschild, *Strangers in Their Own Land: Anger and Mourning on the American Right* (New York: New Press, 2016); and Katherine J. Cramer, *The Politics of Resentment: Rural Consciousness in Wisconsin and the Rise of Scott Walker* (Chicago: University of Chicago Press, 2016). For an earlier example, see Christopher T. Husbands, *Racial Exclusionism and the City: The Urban Support of the National Front* (London: Allen and Unwin, 1983). On the unimportance of shifts associated with globalization, see Fitzgerald, *Close to Home*, pp. 9–10.
11. "Nine Charts That Help Explain Donald Trump's Win," online at www.thoughtco.com (accessed 28 February 2018).
12. If concern over the Socialists' turn toward capitalism had driven disillusioned voters toward the FN, presumably economic concerns would have motivated them. Immigration and crime were already their chief concerns, however, not unemployment, inequality, or rising prices.
13. Lebourg and Fourquet, *La nouvelle guerre d'Algérie n'aura pas lieu*, pp. 5–6.
14. Ibid., p. 72.
15. Marshall Berman, *All That Is Solid Melts Into Air: The Experience of Modernity* (New York: Simon and Schuster, 1982), p. 15.
16. Karl Marx and Friedrich Engels, "Manifesto of the Communist Party," in Robert C. Tucker (ed.), *The Marx-Engels Reader* (New York: W. W. Norton, 1978), p. 476.
17. Antonio Gramsci, *Selections from the Prison Notebooks* (New York: International, 1971), p. 276.
18. Bloch, "Nonsynchronism and the Obligation to Its Dialectics," p. 36; see also Frederic J. Schwartz, "Ernst Bloch and Wilhelm Pinder: Out of Sync," *Grey Room* 3 (Spring 2001), pp. 54–89.
19. Douglas Kellner and Harry O'Hara, "Utopia and Marxism in Ernst Bloch," *New German Critique* 9 (Autumn 1976), pp. 11–34.
20. Ibid., p. 22.
21. "Co-opt and dissolve" is shorthand for "sublation," a word meant to capture the elusive meaning of *aufheben*.
22. FN supporter, born 1930s in Bône.
23. Suzanne Berger, "Populism and the Failures of Representation," *French Politics, Culture and Society* 35/2 (2017), pp. 21–31.
24. On the far right and nostalgia for a golden age, see Fitzgerald, *Close to Home*, p. 8. On deracination, the European Union, and romantic nationalism today, see Adam Kirsch, "The Stranger in Love," *New York Review of Books* (9 February 2017), pp. 37–38.
25. Max Weber, *The Protestant Ethic and the Spirit of Capitalism* (Los Angeles, CA: Roxbury, 2002), p. 124.
26. Elected with FN support in 2014, the mayor of Béziers (Robert Ménard, a *pied noir*, former Socialist, and co-founder of Reporters Without Borders) has defended French Algeria and declared that immigration is colonizing France; see Lebourg and Fourquet, *La nouvelle guerre d'Algérie n'aura pas lieu*, pp. 74–76.
27. Comtat, *Les pied-noirs et la politique*, p. 293. On transmission across generations, see Clarisse Buono, *Pieds noirs de père en fils* (Paris: Balland, 2004).
28. IFOP/CEVIPOF, "Le vote pied-noir 50 ans après les accords d'Evian," *Elections 2012—les électorats sociologiques* 6 (January 2012); online at http://www.ifop.com/media/ (accessed 14 February 2012; no longer online).
29. Buono, *Pieds-noirs de père en fils*; Comtat, *Les pieds-noirs et la politique*, pp. 129–138; and Sung-Eun Choi, *Decolonization and the French of Algeria: Bringing the Settler Colony Home* (London: Palgrave Macmillan, 2015).
30. Branche, *La guerre d'Algérie*, pp. 7–54.
31. Bertrand, *Mémoires d'empire*, pp. 17–18.

REFERENCES

BOOKS AND ARTICLES

Ageron, Charles-Robert. *Histoire de l'Algérie contemporaine 1830–1999* (Paris: Presses Universitaires de France, 1999).
Aissaoui, Rabah. *Immigration and National Identity: North African Political Movements in Colonial and Postcolonial France* (London: Tauris, 2009).
Aldrich, Robert. *Greater France: A History of French Overseas Expansion* (Houndmills: Macmillan, 1996).
Algazy, Joseph. *L'extrême droite en France 1965 à 1984* (Paris: Harmattan, 1989).
Aron, Raymond. *Mémoires* (Paris: Julliard, 1983).
Arreckx, Maurice. *Ça suffit* (Toulon: Presses du Midi, 1998).
Art, David. "Party Organizations and the Radical Right." In *The Oxford Handbook of the Radical Right*, edited by Jens Rydgren (New York: Oxford University Press, 2018), 239–250.
Arzheimer, Kai. "Explaining Electoral Support for the Radical Right." In *The Oxford Handbook of the Radical Right*, edited by Jens Rydgren (New York: Oxford University Press, 2018), 143–165.
Association Culturelle des Français d'Afrique du Nord. *Le Cercle algérianiste* (Narbonne: Cercle Algérianiste, n.d. [circa 2003]).
Baillet, Pierre. "L'intégration des rapatriés d'Algérie en France." *Population* 30/2 (1975): 303–314.
Bancel, Nicolas, Pascal Blanchard, and Françoise Vergès. *La République coloniale: Essai sur une utopie* (Paris: Albin Michel, 2003).
Bancel, Nicolas, Florence Bernault, Pascal Blanchard, Ahmed Boubeker, Achille Mbembe, and Françoise Vergès, eds. *Ruptures postcoloniales: Les nouveaux visages de la société française* (Paris: La Découverte, 2010).
Banfield, Edward C. *The Moral Basis of a Backward Society* (Glencoe, Ill.: Free Press, 1958).
Baudouin, Jean. "Le 'Moment néo-libéral' du RPR: Essai d'interprétation." *Revue française de science politique* 40/6 (1990): 830–844.
Baussant, Michèle. *Pieds-noirs mémoires d'exils* (Paris: Stock, 2002).
Bayle, Marc. "Les droites à Toulon (1958–1994): De l'Algérie française au Front national." Ph.D. dissertation, Aix-en-Provence and Marseille, Université Aix-Marseille I, 2001.
Bell, David S. *French Politics Today* (Manchester: Manchester University Press, 2002).
Berger, Suzanne. "Populism and the Failures of Representation." *French Politics, Culture and Society* 35/2 (2017): 21–31.
Berman, Marshall. *All That Is Solid Melts Into Air: The Experience of Modernity* (New York: Simon and Schuster, 1982).
Bernard, Mathias. "L'opposition de droite après l'alternance de mai-juin 1981." *Histoire@ Politique* 28/1 (2016): 97–107.

Bertrand, Romain. *Mémoires d'empire: Controverses autour du "fait colonial"* (Bellecombe-en-Bauges: Le Croquant, 2006).

Betz, Hans-Georg. "Politics of Resentment: Right-Wing Radicalism in West Germany." *Comparative Politics* 23/1 (1990): 45–60.

Betz, Hans-Georg. "The New Politics of Resentment: Radical Right-Wing Populist Countries in Western Europe." *Comparative Politics* 25/4 (1993): 413–427.

Birenbaum, Guy. *Le Front national en politique* (Paris: Balland, 1992).

Birenbaum, Guy, and Bastien François. "Unité et diversité des dirigeants frontistes." In *Le Front national à découvert*, edited by Nonna Mayer and Pascal Perrineau (Paris: Presses de la Fondation nationale des sciences politiques, 1989), 83–106.

Blanchard, Pascal, Sandrine Lemaire, and Nicolas Bancel, eds. *Culture coloniale en France: De la Révolution française à nos jours* (Paris: Centre national de la recherche scientifique, 2008).

Blévis, Laure. "La citoyenneté française au miroir de la colonisation." *Genèses* 53/4 (2003): 25–47.

Bloch, Ernst. "Nonsynchronism and the Obligation to Its Dialectics." *New German Critique* 11 (1977 [1932]): 22–38.

Bloemraad, Irene. "Becoming a Citizen in the United States and Canada: Structured Mobilization and Immigrant Political Incorporation." *Social Forces* 85/2 (2006): 667–695.

Bornschier, Simon. "Globalization, Cleavages, and the Radical Right." In *The Oxford Handbook of the Radical Right*, edited by Jens Rydgren (New York: Oxford University Press, 2018), 212–238.

Bouchène, Abderrahmane, Jean-Pierre Peyroulou, Ouanassa Siari Tengour, and Sylvie Thénault. "Chronologie 1830–1880." In their *Histoire de l'Algérie à la période coloniale 1830–1962*. (Paris and Algiers: La Découverte and Barzakh, 2012), 45–51.

Bouclier, Thierry. *Tixier-Vignancour* (Paris: Rémi Perrin, 2003).

Bouveresse, Jacques. *Un parlement colonial? Les délégations financières algériennes 1898–1945* (Mont-Saint-Aignan: Publications des Universités de Rouen et Du Havre, 2008).

Branche, Raphaëlle. *La guerre d'Algérie: Une histoire apaisée?* (Paris: Le Seuil, 2005).

Braudel, Fernand. "A propos de L'Histoire de l'Afrique du Nord de Charles-André Julien." In his *Autour de la Méditerranée* (Paris: De Fallois, 1996 [1933]), pp. 151–164.

Brown, Rupert. "Social Identity Theory: Past Achievements, Current Problems and Future Challenges." *European Journal of Social Psychology* 30/6 (2000): 745–778.

Buono, Clarisse. *Pieds-noirs de père en fils* (Paris: Balland, 2004).

Calderon, Désiré. *La Droite française: Formation et projet* (Paris: Messidor, 1985).

Camus, Jean-Yves. "Origine et formation du Front national (1972–1981)." In *Le Front national à découvert*, edited by Nonna Mayer and Pascal Perrineau (Paris: Presses de la Fondation nationale des sciences politiques, 1989), 17–36.

Cantier, Jacques. *L'Algérie sous le régime de Vichy* (Paris: Odile Jacob, 2002).

Çelik, Zeynep. *Urban Forms and Colonial Confrontations: Algiers under French Rule* (Berkeley and Los Angeles: University of California Press, 1997).

Chabal, Emile. "Managing the Postcolony: Minority Politics in Montpellier, c.1960–c. 2010." *Contemporary European History* 23/2 (2014): 237–258.

Charlot, Monica. "L'émergence du Front national." *Revue française de science politique* 36/1 (1986): 30–45.

Chiche, Jean, and Élisabeth Dupoirier. "De Chirac à l'UMP: Mutations et reconquête." In *Le vote de tous les refus: Les élections présidentielle et législatives de 2002*, edited by Pascal Perrineau and Colette Ysmal (Paris: Presses de la Fondation nationale des sciences politiques, 2003), 161–197.

Chiroux, René. *L'extrême-droite sous la Cinquième République* (Paris: Librairie générale de droit et de jurisprudence, 1974).

Choi, Sung-Eun. *Decolonization and the French of Algeria: Bringing the Settler Colony Home* (London: Palgrave Macmillan, 2015).

Cohen, William B. "The Colonial Policy of the Popular Front." *French Historical Studies* 7/3 (1972): 368–393.

Cohen, William B. "Pied-Noir Memory, History, and the Algerian War." In *Europe's Invisible Migrants*, edited by Andrea L. Smith (Amsterdam: Amsterdam University Press, 2003), 129–145.

Cole, Joshua. "Understanding the French Riots of 2005: What Historical Context for the 'crise des banlieus'?" *Francophone Postcolonial Studies* 5/2 (2007): 69–100.

Cole, Joshua. "Constantine before the Riots of August 1934: Civil Status, Anti-Semitism, and the Politics of Assimilation in Interwar French Algeria." *Journal of North African Studies* 17/5 (2012): 839–861.

Compagnon, Antoine. *Les antimodernes: De Joseph de Maistre à Roland Barthes* (Paris: Gallimard, 2016).

Comtat, Emmanuelle. "La question du vote Pied-Noir." *Pôle Sud* 24 (2006): 75–88.

Comtat, Emmanuelle. *Les pieds-noirs et la politique: Quarante ans après le retour* (Paris: Presses de la Fondation nationale des sciences politiques, 2009).

Cooper, Frederick. "Postcolonial Peoples: A Commentary." In *Europe's Invisible Migrants*, edited by Andrea L. Smith (Amsterdam: Amsterdam University Press, 2003), 169–183.

Couto, Marie-Paule. "L'intégration socio-économique des pieds-noirs en France métropolitaine: Le lien de citoyenneté à l'épreuve." *Revue Européenne des Migrations Internationales* 29/3 (2013): 93–119.

Cramer, Katherine J. *The Politics of Resentment: Rural Consciousness in Wisconsin and the Rise of Scott Walker* (Chicago: University of Chicago Press, 2016).

Cuhadar, Esra, and Bruce Dayton. "The Social Psychology of Identity and Inter-Group Conflict: From Theory to Practice." *International Studies Perspectives* 12/3 (2011): 273–293.

Davezies, Laurent. "Fort développement et faible croissance." In *Toulon, ville discrète*, edited by Jean Viard (La Tour d'Aigues: L'Aube, 2014), 83–127.

Davies, Peter. *The National Front in France: Discourse, Ideology and Power* (London: Routledge, 1999).

de Barros Françoise. "Des 'Français musulmans d'Algérie' aux 'immigrés': L'importation de classifications coloniales dans les politiques du logement en France (1950–1970)." *Actes de la recherche en sciences sociales* 159 (2005): 26–53.

della Porta, Donatella, Massimiliano Andretta, Tiago Fernandes, Eduardo Romanos, and Markos Vogiatzoglou. *Legacies and Memories in Movements: Justice and Democracy in Southern Europe* (New York: Oxford University Press, 2018).

Delmonte, Frédéric. "Le Front national à Toulon: De la sous-société des débuts à la contre société de juin 1995." *Recherches Régionales—Alpes-Maritimes et contrées limitrophes* 148 (1999): 51–83.

Delpard, Raphaël. *L'Histoire des pieds-noirs d'Algérie 1830–1962* (Neuilly-sur-Seine: Michel Lafon, 2002).

Denis, Nicolas. "Les élections législatives de mars 1978 en métropole." *Revue française de science politique* 28/6 (1978): 977–1005.

Dermenjian, Geneviève, and Benjamin Stora. "Les juifs d'Algérie dans le regard des militaires et des juifs de France à l'époque de la conquête (1830–1855)." *Revue Historique* 284/2 (1990): 333–339.

Di Iorio, Stéphan. "D'un 'système' à l'autre: Les facteurs explicatifs du vote Front national à Toulon." Mémoire de DEA (Paris: Institut d'études politiques, 1998).

Diani, Mario. *The Cement of Civil Society: Studying Networks in Localities* (Cambridge: Cambridge University Press, 2015).
Dogan, Mattei. "Political Cleavage and Social Stratification in France and Italy." In *Party Systems and Voter Alignments: Cross-National Perspectives*, edited by Seymour M. Lipset and Stein Rokkan (New York: Free Press, 1967), 129–195.
Dowling, William C. *Jameson, Althusser, Marx: An Introduction to The Political Unconscious* (Ithaca, NY: Cornell University Press, 1984).
Drew, Allison. *We Are No Longer in France: Communists in Colonial Algeria* (Manchester: Manchester University Press, 2014).
Duclos, Jeanne. *Dictionnaire du français d'Algérie* (Paris: Bonneton, 1992).
Duprat, François. *Les mouvements d'extrême-droite en France depuis 1944* (Paris: Albatros, 1972).
Duranton-Crabol, Anne-Marie. *Le temps de l'OAS* (Brussels: Complexe, 1995).
Eatwell, Roger. "Plus ça change? The French Presidential and National Assembly Elections, April–June 1988." *West European Politics* 59/4 (1988): 462–474.
Eatwell, Roger. *Fascism: A History* (London: Vintage, 1996).
Eatwell, Roger. "Ten Theories of the Extreme Right." In *Right-Wing Extremism in the Twenty-First Century*, edited by Peter H. Merkl and Leonard Weinberg (London: Frank Cass, 2003), 47–73.
Eatwell, Roger. "Introduction." In *Western Democracies and the New Extreme Right Challenge*, edited by Roger Eatwell and Cas Mudde (London: Routledge, 2004), 1–16.
Eisenstadt, Shmuel N., and Luis Roniger. *Patrons, Clients and Friends: Interpersonal Relations and the Structure of Trust in Society* (Cambridge: Cambridge University Press, 1984).
Eldridge, Claire. *From Empire to Exile: History and Memory within the Pied-Noir and Harki Communities, 1962–2012* (Manchester: Manchester University Press, 2016).
Eldridge, Claire. "Unity Above All? Relationships and Rivalries within the Pied-Noir Community." In *Vertriebene and Pieds-Noirs in Postwar Germany and France*, edited by Manuel Borutta and Jan C. Jansen (London: Palgrave Macmillan, 2016), 133–150.
Esclangon-Morin, Valérie. *Les rapatriés d'Afrique du Nord de 1956 à nos jours* (Paris: Harmattan, 2007).
Evans, Martin, and John Phillips. *Algeria: Anger of the Dispossessed* (New Haven, CT: Yale University Press, 2007).
Fernando, Mayanthi L. *The Republic Unsettled: Muslim French and the Contradictions of Secularism* (Durham, NC: Duke University Press, 2014).
Ferraresi, Franco. *Threats to Democracy: The Radical Right in Italy after the War* (Princeton, NJ: Princeton University Press, 1996).
Fitzgerald, Jennifer. *Close to Home: Local Ties and Voting Radical Right in Europe* (Cambridge: Cambridge University Press, 2018).
Foucault, Martial, and Elisabeth Dupoirier. "Nouvelles régions, nouveaux élus?" *Revue Politique et Parlementaire* 1878 (2016): 85–101.
Fourquet, Jérôme, and Nicolas Lebourg. *La nouvelle guerre d'Algérie n'aura pas lieu* (Paris: Fondation Jean Jaurès, 2017).
Front national. *Le programme du Front national: Défendre les français* (Paris: Front national, 1984).
Front national. *Pour la France: Programme du Front National* (Paris: Albatros, 1985).
Front national. "Le Pen Président." *La Lettre de Jean-Marie Le Pen* (April 1987).
Front national. *Le Front national c'est vous* (Paris: Front national, 1990).
Fulbrook, Mary. *Dissonant Lives: Generations and Violence through German Dictatorships* (Oxford: Oxford University Press, 2011).
Gaignebet, Jean-Baptiste. "A la recherche de nouveaux rôles." In *Histoire de Toulon*, edited by Maurice Agulhon (Toulouse: Privat, 1988), 357–379.
Gest, Justin. *The New Minority: White Working Class Politics in an Age of Immigration and Inequality* (New York: Oxford University Press, 2016).

Girardet, Raoul. *L'idée coloniale en France de 1871 à 1962* (Paris: La Table Ronde, 1972).
Goguel, François. "Le référendum du 28 octobre et les élections des 18–25 novembre 1962." *Revue française de science politique* 13/2 (1963): 289–314.
Goguel, François. "Les élections cantonales des 8 et 15 mars 1964." *Revue française de science politique* 14/3 (1964): 556–562.
Goguel, François. "La signification de la consultation." *Revue française de science politique* 15/5 (1965): 911–917.
Goinard, Pierre. "Dossier: Les rapatriés d'Algérie." *L'Informateur* 1 (May 1977): 5–17.
Golder, Matt. "Far Right Parties in Europe." *Annual Review of Political Science* 19 (2016): 477–497.
Gombin, Joël. "'Nouveau' FN, vieille carte électorale? Les territoires du vote pour le Front national de 1995 à 2002." Paper presented at the Congrès de l'Association française de science politique, Paris, 2013. Online at http://halshs.archives-ouvertes.fr/docs/ (accessed 8 April 2015).
Gombin, Joël. "2015, Les trois visages du vote FN." *Le Monde Diplomatique* (December 2015): 1–6.
Gombin, Joël. "Le changement dans la continuité: Géographies électorales du Front national depuis 1992." In *Les faux-semblants du Front national: Sociologie d'un parti politique,* edited by Sylvain Crépon, Alexandre Dézé, and Nonna Mayer (Paris: Presses de la Fondation nationale des sciences politiques, 2015), 395–416.
Gonnet, Paul, "Toulon dans les premiers drames du XXe siècle (1904–1929)." In *Histoire de Toulon,* edited by Maurice Agulhon (Toulouse: Privat, 1988), 317–341.
González-Enríquez, Carmen. "The Spanish Exception: Unemployment, Inequality and Immigration, but No Right-Wing Populist Parties." Elcano Royal Institute, Working Paper 3 (2017). Online at http://www.realinstitutoelcano.org (accessed 6 June 2017).
Goodliffe, Gabriel. *The Resurgence of the Radical Right in France: From Boulangisme to the Front National* (Cambridge: Cambridge University Press, 2012).
Gosnell, Jonathan K. *The Politics of Frenchness in Colonial Algeria, 1930–1954* (Rochester, NY: University of Rochester Press, 2002).
Gougou, Florent. "Les ouvriers et le Front national: Les logiques d'un réalignement électoral." In *Les faux-semblants du Front national: Sociologie d'un parti politique,* edited by Sylvain Crépon, Alexandre Dézé, and Nonna Mayer (Paris: Presses de la Fondation nationale des sciences politique, 2015), 323–343.
Gracián, Baltasar. *The Art of Worldly Wisdom* (Boston: Shambhala, 2006).
Gramsci, Antonio. *Selections from the Prison Notebooks,* edited and translated by Quintin Hoare and Geoffrey Nowell Smith (New York: International, 1971).
Grunberg, Gérard, and Étienne Schweisguth. "La tripartition de l'espace politique." In *Le vote de tous les refus: Les élections présidentielle et législatives de 2002,* edited by Pascal Perrineau and Colette Ysmal (Paris: Presses de la Fondation nationale des sciences politiques, 2003), 341–362.
Guignard, Didier. "Les crises en trompe l'oeil de l'Algérie française des années 1890." In *Histoire de l'Algérie à la période coloniale 1830–1962,* edited by Abderrahmane Bouchène, Jean-Pierre Peyroulou, Ouanassa Siari Tengour, and Sylvie Thénault (Paris and Algiers: La Découverte and Barzakh, 2012), 218–223.
Guillon, Jean-Marie. "Éclairage: Inauguration d'un monument à l'Algérie Française à Toulon (14 juin 1980)." Online at http://fresques.ina.fr/reperes-mediterraneens (accessed 29 October 2014).
Henry, Jean-Robert. "Le centenaire de l'Algérie, triomphe éphémère de la pensée algérianiste." In *Histoire de l'Algérie à la période coloniale 1830–1962,* edited by Abderrahmane Bouchène, Jean-Pierre Peyroulou, Ouanassa Siari Tengour, and Sylvie Thénault (Paris and Algiers: La Découverte and Barzakh, 2012), 369–375.

Hochschild, Arlie Russell. *Strangers in Their Own Land: Anger and Mourning on the American Right* (New York: New Press, 2016).

Hooghe, Liesbet, and Gary Marks. "Cleavage Theory Meets Europe's Crises: Lipset, Rokkan, and the Transnational Cleavage." *Journal of European Public Policy* 25/1 (2018): 109–135.

Hunt, Jennifer. "The Impact of the 1962 Repatriates from Algeria on the French Labor Market." *Industrial and Labor Relations Review* 45/3 (1992): 556–572.

Husbands, Christopher T. *Racial Exclusionism and the City: The Urban Support of the National Front* (London: Allen and Unwin, 1983).

Ignazi, Piero. "Un nouvel acteur politique." In *Le Front national à découvert*, edited by Nonna Mayer and Pascal Perrineau (Paris: Presses de la Fondation nationale des sciences politiques, 1989), 63–80.

Igounet, Valérie. *Le Front national de 1972 à nos jours: Le parti, les hommes, les idées* (Paris: Le Seuil, 2014).

Ireland, Patrick R. "Race, Immigration and the Politics of Hate." In *The Mitterrand Era: Policy Alternatives and Political Mobilization in France*, edited by Anthony Daley (London: Palgrave Macmillan, 1996), 258–278.

Ivaldi, Gilles, and Christine Pina. "PACA, une victoire à la Pyrrhus pour la droite?" *Revue Politique et Parlementaire* 1078 (2016): 139–150.

Jay, Martin. "The Jews and the Frankfurt School: Critical Theory's Analysis of Anti-Semitism." *New German Critique* 19/1 (1980): 137–149.

Jordi, Jean-Jacques. *De l'exode à l'exil: Rapatriés et Pieds-Noirs en France* (Paris: Harmattan, 1993).

Jordi, Jean-Jacques. "The Creation of the Pieds-Noirs: Arrival and Settlement in Marseilles, 1962." In *Europe's Invisible Migrants*, edited by Andrea L. Smith (Amsterdam: Amsterdam University Press, 2003), 61–74.

Jouve, Bernard. "From Government to Urban Governance in Western Europe: A Critical Analysis." *Public Administration and Development* 25/4 (2005): 285–294.

Judt, Tony. *Socialism in Provence 1871–1914* (Cambridge: Cambridge University Press, 1979).

Kateb, Kamel. *Européens, "indigènes" et juifs en Algérie 1830–1962* (Paris: Institut national d'études démographiques, 2001).

Katz, Ethan B. *The Burdens of Brotherhood: Jews and Muslims from North Africa to France* (Cambridge, MA: Harvard University Press, 2015).

Keeler, John T.S. "Situating France on the Pluralism-Corporatism Continuum: A Critique and Alternative to the Wilson Perspective." *Comparative Politics* 17/2 (January 1985): 229–249.

Kellner, Douglas, and Harry O'Hara. "Utopia and Marxism in Ernst Bloch." *New German Critique* 9 (Autumn 1976): 11–34.

Kibee, Jo. "Aux armes citoyens! Les bibliothèques publiques françaises face à l'extrême droite." *Bulletin des bibliothèques de France* 49/6 (2004): 10–19.

Kirsch, Adam. "The Stranger in Love." *New York Review of Books* (9 February 2017): 37–38.

Kitschelt, Herbert, with Anthony J. McGann. *The Radical Right in Western Europe: A Comparative Analysis* (Ann Arbor: University of Michigan Press, 1995).

Kreuzer, Marcus, and Ina Stephan. "France: Enduring Notables, Weak Parties, and Powerful Technocrats." In *The Political Class in Advanced Democracies*, edited by Jens Borchert and Jürgen Zeiss (Oxford: Oxford University Press, 2002), 124–141.

Lange, Sarah L. de. "A New Winning Formula? The Programmatic Appeal of the Radical Right." *Party Politics* 13/4 (2007): 411–435.

Le Gall, Gérard. "Une élection sans enjeu, avec conséquences." *Revue Politique et Parlementaire* 910 (1984): 9–47.

Le Gendre, Bertrand. *Guerre d'Algérie: Le choc des mémoires* (Paris: Le Monde, 2013).

Le Livre Tricolore du 13 mai au 4 juin 1958 (Algiers: Éditions Œdipe, 1959).

Le Monde. *La Cinquième République 1958–1995* (Paris: Le Monde, 1995).

Le Pen, Jean-Marie. *L'espoir* (Paris: Albatros, 1989).
Lebourg, Nicolas, and Jérôme Fourquet. *La nouvelle guerre d'Algérie n'aura pas lieu* (Paris: Fondation Jean-Jaurès, 2017).
Lees, Christiane. "L'établissement des *Pieds-Noirs* dans le Midi méditerranéen français." In *Marseille et le choc des décolonisations: Les rapatriements 1954–1964*, edited by Jean-Jacques Jordi and Emile Temime (Aix-en-Provence: Edisud, 1996), 105–116.
Legenne, Dominique. *Var, terre d'histoire* (Arles: Actes Sud, 1999).
Levy, Deborah R. "Women of the French National Front." *Parliamentary Affairs* 42/1 (1989): 102–111.
Linz, Juan J. "Crisis, Breakdown and Reequilibration." In *The Breakdown of Democratic Regimes*, Part 1, edited by Juan J. Linz and Alfred Stepan (Baltimore, MD: Johns Hopkins University Press, 1978).
Linz, Juan J. "Political Space and Fascism as a Late-Comer: Conditions Conducive to the Success or Failure of Fascism as a Mass Movement in Inter-War Europe." In *Who Were the Fascists: Social Roots of European Fascism*, edited by Stein Ugelvik Larsen, Bernt Hagtvet, and Jan Petter Myklebust (Bergen: Universitetsforlaget, 1980), 153–189.
Lipset, Seymour Martin. *Political Man: The Social Bases of Politics*, expanded edition (Baltimore, MD: Johns Hopkins University Press, 1981).
Lipset, Seymour Martin, and Stein Rokkan. "Cleavage Structures, Party Systems, and Voter Alignments: An Introduction." In *Party Systems and Voter Alignments: Cross-National Perspectives*, edited by Seymour Martin Lipset and Stein Rokkan (New York: Free Press, 1967), 1–64.
Livre d'or Toulon-Var (Toulon: Clayton Publicité, 1960).
Lorcin, Patricia M. E. *Imperial Identities: Stereotyping, Prejudice and Race in Colonial Algeria* (London: I.B. Tauris, 1995).
Löwy, Michael. "Le concept d'affinité élective chez Max Weber." *Archives de sciences sociales des religions* 127 (2004): 93–103.
MacMaster, Neil. *Burning the Veil: The Algerian War and the "Emancipation" of Algerian Women, 1954–62* (Manchester: Manchester University Press, 2012).
MacMaster, Neil. "L'enjeu des femmes dans la guerre." In *Histoire de l'Algérie à la période coloniale 1830–1962*, edited by Abderrahmane Bouchène, Jean-Pierre Peyroulou, Ouanassa Siari Tengour, Sylvie Thénault (Paris: Editions La Découverte and Algiers: Editions Barzakh, 2012), 539–546.
Mandel, Maud S. *Muslims and Jews in France: History of a Conflict* (Princeton, NJ: Princeton University Press, 2014).
Marcus, Jonathan. *The National Front and French Politics: The Resistible Rise of Jean-Marie Le Pen* (New York: New York University Press, 1995).
Martin, Jean-Clément. "Review of Vendée: Du Génocide au mémoricide. Mécanique d'un crime légal, by Reynald Sécher." *Annales de la Révolution française* 368 (2012): 194–196.
Martin, Virginie. *Toulon la noire: Le Front national au pouvoir* (Paris: Denoël, 1996).
Martin, Virginie, Gilles Ivaldi, and Grégory Lespinasse. "Le Front national entre clientélisme et recherche d'un enracinement social." *Critique internationale* 3/4 (1999): 169–182.
Marx, Karl, and Friedrich Engels. "Manifesto of the Communist Party." In *The Marx-Engels Reader*, 2nd ed., edited by Robert C. Tucker (New York: W. W. Norton, 1978).
Mayer, Nonna. "Du vote lepéniste au vote frontiste." *Revue française de science politique* 47/3–4 (1997): 438–453.
Mayer, Nonna. *Ces français qui votent FN* (Paris: Flammarion, 1999).
Mayer, Nonna. "Comment Nicolas Sarkozy a rétréci l'électorat Le Pen." *Revue française de science politique* 57/3 (2007): 429–445.
Mayer, Nonna. "From Jean-Marie to Marine Le Pen: Electoral Change on the Far Right." *Parliamentary Affairs* 66/1 (2013): 160–178.

Mayer, Nonna. "Le plafond de verre électoral: Entamé, mais pas brisé." In *Les faux-semblants du Front national: Sociologie d'un parti politique*, edited by Sylvain Crépon, Alexandre Dézé, and Nonna Mayer (Paris: Presses de la Fondation nationale des sciences politique, 2015), 299–321.

McDougall, James. "The Secular State's Islamic Empire: Muslim Spaces and Subjects of Jurisdiction in Paris and Algiers, 1905–1957." *Comparative Studies in Society and History* 52/3 (2010): 553–580.

Mendosa, Francette. "Le racisme a commencé à Marseille avec l'arrivée des Pieds-Noirs en 1962." *Pieds Noirs d'Hier et d'Aujourd'hui* 43 (February 1999): 9.

Mendras, Henri, with Alistair Cole. *Social Change in Modern France: Towards a Cultural Anthropology of the Fifth Republic* (Cambridge: Cambridge University Press, 1991).

Merton, Robert. "Manifest and Latent Functions." In *Social Theory and Social Structure: Toward the Codification of Theory and Research* (Glencoe, IL: Free Press, 1949), 21–81.

Meynier, Gilbert. "Les Algériens et la guerre de 1914–1918." In *Histoire de l'Algérie à la période coloniale 1830–1962*, edited by Abderrahmane Bouchène, Jean-Pierre Peyroulou, Ouanassa Siari Tengour, and Sylvie Thénault (Paris and Algiers: La Découverte and Barzakh, 2012), 229–234.

Milza, Pierre. *Fascisme français: Passé et présent* (Paris: Flammarion, 1987).

Monzat, René. *Enquêtes sur la droite extrême* (Paris: Le Monde-Editions, 1992).

Morales, Laura, and Katia Pilati. "The Role of Social Capital in Migrants' Engagement in Local Politics in European Cities." In *Social Capital, Political Participation and Migration in Europe: Making Multicultural Democracy Work*, edited by Laura Morales and Marco Giugni (Houndmills, UK: Palgrave Macmillan, 2011), 87–114.

Mudde, Cas. *The Relationship between Immigration and Nativism in Europe and North America* (Washington, DC: Migration Policy Institute, 2012).

Mudde, Cas. "The Far Right and the European Elections." *Current History* 113 (2014): 98–103.

Müller, Jan-Werner. *What Is Populism?* (Philadelphia: University of Pennsylvania Press, 2016).

Müller, Jan-Werner. "Protecting Popular Self-Government from the People? New Normative Perspectives on Militant Democracy." *Annual Review of Political Science* 19 (2016): 249–265.

Nadeau, Richard, Martial Foucault, Bruno Jérôme, and Véronique Jérôme-Speziari. *Villes de gauche, villes de droite* (Paris: Presses de la Fondation nationale des sciences politiques, 2018).

Nakayama, Yohei. "Associations, Party Models and Party System: Changing Patterns of Party Networks in Twentieth Century France." *French Politics* 7/2 (2009): 96–122.

Nouschi, André. *Algérie amère 1914–1994* (Paris: Éditions de la Maison des sciences de l'homme, 1995).

Perrineau, Pascal. "Les étapes d'une implantation électorale (1972–1988)." In *Le Front national à découvert*, edited by Nonna Mayer and Pascal Perrineau (Paris: Presses de la Fondation nationale des sciences politiques, 1989), 37–62.

Perrineau, Pascal. "La surprise lepéniste et sa suite legislative." In *Le vote de tous les refus: Les élections présidentielle et législatives de 2002*, edited by Pascal Perrineau and Colette Ysmal (Paris: Presses de la Fondation nationale des sciences politiques, 2003), 199–222.

Pervillé, Guy. *De l'Empire français à la décolonisation* (Paris: Hachette, 1991).

Piat, Yann. *Seule, tout en haut à droite* (Paris: Fixot, 1991).

Pinson, Gilles. "Le maire et ses partenaires: Du schéma centre-périphérie à la gouvernance multi-niveaux." *Pouvoirs* 148 (2014): 95–111.

Polanyi, Karl. *The Great Transformation: The Political and Economic Origins of Our Time* (Boston: Beacon, 1957 [1944]).

Porch, Douglas. "Bugeaud, Galliéni, Lyautey: The Development of French Colonial Warfare." In *Makers of Modern Strategy from Machiavelli to the Nuclear Age*, edited by Peter Paret (Princeton, NJ: Princeton University Press, 1986), 376–407.

Putnam, Robert D. *Making Democracy Work: Civic Traditions in Modern Italy* (Princeton, NJ: Princeton University Press, 1993).

Prochaska, David. "History as Literature, Literature as History: Cayagous of Algiers." *American Historical Review* 101/3 (1996): 670–711.

Prochaska, David. *Making Algeria French: Colonialism in Bône, 1870–1920* (Cambridge: Cambridge University Press, 2004).

Recham, Belkacem. "La participation des Maghrébiens à la Seconde Guerre mondiale." In *Histoire de l'Algérie à la période coloniale 1830–1962*, edited by Abderrahmane Bouchène, Jean-Pierre Peyroulou, Ouanassa Siari Tengour, and Sylvie Thénault (Paris and Algiers: La Découverte and Barzakh, 2012), 457–462.

Rémond, René. *Les Droites en France*, revised edition (Paris: Aubier, 1982).

Reuters (France). "2012-Marine Le Pen lance une charge contre Goldman Sachs." (7 April 2012). Online at http://fr.reuters.com/ (accessed 7 November 2017).

Rey-Goldzeiguer, Annie. *Aux origines de la guerre d'Algérie 1940–1945: De Mers El-Kébir aux massacres du Nord-Constantinois* (Paris: La Découverte, 2001).

Robert-Guiard, Claudine. *Des Européennes en situation coloniale: Algérie 1830–1939* (Aix-en-Provence: Presses de l'Université de Provence, 2009).

Roncayolo, Marcel. "L'élection de Gaston Defferre à Marseille." *Revue française de science politique* 15/5 (1965): 930–946.

Roy, Jean-Philippe. *Le Front national en région Centre 1984–1992* (Paris: Harmattan, 1993).

Rydgren, Jens. "The Sociology of the Radical Right." *Annual Review of Sociology* 33 (2007): 241–262.

Saada, Emmanuelle. "The Empire of Law: Dignity, Prestige, and Domination in the 'Colonial Situation.'" *French Politics, Culture and Society* 20/2 (2002): 98–120.

Saada, Emmanuelle. "Race and Sociological Reason in the Republic: Inquiries on the *Métis* in the French Empire (1908–37)." *International Sociology* 17/3 (2002): 361–391.

Saada, Emmanuelle. *Empire's Children: Race, Filiation, and Citizenship in the French Colonies* (Chicago: University of Chicago Press, 2012).

Saëz, Claude. "Mon billet d'humeur." *Pieds Noirs d'Hier et d'Aujourd'hui* 205 (May 2012): 41.

Samson, Michel. *Le Front national aux affaires: Deux ans d'enquête sur la vie municipale à Toulon* (Paris: Calmann-Lévy, 1997).

Savarese, Éric. *L'invention des Pieds-Noirs* (Paris: Séguier, 2002).

Savarese, Éric. "Un regard compréhensif sur le 'traumatisme historique': À propos du vote Front national chez les pieds-noirs." *Pôle Sud* 34/1 (2011): 91–104.

Schain, Martin A. "The National Front in France and the Construction of Political Legitimacy." *West European Politics* 10/2 (1987): 229–252.

Schain, Martin A. "Immigration and Changes in the French Party System." *European Journal of Political Research* 16/6 (1988): 597–621.

Schreier, Joshua S. "Napoléon's Long Shadow: Morality, Civilization, and Jews in France and Algeria, 1808–1870." *French Historical Studies* 30/1 (2007): 77–103.

Schwartz, Frederic J. "Ernst Bloch and Wilhelm Pinder: Out of Sync." *Grey Room* 3 (Spring 2001): 54–89.

Scioldo-Zürcher, Yann. *Devenir métropolitain. Politique d'intégration et parcours de rapatriés d'Algérie en métropole 1954–2005* (Paris: École des Hautes Études en Sciences Sociales, 2010).

Sessions, Jennifer E. *By Sword and Plow: France and the Conquest of Algeria* (Ithaca, NY: Cornell University Press, 2011).

Shepard, Todd. *The Invention of Decolonization: The Algerian War and the Remaking of France* (Ithaca, NY: Cornell University Press, 2006).

Shepard, Todd. "Pieds-Noirs, Bêtes Noires: Anti-'European of Algeria' Racism and the Close of the French Empire." In *Algeria and France, 1800–2000: Identity, Memory, Nostalgia*, edited by Patricia M. E. Lorcin (Syracuse, NY: Syracuse University Press, 2006), 150–163.

Shields, James G. "The Far Right Vote in France: From Consolidation to Collapse?" *French Politics, Culture and Society* 29/3 (2010): 78–100.

Silverman, Sydel F. "Agricultural Organization, Social Structure, and Values in Italy: Amoral Familism Reconsidered." *American Anthropologist* 70/1 (1968): 1–20.

Simmons, Harvey G. *The French National Front: The Extremist Challenge to Democracy* (Boulder, CO: Westview, 1996)

Sivan, Emanuel. "Colonialism and Popular Culture in Algeria." *Journal of Contemporary History* 14/1 (1979): 21–53.

Skocpol, Theda. *States and Social Revolutions: A Comparative Analysis of France, Russia, and China* (Cambridge: Cambridge University Press, 1979).

Slyomovics, Susan. "Algerian Women's *Būqālah* Poetry: Oral Literature, Cultural Politics, and Anti-Colonial Resistance." *Journal of Arabic Literature* 45 (2014): 145–168.

Smith, Andrea L. *Colonial Memory and Postcolonial Europe: Maltese Settlers in Algeria and France* (Bloomington and Indianapolis: Indiana University Press, 2006).

Souillac, Romain. *Le mouvement Poujade: De la défense professionnelle au populisme nationaliste 1953–1962* (Paris: Presses de Sciences Po, 2007).

Souvannavong, Juan, and David Sempere. "Les pieds-noirs à Alicante." *Revue Européenne des Migrations Internationales* 17/3 (2001): 173–198.

Stein, Sarah Abrevaya. "Dividing South from North: French Colonialism, Jews, and the Algerian Sahara." *The Journal of North African Studies* 17/5 (2012): 773–792.

Stora, Benjamin. *Le transfert d'une mémoire: De l'"Algérie française" au racisme anti-arabe* (Paris: La Découverte, 1999).

Stora, Benjamin. *Histoire de l'Algérie coloniale 1830–1954* (Paris: La Découverte, 2004).

Suleiman, Ezra N. *Elites in French Society: The Politics of Survival* (Princeton, NJ: Princeton University Press, 1978).

Swidler, Ann. "Culture in Action: Symbols and Strategies." *American Sociological Review* 51/2 (1986): 273–286.

Taguieff, Pierre-André. "La métaphysique de Jean-Marie Le Pen." In *Le Front national à découvert*, edited by Nonna Mayer and Pascal Perrineau (Paris: Presses de la Fondation nationale des sciences politiques, 1989), 173–194.

Taguieff, Pierre-André. "Annexe: les condamnations pour racisme et antisémitisme de Jean-Marie Le Pen." In his *Face au racisme*, vol.1, *Les moyens d'agir* (Paris: La Découverte, 1991), 235–241.

Tarrow, Sidney. *Between Center and Periphery: Grassroots Politicians in Italy and France* (New Haven, CT: Yale University Press, 1977).

Tarrow, Sidney. "Comparison, Triangulation, and Embedding Research in History: A Methodological Self-Analysis." *Bulletin de Méthodologie Sociologique* 141 (2019): 7–29.

Thompson, Victoria. "'I Went Pale with Pleasure': The Body, Sexuality, and National Identity among French Travelers to Algiers in the Nineteenth Century." In *Algeria and France, 1800–2000: Identity, Memory, Nostalgia*, edited by Patricia M. E. Lorcin (Syracuse, NY: Syracuse University Press, 2006), 18–32.

Thomson, David. *Democracy in France since 1870* (Oxford: Oxford University Press, 1969).

Tissot, Sylvie. "The Role of Race and Class in Urban Marginality." *City* 11/3 (2007): 364–369.

Tocqueville, Alexis de. *Democracy in America* (New York: Harper and Row, 1969).

Tocqueville, Alexis de. "Rapport fait par M. de Tocqueville sur le projet de loi relatif aux crédits extraordinaires demandés pour l'Algérie," in his *Œuvres*, vol. 1 (Paris: Gallimard, 1991), 797–873.
Todd, David. "Review of By Sword and Plow: France and the Conquest of Algeria, by Jennifer E. Sessions." *Revue d'Histoire moderne et contemporaine* 60/3 (2012): 201–203.
Verdès-Leroux, Jeannine. *Les français d'Algérie de 1830 à aujourd'hui: Une page d'histoire déchirée* (Paris: Fayard, 2001).
Verdier, Laurent. "Qui sont les maires qui gèrent le mieux leur ville?" *Challenges* (20 March 2014). Online at http://www.challenges.fr/ (accessed 8 May 2015).
Vermeren, Hugo. *Les Italiens à Bône (1865–1940): Migrations méditerranéennes et colonisation de peuplement en Algérie* (Rome: École française de Rome, 2017).
Veugelers, John. "Social Cleavage and the Revival of Far Right Parties: The Case of France's National Front." *Acta Sociologica* 40/1 (1997): 31–49.
Veugelers, John. "Right-Wing Extremism in Contemporary France: A 'Silent Counterrevolution'?" *Sociological Quarterly* 41/1 (2000): 19–40.
Veugelers, John. "Ex-Colonials, Voluntary Associations, and Electoral Support for the Contemporary Far Right." *Comparative European Politics* 3/4 (2005): 408–431.
Veugelers, John, and Michèle Lamont. "France: Alternative Locations for Public Debate." In *Between States and Markets: The Voluntary Sector in Comparative Perspective*, edited by Robert Wuthnow (Princeton, NJ: Princeton University Press, 1991), 125–151.
Veugelers, John, Gabriel Menard, and Pierre Permingeat. "Colonial Past, Voluntary Association and Far-Right Voting in France." *Ethnic and Racial Studies* 38/5 (2015): 775–791.
Villarreal, Andrés. "Political Competition and Violence in Mexico: Hierarchical Social Control in Local Patronage Structures." *American Sociological Review* 67/4 (2002): 477–498.
Vinen, Richard. *A History in Fragments: Europe in the Twentieth Century* (Cambridge, MA: Da Capo, 2000).
Vovelle, Michel. "Un champ de bataille de la Révolution (1789–1815)." In *Histoire de Toulon*, edited by Maurice Agulhon (Toulouse: Privat, 1988), 179–190.
Weber, Max. "Politics as a Vocation." In *From Max Weber: Essays in Sociology*, edited by H. H. Gerth and C. Wright Mills (New York: Oxford University Press, 1946), 77–128.
Weber, Max. *The Protestant Ethic and the Spirit of Capitalism* (Los Angeles, CA: Roxbury, 2002).
White, Owen. "Roll Out the Barrel: French and Algerian Ports and the Birth of the Wine Tanker." *French Politics, Culture and Society* 35/2 (2017): 111–132.
Williams, Raymond. *Marxism and Literature* (Oxford: Oxford University Press, 1977).
Winock, Michel. *Nationalisme, antisémitisme et fascisme en France* (Paris: Le Seuil, 1990).
Wolf, Eric R. *Peasant Wars of the Twentieth Century* (New York: Harper, 1969).
Wuthnow, Robert. *Communities of Discourse: Ideology and Social Structure in the Reformation, the Enlightenment, and European Socialism* (Cambridge, MA: Harvard University Press, 1989).
Ysmal, Colette. "Le RPR et l'UDF face au Front national: Concurrence et connivences." *Revue Politique et Parlementaire* 913 (1984): 6–20.
Ysmal, Colette. *Le comportement électoral des Français* (Paris: La Découverte, 1990).
Zack, Lizabeth. "Who Fought the Algerian War? Political Identity and Conflict in French-Ruled Algeria." *International Journal of Politics, Culture, and Society* 16/1 (2002): 55–97.

REPORTS AND POLLS

Assemblée nationale. "Répartition de la réserve parlementaire en 2015." Online at assemblee-nationale.fr/reserve_parlementaire/plf/2015 (accessed 6 January 2018).
Association des Maires de Grandes Villes de Frances. "Rôle économique des grandes villes et grandes agglomérations" (Paris: Association des Maires de Grandes Villes de Frances, 2012). Online at http://franceurbaine.org/ (accessed 18 July 2017).

Centre Hospitalier Intercommunal Toulon-La Seyne sur Mer. "Nouvel Hôpital Sainte Musse, Toulon." 2011. Online at http://www.ch-toulon.fr/ (accessed 9 April 2015).
Chambre régionale des comptes de Provence-Alpes-Cote d'Azur. "Rapport d'observations définitives sur la gestion de la commune de Toulon (Département du Var), Années 1995 à 2005" (Marseille: Chambre régionale des comptes de Provence-Alpes-Cote d'Azur, 2007).
Chambre régionale des comptes de Provence-Alpes-Côte d'Azur. "Rapport d'observations définitives sur la gestion de la commune de Toulon, exercices 2009 à 2013" (Marseille: Chambre régionale des comptes de Provence-Alpes-Cote d'Azur, 2014).
Communauté d'agglomération Toulon Provence Méditerranée. "Le Théâtre Liberté: Origines" (Toulon: 2011). Online at http://m.tpm-agglo.fr (accessed 8 April 2015).
Documentation française. "Taux de chômage, 1967–2005." Online at www.ladocumentationfrancaise.fr (accessed 2 March 2018).
Gouvernement-Général de l'Algérie, *L'Algérie du demi-siècle vue par les autorités locales* (Algiers: January 1954).
IFOP. "Le vote pied-noir: mythe ou réalité?" *Focus* 107 (March 2014). Online at http://www.ifop.com/media/ (accessed 20 May 2015).
IFOP/CEVIPOF. "Le vote pied-noir 50 ans après les accords d'Evian." *Elections 2012—les électorats sociologiques* 6 (January 2012). Online at http://www.ifop.com/media/ (accessed 14 February 2012).
INSEE. "Commune de Toulon/Département du Var, Chiffres clés." Online at www.insee.fr/ (accessed 20 May 2015).
INSEE. "Monthly Consumer Confidence Survey." Online at www.insee.fr (accessed 2 March 2018).
OECD. *International Migration Outlook 2016* (Paris: OECD, 2016).
Région Provence-Alpes-Côte d'Azur. "Projets soutenus par des financements européens en région Provence-Alpes-Côte d'Azur" (Marseille: Région Provence-Alpes-Côte d'Azur. 2017). Online at www.europarl.europa.eu/france/ (accessed 14 July 2017).
Région Provence-Alpes-Côte d'Azur, Direction Régionale de l'Environnement, de l'Aménagement et du Logement. "Tunnel de Toulon" (Marseille: Région Provence-Alpes-Côte d'Azur, 2013). Online at www.paca.developpement-durable.gouv.fr/ (accessed 8 April 2015).
Ville d'Alger. "Bulletin municipal official de la ville d'Alger no. 4" (February 1949).
Ville de Toulon. "Aide aux associations." Online at http://toulon.fr/sites/new.toulon.fr/files/aidesauxassociations2013.pdf (accessed 8 April 2015).

PERIODICALS

Actualités Varoises
Alger Républicain
Challenges
Il Secolo d'Italia
L'Algérianiste
L'Aurore
L'Écho
L'Écho de l'Oranie
L'Édile Algérien
L'Express
La Lettre de Jean-Marie Le Pen
Le Figaro
Le Méridional
Le Monde
Le Monde Diplomatique
Le Nouvel Observateur
Le Petit Varois
Le Point
Les Échos
Libération
National-Hebdo
New York Times
Pieds Noirs d'Hier et d'Aujourd'hui
République-Le Provençal
Time
Var-Matin
Var Matin-République

OFFICIAL PUBLICATIONS
Journal Officiel de la République Française
Recueil des actes administratifs de la Préfecture du Var

OTHER MEDIA
Front national. "Radio Le Pen—Emission du 24 décembre 1989" [recorded telephone message].
Immigration: Le Pen s'explique (Paris: Front national, 1989) [audio tape].

INDEX

For the benefit of digital users, indexed terms that span two pages (e.g., 52–53) may, on occasion, appear on only one of those pages.

Note: Page numbers followed by *t* refer to tables.

Algeria
De Gaulle visits, 39–40, 80
French conquest, 17, 49, 106–7, 194n10
national anthem, 99–100
Ottoman rule, 19–20, 22
presidents, 67–68, 99–100, 208n57
Algeria, colonial period
agriculture, 17–18, 21–22, 30
civil administration, 16, 19–22, 24–25, 26–27, 30
civilizing mission, 27, 184
dependence on France, 30
education, 25, 31, 32, 197n73, 199n56
electoral fraud, 42–43, 201n96
ethnic stratification, 16, 18, 19, 27
French law, 26–27
insurgencies, 19–20
in interwar period, 23–27, 42–43
Jewish minority, 22–23, 25, 27, 30–31, 32, 196n48, 196n52
labor unions, 42–43
landowners, 195–96n46
land seizures, 19–20
military, 30, 184
nationalization laws, 18, 22–23, 26, 196n52
poverty, 24
reformers, 24, 27, 33–34, 199n56
residential segregation, 19, 20, 25, 197n72, 198n23
Sétif massacres, 31
subject population decline, 19
Tocqueville on, 17
trade with France, 21–22, 30
World War II effects, 28, 29, 30–31
See also Arabes
Algeria, European settlers
anti-Semitism, 42–43
differences among, 16, 18, 23
elites, 21–22, 31–32, 195–96n45
intermarriage, 19, 23, 195n26
land provided to, 19–20
mass exit, 40, 41, 42
migration encouraged, 17–18
non-French, 18–19, 23, 42–43, 196n53, 197n81
political affiliations, 42–43, 201n97, 201n103
political refugees, 201n97
population growth, 17–18, 194n12
relations with Algerians, 15, 19–22, 25–26, 27, 30–31, 32–33, 36–37
social identities, 17, 19, 27
See also pieds noirs; repatriates
Algerian independence
aftermath, 42
Communist supporters, 198n2
De Gaulle's view, 38–39, 52–53
Évian Accords, 40, 52–54, 64, 200n83
opposition to, 34, 36–38, 39–41, 50–51, 52–53, 64, 192n22
referendum, 39–40, 52–54, 203n26
support in France, 47–48, 53, 203n27
transition government, 41

Algerian War
  beginning, 33–34
  divisions among French, 16, 34, 35–36, 39–41, 53
  effects on French settlers, 16, 29, 34–35, 43
  end of, 39–40
  French casualties, 53, 85
  French forces, 35, 39–40
  international reactions, 35
  public marches, 36–38, 39
  rebels, 29, 36, 38
  in school curricula, 184–85
  terrorist attacks, 34–35, 41, 53–54
  veterans, 103–4, 107–8
Algiers
  anti-Semitism, 23, 196n54
  battle of, 39–40, 150, 181
  European population, 17–18
  Rue d'Isly massacre (26 March 1962), 40, 68–69, 107–8, 125, 175
  terrorist attacks, 34–35
  in World War II, 30
ANFANOMA. See Association Nationale des Français d'Afrique du Nord, d'Outre-Mer et de leurs Amis
anti-communism, 80, 92, 145
anti-Gaullism
  of Arreckx, 54, 58, 59, 78
  in military, 52
  OAS attacks, 50–51
  of *pieds noirs*, 47–48, 65, 80
  in Toulon, 54, 63
  in Var, 58–59
  See also Centre national des indépendants et paysans; Gaullism; May 1968 events
anti-immigration views
  of Arreckx, 108, 109
  of European far right, 3, 15–16
  of French public, 98–99
  of Le Chevallier, 129
  of Le Pen, 96, 134–35, 215n45
  of National Front electorate, 95–96, 176–77, 180, 183, 228n115
  National Front platform, 16, 94–95, 96, 99, 100, 134–35
  of *pieds noirs*, 104–5, 144–45
  in Toulon, 108–9, 110, 111, 129
anti-Semitism
  in colonial Algeria, 23, 25, 27, 42–43, 196n54

Dreyfus Affair, 23, 91
  of European settlers in Algeria, 42–43
  in France, 141, 144, 227n63
  of Jean-Marie Le Pen, 43, 106, 147
  of National Front voters, 228n115
Arabes
  anti-Semitism, 25
  in cities, 25
  cultural assimilation, 22
  education, 26–27, 32, 197n73
  French citizenship, 22, 26
  in French military, 21–22, 23–24
  French views of, 34, 98–99, 216n58
  as lower caste, 16, 19, 24
  migrant workers in France, 23–24, 196n62
  nationalists, 31, 33–34, 36, 38
  relations with Europeans, 15, 19–22, 25–26, 27, 30–31, 32–33, 36–37
  stereotypes, 21
  voting rights and political power, 24, 26–27, 33–34, 197n81
  See also Front de libération nationale; Muslims
Aron, Raymond, 90–91
Arreckx, Maurice
  on Algerian War, 53–54
  anti-Gaullism, 54, 58, 59, 78
  anti-immigration views, 108, 109
  corruption scandal, 113–14, 118–19, 121, 220n72
  death, 114
  Falco and, 165
  Giscard and, 78, 81–82, 84, 85, 106
  life of, 52
  municipal elections (1965), 64–65
  parliamentary elections, 85, 86–87
  political career, 73, 82, 106, 109–11, 113–14, 165
  political power in Var, 111, 112
Arreckx, Maurice, relations with *pieds noirs*
  Commission extra-municipale des rapatriés, 66, 73
  disagreements, 87
  municipal election campaigns, 64, 65
  mutual support, 61–63, 67, 73, 77, 85, 86
  parliamentary election campaigns, 69–70, 71–72, 84–85, 86
  as patron and clients, 59, 65, 77, 87, 106–8, 157–58
  welcome and assistance, 57–58, 59
Arrighi, Pascal, 69–70, 203n23

[252] Index

association funding
　corruption in, 155, 156
　by National Front mayors, 122–23
　parliamentary reserve, 154–55
　patronage and, 123
　state, 154–55
　in Toulon, 123–24, 155–58, 222n53, 230n36
Association Nationale des Français d'Afrique du Nord, d'Outre-Mer et de leurs Amis (ANFANOMA), 206n2, 208n53
Association Nationale des Français d'Afrique du Nord et d'Outre-Mer, 51, 203n16
Association Nationale des Français d'Afrique du Nord et de leurs Amis (ANFANOMA), 51, 203n17
associations
　cross-class, 183
　democracy and, 153–54, 161–62
　in France, 160–61
　in southern Italy, 160–62
　patriotic, 159–60, 161
　patronage and, 161
　Tocqueville on, 153–54
　in Toulon, 154–55, 157–58, 159–61
　in United States, 153–54, 160
　See also labor unions; pieds noirs organizations
Aussaresses, Paul, 150

Boualem, Saïd, 71–72, 85
Balladur, Edmond, 119–20, 221n23
Bandung Conference, 34
Banfield, Edward C., 160
Barre, Raymond, 82–83, 110, 218n25
Ben Bella, Ahmed, 67–68, 208n57
Berbers, 19, 20–21, 26, 195n29, 195n37, 201n91
Bidault, Georges, 68, 79, 203n23, 203n26
Bloch, Ernst, 11, 182, 183
Boumedienne, Houari, 99–100, 208n57
Boutigny, Louis, 68, 70, 73, 84–85, 86, 106, 125
Braudel, Fernand, 27
Britain
　League of Empire Loyalists, 201–2n110
　National Front, 3, 201–2n110

Camus, Albert, L'Étranger, 197n75
capitalism, 179–80, 181–82, 184

Carpentras, 83–84, 144
Catholic Church, 20, 112, 141, 181
Cayagous, 21
Céline (Louis-Ferdinand Destouches), 51
Centre national des indépendants et paysans (CNIP), 16, 52, 58–59, 71, 91, 217n3
Cercle algérianiste, 138–39, 225n38, 229n28
Chirac, Jacques
　cartoon depicting, 141
　military service in Algeria, 145, 146
　as party leader, 82–83, 128–29, 165–66, 213n52
　pieds noirs and, 85, 86, 119–20, 145, 146, 221n22
　presidential campaigns, 110, 119–20, 145, 221n22
　as prime minister, 82–83
civil society. See associations
Clean Hands in the Var, 118–19
Clemenceau, Georges, 81–82
CNIP. See Centre national des indépendants et paysans
CODUR. See Comité de Défense et d'Union des Rapatrié
Colin, Daniel, 219n44
Colombani, Louis, 120–21, 122, 221n40
colonialism. See Algeria, colonial period; imperialism
Comité de Défense et d'Union des Rapatriés (CODUR), 67–70, 71–72, 73, 80, 208–9n60
Comité de Vincennes, 52–53, 203n26
Commission extra-municipale des rapatriés, 66, 73
Communauté d'agglomération Toulon Provence Méditerranée (TPM), 167–68, 171, 233n19
Communist Manifesto, 181–82
Communist Party, Algerian, 24, 25, 43, 198n2, 201n105, 201n107
Communist Party, French
　Algerian expatriates and, 24
　Algeria policies, 36
　alliance with Socialists, 81, 82–83
　deputies, 43
　local governments, 99
　support for Algerian independence, 198n2
　in Toulon, 54, 69–70, 120, 121
　in Var, 127–28
Constantine, 17–18, 23

corruption
- Arreckx scandal, 113–14, 118–19, 121, 220n72
- in association funding, 155, 156
- in Italy, 113–14
- politicians linked to, 169
- in Var, 112–14, 118–19, 125–26, 169, 220n72

Court of Cassation, 155
crime, 112–13, 135. *See also* corruption

Dahmar, Georges, 65, 66, 68–69, 70, 71, 87
Debré, Michel, 39, 62–63, 206n10
Deferre, Gaston, 47–48
De Gaulle, Charles
- Algeria policies, 7, 38–39, 52–53, 145, 146, 208n56
- assassination attempts against, 57, 63, 66–67, 206n17
- foreign policy, 38
- May 1968 events and, 79–80, 92
- parliamentary elections (1967), 71–72
- Poujade and, 90
- as president, 39, 57, 58, 78, 208n56
- as prime minister, 38
- resignation, 81
- son, 53
- supporters, 7, 36, 43, 51, 78, 79, 90–91
- visits to Toulon, 53–54, 63
- visit to Algeria, 39–40, 80
- during World War II, 146–47
- *See also* Gaullism

Degueldre, Roger, 66–67, 107–8, 218n26
Delmas, François, 47–48, 77–78, 83, 207n36
democracy
- far-right views, 2–3, 191n5
- voluntary associations and, 153–54, 161–62

discourse
- back-stage, 133, 140–51, 224n1
- front-stage, 133–37, 138–39, 151

Dominati, Jacques, 84–85, 107–8, 117–18, 212n43, 218n25
Draguignan
- National Front in, 104, 219n41
- *pieds noirs* organizations, 51
- prefecture, 82, 109
- Socialists, 81–82, 127–28

Dreux, 94–95, 100, 144
Dreyfus Affair, 23, 91
Drumont, Édouard, 23, 141, 227n63
Duprat, François, 93

Egypt
- Nasser regime, 90
- Suez Crisis, 34, 90–91

elections
- cantonal, 63, 94, 95, 100, 113–14, 127, 164, 217n13
- in colonial Algeria, 42–43, 201n96
- nonvoting rates, 98
- *See also* European elections; municipal elections; National Front electorate; parliamentary elections; presidential elections

elective affinity, 44, 133, 151, 184
employment, 50, 78–79, 126, 204n57, *See also* unemployment
Engels, Friedrich, 181–82
ethnocentrism, 158
ethnocracy, 27–28
European elections
- of 1978, 94
- of 1984, 95, 97–98, 100, 104, 220n3
- of 1989, 111
- of 1999, 127, 129
- of 2014, 164, 232n4
- National Front voters, 111, 119–20, 164, 189t

European far right. *See* far right, European
European Parliament, far right bloc, 220n3, *See also* European elections
European settlers. *See* Algeria, European settlers
European Union (EU)
- agricultural policies, 83–84
- grants to cities, 168
- immigration policies, 149–50

Évian Accords, 40, 52–54, 64, 200n83

Fabre, Henri, 52–53, 57, 58–59, 70, 71–72
Falco, Hubert
- allies, 165–66, 169
- government posts, 166, 170
- patronage, 169–70
- *pieds noirs* and, 169–70
- political career, 128–29, 165, 166–67
- relations with National Front, 166
- as Toulon mayor, 129–30, 156–57, 164–66, 167–71, 172, 232n9
- Var book fair and, 124

Fargette, Jean-Louis, 112–13, 114
far right, European
- anti-immigration views, 3, 15–16

[254] *Index*

beliefs, 2–3
demand-side and supply-side factors, 5–6
economic factors and, 179–80
in European Parliament, 220n3
fascism, 25, 43, 179
as hidden undercurrent, 10
in interwar period, 89, 179
media coverage, 3
neo-fascists, 93–94
political rise in 1980s, 2–3, 4–5, 10
in postwar period, 2
recent developments, 3–4, 192n12
far right, French
anti-communism, 92
economic conditions and, 96–97
extreme and radical right, 191n5
factors in support, 44, 130, 180, 181
historical roots, 89, 91
internal tensions, 127
in interwar period, 43
moderate-right parties and, 128–29
neo-Nazi groups, 144
in 1960s, 92–93
Ordre Nouveau, 93–94
Parti des forces nouvelles, 94, 103, 217n3
pieds noirs and, 91
in postwar period, 43, 89, 91
reducing influence of, 47–48, 183
supporters, 96, 97, 128, 143–44, 163, 164, 180, 232n2
violence, 105, 217n11
See also National Front
far-right potential
changes over time, 61
Gaullism and, 90–91
in 1960s, 67
of *pieds noirs*, 6, 9, 151, 158–60, 161, 180–81, 183, 184
in Toulon, 67, 173
fascism, 25, 43, 179. *See also* Nazism; neo-fascists
Faurisson, Robert, 141
Fédération du Sud des Rapatriés (FSR), 80, 211n20
FLN. *See* Front de libération nationale
FN (Front national). *See* National Front
FNC. *See* Front national des Combattants
FNR. *See* Front national des rapatriés

FRAN. *See* Front des Réfugiés d'Afrique du Nord
France
colonies, 2, 16, 21, 31
Fifth Republic, 39, 44, 57, 78
Fourth Republic, 36, 57
Jewish minority, 22–23, 77–78
military, 23–24, 35, 52
nationalization laws, 18, 22–23, 26, 196n52
Navy, 49, 50–51, 56, 108
Third Republic, 57, 81–82, 141, 154, 193n25
Vichy regime, 30, 51, 89, 142
Franco, Francisco, 141
Frank, Anne, 141
Frêche, Georges, 77–78, 83, 211n4
Freemasonry, 3, 16, 89, 141, 227n63, 232–33n13
Fréjus
Le Pen visits, 112
mayors, 107–8, 112–13, 164, 169, 172
National Front in, 111, 163–64, 166, 219n41
pieds noirs organizations, 51
French Algeria. *See* Algeria, colonial period; French Algeria
commemorations, 125, 175
Le Pen's support, 51
monuments, 68–69, 85, 86, 106–8, 125, 175, 218n24, 218n26
organizations, 50–51, 52–53, 90–91
propaganda, 37
See also Algeria, colonial period; *pieds noirs*; Poujadism
French Fraternity (Fraternité française), 123–24, 156–57
French Resistance, 29, 31, 43, 52, 91, 107–8, 146–47
Front de libération nationale (FLN), 34, 41, 52, 54, 67–68, 90, 99–100. *See also* Algerian War
Front des Réfugiés d'Afrique du Nord (FRAN), 65, 67–68
Front national (FN). *See* National Front
Front national des Combattants (FNC), 90–91, 103–4
Front national des rapatriés (FNR), 125, 157, 211n17
Front national pour l'Algérie française, 51
FSR. *See* Fédération du Sud des Rapatriés

Index [255]

Gaullism
    far-right affinities, 90–91
    May 1968 events and, 79–80
    municipal elections (1965), 63–65
    parliamentary elections (1967), 69–73, 209n67
    popular support, 47–48
    in Toulon, 52, 64, 87
    See also anti-Gaullism; De Gaulle, Charles
Gaullist parties, 64, 80, 98, 205n74 *See also* Rassemblement pour la République
Gautier, Théophile, 16
Germany, leftists, 182. *See also* Nazism
Ginesta, Georges, 165–66
Giraud, Marc, 165–66, 169
Giscard d'Estaing, Henri, 84
Giscard d'Estaing, Valéry
    Arreckx and, 78, 81–82, 84, 85, 106
    parties, 78, 86, 205n74, 212n29
    pieds noirs and, 82–85
    political career, 81
    as president, 81–85, 86–87
    supporters, 111, 216n50
    See also Républicains indépendants; Union pour la démocratie française
Goux, Christian, 120, 121–22
Government-General of Algeria, 15
Gramsci, Antonio, 181–82
Guillet de la Brosse, Éliane, 113–14
Gulf War, First, 144

harkis (Muslim French Army auxiliaries)
    benefits for, 85, 212n31
    deaths, 42
    in France, 54–55, 77, 85, 143
    French views of, 198n1
    leaders, 71–72, 85, 107
Holocaust denial, 43, 141, 147
Hyères
    mayor, 110–11, 219n60
    National Front in, 121, 219n41
    pieds noirs organizations, 51, 68, 70
    See also Piat, Yann

immigration
    Catholic views of, 112
    EU policies, 149–50
    to France, 16, 23–24, 99, 134–35, 144–45, 178–79
    French policies, 149–50
    French views of, 98–100, 216n57

    of Muslims, 15–16, 23–24, 92, 96, 129, 135, 178–79
    political mobilization factors, 205n1
    See also anti-immigration views; nativism
imperialism
    French, 2, 16, 142–43, 184
    legacies, 2, 11, 184–85
    See also Algeria
Indochina, 21, 31, 33–34, 104, 112, 142
inter-municipal federations, 166–68
International League against Racism and Anti-Semitism., 165–66
interwar period
    in colonial Algeria, 23–27, 42–43
    European far right, 89, 179
    French far right, 43
    immigration, 23–24
    political parties, 42–43
    Popular Front, 42–43
Islam
    fundamentalism, 15–16
    gender relations, 32–33
    law, 25
    See also Muslims
Islamic terrorism, 112, 181
Italy
    fascism, 179
    neo-fascists, 93–94
    political corruption, 113–14
    voluntary associations, 160–62

Jews
    cemeteries, 144
    citizens, 32
    in colonial Algeria, 22–23, 25, 27, 30–31, 32, 196n48, 196n52
    emigration from Algeria, 201n95
    in France, 22–23, 77–78
    French views of, 98–99
    intermarriage, 23, 198n24
    political rights, 32
    See also anti-Semitism
Joan of Arc, 140
Jospin, Lionel, 119–20, 127–28, 224n95

labor unions
    in colonial Algeria, 42–43
    general strike (1968), 79
    power, 136
    in Toulon, 81–82, 123, 124–25, 126, 154, 157–58, 223n69, 223n86

Lanfranchi, Horace, 165–66
Languedoc-Roussillon
  National Front voters, 228n1
  pieds noirs, 153, 228n1
  See also Montpellier
Le Bellegou, Édouard, 68, 203n34, 204n67
Le Chevallier, Cendrine, 123–26, 127–28, 129–30
Le Chevallier, Jean-Marie
  anti-immigration views, 129
  leadership of National Front in Var, 106, 111, 112, 117–20
  as mayor, 122–29, 167–68
  municipal election campaign (1995), 121–22, 221n29
  political career, 117–18, 119, 129–30, 220n3
  resignation from National Front, 127
leftists
  former, 97–98, 216n54
  German, 182
  political refugees in Algeria, 201n97
  in Var, 109, 111, 113, 127–28, 218n34, 219n48
  See also Communist Party; May 1968 events; Socialist Party
Left-Radicals, 63–64, 82–83, 85, 120
Léotard, François
  Arreckx and, 111, 112–13, 219n44
  corruption trial, 112–13
  Falco and, 165
  pieds noirs and, 107–8
  political career, 212n29, 219n59, 224n99
Le Pen, Jean-Marie
  anti-immigration views, 96, 134–35, 215n45
  anti-Semitism, 43, 106, 147
  cultural views, 136–37
  on De Gaulle, 90–91
  Dominati and, 212n43
  economic policies, 134
  Front national pour l'Algérie française, 51
  on Gulf War, 144
  as imperialist, 142
  on Islam, 96
  Le Chevallier and, 117–18, 122–23, 127, 129–30, 220n3
  military service, 90–91, 146
  pieds noirs supporting, 145, 147–48, 158
  political career, 90–91, 95, 100–1
  Poujade and, 90–91
  presidential candidacy (1974), 94
  presidential candidacy (1988), 110, 135, 219n41
  presidential candidacy (1995), 119–20, 221n23, 221n29
  presidential candidacy (2002), 145, 153, 158, 180, 228n115, 231n41, 232n57, 233n18
  presidential candidacy (2007), 158
  presidential election support, 189t
  public views of, 119–20
  reaction to May 1968 events, 92
  rhetoric, 137, 147, 148
  Tixier campaign and, 66–67
  in Var, 105, 112, 113–14, 119–20, 122–23
  visits to Toulon, 119–20, 122–23, 126, 221n21
  See also National Front
Le Pen, Marine
  party leadership, 171–72
  presidential campaigns, 137, 158, 189t, 228n1, 232n1
  rhetoric, 137
Levy, Geneviève, 165–66, 171
Ligue antijuive d'Alger, 23
Lipset, Seymour Martin, 90–91
Living Better in Toulon, 118–19
LR. *See* Républicains, Les

Macron, Emmanuel, 1, 154–55
Maghreb
  French conquest, 16
  French policies, 20
  immigration from, 16, 134–35, 144–45, 178–79
  See also Algeria; Morocco; Tunisia
Maison du Rapatrié, La, 86, 157–58, 169–70
Malraux, André, 40
Mamy, Bernard, 103–4, 105, 217n6, 217n12
Marchiani, Jean-Charles, 128–30, 224n100
Marignane, 47, 122–23, 124, 218n26
marriages
  among European settlers, 19, 23, 195n26
  among Muslims, 20, 195n33, 199n56
  endogamy, 19, 32, 195n26, 198n24
  of Jews and Christians, 23, 198n24
  of Muslims and Christians, 20, 21, 25, 32, 195n28, 198n24

Marseille
  Algerian repatriates in, 47
  anti-Gaullist rally, 80
  city council, 207n39
  moderate-right parties, 163–64
  National Front in, 163–64, 206n17
  pieds noirs and politicians in, 47–48, 144–45, 207n39
Marx, Karl, 181–82
Massu, Jacques, 35, 36, 37, 79, 181
May 1968 events, 79–80, 92–93
mayors. *See* municipal elections; Toulon mayors; *and specific cities*,
Médecin, Jacques, 47–48, 107–8, 207n36, 210n93, 218n26
Mégret, Bruno, 112, 127
Merton, Robert, 59
métissage, 21
Mitterrand, François
  pieds noirs and, 99–100, 208n53
  political career, 33–34, 81–82, 208n53
  as president, 94, 95, 97, 99–100, 110
  supporters, 97–98
  in Vichy regime, 142
moderate-right parties
  appeals to far-right voters, 128–29
  National Front and, 100, 105, 166
  pieds noirs and, 61
  in Provence-Alpes-Côte d'Azur, 168
  in southern cities, 163–64
  supporters, 98, 113, 119–20
  Toulon municipal government, 164–66
  in Var, 121, 128–29
  See also Arreckx, Maurice; Falco, Hubert; Parti républicain; Rassemblement pour la République; Républicains; Républicains indépendants; Trucy, François; Union pour la démocratie française; Union pour un mouvement populaire
Montpellier
  compared to Toulon, 77–78
  far-right support, 211n4
  mayors, 47–48, 77–78, 83, 207n36
  minority communities, 77–78
  OAS attack, 206n18
  pieds noirs in, 47–48, 56, 77–78, 83
Morocco, 16, 51. *See also* Maghreb
Moutardier, Guy, 53
Mouvement National Républicain, 127
Movimento sociale italiano (MSI), 93–94

multiple mandates, 106, 117, 130, 166–67, 170
municipal elections
  of 1965, 63–66
  of 1977, 83
  of 1983, 94–95
  of 1989, 111, 119, 121, 219n46
  of 1995, 6, 117, 118–19, 120–22, 156, 222n41
  of 2001, 128–30, 165–66, 224n109
  of 2008, 232n9
  of 2014, 163–64, 169, 232n9
  National Front voters, 111, 119–20, 129–30, 163–64, 224n109
municipal governments. *See* Toulon municipal government; *and other specific cities*,
Muslims
  anti-Muslim views, 96, 137, 216n58
  immigration to France, 15–16, 23–24, 92, 96, 129, 135, 178–79
  marriages, 20, 21, 25, 32, 195n28, 195n33, 198n24, 199n56
  pieds noir views of, 149
  in Toulon, 106
  women, 21, 25–26, 32–33, 36–37, 199n56, 201n91
  See also Arabes; Berbers; *harkis*; Islam

Napoleon Bonaparte, 22–23, 82, 141
National Assembly
  deputies representing Algeria, 23, 26, 39, 42, 43, 201n109
  deputies representing Var, 52, 58–59, 154–55, 165–66
  far-right deputies, 95
  laws on Algerian repatriates, 84, 85, 203–4n43, 208n56, 212n31, 212n33
  National Front deputies, 7, 105–6, 110–11, 129, 142–43, 154–55
  parliamentary reserve, 154–55
  UDCA deputies, 90–91
  See also parliamentary elections
National Front (Front national)
  Algerian War veterans and, 103–4
  anti-immigration views, 16, 94–95, 96, 99, 100, 134–35
  anti-Muslim views, 96, 137
  back-stage discourse, 133, 140–44
  conservative resistance, 164–65
  critics, 8, 9

deputies, 7, 105–6, 110–11, 129, 142–43, 154–55
Duprat and, 93
early years, 93–94
economic policies, 134, 137, 171–72, 180, 235n9
electoral successes, 94–95, 117, 122–23, 163–64
European elections, 164, 232n4
factors in rise of, 96–98, 100–1, 180, 184
founding, 73, 93
front-stage discourse, 133–37, 151
future of, 171–72
historical consciousness, 29, 140–41
internal tensions, 127
leadership of Jean-Marie Le Pen, 93–94
leadership of Marine Le Pen, 171–72
logo, 93–94, 215n32
publications, 140
recent developments, 137, 225n36
rise in 1980s, 3, 10, 94–98, 100–1
See also Toulon, National Front government; Var department, National Front in
National Front (Front national) electorate
anti-immigration views, 95–96, 176–77, 180, 183, 228n115
anti-Semitism, 228n115
characteristics, 175–76
class membership, 95–96, 97, 128, 143, 164, 180, 215–16n49
European elections, 111, 119–20, 164, 189t
former leftists, 97–98, 216n54, 236n12
growth in 1980s, 95, 97, 98
municipal elections, 111, 119–20, 129–30, 163–64, 224n109
parliamentary elections, 110, 113, 119–20, 188t, 189t, 190t, 230n39
pieds noirs, 6, 9, 153, 158, 180–81, 184
presidential elections, 119–20, 153, 189t, 193n24, 221n23, 230n37
in Provence-Alpes-Côte d'Azur, 163–64, 228n1
racial views, 176–77, 180
regional variations, 10, 96, 163, 190t, 232n2
in Var, 104, 111, 112, 113, 119–20, 164, 190t, 219n41, 221n23, 232n4
women, 215n43
See also Toulon, National Front voters

National Front, British, 3, 201–2n110
National Hebdo, 140–44, 226n55
National Senate, 57, 163–64, 165, 166
Nationaux, 61, 63–64, 65, 66–67, 73, 207n39
nativism, 1, 3, 15–16, 98–99. *See also* anti-immigration views
NATO (North Atlantic Treaty Organization), 70–71, 78, 209n79
Navy, French, 49, 50–51, 56, 108
Nazism
atrocities, 145–46
factors in rise of, 11
Holocaust, 43, 141
leftist resistance to, 182
pieds noirs on, 145–46, 147
supporters in Algeria, 25
neo-fascists, 93–94
nepotism, 124–25, 127, 169–70, 233n27
Nice
mayors, 47–48, 210n93, 218n26
moderate-right parties, 163–64
OAS monument, 218n26
pieds noirs and politicians in, 47–48, 73, 207n36, 210n93
terrorist attack (2016), 181
North Africa. *See* Algeria; Maghreb; Morocco; Tunisia

OAS. *See* Organisation armée secrète
Occident, 93
ON. *See* Ordre Nouveau
Oran
anti-Semitism, 23
European population, 17–18
massacre (5 July 1962), 42, 107–8
refugees from, 54, 55, 56
in World War II, 30
Orange, 122–23, 124
Ordre Nouveau (ON), 93–94
Organisation armée secrète (OAS)
assassination attempts on De Gaulle, 57, 63, 66–67, 206n17
coup attempt, 40, 52–53, 62–63, 66, 68, 99–100, 103–4, 107, 129–30, 142–43, 192n21, 200n75
leaders, 7, 68, 202n12, 206n17
members, 52, 66–67, 79, 91, 142–43
monuments to, 107–8, 218n26
police campaign against, 50–51
supporters, 50–51, 52, 69–70, 192n22, 203n15

Organisation armée secrète (OAS) (*Cont.*)
   terrorist attacks, 40–41, 50–51, 53–54, 57, 62–63, 192n22, 200n78, 206n10, 206n18
organized crime, 112–13
Ottoman Empire, 19–20, 22, 23–24

PACA. *See* Provence-Alpes-Côte d'Azur
Parliament. *See* National Assembly
parliamentary elections
   of 1871, 81–82
   of 1956, 90
   of 1962, 58–59
   of 1967, 67–68, 69–73, 207n36, 209n67, 209n72, 209n73
   of 1973, 81, 93–94
   of 1978, 83–84, 85–87, 213n70
   of 1981, 94
   of 1986, 95, 97, 100, 105, 110–11
   of 1988, 105–6, 110–11
   of 1993, 113, 119–20
   of 1997, 127–29
   of 1998, 127–28
   of 2002, 158, 170
   of 2007, 158
   of 2017, 190*t*, 232n2
   National Front voters, 110, 113, 119–20, 188*t*, 189*t*, 190*t*, 230n38, 230n39
   See also National Assembly
Parti des forces nouvelles (PFN), 94, 103, 217n3
Parti républicain (PR), 86, 212n29
Parti socialiste (PS). *See* Socialist Party
patron-client relations, 59, 65, 77, 87, 109–10, 124–25, 156, 161, 169–70, 205n81
Pétain, Philippe, 89, 90–91, 137, 142, 151.
   See also Vichy regime
Pflimlin, Pierre, 36
PFN. *See* Parti des forces nouvelles
Piat, Yann, 104–5, 106, 110–11, 113–14, 117–18, 219n60
pieds noirs
   affinity with far right, 6, 9, 151, 158–60, 161, 180–81, 183, 184
   during Algerian War, 36
   anti-communism, 80, 145
   anti-immigration views, 104–5, 144–45
   back-stage discourse, 133, 144–51
   economic integration, 78–79
   effects of independence, 42
   employment, 78–79, 204n57

   front-stage discourse, 133, 138–39, 151
   historical consciousness, 68–69, 181, 183
   May 1968 events and, 79–80
   moderate-left supporters, 8–9
   National Front voters, 6, 9, 153, 158, 180–81, 184
   noteworthy, 139, 226n46
   periodicals, 138–39
   political influence, 65, 67–68, 83, 178
   political parties supported, 51, 59, 153, 207n38, 207n39, 213n70
   racial views, 6–7, 148–49, 158
   return visits to Algeria, 159
   Rue d'Isly massacre (26 March 1962), 40, 68–69, 107–8, 125, 175
   settler insurgency (May 1958), 36–38, 39
   social identities, 61–62, 150–51, 184
   subculture, 9, 44, 153, 159–60, 177–78
   unemployment, 78–79, 211n7
   views of *Arabes* and Muslims, 43, 149
   violent activists, 105, 217n11
   women, 78–79, 211n7
   younger generations, 184
   See also Algeria, European settlers; far-right potential; repatriates; Toulon, *pieds noirs* in; Var department, *pieds noirs* in
pieds noirs organizations
   attitudes of members, 231n47
   city funding, 156, 230n36
   non-partisan, 125
   number of members, 184
   political affinities and membership, 9, 158–60, 161, 178, 183, 231n48
   in Toulon, 57, 61–62, 65, 86, 156, 157, 158–60, 161
   in Var, 51–52, 67–70, 80, 83, 105, 125, 204n65
   See also ANFANOMA; Comité de Défense et d'Union des Rapatriés; FNR; FRAN; FSR; RANFRAN; RECOURS; UAVFROM
Pieroni, Henri, 52
Polanyi, Karl, 179
political bosses and machines, 59
political parties
   in colonial Algeria, 42–43
   dealignment, 98
   in interwar period, 42–43
   main, 98
   in postwar period, 29, 43
   See also specific parties

political potential, 176. *See also* far-right potential
Pompidou, Georges, 79–80, 81
populism, 121, 137, 151, 173, 180
Portugal
   ex-colonials from Mozambique and Angola, 201–2n110
   nationalism, 43
   OAS members in, 52
postwar period
   colonial policies, 31–32
   economic recovery in France, 31–32
   European party systems, 4–5
   far right, 43, 89, 91
   French politics, 2
   political parties, 43
   settler relations, 32–33
   in Toulon, 49
Poujade, Pierre, 89–91, 214n8
Poujadism
   influence, 89–90, 141
   Le Pen and, 90–91
   supporters, 16, 29, 50–51, 63–64, 93, 96, 97, 103–4
Poulet-Dachary, Jean-Claude, 121, 126, 127, 129–30
PR. *See* Parti républicain
presidential elections
   of 1965, 66–67, 70, 92, 208n53
   of 1969, 81
   of 1974, 81–82, 94
   of 1981, 94, 97–98, 99
   of 1988, 110, 135, 219n41
   of 1995, 119–20, 221n23
   of 2002, 145, 153, 158, 180, 228n115, 230n37, 231n41, 232n57, 233n18
   of 2007, 158, 166, 230n37
   of 2012, 137, 153, 158, 228n1, 230n37, 232n1
   of 2017, 1, 154–55, 232n1
   National Front voters, 119–20, 153, 189t, 193n24, 219n41, 221n23, 230n37
   voter surveys, 158, 230n37
Provence-Alpes-Côte d'Azur (PACA)
   far-right supporters, 163–64
   National Front voters, 163–64, 228n1
   pieds noirs in, 153, 228n1
   presidents, 155
   regional council, 163–64, 168, 232n3

PS (Parti socialiste). *See* Socialist Party
Putnam, Robert D., 161–62

Quinzaine des Rapatriés, 62–63

Rachline, David, 166
RANFRAN. *See* Rassemblement national des Français d'Afrique du Nord
Rassemblement et coordination unitaire des rapatriés et spoliés d'outre mer (RECOURS), 84–85, 86
Rassemblement national des Français d'Afrique du Nord, 51, 203n18
Rassemblement National des Français Rapatriés d'Afrique du Nord (RANFRAN), 208n53
Rassemblement pour la République (RPR), 82–83, 110, 128–29, 213n52, 213n70
RECOURS. *See* Rassemblement et coordination unitaire des rapatriés et spoliés d'outre mer
Red Cross, 54–55
refugees. *See pieds noirs*; repatriates
Reimbold, Jean, 50–51, 52–53, 202n12
repatriates
   anniversaries of arrival, 157–58
   arrivals in Marseille, 47
   assistance for, 54–55, 77, 144–45, 154, 203–4n44
   compensation claims, 64, 67–68, 69–70, 79–80, 83, 84, 86, 157, 212n33
   emigration from Algeria, 40, 41, 42
   legal status, 203–4n43
   number of, 47, 54
   press coverage, 55–56
   resettlement areas, 56, 67–68, 80, 83, 204n58
   ships, 55
   See also pieds noirs; Toulon
Républicains, Les (LR), 165–66, 168, 169
Républicains indépendants (RI), 81, 82, 84, 85, 205n74, 212n29
Reymond, Jean-Marie, 51, 87
RI. *See* Républicains indépendants
Ricard, Paul, 62
Ritondale, Léopold, 110–11, 219n60
Roseau, Jacques, 77–78, 206n18, 212n47, 212n49
Rue d'Isly massacre (26 March 1962), 40, 68–69, 107–8, 125, 175

Saint-Raphaël
- corruption scandals, 169
- Le Pen visits, 112
- mayors, 165–66, 169
- National Front candidates, 111, 121, 217n16
- *pieds noirs* organizations, 68, 208–9n60

Salan, Raoul
- attempt on life of, 90, 214n10
- coup attempt, 40, 68
- honors, 129–30
- *pieds noirs* and, 107
- supporters, 37, 79, 80
- trial and imprisonment, 66–67, 69–70, 71–72, 79, 80
- wife, 71–72

Sarkozy, Nicolas, 149–50, 165–66, 224n100, 232–33n13

Sergent, Pierre, 7, 202n12

Seyne-sur-Mer, La
- mayors, 69–70, 114
- National Front candidates, 217n13
- shipyards, 50, 69–70, 71–72, 81–82, 108
- Socialist victories in municipal elections, 127–28

social identities, 17, 19, 27, 61–62, 150–51, 184

Socialist Party
- in Algeria, 201n107
- Algeria policies, 36
- deputies, 43
- European elections, 111
- local governments, 127–28
- in Marseille, 207n39
- in 1970s, 81, 82–83
- *pieds noirs* and, 99–100, 159
- recent developments, 1
- in Toulon, 53–54, 64, 65, 120, 122, 123, 156, 207n39
- in Var, 58–59, 68, 78, 81–82, 127–28, 202n3
- *See also* Defferre, Gaston; Frêche, Georges; Goux, Christian; Jospin, Lionel; Le Bellegou, Édouard; Mitterrand, François; Soldani, Édouard

Soldani, Édouard, 81–82, 204n67, 219n60
Solzhenitsyn, Alexander, 136–37
SOS France, 217n11
SOS Racisme, 99–100, 112, 217n11, 222n51
Soustelle, Jacques, 37, 68, 79, 203n26, 208n53
Soviet Union, 80, 92

Spain
- emigration to Algeria, 18–19, 23
- far right, 4, 43, 192n12
- fascism, 141
- immigration, 4
- *pieds noirs* in, 200n75

Stirbois, Jean-Pierre, 94–95, 104, 144, 220n3
subculture of *pieds noirs*, 44, 153, 159–60, 177–78
Suez Crisis, 34, 90–91

Tixier-Vignancour, Jean-Louis
- Le Pen and, 51, 66–67
- life of, 51
- parliamentary candidacy, 70–73
- *pieds noirs* and, 51
- presidential candidacy, 66–67, 80, 92, 103–4, 148, 208n53
- supporters, 73, 148

Tocqueville, Alexis de, 17, 153–55, 157–58, 160–62
Touati, Ahmed, 124–25, 222n68

Toulon
- anti-Gaullism, 63
- anti-immigration views, 108–9, 110, 111, 129
- association funding, 123–24, 155–58, 222n53, 230n36
- associations, 154–55, 157–58, 159–61
- casualties in Algerian War, 53
- Communists, 54, 69–70, 120, 121
- compared to Montpellier, 77–78
- De Gaulle's visits, 53–54, 63
- economy, 50, 172–73, 181
- employment, 50, 126
- far-right potential, 67, 173
- Gaullism, 87
- geography, 49, 172
- history, 49, 82
- housing projects, 119, 144–45, 172
- labor unions, 81–82, 123, 124–25, 126, 154, 157–58, 223n69, 223n86
- Le Pen visits, 119–20, 122–23, 126, 221n21
- Muslims, 106
- naval base, 49, 50, 54, 56, 108, 126, 173, 223n85
- politicians, 47–48, 52, 53–54, 57–58
- population, 6, 50
- port, 47–48, 49, 81–82, 202n7
- Socialists, 53–54, 64, 65, 120, 122, 123, 156, 207n39

[262] *Index*

ties to Algeria, 50–51, 53
tourism, 49, 172–73, 234–35n52
urban renewal and infrastructure projects, 109–10, 114, 126–27, 129–30, 170–71, 234n31
war damage and postwar reconstruction, 49
Toulon, National Front government
achievements, 126–27
administrative issues, 126
association funding, 123–24, 156–58, 222n53
book fair and, 124
city employees, 124–25, 126–27, 170–71
defeat in 2001, 129–30
election campaign (1995), 6, 117, 120–22, 181, 221n29, 222n41
inter-municipal federations and, 167–68
internal tensions, 127
international reactions, 124
isolation, 168–69
leftist responses, 127–28, 168–69
legacy, 164–65, 170–71
nepotism, 124–25, 127
pieds noirs and, 125
in power, 122–28
scandals, 125–26, 129–30
Toulon, National Front in
candidates, 109, 121–22, 129–30
city council members, 111, 119
members, 124–25, 127
offices, 104
politicians leaving party, 217n16
recruiting, 117–19
Toulon, National Front voters
cantonal elections (1985), 104
European elections, 189t
interviews, 6–8
municipal elections, 119, 129–30, 164, 224n109
parliamentary elections, 110, 113, 188t, 189t, 190t, 230n38
presidential elections, 189t, 219n41, 221n23, 230n37
recent elections, 173
Toulon, *pieds noirs* in
arrivals of refugees, 47–49, 54–55, 56, 58, 154
assistance for, 54–55, 144–45, 154, 204n44
associations, 57, 61–62, 65, 86, 156, 157, 158–60, 161

city councilors, 125
Commission extra-municipale des rapatriés, 66, 73
Falco and, 169–70
historical consciousness, 175
interviews, 6–9, 144–51, 183, 227n89
leaders, 61–62, 65
May 1968 events and, 79–80
monuments to French Algeria, 106–8
National Front government and, 125
political affiliations, 63–65, 69–70, 71, 73
political influence, 57–59, 61–63, 64–66, 67, 71–72, 87
share of population, 57, 64, 207n24
social identities, 61–62
voter surveys, 158–60, 230n37
See also Arreckx, Maurice, relations with *pieds noirs*
Toulon mayors, 117, 130. *See also* Arreckx, Maurice; Falco, Hubert; Le Bellegou, Édouard ; Le Chevallier, Jean-Marie; Trucy, François
Toulon municipal government
employees, 124–25, 126–27, 169–71
finances, 126–27, 170–71, 233n30, 234n39
moderate-right, 164–65
See also municipal elections; Toulon, National Front government
Toulon Youth, 123–26, 127, 129–30
Toulouse, *pieds noirs* in, 79–80
tourism, 49, 172–73, 234–35n52
TPM. *See* Communauté d'agglomération Toulon Provence Méditerranée
Trucy, François
anti-immigration views, 110
Arreckx and, 114, 120, 169
as mayor, 109–10, 114, 117–18, 123, 156, 157–58, 219n38
re-election campaign (1995), 120–22, 130, 156, 169, 221n23
supporters, 118–19
Trump, Donald J., 180
Tunisia, 16, 35, 51. *See also* Maghreb

UAVFROM. *See* Union des Amicales Varoises des Français Rapatriés d'Outre-mer
UDCA. *See* Union de défense des commerçants et artisans
UDF. *See* Union pour la démocratie française

UMP. *See* Union pour un mouvement populaire
unemployment, 78–79, 96–98, 108, 134, 143, 180, 211n7, *See also* employment
Union de défense des commerçants et artisans (UDCA), 90–91. *See also* Poujadism
Union des Amicales Varoises des Français Rapatriés d'Outre-mer (UAVFROM), 83, 84–85, 86
Union pour la démocratie française (UDF), 86–87, 110, 112–13, 117–18, 122, 128–29, 213n70
Union pour un mouvement populaire (UMP), 165–66, 170
United Nations, 35
United States
  political bosses and machines, 59
  Trump voters, 180
  voluntary associations, 153–54, 160
University of Toulon, 172

Var department
  agriculture, 49, 108
  anti-Gaullism, 58–59
  departmental council, 109–10, 112, 113–14, 124, 128, 164, 165–66, 219n56
  economy, 49, 108, 113, 126, 128, 204n57
  far right, 103, 119–20
  leftists, 109, 111, 113, 127–28, 218n34, 219n48
  nepotism, 169–70, 233n27
  organized crime, 112–13
  political corruption, 112–14, 118–19, 125–26, 169, 220n72
  political parties, 81–82
  population growth, 108
  prefects, 128–29
  prefecture, 82, 109
  presidential election (1965), 67
  Socialists, 58–59, 68, 78, 81–82, 127–28, 202n3
  ties to Algeria, 50–51
  tourism, 49
  See also Toulon
Var department, National Front in
  candidates, 110–11, 113–14, 217n13, 219n46
  in city governments, 111, 122–23, 124
  deals with other parties, 110–11
  deputies, 105–6, 110–11
  leaders, 103–5, 106, 129–30

  members, 103, 104, 127
  pieds noirs and, 104–5, 125
  politicians leaving party, 217n16
  voters, 104, 111, 112, 113, 119–20, 164, 190t, 219n41, 221n23, 232n4
  See also Le Chevallier, Jean-Marie; Piat, Yann; Toulon
Var department, *pieds noirs* in
  anti-immigration views, 104–5
  influence, 67, 85, 86
  National Front and, 104–5, 125
  organizations, 51–52, 67–70, 80, 83, 105, 125, 204n65
  population, 83, 212n27
  See also pieds noirs
Vendée uprising, 140–41
veterans' associations, 50–51, 159–60, 161–62
Vichy regime, 30, 51, 89, 142. *See also* Pétain, Philippe
Vitel, Jean, 52–53, 57, 58–59, 69–70
Vitel, Phillippe, 165–66, 171
voluntary associations. *See* associations
voters. *See* elections; National Front electorate,
Vox Party (Spain), 192n12

Weber, Max, 44, 59, 133, 184
women
  domestic workers, 25–26
  education, 32
  household roles, 25–26
  interethnic relations, 25–26
  labor force participation, 26, 78–79, 197n79, 211n7
  marriages to French men, 19, 195n28
  Muslim, 21, 25–26, 32–33, 36–37, 199n56, 201n91
  National Front voters, 215n43
  pieds noirs, 78–79, 211n7
  voting rights, 148
working class, far right supported by, 95–96, 97, 128, 143–44, 164, 180
World War I, 23–24. *See also* interwar period
World War II
  effects in Algeria, 28, 29, 30–31
  French military, 31
  French Resistance, 29, 31, 43, 52, 91, 107–8, 146–47

Zeralda, 30–31
Zola, Emile, 23